Shakespeare's *Living Art*

Shakespeare's
Living Art

ROSALIE L. COLIE

PRINCETON UNIVERSITY PRESS

PRINCETON, NEW JERSEY

16 2242

Copyright © 1974 by Princeton University Press

Library of Congress Catalog card number: 72-6520
ISBN: 0-691-06248-X (hardcover edition)
ISBN: 0-691-10018-7 (paperback edition)

All Rights Reserved

Library of Congress Cataloging in Publication Data will
be found on the last printed page of this book.

This book has been composed in Linotype Baskerville

Printed in the United States of America by
Princeton University Press

Preface

My title comes from an early and experimental play, *Love's Labour's Lost*, the first work discussed in detail in this book. Planning to remake his society, the King of Navarre declares himself a creator:

> Our court shall be a little academe,
> Still and contemplative in living art.

For those who, like me, inhabit a larger academe nowadays neither still nor contemplative, there may be nothing but irony in this passage. Its chief words are very important, though, in the themes of this book. What was "academic" for Shakespeare, in both senses of that abused word—that is, what was simple, easy, natural for him, what studied and learned? Fixed into art, things are conventionally "stilled" for our contemplation, which is the more difficult, if the more rewarding, when art seems to "live," to "move" us, out of its stillness, in all the ways art is supposed to do those things and does them. Here I try to revivify, or at any rate revive, what may seem only "academic" in the worst modern sense: those still forms bequeathed to an author by his craft and his culture, the forms by which an artist lives, and therefore by which art must live too. I try to see what the "meanings" of these forms are, in specific literary works and in the making of those works. So the words of a foolish, limited, limitedly learned young man with aspirations to understanding may be my motto too: like Navarre, I have learned a great deal from the experiment.

Where they have existed, for my plays I have used the Arden editions (London and Cambridge, Mass.): *1* and *2 Henry IV*, ed. A. R. Humphreys; *Love's Labour's Lost*, ed. Richard David; *Othello*, ed. M. R. Ridley; *Julius Caesar*, ed. T. S. Dorsch; *Antony and Cleopatra*, ed. M. R. Ridley; *The Winter's Tale*, ed. J.H.P. Pafford; *Cymbeline*, ed. J. M. Nosworthy; *The Tempest*, ed. Frank Kermode; *King Lear*, ed. Kenneth Muir. I used the Norton *Hamlet*, edited by Cyrus Hoy (New York, 1963); and for the rest have depended upon Peter Alexander's edition of Shakespeare's *Complete Works*, in the four-volume version (London, 1951).

v

I want to apologize for something I cannot seem to alter, my entirely-too-attic style. A kind friend said, "You write the way you talk, and there's just nothing we [we!] can do about it." I *have* tried to do something about it in revision, though I know I cannot break a lifetime's bad habit of qualifying each generalization and offering alternatives all in one breath. Since I have strong opinions about literary works and other things, I can only suppose that my failure to state them unequivocally comes from some internal obligation to make sure that the counterargument is known. The argumentative structure of the following chapters seems definite to me, but I know that for some readers the paragraphs seem to spiral from specific to general each time, instead of providing the logical links that my bad eyesight interprets them as being.

I have many and various personal debts, partly to audiences who patiently listened to parts of this book as lectures at Smith College, Williams College, Ohio State University, Michigan State University, the Warburg Institute, the University of North Carolina, and the University of Essex. To my hosts and interlocutors at those institutions, I want to express my thanks: Frank and Constance Ellis, Joan Webber, Julian Markels, Lore Metzger, E. H. Gombrich, J. B. Trapp, Elizabeth Hageman, Philip Edwards, and Philip Long. My debts to students at the University of Iowa, the University of Toronto, Yale University, and Brown University are considerable, and some cannot pass unnamed: John P. Barnes, Elisabeth Holm, Robin McAllister, Willy Melczer; Martha Andresen, Michael Engl, Stephen Greenblatt, Alarik Skarstrom; Sr. Jean Klene; Barbara Bono, June Fellows, Gavriel Moses, David Orsini, Edward de Santis, William Watterson. This book has been especially a "Brown book," since I gave a colloquium on it before I came there to teach, and have worked through many problems with colleagues and students since. I want to thank Cynthia Grant Tucker, Arline R. Standley, Max Yeh, Irene Samuel, and Murray Krieger for special help; Bridget Gellert Lyons, Jessie and Roger Hornsby, Edward Williamson, Alan Trueblood, Maynard Mack, Curt Zimansky, and Sheldon A. Zitner are responsible for almost all that is good in these pages, but are of course absolved from weaknesses. Barbara Lewalski has proved, as always, an ideal colleague, and Sears R. Jayne not only hunted out peculiar references in foreign libraries with exemplary speed and accuracy, but also helped the writer survive the writing. E. H. Gombrich has usually said it all, better, in another context.

Institutions have helped me too: I first worked hard on the book at the rich and wonderful Newberry Library, where work was made easy for me by many people, especially Matt Lowman and James M. Wells; later, a Guggenheim Fellowship granted me leisure to work still harder, and Lady Margaret Hall made the thing come true. I could not have written this book without the kindness of the S.C.R. at Lady Margaret Hall, nor without the friendship of Professor Romila Thapar, like me a guest at that generous college in 1966-67. Brown University helped make the typing possible, and Janet Kubbinga, Patricia Schlosser, and Jennyvee Martin actually typed. The Bodleian and the Beinecke Libraries were, beside the Newberry, "my" libraries for this book. To two readers for Princeton University Press, especially James Calderwood, I am grateful for valuable correctives and advice; my debts to George Robinson are by now unpayable.

Every book has special obligations, marks personal disappointments. Patrick and Helen McCarthy and Harry Berger, Jr., did not give specific advice on this book, but I hope that something of their spirit has entered my formulations. One of the joys at the beginning of this book was the unexpected encouragement and unstinting support of John Crow, who talked everything over, overwhelmed me with bibliography, and was kindly in his manifold correction of my misapprehensions. Without him then, I would have been mired again and again—and now, without him for good, I suppose I must expect regularly to be mired. I want also to thank Kossia Tomasini, whose insights helped more than they may show here. By being so slow in writing, I have lost my chance to tell Heinrich Bluecher how much this book was for him, who as a boy in Berlin found Shakespeare for himself and knew what he had found; the best I can do is to say that without him and his wife, this book would never have been conceived.

Rosalie L. Colie
Old Lyme, Connecticut
July, 1972

Note

Rosalie Colie completed her work on the manuscript of this book, and delivered it to her editor, one week before her tragic death. Subsequent work on it has gone forward without her counsel and good humor. We have changed nothing in the text but have confined ourselves to verifying names, dates, references, etc. We hope, therefore, that the voice and hand remain unmistakably hers, and that errors will be laid at our door.

Bridget Gellert Lyons
Rutgers University

George Robinson
Princeton University Press

Contents

Shakespeare's *Living Art*

Introduction

I

THIS BOOK, OF COURSE, is the result of trying to teach something—
this time Shakespeare—to a group of comparatists (which is what
I call students, of any age, of comparative literature), for whom
his celebrated "Englishness" carried no particular sanction. Trying to make Shakespeare intelligible to students who cared not at
all for morality plays, national chronicles, the language of English
bibles, local stage-conditions, etc., led me to think back not only
to Shakespeare's real or supposed continental "sources" (Boc-
caccio, Cinthio, Belleforêt), but also to that more fertilizing
stream, fed by these sources and so many more, the powerful literary tradition taught in the schools and learned in the Renaissance
literary world. This means, as Claudio Guillén has taught us, that
I had to rethink, in connection with this author, the vexed matter
of "influence." The fluidity of these metaphors may suggest how
difficult it is to attempt "exact scholarship" (the proud phrase of
a historian-friend) in such a subject as this, and why I do not
attempt it here. I am less concerned in this book with the particular documentary or pseudo-documentary origins of Shakespeare's works than with the ways in which he used, misused,
criticized, recreated, and sometimes revolutionized the received
topics and devices, large and small, of his artful craft. To return
to the liquidity of the terms for a moment, a writer does not live
by bread alone. In the body of his work, as in his own body, the
nourishing water from his sources is the major element. So, in a
particular way, it is Shakespeare's relation to his "traditions" that
concerns me here. Of course many Shakespeareans have been concerned with just this—Harry Levin's brief but powerful "Shakespeare in the Light of Comparative Literature" comes to mind at
once; but we are only beginning to understand the critical as well
as the genetic relation of a work to its sources and its analogues.
In Shakespearean studies, I think especially of Bridget Lyons' and
Sheldon Zitner's exemplary work, and of such projects as Louise
Clubb's forthcoming examination of the debt to Italian comedy
owed by Shakespeare.

3

The book has a second aim. I want to try to do for Shakespeare's use of literary *forms* something like what Sigurd Burckhardt, James Calderwood, Hilda Hulme, and Sheldon Zitner[1] have been variously doing for his *words*. To do anything at all with Shakespearean forms means that one owes a great debt to E. E. Stoll, E. K. Chambers, T. W. Baldwin, E.M.W. Tillyard, Alfred Harbage, Harry Levin, Robert Ornstein, and (especially) Muriel Bradbrook and Madeleine Doran, whose books have led the way in this area, as well as to countless other scholars, here nameless, whose contributions have enriched our understanding of the range of Shakespeare's response to the conventions and devices available to him. Nowadays in an era of phenomenological and structuralist criticism, to speak of "forms" sounds hopelessly old-fashioned: formalism is something some critics are "beyond." This implies that its uses in literary study have been exhausted. Obviously, I do not think so, rather that after years of source-study, new-critical readings, rhetorical analyses, and generic debate, we are only now getting ready to hitch "forms"—verse-forms, *topoi*, devices, motifs, themes, conventions, traditional organizations of words, genres—to the culture from which a writer springs and to the particularities of his own organization and selection of materials: to connect "forms" to criticism. Formalism seems to me not a dead end at all, but the ground on which we can enter into and understand the very processes by which a writer becomes what he is, and is enabled to do what he does.

In other words, like E. H. Gombrich, from whose *Art and Illusion*[2] (so memorable, and so modest) we have learned about art as its own social, even sociological system, I think that it is by its norms and forms[3] that an art exists and is borne from imagination to imagination, from generation to generation, from professional to unprofessional public, from creator to lover of art; that it is only by norms and forms, and forms *as* norms, that art can be understood at all. Such a view may seem to threaten

---

[1] See Sigurd Burckhardt, *Shakespearean Meanings* (Princeton, 1968); James L. Calderwood, *Shakespearean Metadrama* (Minneapolis, 1970); Hilda Hulme, *Explorations into Shakespeare's Language* (London, 1962); Sheldon P. Zitner, "Shakespeare's Secret Language," unpublished paper; and *"King Lear* and its Language," *Some Facets of "King Lear"* (Toronto, 1974).

[2] (London, 1960).

[3] The reference is to E. H. Gombrich, *Norm and Form. Studies in the Art of the Renaissance* (London, 1966).

our post-romantic insistence on the novelty of creative intellect
and on the uniqueness of any worthwhile work of art, but in fact
it need not. Rather, I think this view enables us to recognize not
just the actual *conditions* from which any work of art arises, but
also the particular *ways* in which it has been made unique. Certainly for the period in which Shakespeare lived and worked, one
can have it both ways: just as there was no possibility that any
author or artist could "make it new" by abandoning inherited
forms, so also there was an insistence on outdoing and overgoing
earlier achievements, each man newly creating out of and against
his tradition, in conscious competition with the very best that
tradition could offer him.

This means, then, that an author writing from within and out
of a sense of the traditions of his art must write problematically,
must look critically at the customary materials of his workman-
ship—in the case of the literary artist, at the traditional elements
I spoke of earlier—in order to use them anew, or in a new way.

Most of the "forms" a writer uses are of course those particularly embedded in his craft—the genres, the conventions, the devices, the *topoi* of poetics and rhetoric. Other useful forms,
though, as Harry Berger's work especially stresses for us, are the
forms of thought of a given culture—the idea of progress, the
great chain of being, the idea of a world-harmony are classic *topoi*
of this sort. "Hard" and "soft" pastoral have different intellectual
shapes; paradoxes are another case in point. Standard paradoxes
—"It is better to weep than to laugh"; "It is better to live in a
cottage than a palace"; "An absolute tyranny is the best government"; "The pleasantest life [is] to bee always in danger"—bear
both logical and social implications, and frequently offer severe
criticisms both of ways of perceiving ideas and sociopolitical arrangements, and of thinking about such ideas and arrangements.
But for all their criticism of commonplaces and commonplace
habits of thought, by their very fixedness as topics, these paradoxes become commonplaces themselves, "rhetorical" in this sense
(Curtius' sense) as well as in their exploitation of rhetorical devices and strategies.

Again, sometimes a generic or modal theme, such as the debate
between sophistication and primitivism written into pastoral
formulation, becomes a form of thought. The theme can be conventionally expressed (cf. Touchstone's exchange with Corin in
As You Like It); it can be made the vehicle of very sharp social

commentary, as in the exchange between Autolycus and Perdita's foster family in *The Winter's Tale*—or it can sound, faintly but insistently, in the very structure of Castiglione's *Courtier*, or again as the background to so different a work in kind as Locke's *Second Treatise*. In other studies, I have been concerned with patterns of thought, intellectual "forms" of the Renaissance, and with the ways in which these have been made literary—the *tabula rasa* of Locke's baby's mind must owe something to the picaroon's psychology; and Locke's blind man, as Arline Standley's work on Diderot demonstrates, was to become a literary as well as a philosophical *topos* in the eighteenth century. In some cases, a whole literary genre may owe its origins to non-literary forms—the utopia is a case in point, of course; the love-dialogue, the debate of body and soul, the dedicatory letter owe their existence to the formulation of ideas not primarily literary, however generically such ideas may come to be expressed. The point is, simply, that literature is not only a craft mystery, however difficult to master it may be. It draws much of its strength from entirely extraliterary ideas, which then may indeed become subject to the literary process, the rules of craft. Such literarization, I think, happened to the medico-philosophical notions of melancholy, as Mrs. Lyons has shown us: the various but definite "forms" of medical description and prescription were readily adapted to literary uses.

Though in this book I am chiefly concerned with literary forms and the literary uses of extraliterary forms, obviously, I think that all thought is organized and mediated formally, sometimes so naturally and automatically that formal perception, or perception by forms, often goes unmarked, even in the perceiver. If we look for them, "forms" are everywhere to be seen. But for the student of a particular subject—philosophy, history, art history, literature —certain forms are more important, more relevant than others. In the system of the humors, for instance, melancholy *is* important in literature and art, and phlegm far less so, though both humors are equally part of the physician's structural repertory. Though I suspect that future research into Renaissance subjects may involve the identification of different forms of thought and expression, together with their particular functioning in works of art, history, philosophy, etc., such study must always involve the same tact and common sense, as well as the same diligence, that any specialty requires.   .

6

Though I think the study of forms will help interpretation a great deal, it cannot absolve readers and writers altogether from their tasks of criticism. As this book exists to suggest, concepts of form as formulations of craft were of utmost concern to Renaissance writers. Contrary to the dictum of one contemporary school of interpretation, these authors knew that they had to understand their craft in order to master it, still more if they had pretensions of overmastering their illustrious predecessors. They were not so much burdened by the past as made the richer for it, as we know by the welcome accorded ancient texts newly uncovered during the Renaissance. By redistributing the stresses in their own work, artists prevented it from becoming burdensome: they carried their learning lightly, because to them it was simply the condition of craftsmanship and professionalism.

Craft, then, can be seen as a set of problems to be solved, so that an artist's work experiments in problem-setting and problem-solving. In this sense, all Shakespeare's plays, not just those dark comedies written two-thirds of the way through his career, are problem-plays. I have tried to treat the works I have chosen as "problems" in this sense, works exploring and revealing the problematics of this particular writer's craft, this particular writer's assessment of what was problematical. With this aim, I have tried to choose topics for study which connected Shakespeare with the range of Renaissance writing beyond English linguistic boundaries rather than with the practice of island-writers alone—or, have tried to present a comparatist's Shakespeare, of a piece with the long and rich continental Renaissance. Interest in forms does not dictate one course over the other. Of course one could study the place of forms in Shakespeare's problematic art just as well, perhaps better, from an English perspective; it seemed to me that there is room for a book on Shakespeare which opens upon retrospects and prospects beyond national boundaries, a book which might encourage Shakespeare henceforth to seem, as Dante, Cervantes, Voltaire, and Goethe so clearly are, an author essential to a comparatist's education.

In most cases, therefore, I have chosen a single topic dealing with some formal aspect of a play or plays—the operations of styles or genres in counterpoint; the use of stereotypes in building a character highly original in stage-practice; various manipulations of a mode (the pastoral) rich in potentialities—trying to see in what particular ways Shakespeare shaped works that are, still, noticeably "unique." Whenever possible, I have tried to look at an earlier work as a control for the work principally studied, but obviously, in the case of the *Sonnets*, this was impossible. Traditionalists, of course, tend to like "traditions" and the forms by which they are borne and become recognizable; perhaps because they too work in "older" fields of study, the theorists I rely on most heavily have developed arguments in terms of received *schemata*, mental sets, possible alternatives, and even "influences," another dangerous literary concept now being re-examined and revised. Against the broad field of possibility postulated by E. R. Curtius,[4] E. H. Gombrich, and Claudio Guillén,[5] earlier positivistic notions of influence must be altered to allow for an author's choosing among his alternatives. Thus, as Guillén puts it, influence-studies should concern not so much the finished work itself as its own creative biography—what did an author decide to concentrate on? What did he neglect, and did he neglect it deliberately, accidentally, or out of ignorance? Or, as Gombrich wisely asks about everything, "What are the possible alternatives?" Here, I try to shift the emphasis of criticism from the finished work to its *having reached* that finish:[6] I know, for instance, that no one will be surprised to hear from me that Shakespeare wrote in one style to his sonnet-friend and in another to his sonnet-mistress, or that Hamlet was melancholy. In that sense, these essays rarely tell something "new" about the works they treat, nor (in that sense) do they intend to. I am trying instead to see *how* the works came to be formed as they are, how we know that these two major styles operate in the *Sonnets*, or when Hamlet is melancholy. Against what norms are these impressions formed, what forms have been taken over, bent, turned inside out, mixed to make their particular form? Guillén's remark that a genre is an invitation to match form to material[7] is an extremely helpful formulation of a difficult problem—we can see that casting *The Winter's Tale* as a tragicomedy answers a specific invitation to form which, however, did not happen to dictate the author's solution to the prob-

[4] *European Literature of the Latin Middle Ages*, tr. Willard Trask (New York, 1955).

[5] *Literature as System* (Princeton, 1971).

[6] Ibid., particularly "The Aesthetics of Literary Influence" (pp. 17-52); and "A Note on Influences and Conventions" (pp. 53-68).

[7] Ibid., pp. 111, 119.

lem set. Similarly, the revenge-play was an invitation to a recognizable form—but it took a hardy man to decide to make its protagonist an intellectual, and a melancholy intellectual at that. Another way of looking at these special problems is to consider them as mixtures of genres—*two* invitations to form issued at once, which is to turn Sidney's complaint about "mungrell" tragicomedies around. That other people saw *Hamlet* as such a mixture Antony Scoloker's words, in the *Epistle to Daiphantus* (1604), tell us

> . . . or to come home to the vulgars *Element* like *Friendly Shakespeare's Tragedies,* where the *Commedian* rides, when the *Tragedian* stands on Tip-toe: Faith it should please all, like Prince *Hamlet*. But in sadnesse, then it were to be feared he would runne mad.

Since in *Hamlet* the norms of these forms—tragedy, comedy, revenge-play, thinker-in-literature—pull against one another, the problem was somehow to make various decorums blend together. What then does a writer retain, what alter, in the norm, or rather, in the *idea* of the norm? How has, specifically, "tragedy" been treated, how "comedy," in *The Winter's Tale*? How has *Hamlet* profited by its hospitability both to comic and tragic forms, to the revenge-form and the (emergent) form of critical-philosophical hero?

A "critical-philosophical hero" raises other questions: what *is* such a thing, literarily speaking? In what decorum does such a figure belong? We might look for him, say, in Pico's great oration on human potentiality—and there, perhaps, the well-educated Hamlet *did* look for a model for one of his speeches (I.ii.286-96); but Shakespeare evidently did not use this model for his prince. Most literary devices—*vide* E. R. Curtius, who did not mean chiefly to be teaching us this lesson in his great handbook—come charged with implications: to say, for instance, "Siste, viator," is not just to play Ancient Mariner to any passerby out of some private obsession of one's own; rather, a whole formal mode of address is implied by those two words, in which an inscription speaks out its *memorabilia* to an anonymous if individuated audience. Its monumental stasis is played off against *viator*'s passage, its dense meaning stressed by the obligatory brevity of the epigrammatic lines. Again, to write a poem beginning with dawn and to end it with nightfall implies a day somehow idealized, somehow set off from all others, as we can learn from such divergently generic pieces as "Lycidas" and "Upon Appleton House." The debate of arms and letters, so charmingly introduced into *Love's Labour's Lost*,[8] implies an entire decorum in which a literary question turns out to have ethical, moral, and cultural significances. A melancholy man, especially one designated as a traveler, might be expected to bring his own satiric milieu with him wherever we find him: so Jaques even in Arden.[9] But what of a melancholy, sporadically satirical prince? For him, Pico's *Oration* was too fully optimistic to provide much help. His proper *milieu* seems to have been books of medicine, or at best philosophical considerations of the human fabric, decorums rarely found in dramatic literature—what is impressive is Shakespeare's transfer of these diagnostic stereotypes not merely onto the stage, but into a single dramatic character, made thereby to seem to the audience an extraordinarily complex personality.

In the essays which follow, I try to work in both directions, examining what implications a large form (a genre, a mode) may have for a work at least resonating to that form's dominant notes (e.g., *The Winter's Tale* as tragicomedy; epigrammatic elements in the *Sonnets*), and examining as well the implications of its larger natural *milieu* carried by a particular small convention—device, *topos*, stereotype—into its new larger context (e.g., the *aube* in *Romeo and Juliet*; the paradoxy in *King Lear*, studied in an earlier work; Cassio as *adulescens*). If it is true that all such conventional forms are deeply rooted in the culture of craft and in the larger social culture as well, then of course no form-matter dichotomy can be allowed: such a form, large or small, must "inform" the work in which it occurs, must fundamentally contribute to its particularity; it must also "inform"—that is, give information to—beholders and readers about its nature and implications. One can go farther: such a form "informs" beholders and readers in yet another sense, by supplying a needed structure for understanding, providing mental set, "forming" the receiving mind. Forms are those *schemata* which by their cultural accessibility ready us to take in whatever we do take in of an environment, our own lived environment, the environment of another place or time, the environment of a given work of art.

[8] See below, p. 39. [9] See below, pp. 256-57.

Obviously, then, forms are crucial in the translation of ideas, including aesthetic ideas, from mind to mind. They are the media for culture, in this case the literary medium by which ideas are presented, transferred, understood, and judged. An unmediated vision cannot be communicated, still less interpreted: it can only remain in its incommunicable, pristine state—a vision, no less and (certainly) no more than that. Since Shakespeare's work is preeminently mediated and mediating, speaking as it has to so many kinds of men, I need not argue for the presence and importance of forms in his work; we all know they are there. What I must argue for, with some determination, is the presence of "norms" in that work, since he of all authors seems freest in breaking patterns, in unmetaphoring and remetaphoring familiar literary clichés, in creating new forms and patterns to bequeath to successors.

The notion of "unmetaphoring" is simple enough, really: an author who treats a conventionalized figure of speech as if it were a description of actuality is unmetaphoring that figure. Shakespeare's quietly making the garden enclosed of virginal love the locus of Romeo's second exchange with Juliet or his transforming a standard prop in the tableaux of noble melancholy into the specific skull of a dead friend are examples of the sort I mean. In the examination of rhetorical styles in *Antony and Cleopatra*, I should say that the playwright "remetaphorizes" by identifying once more linguistic styles with chosen modes of life. We always know where we are, though, in this particular poetic revaluation: the norms, the common language of a particular writer, are always somehow adumbrated or made clear by implication, even when they are not asserted or "given" polemically in a work. We can recognize consciously or unconsciously the liberties taken with the forms articulated in any work. *Parole* reliably implies *langue*. That is, when King Lear says,

> In such a night
> To shut me out? Pour on; I will endure.
> In such a night as this?
>
> (III.iv.17-19)

we are reminded of the lyrical exchange of Jessica and Lorenzo in *A Merchant of Venice*, of the whole grand tradition of *O qualis nox* lying topically behind them, as well perhaps as of the mechanicals' travesty of it in *Midsummer Night's Dream*. The bitterness of his daughters' treatment of Lear is the more poignant for its being cast, for a moment, in these particular terms of lyric celebration.

Though in most of my chapters, as I have said, I deal with only one problem, in the first and last chapters I have tried to touch, all too briefly, upon the multiple aspects of different plays. Of course studying the forms worked into any one play would reliably provide endless discoveries about Shakespeare's interwoven art (he wasn't a dyer, really, so much as a weaver, like Bottom), and my heart lies with such works. To cite just one study of a single work, Maynard Mack's *King Lear in Our Time*[10] has opened up the almost unbelievable literary richness of the play, and has proved paternally fertile. Some of Mack's notions have been treated in greater detail by such studies as Martha Andresen's of *King Lear*[11] and the essays collected in *Some Facets of "King Lear."*[12] Each analysis of one of the play's informing forms raises the question, ever more mysterious, of how one man managed to get so much, and that much so well, into a single work. In the chapters which follow, I want to disclaim the implication that the particular form I chose for study is the *only*, or even the major, informing element in that work. Of course I do not think that any of these works can be reduced to a single element of its greatness, or that my treatment of a particular *schema* sanctions shrinking a play down just to that particular point of consideration. My own experience suggests quite the opposite. Some years ago, after a heady month of feeling utter mastery over the complexities of *King Lear* as a result of finding the use Shakespeare put in the play's language, plot, and structure of so many of those cliché paradoxes Ortensio Lando anthologized for Europe,[13] I began to realize what paradoxy did not "explain" in the play.[14] In particular, it did not account for the secure sense of rockbed morality which, in spite of all its horrifying contingency, the play makes us feel. Further study suggested some of the literary reasons for such hard-bought security—which suggested, in turn, more

[10] Berkeley, 1965.
[11] Unpublished dissertation, Yale University, 1972.
[12] Toronto, 1974.
[13] *Paradoxia Epidemica* (Princeton, 1966), Chapter 15.
[14] See William Elton's remarkably inclusive study, *King Lear and the Gods* (San Marino, 1966).

topics for investigation. Nor do I think my study of *Othello* here accounts for that play—a similar essay on heroic language, gesture, and psychology, or one on the question of honor in the play,[15] seems to me more central to its meanings than my chapter here; but my subject is, I think, unduly neglected and touches upon problems fundamental to the play's original conceptualization.

As for *Hamlet*, in spite of the many comments on the prince's melancholy, I have not found any study of melancholy, save for Bridget Lyons' exemplary book,[16] which accounts for more than the prince's behavior. Here, I have tried to show how many of the play's, as well as the prince's, puzzles can be solved in the context of melancholy ideas and *schemata*, and to suggest that in the complex melancholy syndrome may lie the secret of the play's baffling unity. Withal, I do not insist that my insights into the play are essential to its being understood, or that all base mechanicals who saw "*Hamlet* when new" recognized such a source of unity in the play—only that Shakespeare could see the potentialities for his art in that syndrome, as in more recognizably literary traditional forms, and that he used the melancholy syndrome just as he used more traditionally literary materials, for his own uses. Much as E. H. Kantorowicz did with the notion of "the King's two bodies" in *Richard II*, I have tried to write of each traditional form as exemplary in its play, regarding it as one might a Japanese paper flower which explicates in solution. That flower is an intricate contrivance which literally expands and unfolds its manifold implications in a favorable environment: so the individual forms in a Shakespearean play.

Much Shakespearean criticism (as, perhaps, criticism of any major artist's work) tends to give the impression that everything else written was produced to be of use to, or to find its apotheosis in, this playwright's work. Trying to naturalize Shakespeare in a context larger than national, I may seem to suggest that Shakespeare is the figural fulfilment of all previous European literature—of course he is *not* the microcosm of the Renaissance, a time-capsule of a culture that would have been great even without him. There is much that is important in the Renaissance decidedly *not* in Shakespeare—echoes of Montaigne, for instance,

[15] Sr. Jean Klene's forthcoming study in *SQ* will deal with the matter of honor in *Othello*.

[16] *Voices of Melancholy* (London, 1971).

are there, but no trace of that Renaissance *novum repertum*, the essay; rogues and roguery, but nothing of the problematical picaresque form; philosophical *topoi* and satire on philosophical positions, but no significant response to the great neoplatonic awakening, and no serious reaction to scepticism save as the common man's common self-protection against novelty and change. All the same, great though Shakespeare might well have been whenever and wherever he was born, he was great in his own way because of his culture, which he exploited with a professional's grasp of its potentialities for his art and with a multiple response characteristic of his personal imaginative power. The chapters which follow aim to give some sense, however inadequate, of that unique response.

II

As will be immediately obvious, several of my chapters discuss questions of genre. Like E. H. Gombrich and E. D. Hirsch,[17] I think it extremely important to locate a work within its genre, simply because genre offers a set of fairly fixed expectations by which to organize one's reaction to a work of literature. Though Croce and new-critical theorists have marshaled strong arguments against a predestinating concept of extrinsic genres, Renaissance students have gradually gained sufficient confidence to insist upon the importance of genre at least for their fields.[17a] Mr. Hirsch has offered a concept of a work's "intrinsic genre," by which he seems to mean something very like the formal particularity attributed to any piece of work by linguistic structuralists. There can be, I suppose, as many intrinsic genres as there are works in existence— but even if that be so, our way of identifying intrinsic genres is by way of received extrinsic genres. I cannot, for instance, identify the genre, intrinsic or extrinsic, of *Troilus and Cressida*, and I remain puzzled by my own puzzlement in this case. I doubt if *Troilus and Cressida* is any more mixed in genre than *Cymbeline*, that comical-tragical-historical-pastoral play in the romance

[17] E. H. Gombrich, "Expression and Communication," in *Meditations on a Hobby Horse* (London, 1963), pp. 66-67; and E. D. Hirsch, *Validity in Interpretation* (New Haven, 1966). Sherman Hawkins gives a fine argument for considering Shakespeare's genres in "The Two Worlds of Shakespearean Comedy," *S. Stud.*, III (1967), 62-80.

[17a] I treat this matter in more detail in my forthcoming study, *The Resources of Kind.*

mode, or than *King Lear*; but *Troilus and Cressida*'s generic components are in such suspension that I cannot assign weight to them. I can identify them (I think), which makes it all the odder that I cannot really discuss the play in generic terms, as it certainly *should* be discussed. All this suggests that Mr. Hirsch is right: until we can assign a work within its genre, interpretation and criticism will not be directed to the play's fundamental problems.[18]

However important we find genres in literary interpretation and criticism, we cannot limit ourselves to *identifying* these genres. To read Julius Caesar Scaliger, or any of the great genre-critics of the Renaissance, one might get the notion that genre was viewed by literary men much as Michelangelo is said to have viewed the marble in which he worked, each piece of stone containing its own essential form, which it was the sculptor's job to liberate from its surrounding mass. Marble-hard, genre seems to resist the inferior technician (as the block that became the David resisted Bandinelli's hand), to submit only to the man who can discover its hidden form, clean and flawless. By such a critical theory, both theory and work of art disdain criticism and interpretation, confident of existing in a near-perfect world indifferent to audience, beholder, or reader.

Shakespeare offers a major argument against such a simplistic view of genre: his interest in the traditional aspects of his art lay precisely in their problematic nature, not in their stereotypical force. As I argue in the chapters which follow, I think he worked from the hypothesis that the problematical in literary theory and practice has to do with the problematical in human life—that the letter exists to point the way to the spirit. No literary dictate can be allowed more importance than the specific demands of the imagination working on a specific problem—but also, an imagination cannot work on its problems *without* recourse to its intellectual and artistic environment, to its literary and moral correlatives. Shakespeare's work relies upon his means of expression for its "meaning," and in turn those means of expression are not neutral or empty forms. They too have their context of ideas, so that literary meanings, in this period at the very least, reach out to involve moral and social situations larger than the

[18] For "intrinsic genres," see *Validity in Interpretation*, pp. 78-89; see also pp. 89-126, on genre; and pp. 127-207, on interpretation and criticism.

containments of a single play or poem. Dependent also practically and aesthetically upon what Gombrich has called "the beholder's share,"[19] Shakespeare could not have allowed himself the luxury, even if his temperament had permitted such self-indulgence, of attempting perfection in a world of platonic forms. Like Spenser, though very differently, Shakespeare accepted the mixed nature of living, the varieties of becoming, as the matter of literary works. For him, literary materials were not Michelangelo's marble.[19a] He worked them as if they were clay, to be shaped into the likeness of life—or shaped, like Adam, into life itself. And like the sculptor's clay, Shakespeare's materials came out of different crocks and were formed of different earths—that is, they came from different categorical and schematic sources, to be combined and recombined as imaginative and technical needs found practical.

On the whole, though Shakespeare's plays are notoriously and gloriously mixed in genre, their dramatic generic associations are usually clearly marked. In *The Winter's Tale* we cannot miss what is "tragic," what "comic," nor can we miss noticing how these two are conjoined under a pastoral umbrella. The non-dramatic genres are usually less clearly visible: in *Romeo and Juliet* the nondramatic generic contribution of sonneteering *is* manifest; far less so, although there it is far more important, in *Othello*. In *Love's Labour's Lost, inter alia,* we can recognize the generic shadow cast by the Renaissance dialogue both in the topics and in the interaction of characters in the play. In a later comedy, *Much Ado About Nothing*, debate has been animated, much as the convention of sonnet-criticism was in Shakespeare's *Sonnets*, into personality, so that debate- and dialogue-points are worked out in the dramatic action between Beatrice and Benedick, not argued pro and contra as in *Love's Labour's Lost*. Finally, in *Hamlet* we see and hear the debate reduced to a *device*, albeit an extremely important one, as Hamlet, that studious princeling, formulates his great soliloquy in scholastic terms. But the terms of his soliloquy on life and death, on living and dying,

19 *Art and Illusion*, pp. 181-290. Important applications and extensions of this principle to literature are provided in the recent work of Stanley Fish, Paul Alpers, and Stephen Booth.

19a Nor, really, was Michelangelo so platonic as is usually supposed: I am indebted for help on this point to D. D. Ettlinger, Sears R. Jayne, and Gavriel Moses.

on action and retirement, are not such as to indicate his studious temperament only, though they surely do that; they are Hamlet's casuistic maneuver to objectify and distance, for a while at least, an overwhelming and immediate life-problem.

In *Love's Labour's Lost*, the dialogue informs much of the play's structure, as the characters work out their comical destinies in a parody of the orthodox form. By no stretch of the imagination, for all its dialectics, could we call *Hamlet* generically a debate, of body and soul, of action and contemplation, important and problematical though those questions are in the play. On the other hand, *The Winter's Tale is* unmistakably a tragicomedy—more obviously so, for instance, than *Cymbeline*, a play which it resembles, and differently so from the terms laid down for the form by Guarini, the inventor of the genre. How free Shakespeare was in his generic experiments and manipulations we can read from Bernard Weinberg's important study of *Cinquecento* literary criticism:[20] genre-theory governed thinking about literature, so much so that it had to be altered, with enormous polemic, every time a major work failed to fit generic categories (the *Commedia, Orlando Furioso, Il Pastor Fido*). Although the contours of the theory of genres changed under the impact of new forms, in fact its ideology did not—Mazzoni's defense of Dante, Guarini's of pastoral drama, Pigna's of romance all insisted on an enlarged canon of acceptable generic categories, never questioning the rightness of genre-theory. In subsequent arguments about the precise nature of tragicomedy and its difference from comitragedy,[21] the clear assumption is present that each genre is somehow unique, and that distinctions between genres can be spelled out. But no such assumption governs Shakespeare's mixtures: though *The Winter's Tale* is tragicomic, neither Guarini nor Pontanus would have allowed it as exemplary, so idiosyncratic is it. Shakespeare's generic mixtures are remarkably independent of rule; however clearly we can see their practical connections with theoretical problems consciously raised by others, their freedom from orthodoxy and academicism remains their most engaging quality. Literary *dicta* were in the air, certainly, called up by the literary problems they were formulated to solve, but they seem never to have dictated to our playwright, who conspicuously flaunts his

[20] *A History of Italian Literary Criticism in the Renaissance* (Chicago, 1960).

[21] See below, pp. 261-65.

freedom and originality, even in the way he *interprets* literary problems, to say nothing of the solutions he found.

In this book, I am not sure whether I am offering "interpretation" or "criticism," recently wedged so far apart by theorists, though I hope to provide both; I am trying, in a sense slightly different from the ordinary one, to offer by example *explications de texte*, a way of explaining why a text is as it is and has taken the particular form it has. Although this requires recognizing literary forms as they appear in given works—requires, then, some sense of literary history—I do not in the least mean to imply that the naming of parts is sufficient tribute to any significant literary work. Rather, I think that what the parts *do* for and in the literary work is what counts, both as interpretation and as criticism. It matters that, just before taking her potion, Juliet utters a systematic meditation on death such as Louis Martz has taught us to recognize;[22] it matters that both Ophelia and Perdita, in very different styles and in very different contexts, imaginatively invoke a catalogue of flowers to "match" the characters from a stranger world who intrude upon their private celebrations.

To develop a familiar example along these lines, Shakespeare offers us in the *Henry IV* plays a splendid creation, Sir John Falstaff, very different from the real and legendary Sir John Oldcastle, sometime companion to Prince Henry. *Why* this Falstaff? Some of the answer lies in the sources of the narrative. In the chronicles and onstage young Henry V had been fixed into a certain shape—a knobby, irregular, inconsistent shape, to be sure, but a shape firm enough to demand fairly strict *mimesis*. His madcap youth, his subservience to his father before and after the deathbed episode with the crown, his exemplary conduct as healer of national breaches and victor over foreign dangers were all fully established: Henry V was "this star of England," the fulfilment of Respublica's long-thwarted hopes. It was difficult to find in the sources the resources to give this English princeling depth of character; some other means had to be found—so Falstaff was evolved as foil to a prince for whom there were insufficient conventional guidelines.

The prince was very "given," in the factual ways of the literary *milieux* in which Shakespeare found him, the chronicles, chronicle-poems (*Mirror for Magistrates* and Daniel's *Civill Wars*), and

---

[22] *The Poetry of Meditation* (New Haven, 1954).

a morality chronicle-play (*The Famous Victories*). For Falstaff the opposite is the case: brilliant studies have identified some of the many literary streams which conjoined to feed his substantial shape. We recognize in him the braggart soldier, the parasite, and the *buffone* of Latin comedy, *commedia erudita*, and *commedia dell' arte*;[23] we recognize in him (as does the English Hal) the Vice of the morality play,[24] *Mundus* with his *Infans*, Gluttony, Appetite, Riot, and the rest of the temptations besetting this important prodigal son; we recognize in him the Lord of Misrule and Carnival of folkish and medieval festivals;[25] we recognize in him, too, the *Roi des sots* of medieval *sottie*, the court-jester accompanying a ruler,[26] and the complex, critical, paradoxical ways of the Renaissance fool.[27] We recognize in this *puer senex* who insists on the privileges, both of youth and of age, in a particular person: Falstaff. Paradoxically, then, this remarkable mixture of generic characters and stereotypes, this man made of whole cloth (buckram) who seems to be, literarily at least, "all the world," is far more mimetically "real" than the actual young man of history whose companion he is.

And what an extraordinary, exceptional exemplar he is of all these types!—a *miles gloriosus* whose brags are transparent, even arranged to suit the prince's expectation, who, when faced with a "real" braggart soldier from the repertory, Pistol, fearlessly drives him offstage; a parasite not just upon a powerful status-figure but also, *literally*, upon a hostel-keeper and a bawd; a Riot, a Master of the Revels, whose chief reveler knows throughout the game that it must one day end for good; a fool whose folly mocks himself as surely as it mocks king and royal justice; a devil whose temptations to this heir-apparent turn out to be as unavailing with that chill and distanced young man as Satan's importuning

---

[23] J. W. Draper, "Falstaff and the Plautine Parasite," *Classical J.*, XXXIII (1938), 390-401; D. C. Boughner, "Traditional Elements in Falstaff," *JEGP*, XLIII (1944), 417-28; and "Vice, Braggart, and Falstaff," *Anglia*, LXXII (1954), 35-61; D. B. Landt, "The Ancestry of Sir John Falstaff," *SQ*, XVII (1966), 69-76; E. E. Stoll, *Shakespeare Studies* (New York, 1942); Northrop Frye, "The Argument of Comedy," *English Institute Essays* (New York, 1949).

[24] J. Dover Wilson, *The Fortunes of Falstaff* (Cambridge, 1943). See also James Monaghan, "Falstaff and his Forebears," *SP*, XVIII (1921), 353-61.

[25] C. L. Barber, *Shakespeare's Festive Comedy* (Princeton, 1959).

[26] Enid Welsford, *The Fool* (London, 1935); J. W. Draper, "Falstaff as Fool and Jester," *MLQ*, VII (1946), 453-62.

[27] Walter Kaiser, *Praisers of Folly* (Cambridge, Mass., 1963), pp. 195-275.

of Christ in the wilderness. Like Erasmus' Folly, Falstaff keeps us all off-balance—all save the prince, who knows even before the play begins that the revels must be ended and their master turned out of the game. In a final turning, perhaps owing something to the traditions of the morality-play, this *chevalier sans cheval*,[28] this riotous glutton, this fool is shown to be off-balance too, surprised by the forms of worldliness his tender lambkin now displays.

By both the morality reading and the Machiavellian reading, the *Henry IV* plays are a mirror of princes, a study in rulers' regimen, where we watch a young man learning to rule his nation, growing into his kingship, building his character into its ultimate calling. But much of this character-building is Shakespeare's, who shows us an increasingly able Hal simply by putting him in relation to various symbolic characters in the play; from these arrangements we see where Hal starts. He is characteristically "between":[29] between Falstaff, the festive mock-king, and grim, lamenting, businesslike Henry IV; between Falstaff, a braggart soldier forced into the field, and another glorious soldier, the over-heroic Hotspur, who throws his cause away for the "honour" Falstaff has the good sense to reject; between Falstaff, careless of his master's cause and of human life ("tush, man, mortal men, mortal men"), and Prince John of Lancaster, so careful of polity that he cares not for his pledged word or for human life; between Falstaff, openly flaunting his cheating, and that intransigent servant of the king, the Lord Chief Justice. These pairings serve to identify for us a prince who, though he does not really develop in the play, is seen responding to more and more situations; even more important are those situations in which Hal is, as it were, bounced off Falstaff himself. From these we learn, unexpectedly, how like the two are. They share real distaste for responsibility. Though Hal bites the biter Falstaff in the Gadshill episode, they are alike in the pleasure they take in deviancy, alike in their different parodies of the highborn robberies in the kingdom at large. Their joint misrule speaks to England's condition: the jests at Eastcheap (for all their underworld character), furthermore, have an innocence which the king and the plotters have long since forfeited. Both Hal and Falstaff are Machiavellian, manipulating others (Mistress Quickly, Francis, Poins) and each other, enigmatically in

28 Harry Levin, "Falstaff Uncolted," *MLN*, LXI (1946), 305-10.
29 Kaiser's discussions of Falstaff are particularly helpful on this point.

the buckram exchange after Gadshill, tolerantly in the judgment-scene and in Hal's permitting Falstaff to steal his honor in Hotspur's death. Though the plays make quite clear that Hal once crowned has no intention of condoning Falstaff, from Hal's first soliloquy, *via* Falstaff's impressment of men and dealings with Justice Shallow and Mistress Quickly, to the morality harshness of "I know thee not, old man," they also unequivocally show Hal's enjoyment of Falstaff and, before the prince's final departure to labor in his vocation, his *need* for a figure of diversion, to take the sting out of his own rebellion against rank, to provide outlet for his dissatisfactions with the quality of life at his father's court. What Falstaff offers Prince Hal is not only the symbolic freedoms of youth, but also a chance to practice at being human.

Shifting the level of discussion from the play itself to the making of the play, we can see how Shakespeare found refuge from a ticklish literary problem in the accomplishments of his profession. From his models, those static chronicles and poems from which he took his story, he had little to go on to make of his prince a credible personality, as he had so brilliantly managed with Richard II; neither had he in Hal's life a steady progression toward ever-greater success, a dramatic paradigm such as that offered by Richard's magnificent fall from fortune. The *schemata* to hand were simply insufficient to make this real king into a dramatic character; so the playwright had to turn elsewhere, to other dramatic contexts, and to make from the jumble of *schemata* available to him a figure (out of whole cloth, wholly out of cloth) allied with and foil to the Lusty Juventus who will, like his medieval forebear, ultimately redeem the time he spent in alehouse anarchy, as well as the time wasted in a misgoverned nation.

To think of Falstaff in connection with these denatured types is in part to denature him of his earthy reality, so convincing is the illusion that this particular character is a real individual. Not for nothing did Prince Hal want to pass the time till Falstaff should arrive, nor Queen Elizabeth want him back (at least, on the stage) after his banishment. This unmetaphored figure for the world ("all the world"), the flesh ("Ribs," "Tallow," belly), and the devil ("old white-bearded Satan"), this voluntary anti-courtly fool forcing the problematics of public life upon us as upon the prince, gives form, in his very bulk and anarchic denial of all forms, to the dialectic which propels Hal out of Eastcheap to Shrewsbury and, finally, to Westminster and the responsibilities of Respublica. Quite simply, as we can see, though nature influences art, art influences art more: Shakespeare's success in making a "realer" person out of the art-generated Falstaff than of the actual Henry Plantagenet is a primary example of the Aristotelian notion that poetry is more powerful than history.

The "comical-tragical-historical method" of this play,[30] to say nothing of its satirical component too, will not have escaped notice. As Falstaff is compounded of character-types from different decorums, and brings something of all those decorums into the play with him, so is this a "mungrell" play, the mingling of kings and clowns that Sidney so deplored. Of what is it made, after all?—a usurping King; Falstaff as burlesque player-king; chivalric Hotspur out of professional epic; the political magician Glendower and his lyrical daughter, out of romance; the tavern-frequenters out of city-pamphlets of city-roguery, with Hal moving enigmatically among them to claim a place and voice, after testing his own voice against under-skinker's and Hotspur's, as his own. As Mr. Empson long ago observed,[31] the superhistorical effect of this is to give the impression that all England is somehow involved in the play as Hal progresses to his exemplary rule: the literary decorums drawn on for the play imply a national culture of great complexity and offer a symbolic texture we may take as the thing itself.

III

Let the prince and Falstaff in their prodigality stand for a moment as metaphor for the poet's own prodigality: Shakespeare throws away more than most poets manage to put in, so that the student of his works and of Renaissance culture often feels (as Whitehead said of Plato) that wherever he goes, he meets Shakespeare coming back. But because the concealments of his art are very great, it is not always obvious beneath the more-than-sufficient play itself that there are literary and literary-theoretical problems just under the surface. Sometimes the problems seem submerged because we can recognize them only after long study; sometimes because Shakespeare took them for granted as we cannot, and therefore had no need to stress them; sometimes because critical concepts and their basic materials are so entirely trans-

---

[30] See Gareth Lloyd Evans' article in *Early Shakespeare*, ed. John Russell Brown and Bernard Harris (London, 1961), pp. 154-63.

[31] *Some Versions of Pastoral* (reprinted New York, 1960).

formed and digested into new forms (as in *Henry IV*) that they are not readily identifiable.

Most important of all, we often miss the literary-critical component of Shakespeare's work because he was doing so much else in his plays which has, as it ought to have, prior claim on our attention. At all ranges, he was prodigal, and we cannot take in everything at once. His illusionism, for instance, forces us to attend to different, often more naturalistic, aspects of his work from those more closely formal and conventional. Shakespeare's prodigality is balanced by his economies: sometimes he took incredible risks with materials and forms, forcing them far beyond their normal limits (the pastoral pattern in *King Lear*; the sonnets to the lady); sometimes he altered a "source" or form minimally and nonetheless set his mark on it (e.g., Rosalind's behavior in the forest; Perdita's language at the sheep-shearing; Parolles' virginity-speech). Read against the works of most of his contemporaries, Shakespeare's plays show great powers of naturalistic illusionism; his generosity in this respect is manifest over and over again. The Nurse's great speech on Juliet's broken brow calls up the whole domestic and psychological life of the Nurse a decade before the play takes place—material, we realize abruptly, with no particular relevance to the play; until we come to understand what the Nurse's realistic, affectionate, lifelong picture of Juliet does to modify Romeo's extraordinary language of idealization. In the Queen Mab speech, Mercutio's wit and invention are displayed in a set-piece, an aria, on a theme irrelevant to the plot's action—after all, Romeo and Juliet never have time to be properly visited by Queen Mab, which is part of the sadness of their situation. But the speech is all the same fundamental to the theme of brilliant youthfulness and to the sociological setting of these glittering, imaginative, under-employed young men. From that speech we get something else, too, aslant of the main action but supportive to the play's theme: that is, a different sense of the wastefulness of the foolish feud. As much as the deaths of Juliet and her Romeo, so young and so alive, the waste of a man like Mercutio cries out for civil settlement of the old men's vendetta. In this case, what seems to be the overflow of prodigal invention turns out to have its own economies: that contradictory double gift of prodigality and economy Shakespeare displayed over and over again. The evidently tedious Polonius is a good example of the way in which the playwright communicates the ethos of an entire family, so that the behavior and fates of Laertes and Ophelia become more realistically intelligible to us, once we know the father's expressions of value and modes of behavior.

In language, Shakespeare is as prodigal and as economical, throwing away lines, speeches, even whole scenes. Whenever we pause over language, we can see the ways in which apparently careless lines and speeches support character, further plot, and stress theme. Imagery tends to work on behalf of the play, as studies from Miss Spurgeon's to Heilman's, Foakes', Clemen's, and Charney's bear out.[32] But in addition, Shakespeare can, with the utmost economy, make his language do two very different things at the same time: he can write, for instance, an exchange between two characters which perfectly matches both characters' assigned roles and in which also one speaker (Hal, Hamlet, Edgar, Lear, in Mr. Zitner's examples),[33] without abandoning his own role or losing his sense of his interlocutor's, speaks through and beyond mere role to appeal to the responsible humanity of his hearer. Lear's press-money speech is, at one manifest level, the disjunctive utterance of an insane old man, an insane old king. It is also highly rational and organized, with classical references—but it takes a bit of distancing to see how that is so.[34] Hamlet's recorder speech, at first hearing so casual, so chancy, so whirling, focuses to comment on the human instrumentalism and manipulation that is a particular theme as well as a major plot-element of this play.

As his language is multiple, so is his use of conventional device. When Lear says to Cordelia, "And fire us hence like foxes," a great deal is called up in that short phrase—farmers putting fire down foxholes to destroy the predators; Samson's trick with the foxes and the corn; the little destroyers of Canticles; the conventional morality which sent the doomed and damned to hellfire.

---

[32] Caroline Spurgeon, *Shakespeare's Imagery and What It Tells Us* (Cambridge, 1935); Robert B. Heilman, *This Great Stage* (Baton Rouge, 1948); and *Magic in the Web* (Lexington, 1956); R. A. Foakes, "Suggestions for a New Approach to Shakespeare's Imagery," *S.Stud.*, v (1952); Wolfgang Clemen, *The Development of Shakespeare's Imagery* (London, 1951); Maurice Charney, *Shakespeare's Roman Plays* (Cambridge, Mass., 1961); and *Style in Hamlet* (Princeton, 1969).

[33] Zitner, "Shakespeare's Secret Language," develops this point.

[34] See Edmund Blunden, "Shakespeare's Significances," in *Shakespeare Criticism, 1915-1935*, ed. Anne Ridler (London, 1962), pp. 326-42, and Zitner, "*King Lear* and its Language."

To take an example different in kind, much like the Falstaff-example, Iago is a masterpiece of mysterious psychological analysis, but he is also a stage machiavel, as such related to another Old Nick, the morality devil, characteristically a presenter of plots and playlets. We know this from Mr. Spivack's book,[35] but we must not forget that Iago is also a parasite, a malcontent, a Brighella,[36] and a braggart soldier as well. Further, as Falstaff also persuades us of a real past, involving Clement's Inn and the revels of Mile-end Green as well as the difficulties of the flea-bitten, down-at-heels, out-at-elbows gentry, so Iago has his correlatives in real life, a new man, a technician making his fortune in a world of changing opportunities by his practical skills and his sense of empirical adaptation. Hamlet is forced to cry revenge, like many another son stuck with a vendetta, but he is also—*why?*—marked with Montaigne's tendency to consideration and doubt. Unlike Montaigne, though, he has the malcontent's sharp vision and sharp tongue. In Falstaff, Iago, and Hamlet many different traditions are gathered up, dramatic and nondramatic, to make highly successful theatrical figures. By combining traditions, sometimes in very simple ways, Shakespeare demonstrates his prodigality and the economy that results from that generosity: he had, evidently, no fear of running out of creativity, could pour out his invention like wine, the wine of Cana at that, multiplying to need. *Multum in parvo*: and in something already large, like a play, how much more!

Critically speaking, this compressed, allusive, suggestive pluralism can be seductive and misleading. Because Shakespeare said so much, and this "much" all at once, it has been easy for readers of his works to assume that, in criticizing or commenting upon them, anything goes: works so inclusive *must* be hospitable, the justification seems to run, to *any* interpretation. So the wildest personal associations with the text can be considered to make some sense; indeed, in extreme instances, the critic can be enjoined to misunderstand the text to create a new insight of his own.

Well, anything did not go into the plays, so it does not make sense to assume that they send random messages out. With a little care and a little learning (small Latin helps here!), one can see what went in and, from that recognition, can even begin to see

[35] Bernard Spivack, *Shakespeare and the Allegory of Evil* (New York, 1958).
[36] For this, I am indebted to June Fellows.

why certain things went in. Further, because of his peculiar openness to the mysteries of his craft and to his audience, Shakespeare played fair, providing us every time with directions to the literary or extraliterary context from which he drew—not, like Jonson, as our schoolmaster, but simply as our playwright, communicating and sharing his insights into his (and our) culture. Shakespeare was neither pedant nor obscurantist nor monopolist: what he took from his culture he gave back with both hands, enriched, transvalued, transfigured.

To take forms—devices, stereotypes, genres, etc.—seriously is both to honor and to criticize them, to involve one's self in the very morality of one's craft. Shakespeare mocked, for instance, conventional forms of expression: in *Love's Labour's Lost*, figurative languages; in *Henry V*, bombast; in *Hamlet*, both stiff and pliable languages of courts. A master of stylistic alternatives, he could parody, could imitate, could write in counterpointed styles, could even "invent" languages; but, excellent as he was at this aspect of his art, he did not do it for *epideixis* alone. In his work, linguistic habits always relate to ways of life, style to morality;[37] by his literary comments, Shakespeare offers, in entirely *literary* terms, moral commentary as well. So with ideas and themes, conventions, genres, modes: he looked "through" them in more than one sense, as in *King Lear* he saw through the most ordinary rhetorical-moral paradoxes to far deeper moral meanings. The forms were transparent for him—in Donne's word, "through-shine"—and in turn become transparent for us. By seeing to the center of his professional artifices, he could present a familiar scheme without losing either its artificiality or its "truth," so that literature itself can be experienced as at once a "new" aesthetic experience and a critical experience. We see it anew, renewed, so that, for instance, the familiar triad of the world, the flesh, and the devil is forever unmetaphored and incorporated in Falstaff, and we know from Falstaff's very particularity how common, even commonplace, "temptation" can be. It would be false to *moralize* Falstaff simply—false to the complex aesthetic experience, false to the sense of layered, interlocking life which the *Henry IV* plays communicate; but the moral *situation*, in all its problematic complexity, is precisely what is conveyed.

With all this to work on, offered in such fascinatingly literary terms, the literary critic has his hands full: a pluralism offering so

---

[37] See below, chapters 1 and 4, for fuller discussion.

many ways to understand art is itself the best argument against the proliferation of private visions, unregulated by textual respect, to which we are nowadays so often tempted.

IV

To look at Shakespeare's work from this perspective makes us take seriously the ways in which he forced conventions, in particular generic limits. As Góngora and others (Morgenstern, Lewis Carroll, Hopkins, Rilke) forced the language to express relations to which normal syntax does not do justice, so Shakespeare (who could also force language in just this way: the sandblind, gravelblind, stoneblind of *The Merchant of Venice*) forced larger devices and conventions—unmetaphoring metaphors and whole metaphorical patterns, springing traditional stereotypes back into a resonant reality, playing different generic languages against each other. It gives us, too, a deeper sense of the ways in which generic habits are, as Guillén repeatedly says, "invitations" to do something else, something *more*, something *new*, with familiar forms. Elsewhere I argue that a period with such remarkable examples of *genera mixta* as we find in the Renaissance (Rabelais, Cervantes, Milton, to name only a few authors conspicuously practising in mixed genres) is somehow special; and that anthological works (often "anatomies" in Frye's sense)[38] answered in a particularly conscientious and demanding way to the sense of cultural multiplicity of the period and of the writer's trade. Whatever the critical arguments against generic studies in our time, then, I know that *not* to be aware of generic boundaries, generic definitions, generic models is, at the very least, to make much of Renaissance literature altogether unintelligible.

I assume, therefore, a background of known materials ("traditions") for each chapter that follows, rather than specific literary "sources." I take for granted that Shakespeare knew Catullus, for instance, but not that he had (as Jonson surely had) Catullus either by heart or at his elbow; the same goes for Martial, Ovid, Plautus, or Seneca. I assume that Shakespeare knew, and knew *about*, various *milites gloriosi*, but not that Falstaff can claim descent from a specific braggart knight; that he knew commentaries on melancholy, and knew something of what contradictory remarks a medical practitioner would be likely to make about the

---

[38] Northrop Frye, *Anatomy of Criticism* (Princeton, 1959).

disease, but did not need to check his projections of melancholic symptoms against specific commentary or specific cases. I tend to think of "traditions" as clusters of meanings and practices, with a stable core but fluctuating contours, and I assume that traditions came thus to Shakespeare, as to other artists.

I know too that there will be complaints against this sort of book. *Cognoscenti* will grow restive at what is not discussed; for other readers this approach will seem hopelessly bookish, bogged down in "traditions," "conventions," "languages" which only pedants can now recognize and which (perhaps) only a pedant could then have used, or known he was using. From such readers, I expect Shakespeare's small Latin and less Greek to be invoked against me, together with statements about his money-making talents as an entertainer and about the low level of his audience (presumably the more "authentic" the more it was illiterate). Such a defense is the modern version of the warbling-woodnotes-wild theory of Shakespeare's genius, the version that takes him to be a man who never blotted line. In response, it is easy enough to point out that his small Latin and less Greek is all the same more than most of us possess, and opened to him a world of literary experience which nowadays we are lucky to have glimpsed through a keyhole; that talent as an entertainer of base mechanicals does not by definition mean that a man is forbidden thereby to know anything about his art; that even if the Shakespearean audience was illiterate (which in good part it was not), it was nonetheless highly experienced in watching plays, knew the conventions of dramatic forms, and could be relied upon to recognize variations on its own expectations.

Finally, as Heminges and Condell knew when they collected the materials for their Folio, these plays, great in performance, are also great reading-matter:

> . . . it is not our province, who only gather his workes, to give them to you, to praise him. It is yours that reade him. And there we hope, to your divers capacities, you will finde enough, both to draw, and to hold you: for his wit can no more lie hid, then it would be lost. Reade him, therefore; and againe, and againe: And if you doe not like him, surely you are in some manifest danger, not to understand him.

The editors knew Shakespeare's pluralism: "againe, and againe" points to their sense of the apparently inexhaustible depths of his plays. Because so many fine works have stressed precisely the theatricality of Shakespeare's art, I may be pardoned for treating it as reading matter. After all, no excuse is needed for treating Chaucer's work as read material, although we know he read it *aloud*, as performance, at the time. My own defense of reading, as against seeing or directing these plays, is simply that by necessity every performance must do what criticism need not do: for simplicity's sake, for coherence's sake, performances must choose a point of view, must take a reductionist stance toward works so plural as these. Readers have an advantage, as Coleridge recognized: let us make the most of it! First of all, we may abandon unnecessary polemic: no need to insist upon an active, acting, alert playwright-manager doing what, and only what, his company and his audience expected and demanded of him; nor yet postulate a bespectacled Shakespeare writing dutiful exercises according to the dictates of Renaissance systematics. There is no reason why Shakespeare, like other playwrights concerned in production, should not have incorporated accidental or incidental findings into his text (after all, poets writing in their closets do just that); no reason, equally, why he should not also have had a subtle understanding of literary practice and theory. There is not the slightest reason to choose, once and for all, between a Shakespeare who so vividly amused and moved men and women and a Shakespeare whose awareness of literary meanings reached far beyond lay appreciation: obviously, the playwright was at least these two Shakespeares, even if he was not Bacon, Marlowe, the Earl of Oxford, or some other claimant to his name.

All the same, it is difficult to believe that any man could be conscious of all that Shakespeare was doing all at once—until we think of analogues. It is only about *writers* that we hear the question asked, "Do you really believe that this author could have realized that he was doing all you say?" Rubens, as Professor Held shows us over and over again, and Rembrandt, as Lord Clark has shown in his study of Rembrandt and Italian art,[39] had prodigious visual memories—they could not have looked up each time they needed them all the "sources" which manifestly enriched their work. If I may be forgiven a low-style analogue to Shakespeare's talent, there is the proverbial mathematical idiot-boy whose mind, dulled in other ways, responds with uncanny speed and correctness to verbal numerical problems which I could never do right,

[39] Kenneth Clark, *Rembrandt and the Italian Renaissance* (London, 1966).

even with paper and pencil (and probably not even with an adding machine). Shakespeare seems to have handled linguistic and literary problems with much the same reflexive accuracy as that classic simpleton who was also, unaccountably, an arithmetical natural. Of course, he was no simpleton, and a "natural" only in a special sense. My Shakespeare, I am sure, knew too much to have been a scholar. "Ease" marks his works, as Heminges and Condell said of him: "His mind and hand went together: and what he thought, he uttered with that easinesse, that wee scarce received from him a blot in his papers." Another high-style analogue to all this, besides Rubens and Rembrandt, is the young Mozart, who could do "anything" and was, like Shakespeare, indecently prodigal with his gifts. A careful if not a hoarding author, Ben Jonson lamented as untidiness the ease in writing Heminges and Condell acclaimed: that Shakespeare never blotted line makes, occasionally, hard reading for us—but it is, of course, what makes his work so magnificently, plurally rich.

To match his richness requires a cultural recreation sufficient to respond to some of the cues in his art. From the language of an author's cues, understanding can come, with something like the author's own professionalism, of what his problems were and the alternatives he saw as leading to their solution. We can the more easily, then, appreciate both his dilemmas and his ways of getting out of them. A very great author can be counted on not to be constricted by any predestination in his traditions: he enlarges possibilities to pour back into traditional currents as much as he takes from them, and often much more besides. Shakespeare was the Prodigal Son of his traditions—but spend as he would, in spite of himself, his talents increased tenfold and tenfold again, to leave his successors with a legacy of alternatives of which his predecessors had little inkling. With that talent the following pages are concerned.

1

Criticism and the Analysis of Craft:
Love's Labour's Lost and the *Sonnets*

I. *Love's Labour's Lost*

FROM THE VERY BEGINNING of his career, Shakespeare showed remarkable adeptness with the stuff of literature—with literary
conventions, traditions, genres, modes, all the elements and the
tools of his craft available to him. His alterations to the Senecan
model on the side of expansion are recognizable in *Titus Andronicus,* his enrichment of the Plautine pattern a major reason
for the particular fun of *A Comedy of Errors.* In another early
comedy, *Love's Labour's Lost,* the playwright worked in an entirely different area, significantly extending the implications of
the fashionable courtly play so splendidly practised by Lyly, in an
examination of the relation between language and dramatic personality. In *Love's Labour's Lost,* Shakespeare exploited the question of "language" to the full, so that even the play's plot is made
up of what might be called linguistic situations, as styles of behavior and speech—the King's pretentious academy (with its
inept fulfillment in its unlearned members), the Princess's courtly
progress with its masque-entertainments (such as actually were
used to beguile royalty on progress), and the rustics' ordinary life,
with its real fantasies and its interruptions by noble obsessions, all
cast in different imaginative and literary styles—are made into
what "plot" there is in the play. These elements, expressed almost
as set-pieces, continually impose upon one another, threaten, undermine, and expose one another simply by juxtaposition. It is
possible to see the play as a competition of different styles of
speech and of life, all jockeying for their rights and even for their
existence. Like those educated wits Lyly and Greene, Shakespeare
seems to have been responding to the challenge of many con-
comitant but mutually separate literary traditions, to be testing
himself as a writer as well as testing those traditions as valid elements of his craft. He drew, then, for this play, on different literary reservoirs, from different literary stores, in such a way as to
point to the peculiar qualities of each particular literary device

31

displayed—and to point, finally, at the problems involved in making fictions as a whole. Superficially, at least, there is no question about the parodic element in *Love's Labour's Lost*; a good part of its contemporary appeal, even some of its delight for us, lies in its confident mockery of linguistic fashions, manners, and mannerisms—in its high-hearted competence precisely with the conventionality of contemporary dramatic writing. The parody is present—but, as criticism of the play abundantly shows,[1] more seems to be involved in it than mere parody.

Because the play has no known principal "source," it has invited many "solutions" in terms of source and analogue. Though this essay certainly deals with "background" for the play, it does not appeal to specific visits by Marguerite de Navarre to her husband, or excursions on her mother's part to that same free-wheeling prince; nor do I turn to those ever-fascinating speculations about the presence of a School of Night in the play or out of it.[2] Its own implications ask for unfolding, certainly: C. L. Barber is right to subsume this play under his umbrella-term "festive"; its gamesmanship makes it a prime candidate for the Huizingesque discussion now so current. It is festive also in the game it makes of learned wit, here taken as academicism, as pedantry, or as linguistic mannerism—but it is, as James Calderwood has beautifully shown,[3] a great deal more than that. For here, Shakespeare plays with many traditions of learning in terms of language: of learning through language and of learning (finally) in spite of language and at language's expense. Conspicuously, the playwright handles various traditions, modes, manners, and styles *as if* they

---

[1] For some comment on the play's linguistic aspects, see G. D. Willcock, *Shakespeare as a Critic of Language* (Shakespeare Association Pamphlet, London, 1934); B. Ifor Evans, *The Language of Shakespeare's Plays* (London, 1965), pp. 1-16; C. L. Barber, *Shakespeare's Festive Comedy* (Princeton, 1959); Philip Edwards, *Shakespeare and the Confines of Art* (London, 1968), pp. 37-48; and especially Calderwood, *Shakespearean Metadrama*, Chapter 3.

[2] Valuable though both Miss Yates' and Miss Bradbrook's studies are, I do not think that a "School of Night" can be held accountable for this play: see M. C. Bradbrook, *The School of Night* (London, 1936); and Frances A. Yates, *A Study of "Love's Labour's Lost"* (Cambridge, 1936). Miss Yates' book stresses Florio's connections with the language of the play in a particularly interesting way.

[3] Calderwood, pp. 64-76; cf. Cyrus Hoy, *The Hyacinth Room* (New York, 1964), pp. 21-38, for a discussion of the moral education and self-education of the characters in the play.

were simply language and no more, by the flexibility of those languages measuring both their strengths and their vulnerabilities, to render at the last a serious comment on the connections between word and deed, language and behavior, vows and the limits of necessity. Primarily, in this play, we see the playwright's emptying out his traditions—though to say that, so bluntly, is to ignore how also their empty shells are shown to be the beautiful, well-made, delightful counters in a continuing translation of critical importance to the persons playing it.

Love's Labour's Lost is unquestionably one of the most overtly stylized plays in Shakespeare's repertory. As I suggested at this chapter's beginning, in it the habit of set-piece is doubly "set," both as an opportunity for showing and for showing off, and as the "set" of a given convention or frame of mind, the setting for a certain role and dictated by that role. In still another sense, a passage, a scene, an interchange is hardened or "set" into a firm, familar form, suitable to a specific rhetorical or intellectual posture, role, stance. The play begins with such a standard piece, the King of Navarre's sonorous version of the praising of "a little academe," that proud discovery (which they considered a "recovery") of Renaissance princes, persuaded by their humanist servants to create among their court ornaments an ecphrastic figure for learning, a local academy, "Still and contemplative in living art."[4] Castiglione's normative work magnificently shows us how a Renaissance court could be deliberately conceived as a work of art, each of its elements a courtier perfectly "finished" in his own self-development, an aesthetic achievement in words and manners analogous to those pictures, by Piero or Raphael, commanded by successive Dukes of Urbino to beautify their already beautiful palace. So Navarre's aim that "Navarre shall be the wonder of the world," where fame shall be "register'd upon our brazen tombs," records princely efforts to make of princely environments models of social and intellectual perfection for the rest of the world—and above all other princes, other courts—to look to.

Shakespeare gives us all this, in the grand and eloquent words of humanist advertisement, but what he *shows* us is another matter. We never see the King and his squadron engaged in contemplation, in debate, or in speculation, save on subjects directly contradicting their stated programmatic aims. For a real knowl-

---

[4] I use the Arden edition, ed. Richard David (London and Cambridge, Mass., 1956).

edge of the mode referred to in the King's first speech, we must read Castiglione and listen to his courtiers' exchanges, repair to Ficino's letters and to Vittorino da Feltre's programs, look at the palaces in Mantua, Gubbio, Urbino, or Asolo to understand the environment of such seriously undertaken learned games—or, we may take the fine shortcut to such understanding offered by Frances Yates' *French Academies of the Sixteenth Century*.[5] Shakespeare simply conjures up the plan, the *schema*, of fashionable academic life and severely truncates its realization by the accidents of the play. In *Love's Labour's Lost*, courtly academicism remains (as perhaps it was always to remain in England) an outdated, alien, nostalgic dream.

We meet at once the dramatic figure who mediates these schemes, Berowne, a man who knows from the beginning the pitfalls of academic life. His friends fall in easily enough with the King's suggestion, but Berowne recognizes not only the weakness inherent in such vows (especially when taken by young men who have already danced in Brabant) but also the trickiness of the ethos such a vow entails. Expressed humanist misogyny was common enough, and it is unquestionably true that women can, even today, divert men from contemplation and even from study; but the humanist who shut women altogether out of his world had already come to seem old-fashioned, long before Berowne on stage realized how unlikely it was for Navarre to find fulfillment in his vows. Castiglione, among others even more authoritative, was to argue for the full sharing of women in the courtier's life and the life of any court. His model for the education of the court lady grew out of and in its turn nourished many defenses of women's proper place, intellectually as well as decoratively, in cultivated society. In this respect, Berowne's realism, in comparison to his companions' exclusionism, makes him a fit choice (in a comedy at least) for the realistic Rosaline, who knows as well as he that "Necessity will make us all forsworn," and who knows too how little may come to seem "necessity." Life cannot stand on oaths, especially those taken against human nature; a man's word is held up to examination in this play—or, better said, the relation of a man's word to his capacity for keeping it is one point explored in the play.[6]

5 Frances A. Yates, *French Academies of the Sixteenth Century* (London, 1947).

6 For a study of the meanings in several other Shakespearean plays of a

So we are little surprised that Navarre's edict is brought into question before it can be put into effect, comically qualified by the arrival of a guest who cannot be gainsaid. A Princess of France amiably camps, in a courtly pastoral gesture, outside the walls of Navarre's court, and must be royally entertained in spite of vows. At the other end of the social scale, the hind Costard appears to be doomed by the new law's impositions to suffer a year in prison after being taken with a wench (or a demsel, or a virgin, or a maid); but Costard is spared punishment to move through the play testing the verbal strata into which he comes. And this same wench (demsel, virgin, maid) Jaquenetta turns out to be irresistible not just for Costard; the "refined traveller of Spain," Don Armado de Adriano, falls in love with her quite as demandingly as Costard. That for Don Armado Jaquenetta is what Dulcinea was to be to his more famous traveling countryman, a fictional creature answerable to a man's internal needs and not the "wench" Costard knows her to be, simply makes more obvious how foolish are the King's regulations: men will love, and will love what they can find. So we are unsurprised again when Navarre himself, without acknowledgement of the foolishness either of his renunciation of women or his attraction to a woman, falls in love, according to the dictates of neoplatonic love-theory, *à coup de foudre*, and with a woman of highest rank and spiritual qualities. We watch his dutiful co-swearers, Dumain, Longaville, and Berowne, following him in falling in love, as they had followed him in other things—and all this also in obedience to the decorum of formal comedy as well as to the decorum of courtiers dutifully mirroring their prince.

Such academic traces as we find in the play are properly "academic," but sometimes they run counter to the particular academic program Navarre conceived. Much later in the play's unraveling, when King and lords have been revealed as conventional doting lovers, Berowne is called on to offer the salving academic excuse for their breaking their vow. He assures them that true contemplation begins, as a host of love-theorists and sonneteers insisted, in a woman's face. That is, Berowne knows more programs than his master admits, and can provide the choplogic dialectic necessary to save his master's reputation as an academic:

---

man's word and his capacity for keeping it, see Burckhardt, *Shakespearean Meanings*, especially chapters II and VIII.

From women's eyes this doctrine I derive:
They are the ground, the books, the academes,
From whence doth spring the true Promethean fire. . . .

For where is any author in the world
Teaches such beauty as a woman's eye? . . .

And where we are our learning likewise is:
Then when ourselves we see in ladies' eyes,
Do we not likewise see our learning there?

(IV.iii.299-301, 309-10, 312-14)

He knows then, the doctrine of the religion of beauty in women, a doctrine preached by a host of theorists on love in both prose and verse,[7] a doctrine borrowed by sonneteers engaged in ennobling the simplest of human passions, the love of a man for a woman. Berowne produces the clichés of that program with as much agility as he had produced his earlier justifications of a different view entirely: that he rescues his companions from one academic position by offering them another equally sanctioned in the courtly schools (and far richer in developed rationale than the excerpts here suggest) is typical of Shakespeare's strategy in this play. In *Love's Labour's Lost*, intellectual and stylistic decorums are played off against fictions of reality, in which one set of conventions is faced with another, so that we accept the less programmatic, however artificial and stylized it may be, as the truer to some unexplained "reality." But in fact, Berowne's new doctrine, that philosophy resides in women's eyes, is in fact as stylized, as "set," as the King's temporary misogyny—it is this new doctrine, for instance, which Shakespeare attacks in another work, in another context, the sonnets to a mistress.[8] But in *Love's Labour's Lost* we are shown how academic doctrine can be a resource as well as a limitation: in Berowne, we recognize its nourishment as well as its sterility.

In the context of his peers, Berowne is the educative figure, acknowledged as leader among these clever young men, these would-be intellectuals; his is the quickest wit in the trivial performances of rhetoric and argumentation the play demonstrates before us. Berowne sets questions the others try to answer—"What

[7] See John Charles Nelson, *Renaissance Theory of Love* (New York, 1958), for background and discussion of academic debates and theory of love.
[8] See below, p. 119.

36

is the end of study, let me know?"—and Berowne turns their answers to his own equivocal ends. He can match them all in both rhyme and reason, outdoing their aphorisms and proverbs (I.i.97), rhyming and outrhyming his fellows, winning the cleverest lady. To him his companions automatically turn to get them out of their dilemma—"and good Berowne, now prove/ Our loving lawful, and our faith not torn"; his dialectic is equal to the task.

Not only does Berowne fulfill various intellectual needs of the play, he also knows his own place in the drama as active presenter as well as the major representative of the courtly party. He serves, as Anne Barton has rightly observed,[9] as a chorus commentary upon the behavior and occupations of the people he sees before him; he is master of the revels, literally supervising his companions (from a higher position on the stage) as they present their programmatic expressions of love. Berowne is the only one among the young men to project his own personality: he recognizes Rosaline's true wit and character, in spite of her uncanonical good looks. The eyes he learns his philosophy from are "pitchballs stuck in her face," but in spite of that, and of the harsh commands she lays upon him, he sticks to his instinctive choice, bends his will to hers, sharpens wit and wisdom upon her abrasive intellect. Berowne is, then, both chorus and hero, an unexpected combination which accounts for considerable tension in his role, as his detachment is always challenged by his singular commitment. His wordy wits are forced to match the potentialities of, first, his intellectual and then his moral self; his accommodations and his capacities come to support his increasing self-knowledge. In other words, Shakespeare has double-cast Berowne, fused conventional dramatic roles in a single part; by that very fusion, the playwright manages to examine and to criticize both roles—and we reckon their power by the force they exert upon Berowne's personality.

Berowne takes refuge in language games, but his games with language are only part of the larger preoccupation with language and the various conventional lingos with which the play is concerned. For this play is, as the word-clever Moth observes, "a great feast of languages," a symposium in which, quite specifically, various languages are tested. Here too, Berowne is both

[9] Anne Barton (also writing under the names Bobbyann Roesen and Anne Righter), "Love's Labour's Lost," *SQ*, IV (1963), 411-26.

chief practitioner and chief tester, from well inside their limits, of the polished language-systems of the court. When the King describes Berowne as "like the envious sneaping frost/ That bites the firstborn infants of the spring" (1.i.100-101), he shows that talent for simile essential to a Renaissance poet; but Berowne, turning the whole thing into an opportunity for extended metaphor, shows his mastery of the craft to be far greater than his master's.

> Well, say I am; why should proud summer boast
> Before the birds have any cause to sing?
> Why should I joy in any abortive birth?
> At Christmas I no more desire a rose
> Than wish a snow in May's new-fangled shows;
> But like of each thing that in season grows.
>
> (1.i.102-107)

This statement that "toutes choses ont leur saison" (Montaigne, *Essais*, 11, 28) becomes the final assertion of the play. Berowne is at the right age to fall in love, even as he recognizes the irony of his doing so: "I, that have been love's whip" must now recant and subscribe to other rules. He abjures the role of woman-free bachelor which he has so long been playing ("A very beadle to a humorous sigh;/ A critic, nay, a night-watch constable,/ A domineering pedant o'er the boy,/ Than whom no mortal so magnificent!"), to undertake a new style, as servant of

> This wimpled, whining, purblind, wayward boy,
> This signor junior, giant-dwarf, dan Cupid;
> Regent of love rhymes, lord of folded arms,
> The anointed sovereign of sighs and groans,
> Liege of all loiterers and malcontents,
> Dread prince of plackets, king of codpieces,
> Sole imperator and great general
> Of trotting paritors. . . .   (III.i.176-83)

After dispraising his love in terms that show (as in Shakespeare's poems to his mistress) his willing commitment to her unfashionable style of beauty and of being, he submits to the requisites of a lover:

38

Well, I will love, write, sigh, pray, sue, and groan:
Some men must love my lady, and some Joan.
                                        (III.i.201-202)

In this Berowne behaves, though on another plane, in parallel
to Don Armado, who must love "Joan." That is, these lovers free
themselves from some preconceptions in their loving, but they
still love by the book: at the end of Act I, Don Armado abandons
his martial pose for the chamberer's graces in one of the briefest
debates on record of *armas y letras*:[10] "Adieu, valour! rust, rapier!
be still, drum! for your manager is in love; yea, he loveth. Assist
me, some extemporal god of rhyme, for I am sure I shall turn
sonnet. Devise, wit; write, pen; for I am for whole volumes
in folio" (I.ii.171-75). It is all pose, of course: we have no sense
of the reality of Armado's previous militarism, and we watch his
ineptitude in love. Again and again, by these and other displays,
we are forced to consider how roles are expressed in styles—and
how, indeed, it is precisely in style that the adequacy or inadequacy of role can be detected. Just as the two roles Berowne
plays throughout the play cause a tension in him, so do the various modes, tones, and styles in which different characters in the
play react to similar situations work both with and against one
another to maintain tension in the play as a whole—and this in
spite of the skimpy and blatantly artificial plot. The perspectivism includes, as well as all the games with convention and
tradition, with *topos* and truism, some psychological realism as
well. More than all the other lovers, these two, Berowne and Armado, come to learn something more about love itself than they
could have merely by acting through the social poses they had
chosen. By outgrowing their poses, linguistic costumes become
too tight for them, they learned this peculiar "more": Don Armado realizes, as James Calderwood has shown, that loving
Jaquenetta (wench, demsel, and so on) involves more humanly
felt responsibility than he had earlier imagined, involves leaving
off his knightly role to resume the plow for her. Berowne gives
up for Rosaline's sake his "Taffeta phrases, silken terms precise,/
Three-pil'd hyperboles," to take upon himself "russet yeas and
honest kersey noes"; he endures for her sake, too, criticism of this
hardwon stylistic reformation ("Sans 'sans,' I pray you"). At

---

[10] E. R. Curtius, *European Literature in the Latin Middle Ages*, pp. 178-79.

the play's end, the task she sets him—to fill up the year and a day before their next meeting, to

> Visit the speechless sick, and still converse
> With groaning wretches; and your task shall be,
> With all the fierce endeavour of your wit
> To enforce the pained impotent to smile
>
> (v.ii.841-44)

—speaks her recognition of his basic frivolity, his fondness for words over matter, his extravagance with the language of which he is too much a master.

Before the play ends, with Rosaline's solution to Berowne's particular moral and rhetorical problems, however, we see him at work on his love-pose, working perhaps at loving as well, in a hexameter sonnet sent to Rosaline which, in the manner of stage-letters, miscarries. It comes into the hands of the literary-critical Nathaniel and Holofernes, later into those of Berowne's unmasked confederates: by means of this poem, traditional and correct as it is, Berowne is as naked to the public's gibes as that public had always been to his critical wit. His sonnet touches on the question of oaths, debated earlier in the play, turns the lady (as his dialectical offering to his friends did later) into a proper study-book, and establishes the conventional dominion of lady over lover.

Berowne's is not a distinguished poem, as his critics pompously demonstrate; but when we hear his friends' verses, we return to his with some relief. The King's poem, a pentameter sonnet with two final couplets, checks through unrelated generic phrases belonging to the "sonnet," offering a convenient locus for many entirely unrelated sonnet-conceits. That Shakespeare could so manipulate sonnet-devices at the same time (as some think) when he was at work on his own sonnets, demonstrates his masterly detachment from a form to which he showed considerable commitment. Longaville offers a pentameter sonnet, from which we learn that "Vows are but breath," mere vapors exhaled from the sun that "is" his lady; Dumain's tetrameter couplets celebrate, metrically as well as topically, the spring as love's right season. Among them, the young men run through the correct sorts of love poetry in the continental and English Renaissance: their awful poems are, merely, the attributes and gestures of young men in love and in love with love, young courtiers steeped in the values of the romantic, aspiring, Renaissance. But the young men are no more naturally gifted for this pose than they were for the academic pose: born to the court though they may have been, except for Berowne they all fall short in *sprezzatura*. If love demanded that these men play their linguistically ambitious roles well, then they were better off in a womanless world. But such realistic assessment we are not allowed in the context of the play, since the role of lover seems far more natural to nice and nice-looking young men, even when they cannot rhyme, than the role of academician.

Fortunately, they show that they know modes of communication other than the solipsistic school-poems of compliment to ladies. The ladies help them loosen up: they are freer than the men in the languages they use, more at home in the witty exchange canonized by Castiglione's Emilia Pia—although this may only mean that the ladies are better schooled than the men in the languages they employ. Interestingly enough, the ladies have distinct styles of expression: we can tell them apart by what they say, though except for Berowne's (and that only marginally), none of the poems produced by the noble lovers seems really "written," and none seems surely the utterance of any one of them.

All this high-style utterance is parodied at a lower social level in the subplot, that counterpointing action of *commedia dell' arte* characters (whom Berowne recognizes at once: "The pedant, the braggart, the hedge-priest, the fool, and the boy").[11] Don Armado, the braggart, is not so simple a figure as he at first seems. He is certainly like Captain Spavento, often cast as a Spanish braggart soldier by the Italians, familiar with such types from the Spanish Occupation; but he has something too of the intense, obsessional melancholy of another Monsieur Traveler, Jaques in *As You Like It*, as well as the serious aspirations to learning usually associated with the *commedia dell' arte* doctor. In their different pedantic styles, Don Armado and Holofernes share some

---

[11] O. J. Campbell, "*Love's Labour's Lost* Restudied," *Studies in Shakespeare, Milton, and Donne, University of Michigan Studies in Language and Literature*, I (1925), 32-45. K. M. Lea, *Italian Popular Comedy* (Oxford, 1934, 2 vols.) is the authoritative study of *commedia dell' arte*; cf. also Allardyce Nicoll, *The World of Harlequin* (Cambridge, 1963); Maurice Sand, *History of the Harlequinade* (London, 1929), Vol. I; and Pierre Duchartre, *La comédie italienne* (Paris, 1925).

of the doctor's traditional qualifications, although Holofernes' miscarried pedantries bear the mark of the newly-reformed grammar schooling by which, we must suppose, Shakespeare gained access to Ovidian and Horatian topics as well as acquired the rich sense of classical etymologies and verbal structure so marked in his work. Holofernes is, surely, a wretched scholar and doubtless was an even more miserable schoolmaster. Don Armado's touching aspirations to the grand style set him off from Holofernes, whose malapropisms associate him far more closely with the social and linguistic environment of Jaquenetta, Costard, and Dull. Costard is, I suppose, the zany: but the purity he manages to maintain criticizes the verbal posturings of his betters, as he twists and turns with his wench-demsel-virgin-maid and tries to learn the value of guerdon and remuneration. The parasite Nathaniel is an extra verbal delight, with his own specialty: "Sir" Nathaniel is a gentleman and the curate; he has seen the university and learned to parse a sentence and to follow out a conceit. He can, as the country parson should, cite a proverb to his purpose. That is, each figure in this troupe has his linguistic garb, as fully identifying as his social role and costume.

Among these figures, there are poets, too: Don Armado, who promised to "turn sonnet," provides a sample of his verse at the end of his glorious letter to Jaquenetta, delivered by mistake to the Princess. Holofernes has written, in the alliterative fourteeners of his youth, "an extemporal epitaph on the death of the deer" killed by the Princess, in which he showed his wit by the comical alliterations and in his rebus with Roman numerals. Nathaniel is a proper critic—"O rare talent!"—although the analphabet Dull, with his sharp hearing, misunderstands all the words creatively, to come nearer the mark with his "If a talent be a claw, look how he claws him with a talent" (IV.ii.64-65). The courtiers provide us with literary, the rustics with semiliterate puns; and we are made to know without doubt which are the better.

The miscarriage of letters, a stage-device common enough, derives in this case from the fact that Costard and Jaquenetta cannot read: the more significant, then, that for all their verbal mistakings, these countrymen are sensitive to language, aware of the importance of style, industrious in learning new words and in correcting the misapprehensions of the learned. So Dull, mishearing Holofernes' "haud credo," corrects to "pricket," and can stick to his countryman's knowledge of deer in spite of sneers at his lack of Latin: perhaps therefore he deserves Holofernes' patronage in the matter of a dinner. The farborough and the priest-knight-parasite are gathered into the schoolmaster's retinue, to accompany him to "dine at the father's of a certain pupil"— where, in keeping with the literary-critical theme of the play, Holofernes promises to offer his guests a literary feast in which he proves Berowne's verses "very unlearned, neither savouring of poetry, wit, nor invention." To this culinary and critical recreation (Holofernes' word) they go, while the gentles go to their "game." Both groups, then, make of their pastimes their very lives: in their great feast of languages, a man *ist, dass was er isst.* In short, these characters, from the tender satirist Moth to the constable Dull, are all simply styles animated into stage-characters. Or so it seems, until we realize the degree of their self-criticism: Costard and Dull work to master the verbal skills demonstrated by their social betters; Moth promises more than merely style, with his highly-developed youthful Berownisms, all cutting into the truth of his situations; Don Armado breaks out of stereotypical constriction by beginning to understand what is entailed by loving someone other than one's self.

The attitude toward conventions implicit in most of the play impels toward ever more formal uses of language, while the pull toward naturalness, away from artifice, tends to undermine whatever successes the characters enjoy over recalcitrant languages. Are Costard and Dull *rewarded* by a knowledge that their striving toward a "better" language was for nothing? The whole play, much as it questions linguistic artifice, is constructed in terms of linguistic artifice, and leaves no room for alternatives other than linguistic. Its language can only be highly formalized, whether in mockery or in praise; and because of the fun constantly poked at formal linguistic structures, we must suspect the whole play. A case in point is the play's high incidence of rhyme. Compared with Shakespeare's sonnets, *Love's Labour's Lost* offers a counterweight to the language of the constricted sonnet-world, so self-centered and enclosed, by examining the superficial social world of love-convention. At the same time that it mocks and challenges this artificial world of love, it measures (as the *Sonnets* also so masterfully do) love and its expression against varied social conditions, varied temperaments, varied situations, to understand why that intense emotion should be expressed in the forms allotted to it.

43

And in the play, the formal conventions are in fact often pointers to personality: rhyme is one such case. Berowne is the quickest and the "best" rhymester, who can both set and resolve the rhyme-schemes of his fellow-players. When in Act IV, for instance, Longaville threatens to turn to prose—"These numbers will I tear, and write in prose" (IV.iii.57)—Berowne thwarts him and rewards us by maintaining the rhyme by force: "O! rhymes are guards on wanton Cupid's hose." Unseen by one another, the courtiers nonetheless fill out each other's lines, observing both rhyme and metre (IV.iii.87-91); unconscious of each other, they present an unbroken decorum for our delight. As they emerge to chide one another, their rhyme moves faster and faster. The King, for instance, takes over Berowne's usual prerogative of controlling the rhyme to fill out the crossed couplets by that quick poetic dialectic of which hitherto only Berowne had been master (IV.iii.265-69). In this amendment of wit, the King is followed by Dumain and Longaville, until Berowne re-establishes his leadership in his long speech (this time in blank verse, to suit the decorum of philosophy) on the philosophical resources of a lady's face. In that speech, of course, Berowne shows what he can do, adducing material from physiology to explain psychology, chopping logic in a shower of pseudo-empirical examples ("Say, can you fast?" "For when, my liege, would you, or you, or you . . . ?"), likening love to a list of attributes drawn from the bestiaries and classical mythology. From such magniloquence he shifts to dialectic:

> Then fools you were these women to forswear,
> Or, keeping what is sworn, you will prove fools.
> For wisdom's sake, a word that all men love,
> Or for love's sake, a word that loves all men,
> Or for men's sake, the authors of these women,
> Or women's sake, by whom we men are men,
> Let us once lose our oaths to find ourselves,
> Or else we lose ourselves to keep our oaths.
>
> (IV.iii.352-59)

The shift in style is from ornamental to plain—or from the rich language of rhetoric to the logical language of statement. If we think, though, that the speaker has moved away from three-pil'd velvet to the honest kersey of his being, we are wrong, of

44

course: the vocabulary and syntax of this passage are plain enough, but the rhetorical knitting is as intricate as ever. Berowne is a man whose medium is words, as Rosaline knew, and tried to do something about, in her final command laid on him. When we contrast the strict regulation of verbal association in this speech with the wild associationism of the scene's first speech, in which he verbally yaws through an emotional sea—"pitched a toil," "toiling in a pitch," "pitch that defiles," etc.—we hear the same man's voice, if in a totally different style. "For women's sake, by whom we men are men," though, gives promise of that world of real emotion and real consequences, of which Rosaline wants to make Berowne aware. We come to recognize, if not to analyze, how wordplay approaches ever more nearly the procreative powers of life.

We might have been expected to have learned that from so loving and so clever a man as Berowne, but that Costard should teach the same lesson is unexpected. Before our eyes, we see Costard catching on to language—admiring Rosaline's crude exchange with Boyet ("hit it, hit it, hit it"), he begins to take part in such proceedings himself and to offer a rhyme to match Margaret's. When Boyet draws him on, Costard acquits himself so well in rhyme, metre, and sexual *double-entendre* that he earns a rebuke from one mealy-mouthed lady. As the courtiers leave him, he cannot help a little gloating at Boyet's expense—"By my soul, a swain! a most simple clown!/ Lord, Lord, how the ladies and I have put him down!" His delight is at once a misjudgment of Boyet's impregnable decorum and a recognition of the fact that he too can play the language game and thus climb (as bright boys did) the social ladder as well as poetic trees in the Hesperides that had been the property of university wits.

Critics have stressed the holiday, the gaming spirit of this play, with its remarkable reduction of human relations to roles, games, masques, rhetorical and poetical contests. It comes as some disappointment, then, to see Costard decline from his upwardly mobile linguistic role to make a muddle of his part as Pompion the Great, Pompey surnamed the Big. The same Costard who recognized himself in the play's first scene even through the screen of Armado's fustian, because he knew for a fact that it was he who had been taken with a wench, loses his self-control when he must act the part of a Worthy, so that he cannot even recite the lines tinkered together by Holofernes and Nathaniel. All one can say is that Costard in his own person is someone, and in another's he is not.

Perhaps that is one point of this play. Certainly the frequency of disguise, either as costume-party or as travesty, constitutes one element of the criticism: chiefly, characters are unmasked, forced out of their chosen styles, removed from their roles, but they cling to their various disguises. The ladies conceal their attraction to the young men, the young men hide from one another their response to the ladies. Lords dress up as Muscovites; the pedant, the braggart, the hedge-priest, the fool, and the boy enter from a world conventionally taken as "real" to appear in the utterly penetrable characters of the Nine Worthies; the self-presentations of Don Armado, Holofernes, and Nathaniel are as vulnerable as the rustic *commedia*. We are never in doubt, really, as to who is who, or who belongs where: we know from the start, or so it seems, what this play "is." And just at this point the playwright plays us false: this "wooing doth not end like an old play; Jack hath not Jill," as Berowne says. With that, we are brought up hard against a last layer of protective dramatic illusionism that this play asks us to inspect. Throughout, we are asked to notice games—children's games, like Hoodman Blind and Flapdragon, card games and gaming with dice, songs as games played by more than one person, dances as games (branle, morris-dance, hay, courtly measures at the masque's end), courtly pastimes ranging from verbal exchange to the royal hunt. The moment of court-country pastoral when the Princess appears at Navarre's gate is a game; she agrees to his new rules and makes a moral virtue of sleeping in a field. The academic vow, as Berowne let us know from the start, is a game; all this comes to a peak in the stagey, choreographic scene in which Berowne oversees and presents his friends in their self-revelations and is, in his own turn, revealed as a biter bit.

There is a choreography of conventions and of ideas, too, in this play about patterns, models, roles assigned by society and self-assigned. The medium in which these patterns are displayed is in the most consistent and formal way linguistic. The "Sweet smoke of rhetoric"—and of grammar, syntax, etymology, and poetics—blows through the play, as everything about language is brought up, from a single letter ("red dominical," "golden letter") through pronunciation ("det," "cauf," "nebour," puns and quibbles) to choice of lingo (*haud credo* as against pricket);

from an inclusive single word, the *commedia dell' arte* construction *honorificabilitudinous*, through the *copia* of the written epistles, the literary criticism, and the poetic and academic defenses of love, to the moral criticism of linguistic styles offered by the exchanges between Rosaline and Berowne. The potentialities of language for good and ill are dramatized, always with a delight in the possibility of any given linguistic creation. Though there is much corrective of linguistic fallacy and *hubris* in the play, such corrective is not sought until words are, in one and another context, found wanting.

In the play, the concept of language is extended to include what might be called generic or thematic styles. Berowne knows at once that a *commedia dell' arte* troupe has straggled in when the haggard rustic types, incongruously inhabiting a countryside just outside the bounds of a king's court, arrive to put on their entertainment; they are, whether they know it or not, fixed characters from an assigned decorum. Though we see them as far more than that—as personalities straining the seams of their dramatic dress—they never entirely abandon their predestined literary personalities. Though Don Armado can say, in the first version of love's insistence on plain-dealing, "Boy, I do love that country girl I took in the park with the rational hind Costard," and at the end insist, "I have vowed to Jaquenetta to hold the plough for her sweet love three year," he has in between also composed, according to received convention, his second letter and his poem, has discussed the relative merits and relationship to one another of arts, arms, and love, like any academician. Armado lays claim to companionship with the King of Navarre who, of course, recognizes him for the pretentious upstart that he is; but these pretensions are doffed for Jaquenetta, as he reverts to what must be, at the most, yeoman's status. He vows for three years, in the impossible, imperious swearing with which the play began, but his vow lays great claim to a simple act of love: perhaps there *is* more in Don Armado than the King at first could see. In spite of his good sense and his successful sallies out of his analphabet language, Costard too returns to rustic foolishness, confusing his role with his person and at a loss for words. In Navarre's court, the folly of academic celibacy is displayed, but so is the folly of loving by the book. From Holofernes the schoolmaster and Nathaniel the curate, we learn the corruptions of the book at their source in school and pulpit, as these two functionaries are seen

47

to represent the educational possibilities for all Costards, all Armados. The ladies manage to invalidate the original academicians' vow, but they lay upon their lovers another version of conventional oath-taking, with their exacting tests of a year's hermitage for a king and a year's jesting in a hospital for a young man with a short attention span. That is, the ladies substitute one convention for another, impose an older style of love-service upon their suitors, aware of the fantastic inappropriateness to reality of any such commitment. The vows exacted are gestures in the dialectic exchange, honoring seasonal maturation, but also highly literary devices with which to end the play.

This comedy is enclosed, but not in the conventional comic fashion; as such, it is extremely open-ended. It is enclosed, though, by its very topic, the conventions it treats. Here, again, one must consider the *number* of conventions handled in this play, almost an anthological display of particular *tours de force*. In the last act alone, a remarkable array is spread out: the *questione della lingua* handled overtly by Holofernes and covertly by him and Nathaniel; the confrontation of inflated styles offered in Holofernes' meeting with Armado, this pair flanked by the sophisticated, hypercritical Moth on one side and on the other by Costard and Dull; the ladies' quibbles; Boyet's management of their side of the Muscovite masque; Moth's burlesque of that masque as it is being played out; the dance of the ladies with the wrong suitors and that dance realigned; the play-within-the-play of the Nine Worthies; the abrupt appearance in the action of Marcade, the messenger of death who, in one unfinished speech, banishes the lighthearted literary playground that the court has been;[12] the ladies' imposition of new vows; the final, thoroughly ceremonial literary device of seasonal passage, the skeletal debate between Winter and Spring, in which owl and cuckoo speak their genrepieces from a long tradition of dialectics between the chilly inward life of winter and the open procreation, licit and illicit, of spring.[13] On this utterly traditional note the play ends—with

[12] Barton, op. cit., and Calderwood, p. 67.

[13] For background on medieval debate literature generally and for the specific background of this debate of winter and spring, I am indebted to my colleague, Michel-André Bossy, whose unpublished dissertation, "The Prowess of Debate: A Study of a Literary Mode" (Yale University, 1970), p. 15, specifically mentions *Love's Labour's Lost*. See also B. H. Bronson, "Daisies Pied and Icicles," *MLN*, LXIII (1948); and Caroline M. McLay, "The

nothing resolved, with closure denied. The two songs, related to the whole play by their subterranean connections with barrenness and creativity, offer one last sample of the many literary conventions, barely compatible with one another, of which this play is made.

What are we to make of such an anthology, such a textbook of literary *copia* and resource? Is the playwright just showing off, making fun of us? Certainly the characters in the play are impelled by their roles' limitations to seek something else: even the nobles slip the traces of *politesse* in their mockery at the Worthies' playlet and their revelation to the world of the poverty Don Armado has worked so hard to conceal. Just as things promise to spin entirely out of control, Marcade enters to recall them, and their audiences, to another dimension of life, one which involves death. He comes from the world of *negotium*, of rule and rulers, of living, working, and dying, to empty the cosmic cornucopia of its plenty, and to underscore the meaning of "time" which has, for the play's duration, apparently been kept at bay. But we remember how often time has made its appearance—the three-year oaths, the two-months' pregnancy, the truncated playlet and the official play itself without a proper closure, as Marcade cuts the comedy and forestalls the world-without-end bargain of man and maid. Time is measured out anew, in new formalities, not of word only but in the real world of things as well, in the twelvemonth-and-a-day of mourning, in Armado's three-year husbandry for Jaquenetta, in the symbolic seasons of winter and summer (for in winter, not even a king can make a princess camp in the fields). Time offers the protagonists another chance, an end to madcappery and foppery, an opportunity to accept commitment to their own words, feelings, and deeds.

Even at this end, for all Marcade's dark symbolism and the severity of cuckoo and owl, the play insists on its own lightness as a literary construct. The final equivocal setting of the competitive song of Apollo and words of Mercury[14] carries through the magnificent verbal texture of juxtaposed contrasts, the preoccupation with words in themselves and in their allusive plenty that is the peculiar quality of this play. Like the styles in which they are

---

Dialogues of Spring and Winter, A Key to the Unity of *Love's Labour's Lost*," *SQ*, XVIII (1967), 121-27.

[14] Calderwood, p. 80.

expressed, the conventions delight even as their nature is discovered to be sham. The play's concern has been, in several senses, with those "things hid and barr'd from common sense" of which Berowne spoke in the first scene. The persons in the play have all shown their allegiance to one or another, to one *and* another stylistic role, and have been, by different means, forcibly dislodged from that role. But not without some nostalgia on our part for the roles and the worlds those roles imply: follies like these (as Erasmus and others knew) may conceal precious truths. From the comic decorum or the counterpointing clowning *commedia dell' arte*, spokesmen have emerged to comment on the delight as well as the artificiality of words-in-pattern. Only when artificial patterns hardened into personalities are brought up against such crises as love and death can some measure be taken of the resources of the patterns—and then, as this play tactfully shows, chosen styles of speech and of life can be assessed.

That the play rejects a play's proper closure is part of its whole strategy: the ladies' impositions are as stylized as the vows sworn to at the play's opening. This "new" play rejects the traditions of "an old play" to move altogether out of the play-world, into time "that's too long for a play," into a world, then, very much like life, from which, mediated by the archaism of a *Dialogus Hiemis et Veris*, the generative traditions of comedy and of conventional comic language and character can be reassessed and revalued. *Love's Labour's Lost* makes critics of us willy nilly.

II. The *Sonnets*

By the *Sonnets* we are also invited to become critics, urged to experience something about the writing of poetry, the making of fictions, and the meanings of poetry to a poet and to any literate man.[15] Where *Love's Labour's Lost* played with the literary stock conventions and devices, imposed a literary-critical skepticism upon the play's plot, action, and characterization, the *Sonnets* do something else, dramatize literary criticism. Where *Love's La-*

15 Murray Krieger's *A Window to Criticism* (Princeton, 1964) is the most radical metapoetic reading I know of the *Sonnets*. I am, here as elsewhere, deeply indebted to Mr. Krieger. See also Philip Edwards, *Confines*, esp. pp. 21-31; and Hilton A. Landry, *Interpretations in Shakespeare's Sonnets* (Berkeley, 1964) which provides valuable material, as does Joan Grundy, in "Shakespeare's Sonnets and the Elizabethan Sonneteers," *S.S.*, xv (1962), 41-49.

bour's Lost emptied so many conventions of their conventional freight, the *Sonnets* animate, among other significant and characteristic conventions of the genre, the self-referential, self-critical tendency in sonneteering itself.

Critics of Shakespeare's sonnets consistently remark on the dramatic quality of the sequence (or sequences, or series, or cycle, or cycles: the exact relation of the poems to one another is difficult to establish); and compared with other great Renaissance sonnet-sequences, English and Continental, the marked quality of Shakespeare's sonnets is, certainly, that dramatization into personality of Renaissance sonnet *personae* and conventions.[16] Whatever the order of composition or the poet's "intent," the arrangement of the poems (by the author? by the editor? by the printer? by chance?)[17] manifests someone's awareness (for simplicity's sake I assume that someone to have been the poet) of a loose but nonetheless involved and involving "plot." The arrangement of the characters into two triangles—poet-friend-mistress; poet-friend-rival poet—is, so far as I know, unparalleled in Renaissance sonneteering, although there are adumbrations of both relationships in sonnet literature. Two friends' love for the same lady is by no means unknown in romance and comedy; literary theory and practice sanctions sonnet-commentary on stylistic subjects. Shakespeare's sonnets work with the conventions of the literary genre in a remarkable way, possibly most boldly in this triangulation of personalities, by which the poet turns tradition upside down and inside out to examine the "real" implications of conventional utterance and, in some cases, to force these implications to new limits in the situation, poetical as well as psychological, which is the poems' *donnée*. What other Renaissance poet praises his cult-friend in terms normally reserved for the sonnet-mistress *and* devotes considerable sonnet-time to a mistress as well—a mistress who is herself notably atypical in the genre?[18] Further, though many sonneteers qualify conventional admiration of ladies by

---

[16] For comments of this sort, see the *Variorum Sonnets*, ed. Hyder E. Rollins (Philadelphia, 1944), as well as most studies of the sonnets written since; here I cite Richard Levin, "Sonnet CXXIX as a 'Dramatic' Poem," *SQ*, XVI (1965), pp. 175-81.

[17] For a radical revision of the sonnet-order, see Brents Stirling, *The Shakespearean Sonnet Order: Poems and Groups* (Berkeley, 1968); an earlier revision of the order is C. F. Tucker Brooke's, in his edition of the *Sonnets* (New Haven, 1936); and see the *Variorum* commentary on the subject.

[18] James Winny, *The Master-Mistress* (London, 1968).

denouncing their particular ladies for one or another real or fancied fault of love, what sonneteer settles down to love his lady, knowing that she has played him false and doubtless will do so again? Merely in the development of his psychological story, Shakespeare has managed to make important statements about the relation of a literary love-code to specific experiences of loving. As in his other works which deal with love, Shakespeare investigates that difficult, involving, threatening, fulfilling experience, examines both its *mores*—its customs and its morality—and its rhetoric, or, to stretch definitions for rhetoric, the poet examines the relation of its expressive style to behavior.

What are the psychological situations of love which can or should be expressed in lyric poetry, and what are valid ways of speaking about these problems? How does a poet deeply committed to his craft manage to honor the traditional conditions of love-literature *and* to express the particularities of a man's emotional response to his particular experience of love? In the *Sonnets*, many kinds of disappointment are examined: disappointment in a continuing relation to a cult-friend; disappointment in a mistress; disappointment by these two in concerted preoccupation with one another, shutting the poet out of both relationships; disappointment with the self as lover and as poet; even, at times, disappointment with poetry itself. That is not the only mood, of course; it is, though, a mood at variance with the traditional attitudes of love-poets writing sonnets—and the persuasiveness of this poet's disappointment is in part a result of the rarity of that mood in sonnets. Certainly the sonnet-lover conventionally presented himself as constantly analyzing and revising his psychological condition, but Shakespeare manages to treat the human relationships postulated in his sonnets so problematically, to make such "real" problems of them, that a standard self-analytic pose has been considerably enriched and deepened. For instance, when love for a friend conflicts with love for a mistress, what happens to the lover of both? Another way of saying this, pointing more exactly to the literary problem, is: How does a writer handle these two versions of idealized love, faced off against one another? What decorum suits such a conflict, and in what *persona* ought the poet to speak? Unlike *Love's Labour's Lost*, where he tackled the "mereness" of the love-conventions, in the *Sonnets*, Shakespeare set himself to realize—that is, to provide body and mind for—the psychological and literary problems raised by love and the literary love-plot, problems to which he returned again and again through his productive life.[19]

In his sonnets Shakespeare experiments with materials repeatedly used in the sonnet-genre and alters these materials so that his series, though perfectly traditional in shape and in topic, almost leaps from the official limitations altogether.[20] As one reads through, for instance, the English sequences gathered in Sir Sidney Lee's collection, one is first struck by the fact that this genre itself seems to be an invitation to repetitiousness—or, if one prefers the term, to *copia*; and not from poet to poet merely, but within a single poet's work as well. The genre itself requires acceptance of a theme and that theme's variations. Second, one cannot help noting how deviant Shakespeare's sonnets are, not in their repetitiousness, but from the *norms* of repetitiousness—even when, as he does, he asks a young man to marry in seventeen different sonnets!—how peculiarly personal the poems are, within a genre in which conventions of self-expression, self-analysis, and self-reference are extremely highly developed.[21] Some of this independence on Shakespeare's part may be "merely" historical, a factor of the decade in which he came to sonneteering, as Patrick Cruttwell's perceptive essay suggests.[22] No doubt Shakespeare was favored by the generation into which he was born, but so is any gifted poet, as we see after the fact. Shakespeare took advantage of his advantages; not only as inheritor but as legator too of poetic and dramatic practice, he was partly responsible for changes in modes of expression in English writing at the turn of the century. Shakespeare's talent was such that it could not be buried in the earth, or hid under a bushel: in the sonnets, as in his dramatic ex-

[19] For some applications of sonnet-traditions to dramatic love-plots, see below, chapters 3 and 9.

[20] For such understanding as I have of sonnets and sonnet-theory, I owe much to Dr. Cynthia Grant Tucker, whose work on the essentials of sonneteering has proved both instructive and stimulating; see her dissertation, "Studies in Sonnet Literature" (University of Iowa, 1967). The fullest background to the subject is provided by Walter Moench, *Das Sonett* (Heidelberg, 1955).

[21] As Dr. Tucker's work shows, sonnets have a particular kind of self-reference; see my *Paradoxia Epidemica*, chapter 2, for some comments on this topic. Obviously, sonnet-sequences provide one kind of document for twentieth-century studies of literary and psychological self-consciousness: sonnets also show a marked metapoetic, critical self-consciousness, as well as taking self-analysis for one of their substantive *topoi*.

[22] Patrick Cruttwell, *The Shakespearean Moment* (New York, 1955).

periments, he tackled difficult problems, penetrated deeply into the traditions he was using, with the result that those traditions were themselves permanently altered by his having submitted himself to them.

However deviant Shakespeare's sonnets seem when set against contemporary practice, nonetheless they are just as profoundly rooted within the sonnet-tradition. Dante set the mode for a concerted sequence in which repeated quatorzains were a major element; and once Petrarca had written his extraordinary sequence, inevitably the extended lyric narrative, made up of short poems, became one of the great Renaissance forms, a "modern" invention apparently owing little to antiquity.[23] By giving his verses a surround of prose commentary which filled in narrative gaps, commented on his own poetic efforts and intentions, and examined his own lyric feelings in greater detail than the short poetic form then permitted, Dante built into the sonnet-sequence its tendency to *literary* as well as private, personal, and lyric self-criticism; the same scrutiny was directed at the poet and the poetry he was writing, a tendency which left its mark on the whole sonnet-tradition. The sonnet was by no means the only lyric form to comment on itself: several medieval forms, especially the *canzone*, permitted and encouraged comment by the poet on his own verse and his aspirations for it, and poetical self-reference occurs in many classical forms (lyric, epigram, ode). In sonnet-sequences, anyway, such self-commentary was accepted as a sub-theme, until there were sonnets on sonnets, sonnets on the sonnet-form, long before Wordsworth or John Updike produced their sonnets-on-sonnets.

The literary-critical sections of the *Vita Nuova* are in prose, not poetry: the verses lie, separate jewels, in display cases of prose which serve several different purposes, only one of which was Dante's self-explication. Petrarca wrote his sonnet-commentary into his sonnets themselves; Lorenzo de' Medici prefaced his with a prose disquisition, the *Comento*; in Bruno's *Gli eroici furori*, at the end of the long tradition, the sonnets are set, like occasional marks of punctuation, in a sea of discursive prose, as illustrations for the topics under discussion.[24] Petrarca's poetry, originally in-

---

[23] But see below, chapter 2, pp. 80-88, for critical assimilation of the sonnet to ancient poetic categories.

[24] Giordano Bruno, *De' gli eroici furori* (*Des Fureurs héroiques*), ed. and tr. Paul-Henri Michel (Paris, 1954). Bruno's work is extremely interesting as an example of *genera mista*: it is (at least) a philosophical treatise, a love-

nocent of prose, did not lack prose commentary for long; his editors, some of them petrarchan poets themselves (as Bembo was),
provided explanation, explication, critical commentary, and justification for Petrarca's lines. Many *petrarchisti* made their repu-
tations both by their own poetry and by commenting on their
master's. Lecturing on Petrarca, like lecturing on Dante, became
a major critical enterprise in Florence, so that a poet like Tasso,
for instance, could write significant essays on single poems by
Petrarca, by Della Casa, and by himself. In imitation of such respectful treatment of Petrarca, editors sprang up for the other vernacular lyric writers of the Renaissance, of whom Muret is the
most distinguished, who edited Ronsard—indeed, one mark of
Ronsard's official success was the attention his verse received from
humanist and fellow-poet editors, conscious of their models to the
south.[25]

Clearly, then, sonnets could and did become one major opportunity for literary self-reference and self-commentary, not only in
the poet's official duty to examine his own inward self, but also in
his opportunity for critical comment on his own work and on the
traditions in which he was at work. Dante's prose commentary on
the verses of the *Vita Nuova* offers one kind of self-concern, Petrarca's stylized, romantic self-presentation of his maturing self
another. Ronsard everlastingly commented on himself and his
earlier poetical achievements (even, by extension, the ladies celebrated in earlier sequences), and Du Bellay's lyric poetry records
his relation to his own poetry. Ronsard quotes himself so playfully as to raise interesting questions of tone and dedication, in a
genre primarily epideictic. Sidney, who was much indebted to
Ronsard's example, played his own self-referential games in *Astrophil and Stella*—at the linguistic level, often self-consciously skirt-
ing the destruction of the very poems he was writing, as he denied

---

dialogue (see J. C. Nelson, pp. 163-233), a sonnet-anthology, and a work of
literary criticism.

25 As an edited modern text, Petrarca was an early classic: commentaries
by Filelfo, Antonio da Tempo, Vellutello, Bembo, Daniello, and others ex-
plicate the poems in the context of the critics's values and interests, and often
attempt to provide readings of individual poems as well as the general background needed for a great sequence taken as a whole. A good study of these
editions, in the light of polemics over style, is very much needed. Muret and
Belleau, working on Ronsard's *Amours*, were offering their countryman the
same kind of respect as a classic accorded by his editors to Petrarca.

his poetic and stylistic aims in sonnets which set out to demonstrate and to illustrate (masterfully, I think) those very aims he criticized.[26]

Sidney's sonnets celebrate a lady, though quite differently from Petrarca's orderly, clear, sequential celebration in the *Canzoniere*, and differently too from Ronsard's ultimately sequential series of sequences, which "progress" from the childlike nymph Cassandre to the mature, high-born, well-named Hélène. But again and again, Sidney returns to consider, and sometimes to celebrate, poetry; he tests the limit of possibilities of his conventional resources, and of language itself. "What may words say, or what may words not say?" becomes one of the major preoccupations of his lyric sequence, and stands as the fundamental, eminently quotable, classically succinct question about all utterance. His debate is conducted in fairly conventional terms—of Muse, of purling spring, of Aganippe well—thoroughly relevant to sonneteering; but so is the larger question of celebration as truth or as flattery:

> What may words say, and what may words not say,
> Where truth it selfe must speake like flatterie?

The "given" of the sonneteer is the beloved's perfection: what have grammar rules, dictionary's method, or allegory's curious frame to do with such self-evident revelation as Stella's beauty?

Sidney writes directly into his verse those problems peculiar to the sonneteer's exercise; he knows his own, and his models', relation to "poore *Petrarch*'s long deceased woes," and knows too that if he manages to persuade of the uniqueness of his lady and his love, he must do so by a native, not a denisened, wit. Part of the fascination of Sidney's sequence lies in the tension between his exploitation of the tradition, with all its grandiloquence of language and allusion, and the criticism to which the tradition is so overtly subjected.[27]

Perhaps because Sidney's sonnets so manifestly do just this, Shakespeare's sonnets do not explore that paradoxical self-contradictoriness which so punctuates Sidney's *Astrophil and Stella*.

[26] See my *Paradoxia Epidemica*, chapter 2.

[27] For excellent commentary on Sidney, see David Kalstone, *Sidney's Poetry* (Cambridge, Mass., 1965); Richard B. Young, "English Petrarke: A Study of Sidney's 'Astrophel and Stella,'" in *Three Studies in The Renaissance* (New Haven, 1958); Robert Montgomery, *Symmetry and Sense* (Austin, 1961); and Douglas L. Peterson, *The English Lyric from Wyatt to Donne* (Princeton, 1967), pp. 186-201.

Though they have their share of the conflicting rhetorical tropes, oxymoron and paradox, Shakespeare's sonnets rarely rely on technical manipulation of grammar and rhetoric to overcome deliberately self-courted poetic self-destruction. This is not to say that Shakespeare has not his own ways of making us note his skill at sonneteering: he makes impressive variations on the subjects and themes conventional in sonnet-sequences and expected by their experienced readers. As Stephen Booth has so brilliantly demonstrated in his modestly stated and important study,[28] Shakespeare could and did manipulate several linguistic and structural systems in his sonnets at once, balancing one off against another to achieve effects very different from those of other sonneteers. Like Sidney, Shakespeare came at the end of a long European preoccupation with the sonnet, and was therefore able to range from one to another end of the stylistic and thematic gamut appropriate to the genre, from conventional petrarchan opposition and hyperbole, through the sweet fluency of Bembo and Ronsard, to the relative simplicity of Du Bellay's or Wyatt's vernacular styles. Here, I want to touch only on his ways in the *Sonnets* of commenting on poetry, his own and other poets', his ways of managing criticism within the narrative frames he constructed.

We might begin with the standard trope for poetic immortality, the *monumentum aere perennius*—"Not marble, nor the gilded monuments/ Of Princes shall outlive"; "Devouring Time, blunt thou the lion's paws"; "So long as men can breathe, or eyes can see,/ So long lives this, and this gives life to thee"; "Since brass, nor stone, nor earth, nor boundless sea"; "His beauty shall in these black lines be seen,/ And they shall live, and he in them still green." Again and again, the poet reiterates the poet's boast that verse can distill the truth of a man's transient life to its purest essence, that verse is a vial to hold that essence forever. And the classical immortality conferred by verse lives wholly in the poet's gift; he offers or withholds—though with this generous poet, there is no question of withholding whatever he might give. This poet, as his verse records, spent his talents only to find them still green, still growing with (significantly mixed metaphor) "spending" and "use."[29] Gradually, poetic immortality moves out from a trope of

---

[28] Stephen Booth, *An Essay on Shakespeare's "Sonnets"* (New Haven, 1969).

[29] Krieger is particularly eloquent on the implications of this cluster of images.

art (*monumentum*) to images of natural creativity: in Sonnet 115, for instance, the poet incorporates his growing poetic capacity and his present love in a single body—"Those lines that I before have writ do lie;/ Even those that said I could not love you dearer." But since "Love is a babe," in the conventional reference to Cupid, as love grows, so does creative power, closely allied with, dependent upon, the love "which still doth grow."

The *monumentum* trope in many variations is proudly displayed in these poems proud of their subject. The poet recognizes no equivocation about the value either of friendship or of the poetry celebrating this friendship, as the verse itself becomes a monumental epitaph to the friend's perfections. Implied in the trope itself is the memorial function of verse, officially centered in the epigrammatic tradition, of which the epitaph was a part. Navarre's opening speech in *Love's Labour's Lost*, notes the relation of fame, epitaph, and poetry. Here, poetry, that implying art, comes to replace the monolithic precision of incised epitaph:[30]

> Who will believe my verse in time to come,
> If it were fill'd with your most high deserts?
> Though yet, heaven knows, it is but as a tomb
> Which hides your life and shows not half your parts.
>
> (17)

> Or I shall live your epitaph to make,
> Or you survive when I in earth am rotten. . . .
> The earth can yield me but a common grave,
> When you entombed in men's eyes shall lie.
> Your monument shall be my gentle verse,
> Which eyes not yet created shall o'er-read;
> And tongues to be your being shall rehearse,
> When all the breathers of this world are dead.   (81)

The appeal, across the grave and across the monuments marking men's lives, to any reader—*our* eyes, then "not yet created," now o'er-read these lines, to fulfil the poet's prophecy and his boast—extends the meaning of the bookish convention to include an on-

---

[30] See below, pp. 80-83, for the relation of sonnet to epigram, and thus to incised epitaph. For an interesting hypothesis, reached by counting lines, about the poems' "pyramidal" monumentality, see Alastair Fowler, *Triumphal Forms* (Cambridge, 1970), pp. 183-97.

going life; "breathers" marks life's simplest function, and at the same time reminds us of the etymology of poetic inspiration. With a poet in hand, a poet's friend can economize on marble and gilded monuments, may trust to the poet's muse, with whom it lies

> To make him much outlive a gilded tomb,
> And to be prais'd of ages yet to be.   (101)

The poet invokes, then, both the precise and cryptic quality of epitaphic praise and the grandiose boast of the lyric poet's conference of immortality upon his subjects—the poetry of statement and the poetry of praise fuse in this remarkable conflation of traditions generally quite separate.[31]

This method of taking a metaphor literally, of forcing its implications on readers, is of a piece with Shakespeare's practice generally and is one indication of his essentially critical attitude toward his materials. Perhaps even more telling are those examinations of his work as he goes along, writing, it seems, with one eye on himself writing:

> Who will believe my verse in time to come . . . ?   (17)

> Let this sad in'trim like the ocean be. . . .
> Or call it winter. . . .   (56)

> Shall I compare thee to a summer's day?   (18)

—with its implied "no," and its given reasons why such a simile is inadequate to the subject. In Sonnet 21, the poet rejects "couplement of proud compare," to describe his love's excellence for its simple, plain truth; in Sonnet 59, he considers the whole problem of "invention":

> If there be nothing new, but that which is
> Hath been before, how are our brains beguil'd,
> Which labouring for invention bear amiss
> The second burden of a former child!

Love, inextricably joined to poetic creativity, has been a "babe," "still growing"; the poem-monument had appealed, across death, to living generations yet to come. Now, in 59, even searching for poetic language is likened to the labor-pains of a mother, disappointed in her second, counterfeit issue:

---

[31] See below, pp. 99-100.

O, that record could with a backward look,
Even of five hundred courses of the sun,
Show me your image in some antique book,
Since mind at first in character was done!
That I might see what the old world could say
To this composed wonder of your frame;
Whether we are mended, or whe'er better they,
Or whether revolution be the same.
   O, sure I am, the wits of former days
   To subjects worse have given admiring praise.

The sonnet plays with the idea central to the *de inventoribus* trope; Shakespeare assumes as true the burden of Curtius' rediscovery for us, that classically-influenced literature (to say nothing of human habits of thinking) was marked by a series of formulae, schemes, *topoi*, by which a man was relieved of the responsibility for "invention" required of poets since the Romantic revolution. The poem also looks toward the possibility of cyclic return, less a cultural than a natural return, by which this young man may simply be seen, wonderfully, as a later manifestation of some beauty authoritatively commented on "in some antique book." The whole question, then, is raised of a poet's relation to his profession's past, without losing sight of his ever-present responsibility for *epideixis*, the praise of a specific "you," an identifiable subject. Although the poet sounds as if his own invention were exhausted and suggests also that, all invention being merely repetition, either of words (*topoi*) or of a reincarnated beautiful object, he welcomes a literary situation in which he is required to parrot ancient phrases and tropes, he nonetheless belongs to the self-consciously modern era, and must bring into question that authoritative ancient achievement. "Whether we are mended, or whe'er better they,/ Or whether revolution [i.e., cosmic time-changes] be the same" may repeat some ancient notions about historical events, but it calls into question the conviction that the ancients had a monopoly on correctness. The couplet has a weary ring, as if the poet, knowing the bad habits of poets in his day too easily persuaded to mere sycophancy, could not trust his dead colleagues, those unquestioned ancient masters, to have been more accurate than contemporary poets in praising their subjects.

The poet who called his friend "the tenth Muse, ten times more in worth/ Than those old nine which rhymers invocate"

(38), and who so identified his verse with his love and himself with his friend that he could write "O, how thy worth with manners may I sing,/ When thou art all the better part of me?" (39), recognized that actual "breath"—his friend's presence, conversation, and company—was the inspiration of his poetry. Not of his "invention" merely, which could work even in the friend's absence (27, 98), but of his creativity—Sonnet 27 records how the image of the friend blots out all others, and 98, a "Zefiro torna" with a difference, how

> Yet nor the lays of birds, nor the sweet smell
> Of different flowers in odour and in hue,
> Could make me any summer's story tell. . . .
>
> Nor did I wonder at the lily's white,
> Nor praise the deep vermilion in the rose:
> They were but sweet, but figures of delight,
> Drawn after you, you pattern of all those.

Sonnet 113, on the other hand, demonstrates the poet's metaphorical powers at work: whatever he sees, in his friend's absence, he converts into the image of his friend:

> The mountain or the sea, the day or night,
> The crow or dove, it shapes them to your feature . . . ;

and, in 114, he can "make of monsters and things indigest/ Such cherubins as your sweet self resemble." In these poems, we see the image-making process at work, watch the poet watching his own figuring forth in verse, his impossible matching of all things, good and bad, crow and dove and monster, to his obsession.

This record, however, runs counter to the constant stress on poetic "truth"—the friend is the poetry's ornament, which thus needs no ornament drawn from the manuals of rhetoric and poetics. "Couplement of proud compare" is rejected for "the sweet ornament which truth doth give." A poet with such a subject has no need for art, no need for figure, no need for invention, since the subject itself, simply named, confers sufficient perfection upon verse.

In this connection, the slander-sonnets are interesting, in that they recognize in the slanderers' fictions a kinship with the poet's problems of expression. First of all, the very perfection which, by its signaling in verse, confers upon that verse a special value

61

causes slander in real life, "the ornament of beauty is suspect," by its mere existence. But at the same time, there may be some truth in the slanderers' comments (69), since his detractors judge the friend by his behavior—in the conventional overstatement of slander, as in the conventional overstatement of poetry, there is some matching of this particular, specific young man's qualities. Withal, in the end, the poet must charge the friend's enemies with fiction, though, as with the overstatements of his own poetry, he must count, even in its apparent dispraise, their fiction as a kind of praise:

> That tongue that tells the story of thy days,
> Making lascivious comments on thy sport,
> Cannot dispraise but in a kind of praise:
> Naming thy name blesses an ill report. (95)

When his own reputation was at stake, however, the poet did not find things so easily resolved: "ill report" running about him was not so quickly turned to the service of fictive praise. On the contrary, that ill report sent him back, as proper sonneteer, to face himself as he was in naked self-examination, to assess himself and the slander about him. " 'Tis better to be vile than vile esteemed" is a line unthinkable about the friend; but he makes it, with its elaborate defense, about his own condition:

> When not to be receives reproach of being,
> And the just pleasure lost, which is so deemed
> Not by our feeling, but by others' seeing. (121)

As in the poems to his mistress, in which the poet's reproaches turn into an opportunity for self-assessment apparently detached, here too others' disapproval, however painful, offers a chance to make his own critique of himself, far closer to the facts of the matter than any outside criticism:

> For why should others' false adulterate eyes
> Give salutation to my sportive blood?
> Or on my frailties why are frailer spies,
> Which in their wills count bad what I think good?

This sonnet is remarkable for its prosiness: "When not to be receives reproach of being" is exact and euphonious, but entirely without imaginative, figurative imagery. Quite different from the effort in the poems to the friend, the language here strives toward bareness and simplicity of statement, as in the remarkable turning:

> No; I am that I am; and they that level
> At my abuses reckon up their own. . . .

Nothing could be plainer, and nothing more daring, than this paraphrase of the Almighty's self-declaration in an unadorned poetic language which, precisely for that reason, commands belief.

The poet's plainness of statement becomes a poetic position, polemically defended in the Rival Poet series. Once upon a time he could say, fearing no particular threat, that he wrote of his friend "without all ornament"; once upon a time, could imagine his friend favoring his poems, after his death, even though they were mere "poor rude lines" compared with "the bett'ring of the time." Then the friend might be imagined as saying,

> "But since he died, and poets better prove,
> Theirs for their style I'll read, his for his love."
>
> (32)

But when an "alien pen" has actually attracted the attention and favor of this friend, then the poet must reconsider his whole relation to poetry, and to poetry specifically as persuasion, as a means to the beloved's grace. Unquestionably, his style is not high —he is "a worthless boat," a "saucy bark" compared to the vessel "of tall building and of goodly pride" now riding on the "soundless deep" of the friend's patronage (80). Now his own "gracious numbers are decay'd," his Muse is sick: he must "grant, sweet love, thy lovely argument/ Deserves the travail of a worthier pen" (79); but, like himself and all the poets instructed by and in their connection with his friend, this new poet can do no more than repeat, as he so long has done, the subject's beauty. The question of matching comes up in another context: "I never saw that you did painting need," he says, plaintively,

> I found, or thought I found, you did exceed
> The barren tender of a poet's debt;   (83)

> Who is it that says most which can say more
> Than this rich praise—that you alone are you?   (84)

Because of the plainness of his style, then, his critical friend, recognizing how short the celebration has fallen of his true worth,

must "seek anew / Some fresher stamp of the time-bettering days."
But rhetoric alone, the verbal instrument designed for persuasion,
cannot persuade:

> yet when they have devis'd
> What strained touches rhetoric can lend,
> Thou truly fair wert truly sympathiz'd
> In true plain words by thy true-telling friend. . . . (82)

Finally, because of the misery of the separation and the misery
of his own inadequate inspiration, he can only be tongue-tied,
dumb, and mute (83, 85), trusting in silence an eloquence more
persuasive than "the proud full sail of his great verse" (86).

Sonnet 76 shows an enlarged perception into the psychology
and also the sociology of poetry:

> Why is my verse so barren of new pride?
> So far from variation or quick change?
> Why, with the time, do I not glance aside
> To new-found methods and to compounds strange?

In these lines, there is the recognition that, in literary fashions,
novelty counts, and that his own verse is not, in this sense, fashionable. The next quatrain moves from the general situation, in
which time is taken to confer a "bettering" upon poetry, to his
personal situation within the craft:

> Why write I still all one, ever the same,
> And keep invention in a noted weed—

to his own style of "clothing" his thoughts:

> That every word doth almost tell my name,
> Showing their birth, and where they did proceed?

Here, style as fashion comes into the sharpest conflict with style
as individual expression—and, we gather from the plot constructed around the problem, which has provided "reason" for examining the problem in the first place, individual style must go down
before the time's dictation. But, by the compliment's familiar
turning, the poem's logic defends the poet's tautological reiteration of the friend's perfections, justifies the poet's practice altogether:

O, know, sweet love, I always write of you,
And you and love are still my argument;
So all my best is dressing old words new,
Spending again what is already spent;
    For as the sun is daily new and old,
    So is my love still telling what is told.

In the triumphant, and entirely conventional, figure of the sun's faithful return after its nightly extinction, bringing light and fertility to the world each day, the poet establishes the essential nature both of his love, and of his way of expressing that love. Human expression must triumph over fashion, and even over art.

The Rival Poet sonnets form one of several groups of separation-poems, in which the poet sings, studies, and comes to terms with his estrangement from his friend. Certainly he has been "absent" from the friend in earlier sonnets, and he has incurred the friend's displeasure too. But *this* separation is cast entirely in poetic terms: not only is the poet's love called into question, but so is the language he uses, his professional personality. Restoration of the friend's favor brings poetic reunion (97-103) as well, and the Muse is roused to celebrate the refound love—"return, forgetful Muse"; "Rise, resty Muse"; "O truant Muse"; "Make answer, Muse"; "Then do thy office, Muse"—which is, to reassert the values of the poet's poetic convictions:

"Truth needs no colour with his colour fix'd;
Beauty no pencil, beauty's truth to lay;
But best is best, if never intermix'd. . . ."   (101)

The repetitiousness, the familiarity of the poet's style is, finally, justified by a perverse application of the doctrine of imitation: "Fair, kind, and true" must be his only argument because those are the intrinsic qualities of the young man praised. Fashion is rejected, finally, for the truth of plain speaking:

What's in the brain that ink may character
Which hath not figur'd to thee my true spirit?
What's new to speak, what new to register,
That may express my love or thy dear merit?
Nothing, sweet boy; but yet, like prayers divine,
I must each day say o'er the very same;
Counting no old thing old, thou mine, I thine,
Even as when first I hallowed thy fair name.   (108)

65

Sonnets 108 to 113 reconsider the separation now happily ended: the poet examines himself, in some of the sharpest analytical sonnets he ever wrote. In "Alas, 'tis true I have gone here and there/ And made myself a motley to the view," the poet gives himself no quarter, save in the assertion that "worse essays prov'd thee my best of love." Fortune has not favored him, by committing him to a life which forces him to deviation from his best self:

> O, for my sake do you with Fortune chide,
> The guilty goddess of my harmful deeds,
> That did not better for my life provide
> Than public means which public manners breeds.
> Thence comes it that my name receives a brand. . . .
>
> (111)

In a marvelous image, full of self-disgust and yet speaking through that disesteem to his own professional commitment to his art, the poet comments on the "public means" which so threaten him:

> And almost thence my nature is subdu'd
> To what it works in, like the dyer's hand.

"Like the dyer's hand"!—stained by the dyes, marked by its service to the materials of its art, that hand can nonetheless make new patterns, must prepare cloth to useful and decorative functions, as the poet, his whole being steeped unmistakably like the dyer's hand in the materials of his own craft, shapes new patterns for new poetic purposes, chooses the colors (of rhetoric and of poetics) to make social ends beautiful. The poet's verse, to which he is servant, speaks to other people and will do so "Till all the breathers of this world are dead."

Clearly, the relation of poet to this friend is based on poetry: poetry is not only the conventional instrument of appeal to patron, friend, and lover, the conventional voice in beauty's praise; but poetry is also the poet himself, ingrained in his personality and thus marking (the dyer's hand) all his human realizations and relations. That Shakespeare has provided poetic theory with a body and a personality in the fictive Rival Poet, around whom he organized a drama of verse and about verse, thereby invigorating an entirely academic convention of sonnet metapoiesis, is less surprising than that he thereby intensifies and dramatizes recurrent questions of styles—of praise, of imitation, of self-projection. The Rival Poet is invoked not as a voice for "style" of verse simply,

66

though he unquestionably is made into a topic for discussing that subject. Because in this poet's prodigal economy, verse so clearly *is* the man, and a chosen style so interpenetrated with its poet's personality, the Rival Poet becomes an animate, breathing threat to our poet's continued life as poet, as friend, as man, a threat which can only be warded off by a purified rededication to poetic integrity. What Shakespeare's whole creative effort demonstrates is, I think, that for him poetic integrity lay in the continual re-examination of poetic values, the continual confrontation of those problems literature always sets for poets. In *Love's Labour's Lost*, the mereness of style is endlessly and lovingly exposed as the fraud that it is, the miracle of creation reduced to an examination of craft—and the value of skill in the service of literary creativity reaffirmed even as its illusionism is exposed. From the *Sonnets*, we learn something else: how a man's fundamental moral existence can be a matter of style.

2

Mel and *Sal*:
Some Problems in Sonnet-Theory

I. *Mel* and *Sal*: the Couplets

FOR A GREAT MANY talented readers, Shakespeare's sonnets have
proved a serious problem. That so great a writer, so resourceful
and tactful a poet, could have written so many poems manifestly
disappointing has brought out some very sharp criticism indeed,
from Yvor Winters and from John Crowe Ransom, in particular,
poets themselves and major theorists of twentieth-century poetics.
These critics' dissatisfaction tended to focus on the sonnets' endings, the couplets; and even such defenders of the poems as Edward Hubler and C. L. Barber have apologized for the "pallid-
ness" and "defect" of so many of the couplets.[1] Doubtless such
dissatisfaction was a necessary result of a poetics which, though it
values surprise in a poem, insists on internal coherence and tonal
consistency, or permits apparent incoherence and inconsistency
only in the service of a larger harmony—absence of which, in
poems so short as sonnets, seems an intolerable poetic error. Often
Shakespeare's couplets offer alterations of tone and topic blatantly
unmodulated or unaccommodated to the rest of the poem—and to
the New Critics of the nineteen-thirties and -forties, it seemed
foolish to trump up excuses for such lack of poetic tact. Even a

[1] Yvor Winters, "Poetic Styles, Old and New," *Four Poets on Poetry*, ed.
Don Cameron Allen (Baltimore, 1959); see also Winters' "The Sixteenth
Century Lyric in England," *Poetry*, LIII (1939), 258-72; 320-35; LIV (1939),
35-51; John Crowe Ransom, "Shakespeare at Sonnets," *SR*, IV (1938), reprinted
in Barbara Herrnstein Smith, ed., *Discussions of Shakespeare's Sonnets* (Boston, 1964), pp. 87-105; Edward Hubler, *The Sense of Shakespeare's Sonnets*
(Princeton, 1952), p. 27; C. L. Barber, "Introduction to the Laurel *Sonnets*"
(New York, 1960), p. 14. Arthur Mizener's essay on Sonnet 124, "If my dear
love were but the child of state," is a valiant attempt to counterbalance Ransom's reading of this and other sonnets: "The Structure of Figurative Language in Shakespeare's Sonnets," *SR*, v (1940), 730-37. A more tolerant and,
I think, sophisticated version of Winters-descended criticism can be found
in Douglas L. Peterson's *English Lyric*, Chapter 6. See also Claes Schaar, *An
Elizabethan Sonnet Problem, Lund Studies in English*, XXVIII (1960), which
deals with some of the commonplaces of sonneteering.

critic like Barbara Herrnstein Smith, specifically concerned with how poems end, by no means defends all Shakespeare's couplets, some of which seem to her blatantly to display failure in poetic closure.[2] Stephen Booth's sensitive study of Shakespeare's *Sonnets*, devoted to the proposition that the poems are individually extremely complex and work simultaneously in several "systems" (of sound, of syntax, of logic, of "sense," of theme), goes far toward providing a poetic context for the radical "difference" from the preceding quatrains of so many of the couplets.[3] I want to look at Shakespeare's sonnets as a whole sequence, with particular attention to the possibility that they exemplify certain problems within sonnet-theory; and at some of the couplets specifically as a "problem," to see if a poetic and theoretical context can be established in which the *Sonnets* need not be read as a breach of decorum or as a failure in poetic mastery. Of course I do not mean to justify *all* the couplets, or even all the sonnets, any more than I mean to suggest that each word in the whole sequence (or in all the groups) is the best-chosen of all possible alternatives—only to consider why, in the work of a man universally acknowledged to be one of the world's greatest writers, there should be so consistent a poetic "mistake" as it has seemed to so many able and sensitive critics.

Some help comes from linguistics: Jiří Lévỳ's analysis[4] shows us the reasons why, from deep within the English language, English sonnets had to end in a couplet, as their Continental (i.e., Romance) cousins had not. Lévỳ makes clear, too, why the English

---

[2] Although she has some very interesting pages on "Epigram and Epigrammatic," in her valuable *Poetic Closure* (Chicago, 1968), Barbara Herrnstein Smith does not deal with Shakespeare's sonnets under this rubric. Elsewhere, she has important things to say of the sonnets: pp. 142-45, 158-59, 170, 214-22, 227-29, and especially pp. 121 and 148.

[3] Stephen Booth, *An Essay on Shakespeare's Sonnets* (New Haven, 1969). By the sensitivity and tact with which he has pointed to the extraordinary technical variety within Shakespeare's individual sonnets, Booth has put all subsequent commentators in his debt, as well as saving them a great deal of time. Without apology, but with considerable gratitude for his fundamental discussion, I now proceed to do something which, by modern standards of poetics, ought never to be done: that is, I detach the couplet-problem from the sonnet-problem as a whole, in order to indicate the range of these couplets, both in themselves and in relation to the poems they close.

[4] Jiří Lévỳ, "On the Relation of the Language and the Stanza Pattern in the English Sonnet," *Worte und Werke: Bruno Marckwardt zum 60. Geburtstag* (Berlin, 1961), pp. 214-31.

sonnet as a whole is organized by "couplets"—crossed couplet quatrains ending in a rhymed distich—and how that organization supports the noticeable tendency in English poems toward antithetical structure. Certainly the English sonnet departed radically in rhyme-scheme and therefore in logic[5] from its Continental models (a fact sometimes adduced in praise of English independence of models and authorities, of English poetic self-determination). What Lévy's analysis tells us is that, given the structure of the language, the peculiarly couplet-sonnet is hardly a surprising development in English.

Since English sonnets generally ended in couplets, and Shakespeare's completed sonnets all do so, it may seem foolish for me to spend so much time on so obvious a topic, linguistically natural as the couplet seems, in English anyway. Nonetheless, I think Shakespeare's couplets are important critically because, although most English sonneteers indeed used the couplet closing, very few of them wrote, as Shakespeare has seemed so often to have done, couplets which notoriously fail in their relation to the poems as a whole or to demand consideration as free-standing distichs. If this habit is (as Ransom and Winters have suggested) a serious defect in Shakespeare's practice, then not only are Wyatt, Surrey, Sidney, and Spenser all better sonneteers than he (a proposition defensible in whole or in part), but so also are Thomas Watson, Michael Drayton, and Barnabe Barnes, to name three poets taken almost at random from Sir Sidney Lee's handy collection[6]—poets rarely taken to task for their indecorous or maladroit couplet-closures. In other words, although one should not abandon twentieth-century poetics utterly for the sake of only one aspect of Shakespeare's multiple sonnet-accomplishment, we may find, looking elsewhere for authority, that the couplets may seem less careless, less accidental, less unrelated to their full poems than has been stated.

Shakespeare's couplets do not, of course, follow a single formula: they work in very different ways, often "say" very different kinds of thing. Sometimes they answer questions set in the quat-

[5] For linguistic governance of logic, see in particular Roman Jakobson and Lawrence F. Jones, *Shakespeare's Verbal Art in "Th' Expence of Spirit"* (The Hague and Paris, 1970); see also Jakobson, "Poetry of Grammar and Grammar of Poetry," *Poetics* (Warsaw, 1961).

[6] *Elizabethan Sonnets*, ed. Sidney Lee (*An English Garner*), reprint (New York, 1964), 2 vols.

rains, as in Sonnet 13 ("O that you were yourself!") and Sonnet 65 ("Since brass, nor stone, nor earth, nor boundless sea"); sometimes they give a sharp point, or turn, to the argument of the quatrains, as in 21 ("So is it not with me as with that Muse") and 106 ("When in the chronicles of wasted time"); sometimes they pick up the theme of the quatrains to bring it, in a single word, into sharper focus, as in 109 ("O, never say that I was false of heart"), where the dialectic is made even more powerful by the couplet's action. Again, a couplet may seem to be really "wrong" for its poem, as in 95 ("How sweet and lovely dost thou make the shame"), where the knife-image is confusing in a poem with many juxtaposed images already—of roses, tongues, mansions, and veils. The repeated couplet of 36 and 96

> But do not so; I love you in such sort,
> As, thou being mine, mine is thy good report,

whether the result of printing-house muddle or the poet's carelessness, must raise questions of the couplet's fit. In neither 36 nor 96 has this couplet an air of inevitability; indeed, in 96 ("Some say thy fault is youth, some wantonness"), the poet's involvement with his friend's "good report," though stated in the first quatrain, runs quite counter to the sentiment of the eleventh and twelfth lines, where the friend's capacity to seduce "all gazers" is by no means wholly approved. In Sonnet 36 ("Let me confess that we two must be twain"), the couplet has indifferent success, since in the quatrains poet and friend, poet's honor and friend's, have been intertwined from the second line—although even here, the youth's "good report" seems a remarkably poor incentive for this poet to adduce, concerned as he was with ideal fidelity and ideal behavior in love and out of it.

Quite often a couplet's connection with images in the body of the poem is demonstrable, but interrupted by intervening imagery, as for instance in 6 ("Then let not winter's ragged hand deface") and 56 ("Sweet love, renew thy force"), where the couplets certainly gather up some of the meanings expressed in the quatrains, but let other meanings fall slack. Mrs. Smith has pointed to the differently successful endings of Sonnets 148, 18, and 29.[7] Both she and Booth stress the intellectual quality, even the intellection, of Shakespeare's couplets;[8] in contrast to successful sonnets by, for

---

[7] Smith, pp. 142, 159, 162. [8] Booth, pp. 30-31, 41.

instance, Sidney and Spenser, Shakespeare's often show a particularly brainy, calculated incisiveness. Another way of saying this is that Shakespeare's couplets tend to stress thought over figure, to move away from figures of speech toward figures of thought—and sometimes to move into a poetry of statement remarkable precisely for its austerity and abstention from figure. Often the couplets play on words so as to induce thinking; one accepted trick of this sort is the use of different forms of inflectional variation, sometimes very slight, as in the couplet of 28:

> But day doth daily draw my sorrows longer,
> And night doth nightly make grief's strengths seem stronger

and sometimes more radically, as in 146:

> So shalt thou feed on Death, that feeds on men,
> And, Death once dead, there's no more dying then,

where the doctrinal commonplace is reshaped in sharp and memorable language. In such inflectional conclusions, there is much "point," certainly, that verbal wit associated with epigrammatic theory and practice. A great many other couplets are, though, far less sharp, less decisive, less intellectually coercive:

> Lo, thus, by day my limbs, by night my mind,
> For thee, and for myself, no quiet find.   (27)

> Look what is best, that best I wish in thee;
> This wish I have; then ten times happy me!   (37)

> For thee watch I, whilst thou dost wake elsewhere,
> From me far off, with others all too near.   (61)

> Tir'd with all these, from these I would be gone,
> Save that, to die, I leave my love alone.   (66)

In almost every case, these couplets demand no preceding *raison d'être*, in twelve lines or less: at once brief and clear, they evoke a specific, recognizable situation to which they speak directly, sufficiently expressive in themselves. They do not tell much, but at the same time they are not cryptic, do not partake of that elusiveness of syntax and thought we have come to associate with the "metaphysical" style: we understand, and could supply, a context for what is said.

To press this point a bit farther, the couplet of 22 ("My glass shall not persuade me I am old"), which altogether abandons the mirror-images, the images of youth and age, of flourishing and death developed in the quatrains—

> Presume not on thy heart when mine is slain;
> Thou gav'st me thine, not to give back again.

—stands *better* alone than at the tail of the sonnet to which it is assigned.[9] The couplet's conceit—the exchange of hearts by devoted lovers—is familiar enough, but the couplet is slack compared to the quatrains' vividness. Alone, however, it is an excellent amatory epigram, relying on the reader's knowledge of official love-conceit, making a familiar statement about lovers' falling-out. Again and again, one can identify final couplets which seem to be enough in themselves to be, in effect, free-standing distichs.

> Thy unus'd beauty must be tomb'd with thee,
> Which, used, lives th'executor to be.   (4)

for instance, is resonant with *carpe diem*, and entirely within the language of incised epitaph. Another, on another theme, is equally resonant to a traditional theme, this time to classical and Christian notions of eternity:

> So long as men can breathe or eyes can see,
> So long lives this, and this gives life to thee.   (18)

No need to say what "this" is: we enter into the poet's immediacy by the transaction of the poem itself, to understand that literary immortality is the topic, poetry the means to that eternity. Sometimes the couplets are fully celebratory in tone, working out a conventional image to its full extent:

> Ah! but those tears are pearl which thy love sheds,
> And they are rich, and ransom all ill deeds.   (34)

or

---

[9] Sitting before *La Grande Jatte* in the Chicago Art Institute, Donald Justice remarked that Shakespeare probably had a lot of couplets lying around (the book of epigrams he never wrote?), to which he then thought up quatrains. This chapter takes seriously the proposition that the couplets are in an important sense "composed," not merely aphoristic appendages, often applied hit-or-miss, to three sets of crossed couplets.

> More flowers I noted, yet I none could see
> But sweet or colour it had stol'n from thee.   (99)

Sometimes, the compliment is epigrammatically backhanded, as in 82:

> And their gross painting might be better us'd
> Where cheeks need blood; in thee it is abus'd.

or in 148:

> O cunning Love! with tears thou keep'st me blind,
> Lest eyes well seeing thy foul faults should find.

or in 57:

> So true a fool is love that in your will,
> Though you do anything, he thinks no ill.

The couplet in 84 takes the beloved to task in a particularly open but unsonnet-like way:

> You to your beauteous blessings add a curse,
> Being fond on praise, which makes your praises worse.

In the couplets of 129 and 131, sharpness turns to bitterness—

> All this the world well knows; yet none knows well
> To shun the heaven that leads men to this hell.

> In nothing art thou black save in thy deeds,
> And thence this slander, as I think, proceeds.

Whatever else they do in the contexts of separate sonnets, Shakespeare's couplets have a curious force in and of themselves, can often be read, even when they are syntactically hooked to the quatrains preceding them, as if they were intense, dramatic epigrams pointing directly to an intelligible social situation or state of mind. The context is readily supplied for couplets such as these:

> And so of you, beauteous and lovely youth,
> When that shall vade, by verse distills your truth.
>
>   (54)

> But if the while I think on thee, dear friend,
> All losses are restor'd, and sorrows end.   (30)

74

Yet him for this my love no whit disdaineth;
Suns of the world may stain when heaven's sun staineth.

(33)

Unless this general evil they maintain:
All men are bad, and in their badness reign.   (121)

"And so," "But if," "Yet," "Unless": in spite of the logical or pseudo-logical connectives to the matter preceding, we know what is going on in the couplets without needing earlier explanations; we recognize both literary and social situations, bring in our readers' share to fulfill the transaction initiated and preferred by the poet.

All this leads up to the relatively obvious suggestion that, in his sonnets, Shakespeare was working in the epigrammatic as well as the sonnet mode, was playing off two generic styles against one another, sometimes in concert, sometimes in opposition to one another. Indeed, in the epigrammatic tradition, as understood by Renaissance theorists and schoolmasters, some answer may be found to what has puzzled critics of the sonnets for so long: especially in its curious connections in Renaissance theory with the sonnet, epigrammatic theory has much to teach us.[10] Some stylistic problems in Shakespeare's sonnets, so long handled in terms of the poet's sincerity (whatever that may mean), may also appear less compelling when seen in relation to the poet's highly experimental attitude toward the topics, styles, and voices of these two very different although related short forms of verse.

In the body of Renaissance criticism, we can find ample evidence that the sonnet and the epigram were regarded as "like" one another, were sometimes taken almost as twins, sometimes as brother and sister. The epigrammatic syndrome was, in any case, interpreted as enough like the sonnet-syndrome to cause various kinds of confusion, in form, subject-matter, and language, be-

[10] On this subject, see Moench, *Das Sonett*, p. 37; James Hutton, *The Greek Anthology in Italy to the Year 1800* (Ithaca, 1935), p. 57. Though the point has been mentioned in passing by many critics, no one so far as I know has examined the possible significances of the much-commented upon "epigrammatic" aspect of Shakespeare's sonnets. In his *Elizabethan Sonnet Themes and the Dating of Shakespeare's Sonnets, Lund Studies in English*, xxxii (1962), Claes Schaar mentions and cites many Renaissance epigrams as analogues to Shakespeare's commonplaces, but does not deal with the possible significance of an epigrammatic element in the poems.

75

tween the two types. To look at Shakespeare's sonnets in the light of this critical association may make more intelligible his much-discussed mixture of styles, the "golden" and "drab" of one school, the "ornamented" and "plain" of another. Sonnets may not seem appropriately either "drab" or "plain," but the epigram's tendency is, one accepts, toward a poetry of statement which can, in rhetorical terms, be very drab and, in terms of tact, be plain indeed. Against this background, too, the emotional and descriptive language used of Shakespeare's mistress-figure makes a kind of sense it hitherto has not always seemed to do;[11] and an epigrammatic frame of reference may give force to several critics' observation of the "satiric" quality of the *Sonnets*.[12] But, for the moment, it is still with the couplets that I am concerned.

If these distichs were printed alone, readers would hardly be in doubt as to "what" they were, what genre they belonged to:

> How like Eve's apple doth thy beauty grow,
> If thy sweet virtue answer not thy show!　　　(93)

> For thy sweet love rememb'red such wealth brings
> That then I scorn to change my state with kings.　　(29)

> Him have I lost; thou hast both him and me;
> He pays the whole, and yet am I not free.　　(134)

> For sweetest things turn sourest by their deeds:
> Lilies that fester smell far worse than weeds.　　(94)

Such epigrammatic quality as these couplets display, though present in other English sonnets (Wyatt's above all), is surely especially Shakespeare's: Daniel's, Watson's, Barnes', even Spenser's couplets do not make the kind of independent sense, do not carry

---

11 Edward Hubler's chapter, "Shakespeare and the Unromantic Lady," is the most sensible of the voluminous commentaries on this figure; most critics, with an understandable mental set, consider the woman in Shakespeare's sequence in terms of petrarchan and anti-petrarchan conventions of language and attribute—which, although it serves to make Shakespeare's cleverness seem the greater, provides a limited context for what I think are the radical innovations in the mistress-poems. See the discussions by James Winny in *The Master-Mistress* (London, 1968); Northrop Frye, Leslie Fiedler, and R. P. Blackmur in *The Riddle of Shakespeare's Sonnets* (Princeton, 1962); and by Philip Edwards, *Confines*, Chapter 8.

12 For the satiric elements in Shakespeare's sonnets, see principally Cruttwell, p. 19; and J. W. Lever, *The Elizabethan Love Sonnet* (London, 1956), p. 174.

the sharp message, that these do. Drayton and Sidney only, of English sonneteers, occasionally wrote couplets which could be presented as free-standing epigrams—and they far less often than Shakespeare did.

Though it is by no means easy to be sure what the limits (of subject, of size, of form) of an epigram are, Renaissance critics and scholars were less puzzled by the genre than scholars today. Renaissance writers, furthermore, were trained in the writing of epigrams, in Latin, in Greek, in the vernaculars; the epigram, with all its taxing problems of expression, was a major whetstone of poetic wit and wits. Shakespeare is an exception to most serious poets' habit of producing obligatory epigrams, short and sharp, short and sweet (as Davies said of John Owen's epigrams)[13] —and, although critics from Martial onward believed that *brevitas* was the epigram's first qualification, some Renaissance epigrams, even Martial's, were by no means short.

In England, vernacular epigrammatists were not, I think, quite so common as in the major Continental literatures of the Renaissance,[14] but the forms of epigram commonly used in English were very close to the sonnet: English epigrams, like English sonnets, tended to be written in couplets and crossed couplets. Given Lévÿ's analysis of the resources of the English language with respect to rhyme, and its tendency to binary construction as a natural result of grouping by twos, it is hardly a surprise to find that the verse-forms of the English sonnet and the English epigram closely resemble one another.[15] Lévÿ's comment on the English sonnet applies as well to the English epigram, so often cast in

[13] John Davies of Hereford, *The Scourge of Folly* (London, 1611), p. 217.

[14] T. K. Whipple, *Martial and the English Epigram from Sir Thomas Wyatt to Ben Jonson, University of California Publications in Modern Philology*, x (1920-25), 279-414; Hoyt Hopewell Hudson, *The Epigram in the English Renaissance* (Princeton, 1947), which, though left unfinished at Hudson's death, is full of good ideas and information.

[15] George Gascoigne, *Certayne Notes of Instruction*, in G. G. Smith, ed., *Elizabethan Critical Essays* (Oxford, 1904), II, 55: "Then have you Sonnets: some thinke that all Poemes (being short) may be called Sonets, as in deede it is a diminutive word derived of *Sonare*, but yet I can best allowe to call those Sonnets whiche are of fouretene lynes, every line conteyning tenne syllables. The firste twelve do ryme in staves of foure lines by crosse meetre, and the last two ryming togither do conclude the whole. . . . There are Dyzaynes, and Syzaines, which are of ten lines, and of six lines, commonly used by the French, which some English writers do also terme by the name of Sonettes."

crossed couplets with a final, nearly independent distich: "The possibility of different patterns imparts a *potential independence* to a line of the English sonnet and—in some types of verse—an *obligatory independence and unity to the distich*; hence the grouping by twos which is reflected in both syntax and rhyme-scheme."[16]

Very often the epigram in English was a distich, of course, though the longer forms tended to crossed couplets with a distich-ending or were composed entirely of couplets. Thomas Bastard's book of "epigrams" contains several quatorzains which, judged by their content, are perfectly conventional sonnets, such as his introductory poem, "Ad lectorem de subjecto operis sui," and his quatorzain on the Queen, with the usual complimentary tropes.[17] Francis Thynne's *Emblemes and Epigrames* is made up of poems either in couplets or crossed couplets; several are quatorzains, of which one (on the Queen) might well have been written to any metaphorically sovereign sonnet-lady; another, to Fortune, might just as well be addressed to the whimsical, arbitrary, cruel mistress of a sonneteer.[18] Davies of Hereford's *Scourge of Folly* was a collection of epigrams, some satirical, some not; those that were not were often in quatorzain form and, in another kind of book, could have been assumed to be sonnets of compliment. One manifest quatorzain is called "Of Poetry," another "To the Reader." These blameless sonnets on verse are, as we know, solidly within the self-critical tradition of the form.[19] Sir John Davies' "Gulling

16 Lévy, "Language and Stanza Pattern," p. 224. John Crow provided me with a list of quatorzains, including Greville's *Caelica*; Tottel's *Miscellany*; Surrey's *Poems*; Grimald's poems; Davies' *Epigrams*; Weever's *Faunus and Melliflor*; Goode's poems; *A Gorgeous Gallery* (ed. Rollins); *Poems from Romances*, ed. Bullen; Herbert of Cherbury's poems; Sootherne's *Pandora*; *England's Helicon*; Gascoigne's *Posies*; T. Rogers, *Celestiall Elegies*; Emaricdulfe's verse; Ayton's poems; *Poetical Rhapsody*, ed. Bullen; Gervase Markham, *Devoreux*; Campion, *Poems*; Chapman, *Poems; Phoenix Nest*; Drayton's poems; Gorges' poems; Sidney's poems; George Herbert's *Temple*; Henry Lok's sonnets; Thomas Watson's poems; Alexander's poems. That is to say, this listing offers a basic range for the subjects dealt with in quatorzain form, showing how the couplet may be related to its preceding crossed couplets.

17 Thomas Bastard, *Chrestoleros. Seven Bookes of Epigrames* (London, 1558), in *Poems*, ed. A. B. Grosart (Manchester, 1880), pp. 6-7, 37.

18 Francis Thynne, *Emblemes and Epigrames* (1600), ed. F. S. Furnivall, *EETS*, LIV, 35, 44.

19 Davies of Hereford, *Scourge*: the poems addressed to King James and Prince Henry.

78

Sonnets," of which more below, are an important link between sonnet and epigram, written by a man practised in both lyric celebration and official epigrams (interestingly enough, usually in crossed couplets with a final couplet; then, in precisely the same form as the Gulling Sonnets). In Shakespeare's sonnets, one (126) is only twelve lines long, and rhymes by couplets;[20] it ought to be, then, an epigram, and is certainly a significant variation in a series otherwise broken in form only by a single other poem, Sonnet 145 in tetrameter.

All this is only to say that in English practice, sonnet and epigram shared a number of formal elements, in particular the quatorzain; and few epigrammatists or sonneteers made strict *formal* distinctions between the sonnet and the quatorzain epigram. Against this background, Sir John Harington's "Comparison of the Sonnet and the Epigram"[21] makes a great deal of sense:

> Once, by mishap, two Poets fell a squaring,
> The Sonet and our Epigram comparing;
> And *Faustus* having long demur'd upon it,
> Yet at the last gave sentence for the Sonnet.
> Now, for such censure, this his chiefe defence is,
> Their sugred tast best likes his likresse senses.
>> Well, though I grant Sugar may please the tast,
>> Yet let my verse have salt to make it last.

Harington's terms, sugar and salt—like so much in Renaissance criticism, of Italian origin—came to stand, indeed, for the genres of sonnet and epigram in very interesting ways. Both preservatives, "sugar" (or, more properly, "honey") and "salt" became metaphors for whole modes of poetry. These spices, sweet and sharp, kept poetry alive, as well as prepared it for whatever taste reader and writer preferred. How the terms came into use, and why they occurred so often together, can be seen from tracing Renaissance theories of epigram and sonnet, to which cluster of ideas, theories, definitions, and notions I now turn.

[20] F. T. Prince, *Shakespeare: the Poems* (British Council, 1963), p. 26, notes that this poem may be the *envoi* to a manuscript of a "first series" of the sonnets.

[21] Sir John Harington, *The Most Elegant and Wittie Epigrams* (London, 1633), p. 37. See also William Nelson, *The Poetry of Edmund Spenser* (New York, 1963), pp. 85-86.

II. Sonnet and Epigram in Renaissance Literary Theory

Unlike the sonnet, manifestly a modern form, the epigram was a form or genre recognized in and from antiquity, for which Martial, a poet notably "sharp," provided the single great model.[22] With the recovery of the Planudean Anthology and its publication in 1494, however, the "Greek epigram," with its vivid images and conceits, its emphasis on "point" markedly less strong than in the Roman epigram,[23] and its stress on amatory subjects, became a source of widespread imitation and inspiration for subsequent poets. The kind of epigram considered "Greek," particularly the amatory epigram, immediately affected lyric writing, in particular the sonnet and its associated forms, including that remarkable invention of the Renaissance, the emblem.[24] In England, the influence of the Anthology is readily visible in Thomas Watson's *Hekatompathia*, although for us, Shakespeare's final sonnets, 153 and 154, "Cupid laid by his brand, and fell asleep," and "The little love-god, lying once alone," will serve as typical Renaissance adaptations of one major topic, with its attendant figures, of the Greek amatory epigram.[25] To these, many parallel poems may be found in Latin, Italian, French, Dutch, and English, and in other vernaculars as well. The principal thing about epigrams, whether Latin or Greek, as all the theorists agreed, was their brevity: the shorter the better (with the moral for this doctrine in Marital, Bk. I, cx).

[22] For material on this, see T. K. Whipple, *Martial and the English Epigram*; and Hudson, *The Epigram in the English Renaissance*.

[23] The anecdote about "pointless" epigrams *à la grecque* is given in *Menagiana*: Racan visited Mlle. de Gournay, who showed him some of her epigrams. When he complained that they lacked point, she answered that they were epigrams *à la grecque*, and therefore did not require point. Later they were served a tasteless soup, of which Mlle. de Gournay complained; Racan responded that it was soup *à la grecque*. Cf. Hudson, p. 6; James Hutton, *The Greek Anthology in France* (Ithaca, 1946), p. 252.

[24] For material on this literary complex, see the invaluable, compendious studies of James Hutton; his are both critical examinations and bibliographies on the subject. It might be worth noting here that the connections between emblem and epigram are very close, as one can tell even by a casual glance at Alciati's or Scève's work. This matter, too, needs more attention than it has so far received.

[25] James Hutton, "Analogues of Shakespeare's Sonnets 153-154," *MP*, XXXVIII (1941), 385-403.

So long as Martial was taken as the archetypal epigrammatist, then the epigram could reasonably be regarded as a poem no shorter than a distich, stylistically pointed, likely to be directed to abuses or inconsistencies in individual or social behavior, sometimes celebrating the excellence of a person or institution, very often an epitaph. Martial wrote about a range of subjects and in various tones (or, better, in a good many vocabularies). Some of his poems, too, are very short and others are quite long, as he moved from stately celebration of emperors and public figures to manifest obscenity; his style, as Renaissance critics agreed, was properly pointed. Once the Anthology spread through the humanist world, however, the distinctness of the epigram, both in its subject-matter and in its tone, was considerably blurred, as its official range was radically widened. What Renaissance poets found in the Greek epigrammatists was a reservoir of image and conceit for their amatory compliments, already well-domesticated in European poetic circles; the Anthology provided short poems on love, not limited as the Roman epigrams were to sexuality—that is, to prostitution, prostitutes, paederasty, incontinence, infidelity, and deceit—but concerned as well with a felt and acknowledged emotion. Via Roman roads, many of the characteristic sonnet-images had already come down, unknown to the sonneteers writing them, from Greek amatory epigrams; but once the Anthology was made known officially to Renaissance writers, the models it offered became authoritative, and its figures passed at once into the verbal storehouse drawn on by neo-Latin and vernacular love poets.[26]

Throughout, Martial remained the chief standard for sharp, pointed, or "salty" writing. Recognizing his derivation from the Greek lyricists, Renaissance critics identified in Catullus' verse a form of "epigramma amatoria" to counterpose to Martial's sterner, more public sort. From Catullus, evidently via Petrarca, a line of amorous epigrammatists could be (and was) cited, reaching into the modern period; with that heritage established, the

[26] That is, both were "short forms," the sonnet made retroactively a descendent of the amatory epigrams of the Anthology, with Catullus cited as the Roman exemplar of the genre and the link between the Greeks and Petrarca. After the Anthology became known, the influence of its amatory language on Renaissance love-poems (in ancient languages and in the vernaculars) reinforced that notion of the sonnet's descent from the Anthology via Catullus to Petrarca.

boundaries of form and content between strict sonnet and epigram became even more indistinct. The fact that in English the quatorzain so conveniently served both sonnet and epigram is one example of the close connection of the two forms.

What *was* the epigram? Various critics defined the matter in various ways, but all stressed the necessary brevity of the epigram, as well as its historical origins in incised inscription—its brevity was seen, indeed, as a function of that origin. Some thought the epigram connected with, or derived from, longer forms like comedy, satire, or even tragedy; others thought that the form had always enjoyed a separate existence and was not to be considered merely a pithy distich or sententia extracted from a longer work, say, by Homer, Hesiod, or another poet working in longer forms.

Though certainly Martial was admitted by all Renaissance epigrammatic theorists to be its practitioner *par excellence*, Catullus played a consistently important role in these discussions. The Aristotelian critic Francesco Robortello, for instance, cited his work as derived from inscription-traditions and, imitating those forms of inscription, "Phasellus ille" and "Paene insularum, Sirmio" were, he thought, obviously inscriptions on, first, an object and, second, a memorable place. Epigrams themselves, Robortello noted, could be written in several different tones and were thus, in small, "like" greater forms of poetry. When they demonstrated "dolor," as in memorial poems (epitaphs), they were like tragedy; when they praised famous men (as Catullus praised Cicero, and Martial Domitian), they were odes in little. When they demonstrated *facetiae*, or witticism, in their choice of subject or in verbal play, they were like comedy and satire.[27] Later, in his influential literary handbook, Pontanus cited Martial and Catullus as the two great composers of epigram, and divided the form into three parts, *iudicatio, deliberatio*, and *exornatio*; the epigram's chief art lay in its *brevitas* and *argutia*. Pontanus praised the Catullan epigram for its *suavitas*, this sweetness shared with many Greek epigrams, particularly those on amatory subjects.[28] Gradually, Renaissance theorists came to

[27] Francesco Robortello, *In Librum Aristotelis de Arte Poetica Explicationes* (Basel, 1555), pp. 27-30; and Tomaso Correa, *De Toto eo Poematis Genere quod Epigramma vulgo dicitur* (Venice, 1569), pp. 50-51.

[28] Jacobus Pontanus, *Poeticarum Institutionum Libri III* (Ingolstadt, 1597), pp. 160, 190, 192-98.

insist on *argutia*, or wit, or point, though this was never an overt feature of classical theory, nor indeed demonstrated in many of the poems ("à la grecque") of the recovered Anthology; it was, however, a marked quality of Martial's strongly satirical epigrams. In discussions of the matter, the juxtaposition and counterposition of Martial and Catullus came to be taken as a trope of critical commentary on the epigram, until one could expect to find, in little and in large, their official rivalry as epigrammatists to occur in any major debate on proper epigrammatic style.[29]

From this material alone, it is easy to see how epigrammatic theory carried strong implications for the sonnet, a short form on (usually) an amatory subject, but which might concern the celebration also of a famous public figure. Sébillet's famous statement of 1548 is hardly surprising, that the sonnet "suit l'épigramme de bien près, et de matière, et de mesure: Et quant tout est dit, Sonnet n'est autre chose que le parfait épigramme de l'Italien, comme le dizain du Françoys."[30] Earlier, in his *Comento* on his own sonnets, an essay embodying his sonnet-theory, Lorenzo de' Medici had noted[31] the epigrammatic qualities of the sonnet:

> La brevità del sonetto non comporta che una sola parola sia vana; ed il vero subietto e materia de' sonetti per questa ragione debbe essere qualche acuta e gentile sentenzia, narrata attamente ed in pochi versi ristretta, fuggendo la oscurità e durezza. Ha grande similitudine e conformità questo modo di stile con l'epigramma quanto all' acume della materia e alla destrezza dello stile, ma è degno e capace il sonetti di sentenzie più gravi e pero diventa tanto più difficile.

In Minturno's discussion of epigram and sonnet, which he associated with one another in his vernacular study of poetics,

---

[29] For something on the Martial-Catullus rivalry, see Hutton, *Anthology in France*, p. 51 (citing Montaigne); and *Catullus et in eum Commentarius*, ed. Antonius Muretus (Venice, 1554); Pierre Nicole, *Epigrammatum delectus* (Paris, 1659); *Martialis Epigrammata*, ed. Matt. Raderus (London, 1832), citing Janus Lernutius and Paulus Jovius; see also Guillaume Colletet, *Traitté de l'épigramme et du sonnet*, ed. P. A. Jannini (Geneva, 1965), pp. 55, note 1; 86, 89-101.

[30] Thomas Sébillet, *Art poétique françoyse* (Paris, 1548), f. 43v.

[31] Lorenzo de' Medici, *Scritti d'Amore*, ed. G. Cavalli (Milano, 1958), p. 114.

the distinction between the two forms is one of subject and diction:[32]

> Bernardo Rota: Adunque voi non assomigliate il Sonetto a quel, che e Greci e di Latini chiamano Epigramma? Minturno: Anzi credo, che da lui sia molto differente. Perciocchè l'Epigramma è particella dell' Epica Poesia, il sonetto della Melica. Oltre a ciò nell' Epigramma nè vaghezza, nè leggiadria di composizione si richiede; ma agutezze di motteggio, o di sentenza. Nel Sonetto con le parole elitte, e vagamente, e leggiadramente ordite, e composte o grave, o aguto, o dolce sentimento. Nell' Epigramma non si prescrive certo numero di versi, quantunque s'egli n'ha più di due, o di quattro, Elegia più tosto si debba chiamare. Nel Sonetto è determinato il fine, il qual non si può trapassare.

In spite of the difference in emphasis between the two kinds, for Minturno as for others, the sonnet and epigram worked on the same fundamental formal problem, of *brevitas* or diminution. Minturno made careful distinctions between the particular qualities of the two kinds, the epigram depending on its acuteness and the sonnet (*poesia melica*) on its sweetness (with examples from Petrarca)—"Ne pero nego, che 'l Sonetto nella materia non sia tavolta tiene altro modo, ed altro stile." The epigram's chief characteristic, its *argutia*, its pointedness, is not, according to Minturno, a paraphrasable thing, for which prescriptive models can be supplied: it is remembered because of the feelings it arouses, and is not explicable in the normal way.[33]

Other critics deal with the topic. Giovanni Pigna, in his *I Romanzi*, primarily a discussion of another burning critical question, touched on the epigram in his handling of the minor forms; the epigram was, he said, clearly associated with the sonnet and the madrigal:[34]

> & all' uno & l'altro per diversa strada il Sonetto: il quale nondimeno alle volte è tale, che ne in Lirico, ne in Epigramma il

---

32 Antonio Sebastiano Minturno, *L'arte poetica* (Venice, 1563), pp. 240-42; cf. his other poetics, *De poeta* (Venice, 1559), pp. 411-12, where he deals with the epigram (but not with the sonnet, since it was not an ancient form). For an opposite view of the relation of sonnet and epigram, see Girolamo Ruscelli, *Del modo di comporre in versi nella lingua italiana* (Venice, 1558), p. 155.

33 Minturno, *De poeta*, p. 412.

34 Giovanni Pigna, *I Romanzi* (Venice, 1554), p. 55.

suo sentimento spiegare non si potrà: si comè spesso quello che nell' uno ò nell' altro si contiene, in un sonetto malamente s'accommoda, ò che in effetto bene non vista.

For Benedetto Varchi, "il sonetto corrisponda all' epigramma." as did the madrigal also; that is, he felt that for symmetry's sake a short lyric form needed to be identified to "match" the independent epigram.[35] Tasso too discussed an epigrammatic topic, "point," in relation to the sonnet, noting that the final line or lines of the sonnet was the best place for point.[36]

All this simply means that several vernacular forms were associated with the epigram and that, because an amatory parallel was needed, the sonnet, with its Catullan derivations, was often taken as standard, although the *madrigale*, the *huitain*, the *dizain*, and the *douzain* were also mentioned by various critics. One form rarely mentioned in the theoretical works, though cited often by modern critics of the sonnet, is the *strambotto*, an Italian short form with a final rhyming couplet. Frequently, though by no means invariably, its subject was public, political, or even satirical, although Serafino's *strambotti* are an important stage in the spread of petrarchan love-poetry and love-conceits.[37] None of the English theorists or critics touches on the formal problem connecting the sonnet with "sharper" types of verse, so that it is difficult to know how or whether Shakespeare's contemporaries assessed the relation of *strambotto* to other short forms. Certainly the final couplet of the *strambotto*, like that of the English sonnet, fell into the much-discussed domain of epi-

[35] Benedetto Varchi, *L'Hercolano* (Venice, 1570), p. 217.

[36] Torquato Tasso, *La Cavaletta ovvero della Poesia Toscana, Dialoghi*, ed. E. Raimondi (Firenze, 1958), II, 623 (on the ending of a poem, like the sting of a bee); p. 629 (sweetness above all, above even *gravità*, with Petrarca as exemplary); p. 634 (*testura de' sonetti*); p. 635 (*bassezza e stile umile* in Dante's sonnets). I am indebted for help on this point to Irene Samuel.

[37] Serafino's work was certainly known to Wyatt, who translated and adapted some of his poems, and for this reason the final couplet of the English sonnet has often been attributed to the influence of the *strambotto*, but nowhere (so far as I can see) by any contemporary poet or critic. For more on this, see Hutton, *Anthology in Italy*, pp. 297-98; *Anthology in France*, p. 33; Whipple, p. 312; D. G. Rees, "Italian and Italianate Poetry," *Elizabethan Poetry* (Stratford-upon-Avon, 1960), p. 58; Patricia Thomson, *Sir Thomas Wyatt and His Background* (Stanford, 1964), p. 211; J. W. Lever, *Elizabethan Love-Sonnet*, p. 31, who associates Wyatt's sonnet-form with the *strambotto* and the epigram.

grammatic *clausula* and point, so recurrent in Italian and French theory. "Point" was by no means synonymous with closure, but it tended to occur, or to be expected, in the final lines of the sonnet; many of Petrarca's sonnets were cited to show how successful he was in his final lines. But point could also occur at one or another turning, earlier in the poem. In the petrarchan sonnet, there was no final couplet, of course, so that point tended to be either a verbal play in the final line or, often, an arresting verbal device at the turning from octave to sestet. French theorists had much to say about point; they thought of it in terms of rhyming lines, so that their formulations were readily transferable to the final couplet of the English sonnet-form.

A major contributor to literary theory and himself a writer of epigrams in Latin, Julius Caesar Scaliger managed in his short disquisition on the epigram to make most of the points stressed by earlier critics, and to provide as well a metaphoric vocabulary with which to categorize epigrams. He found *brevitas* and *argutia* to be essential; the prescriptive brevity is not, however, precisely definable. Epigrammatic point must be felt, or experienced, in the paradoxical or otherwise clever, unexpected clausula: it is not merely memorable, but actually *to be remembered*. For Scaliger, Martial is unquestionably the master epigrammatist, Catullus having failed now and again; but he accords Catullus the laurel for amatory epigrams, his poems providing the best example of *mel*, or honey or sweetness: "Haec esse decet candida, culta, tersa, mollia, affectum plena. Alia contra, vivida, vegeta, aeria, qualia Martialis." Of the other type, "alia contra," he distinguished four sorts, each with its categorical metaphor:[38]

> horum Ideae quattuor. Una, in qua foeditas est. . . . Una in qua fel. Amarulenta species haec, obiurgatoria, obtrectatrix, maledica, virus olens. . . . Una in qua est acetum. Mordax genus hoc carpit sine maledictis. . . . Una in qua est sal ex iis captatur risus sine ulla vituperatione, atque haud multa mordacitate.

Of these categories, the first, those epigrams remarkable for their *foeditas* or vileness (in particular, filthy smell, actual and metaphorical), were altogether unsuitable for the serious author; the

---

[38] Julius Caesar Scaliger, *Poetices Libri Septem* (Lyon, 1561), pp. 169-70, italics mine. Cf. Correa, pp. 19, 20, 31, 38.

other categories were those practised in by good poets.[39] These, then, are *mel* or honey (sweet, amatory epigrams); *fel*, gall; *acetum*, vinegar; and *sal*, salt. No wonder Harington spoke of the sonnet as "sugar" and the epigram as "salt" in his "Comparison"; like vinegar, these were the preservatives of verse, among which a poet might choose. Gall is medicinal in another way, providing a purge; in that metaphor, "gall" was one quality of satiric writing, with which epigrams often overlapped. As Ben Jonson wrote in the introductory epigram to his book,[40]

It will be look'd for, booke, when some but see
    Thy title, *Epigrammes*, and man'd of mee,
Thou should'st be bold, licentious, full of gall,
    Wormewood, and sulphure, sharpe, and tooth'd withal. . . .

noting thereby the predominance of *fel* in contemporary English epigrammatic theory.

Generally speaking, *mel* and *sal*, or *mel* and *fel*, were the common categories under which the sweet and the sharp epigrams were discussed; Catullus and Martial were the classical examples most commonly cited for these two half-related, half-opposed types. In France, Sébillet regarded Scève (who wrote not sonnets, but dizains) as the best writer in the *mel* category, Marot in the *sal*, the first true writer of vernacular sharp epigrams. Sébillet recommended epigrams of eight and ten lines (huitain and dizain), eight for "matières plus légères et plaisantes," ten for mat-

---

[39] English epigrammatists were concerned with the epigram's chastity of content: of his epigrams, Timothy Kendall wrote, "I have weeded away all wanton and woorthlesse woordes; I have pared away all pernicious patches: I have chipt and chopt off all beastly boughes and branches, all filthy and fulsom phrases. . . ." (*Flowers of Epigrames* [1577], reprinted for the Spenser Society, 1874); Thomas Bastard: "I have taught Epigrams to speak chastlie besides I have acquainted them with more gravitie of sence, and barring them of their olde libertie, not onelie forbidden them to be personall, but turned all their bitterness rather into sharpness." (*Chrestoleros*, 1598, in *Poems*, ed. Grosart); John Davies of Hereford, on Heywood's epigrams:

    Thou lawdst thine Epigramms for being chaste:
    No marvell: for the dead are ne're embrac'd. . . .

(*Scourge*, p. 252). See also John Heywood, *The Workes* (London, 1587), "To the Reader" (preceding "the First Hundred of Epigrammes"), for Heywood's expressed "good will" as an epigrammatist.

[40] Ben Jonson, *Complete Poetry*, ed. William B. Hunter, Jr. (Garden City, 1963), p. 4.

ters "plus graves et sententieuses." The epigram was to be as "fluid" as possible; the one rule for young poets was to be sure that "les deux vers derniers soient agüe en conclusion: car de ces deux consiste la louenge de l'épigramme." Those French poets best at point in the final lines were, he thought, Marot and Saint-Gelais, "pour le sel de leurs epigrammes." As observed, Sébillet considered the sonnet simply the perfect Italian epigram, as the dizain was the perfect French epigram: the sonnet's matter should be "facétieuse," following the model of "le prince des Poètes italiens, duquel l'archétype des Sonnets a esté tiré"; the sonnet "reçoit plus proprement affections et passions grèves. . . ." Neither the petrarchan sonnet nor the dizain ended on a couplet, so although the final line was often "sharp," the point associated with couplets (in the English sonnet) had to be placed earlier in the petrarchan. In the case of the dizain, this was at the fifth and sixth lines, or at the seventh and eighth. In the petrarchan sonnet, Sébillet thought, the point should occur either in the rhyming second and third lines or (better) in the sixth and seventh; it might also be an aphorism or verbal play in the final two, non-rhyming lines.[41]

In his *Deffense et illustration de la langue françoyse*, Du Bellay, himself a master of the sonnet's final line, made fun of weak epigrammatists writing dizains, who wasted, he said, nine lines merely for the point in the tenth; he advised scrupulous imitation of Martial throughout for really forceful effect.[42] For Jacques Peletier du Mans, the epigram had to be brief, familiar, capable of managing a witty topic as well as more serious subjects; also subtle, pointed, and effective in its close. Martial was "le professeur du genre." As for the sonnet, in his view best worked out by Petrarca and Bembo, "il a du commun avec l'épigramme, qu'il doit se faire apercevoir illustre en sa conclusion."[43] The epigram properly had one conclusion, but the sonnet might have more:[44]

---

[41] Sébillet, ff. 39r-44v.

[42] Joachim du Bellay, *Deffense et illustration de la langue françoyse*, ed. Henri Chamard (Paris, 1948), pp. 108-10.

[43] As Muret and Pontanus (and almost everyone else writing on the subject) put it: "Idcirco epigramma quidem cum scorpione contulerunt. Nam scorpio, quanquam minatur undique, tamen in cauda gerit aculeum, quo lethalem plagam infligit" (Muret's ed. of Catullus, cited above, p. 83).

[44] Jacques Peletier du Mans, *L'Art poétique* (1555), ed. André Boulanger (Paris, 1930), pp. 161-62; 165-66 (spelling conventionalized).

Mais il y a de plus, qu'il doit être élabouré, doit sentir longue reconnaissance, doit resonner en tous ses vers sérieusement: et que quasi tout philosophiquement en conceptions. Bref, il doit être fait comme de deux ou de trois conclusions.

Vauquelin de la Fresnaye noted the relation of the Italian sonnet, a quatorzain form, to the dizain of Scève and Saint-Gelais; after praising Pontus de Tyard and Ronsard, he observed the significance of Du Bellay's shift from the love-sequence *Olive* to the sonnet-sequences *Rome* and *Regrets*:[45]

> Et du Bellay quitant cette amoureuse flame,
> Premier fist le Sonet sentir son Epigramme. . . .

In other words, the term "epigram" was loosely applied. Scève himself, whose dizains made up the first major love-sequence in French, heavily dependent upon late petrarchan practitioners, wrote in his book's introductory huitain,[46]

> Ie sçay asses, que tu y pourras lire
> Mainte erreur, mesme en si durs Epigrammes:
> Amour (pourtant) les me voyant escrire
> En ta faveur, les passa par ses flammes.

To take examples at random of the close association, even sometimes the interchangeability, of the terms sonnet and epigram, Jean de la Taille called his collection *Sonnets et Epigrammes*, and published as well little collections called *Sonnets d'Amours* and *Sonnets satyriques du camp de Poictou*, as well as *Epigrammes*, some of which were in sonnet-form. In England, William Webbe associated "Epigrammes, Elegies, and delectable ditties" with the "comicall mode": sonnets and epigrams came under one umbrella.[47] Francis Thynne's *Emblemes and Epigrammes* displays many quatorzains, as well as epigrams both longer and shorter than that norm, largely in crossed couplets with a final couplet. Spenser called some of the poems in his contribution to the *Theatre of Worldlings* "epigrams" and some "sonnets": they are certainly short poems of irregular meter and

[45] Jean Vauquelin de la Fresnaye, *L'art poétique*, ed. Georges Pelissier (Paris, 1885), p. 35.

[46] *The 'Délie' of Maurice Scève*, ed. I. D. MacFarlane (Cambridge, 1966), p. 119.

[47] William Webbe, *A Discourse of English Poetry* (1586), in *Elizabethan Critical Essays*, ed. Smith, I, 249.

rhyme, with a marked family resemblance to each other. In his *Complaints* volume, Spenser regularized a great many of his earlier, very irregular versions to quatorzains. By the time we come to Davies' Gulling Sonnets, we can see that sonnet-form and sonnet-language have fused remarkably with epigrammatic and satiric modes. Davies was officially a sonneteer and an epigram-matist; in his book of epigrams, the first poem (like Martial's and Catullus' introductory poems, about the book to come) is on the epigram, and is a quatorzain. He takes leave of his book, at the other end of it, in an eighteen-line poem, crossed couplets with a final rhyming couplet.[48] Several of Davies' epigrams are on character-types, spoken in the acute, critical analysis customary in epigram. One, "In Gellam," is particularly to our point:[49]

> If *Gellas* beauty be examined
> She hath a dull dead eye, a saddle nose,
> An ill shapte face with morphew overspread,
> And rotten teeth which she in laughing showes.
> Briefly, she is the filthiest wench in towne,
> Of all that do the art of whoring use:
> But when she hath put on her satin-gown,
> Her cut-lawne apron, and her velvet shooes,
> Her greene silk stockings, and her petticoat
> Of taffaty, with golden friendge a-round,
> And is withal perfumd with civet hot,
> Which doth her valiant stinking breath confound:
> > Yet she with these addicions is no more,
> > Than a sweet, filthy, fine ill favoured whore.

The topic, a whore, is properly epigrammatic. The tropes of clothing, carefully developed, and the list of personal attributes are typical of epigram. All this is presented in a perfect quator-zain, with manifest affinities to the standard palinode-sonnet which inverts all the qualities, as well as the language applied to those qualities, of the traditional sonnet-beloved, in this case com-plete down to the near-obligatory sonnet-contradictions of the final line (point!).

[48] *All Ovids Elegies: Three Bookes, by C. M. Epigrams by J. D.* (Middel-burg, n.d.); modern edition by Frederick Etchells and Hugh Macdonald (London, 1925).
[49] Sir John Davies, *Epigrams*, ed. Etchells and Macdonald, p. 93.

The poem is, then, in a familiar Continental tradition, of which Francesco Berni's antipetrarchan blason-sonnet is the norm:[50]

> Chiome d'argento fine, irte e attorte
>   Senz' arte intorno a un bel viso d'oro;
>   Fronte crespa, u'mirando io mi scoloro,
>   Dove spunta i suoi strali Amore e Morte;
> Occhi di perle vaghi, luci torte
>   Da ogni obbietto diseguale a loro;
>   Ciglia di neve, e quelle, ond' io m'accoro,
>   Dita e man dolcemente grosse e corte;
> Labbra di latte, bocca ampia celeste;
>   Denti d'ebano rari e pellegrini;
>   Inaudita ineffabile armonia;
> Costumi alteri e gravi; a voi, divini
>   Servi d'Amor, palese fo che queste
>   Son le bellezze della donna mia.

In just such antipetrarchan spirit Nashe, fed up with overpraise of ladies, wrote,[51]

> Hence come our babling Ballets, and our new found Songs & Sonets, which every rednose Fidler hath at his fingers end, and every ignorant Ale Knight will breath foorth over the potte, as soone as his braine waxeth hote. Be it a truth which they would tune, they enterlace it with a lye or two to make meeter, not regarding veritie so they may make uppe the verse. . . .

Davies' Gulling Sonnets—sonnets that gull, sonnets for gulls— are a concerted exercise in sonnet-language and in sonneteers' truth; they emerge from the same literary world depicted in Donne's, Hall's, Marston's satires, in which the seamy side of London is the locus; and they make fun of all the great conventions of sonnet-rhetoric, those figures of speech and thought all hyperbolized in such writers as Barnabe Barnes, William Percy, and even Sir Philip Sidney himself, here trivialized, made nonsensical by Davies' "Camelion Muse." The Gulling Sonnets strike deep at sonneteering. For instance, the first poem in the series, "Here my Camelion Muse her selfe doth chaunge," is self-

[50] Francesco Berni, *Rime, Poesie Latine*, ed. A. Virgili (Firenze, 1885), pp. 137-38.

[51] Thomas Nashe, from *The Anatomie of Absurditie* (1589), in *Elizabethan Critical Essays*, I, 326-27.

referential in the critical manner we have come to regard as peculiar to the sonnet. The poem not only states the poet's intentions but also gives an overview of sonneteering. Davies' quatorzains offer an epigrammatist's perspective on the sonnet-world, a social, realistic, tough consideration of an idealistic genre, gulling readers who are, or have been, gulled by the lies of love-poets. The poems, with their gross inversions of convention, address themselves to the specific hyperboles of sonnets, compliment, figure, and syntax, in a way which suggests that the great vogue was seriously threatened, as their verbal formulations so readily empty out all beautiful meanings. These quatorzains are sonnets, all right, but parody-sonnets, thus plainly satirical. Even the readers of *these* sonnets are gulled, as the naked Cupid, clothed in the symbolic costume of suffering sonneteer, turns out to be no love-god but a lad from the underside of the city, causing trouble wherever he goes.[52]

Davies' poems, with their salty satire on "sweet" language, are a true bridge between epigrammatic and sonnet forms—the final line on Cupid's garments, for instance, returns us to the pantry-vocabulary systematized by Scaliger. After speaking (of all things) about each separate piece of Cupid's clothing, Davies ends his head-to-toe inventory with the line "and Sockes of sullennes exceding sweete." Sullen; sweet—we may be reminded of Du Bellay's famous poem beginning "J'ay oublié l'art de pétrarquizer," in which the following lines occur:[53]

> De voz doulceurs, ce n'est que sucre & miel,
> De voz rigueurs n'est qu'aloës & fiel. . . .

Du Bellay used the terms carefully; in his "Ad Lectorem," a Latin epigram prefacing the sonnets *Les Regrets*, he wrote,[54]

> Quem, Lector, tibi nunc damus libellum,
> His fellisque simul simulque mellis
> Permixtumque salis refert saporem.
> Si gratum quid erit tuo palato,
> Huc conviva veni: tibi haec parata est
> Coena. Sin minus, hinc facesse, quaeso:
> Ad hanc te volui haud vocare coenam.

52 Sir John Davies, *Poems*, ed. Clare Howard (San Marino, Calif., 1941), 223-27.
53 Du Bellay, *Œuvres poétiques*, ed. Chamard, IV, 206.
54 Ibid., I, 45.

Though it provides a neat reference to *fel, mel,* and *sal,* Du Bellay's introductory poem is important in showing something of his inventions in the subsequent cycle of sonnets, nostalgic, critical, personal, public poems about public life, public men, public events, encomia of (a few) virtuous men, diatribes against wicked men and wicked customs. Du Bellay borrowed heavily, in both tone and vocabulary, from the attacks upon urban (specifically, upon Roman) customs mounted by Juvenal and Martial, to provide us with a remarkable sonnet-sequence specializing, deliberately, in *fel* and *sal.*

One can find the metaphor for the poetic modes and genres in the general poetic store of reference: another such shorthand reference, relying upon the code Scaliger formalized, occurs in *Love's Labour's Lost,* in an exchange between Berowne and the Princess:

Berowne: Whitehanded mistress, one sweet word with thee.
Princess: Honey, and milk, and sugar; there is three.
Berowne: Nay, then, two treys, an if you throw so nice,
Metheglin, wort, and malmsey; well run dice!
There's half a dozen sweets.
Princess: Seventh sweet, adieu!
Since you can cog, I'll play no more with you.
Berowne: One word in secret.
Princess: Let it not be sweet.
Berowne: Thou grievest my gall.
Princess: Gall! bitter.
Berowne: Therefore meet.
                              (v.ii.230-37)

Of his book, *Epigrammes in the Oldest Cut and Newest Fashion* (1599), John Weever wrote,[55]

Nor dost thou like a love-sicke milke-sop gull
Unto thy Mistris for a kisse make mone:
But salt with sugar, honnie mixt with gall,
Must needes be praisde, must needes be likt of al.

And Matthew Grove:[56]

[55] Weever, *Epigrammes,* ed. R. B. McKerrow (London, 1911), p. 5.
[56] Matthew Grove, *The most famous and Tragicall Historie of Pelops and Hippodamia. Whereunto are adioyned sundrie pleasant devises, Epigrams, Songes and Sonnets* (London, 1587), Iiiijv.

Of Sugar and Salt

Sugar and Salt begyn with like letter,
   Though sugar be good, yet salt is better:
This sugar is sweete in mouth to the taste,
   Yet doth the Scripture shew us at the last,
That salt doth season all things that there be,
   And no such mention of sugar we see.

Daniel says of his Delia, "her disdaines are gall; her favours hunny," the term standing for whole areas of feeling, as of writing. The generic language sets the rhetorical tone and provides "content" as well for the poems. That a poet writes of "sweet," that he writes "sweetly" of sweet, means that he evokes a decorum in which he is confident his readers are at home. Berowne's exchange with the Princess or Daniel's attributing gall and honey to Delia's behavior (really, a transfer from his evaluation of her behavior to that behavior) may be mere decoration, or mere game; but both phrases, in their contexts, are charged with literary meanings signaling to readers the particular literary contract under discussion. So the bright young men of *The Returne from Parnassus* speak of Spenser ("A sweeter Swan than ever song in Poe"), of "Sweete *Constable*," of "Sweete hony dropping *Daniell*," of "*Draytons* sweete muse," and of Shakespeare[57]—

Who loves [not] *Adons* love *or Lucre[ce]* rape?
His sweeter verse contaynes hart [th]robbing li[n]e. . . .

exaggerating the chief quality attributed to high Renaissance amatory verse. In the poems themselves, though, such literarily significant words are not just critical signals, starting out of the text as messages to earnest readers; they must also fulfill their primary obligations to the texts in which they occur, must be tempered and harmonized within their literary environment. They must operate, first of all, in their proper context. Berowne's exchange, in the play, is a contest between courtly equals of fashionable wit, in a game proper to the decorum of class and occasion; further, these phrases, shorthand as they are, are entirely appropriate to a play in which language and rhetoric are the play's chief topics. Daniel's line fits nicely into the rhetoric of oppositions developed by practitioners in the petrarchan mode;

[57] *The Returne from Parnassus* (1601), in *Elizabethan Critical Essays*, II, 400-402.

they belong in a poem beginning, as this one does, "Faire is my love, and cruell as she's faire." At the same time, the tonal words are, as Berowne's exchange indicates, significant beyond their immediate primary context, force a literary-critical point to the surface of the quickly-moving text. Sonnets are *mel*, honey, sugar, sweetness; epigrams are salt, vinegar, or gall, their vocabularies and therefore their figures designed to make a metaphorical contrast between poetic styles contrasted in actual practice.

As can be seen from the Continental theorists cited in this section, the sonnet-epigram alliance, though secure, was uneasy. Sometimes the two are regarded as twins, one fair and one dark; sometimes they are regarded as antithetical. They are paired and discussed as a pair, though they are understood at the same time to be very different poetic alternatives, commanding different tones and vocabularies. Unlike any other sonneteer in English (Sidney is surely in this respect his nearest rival), Shakespeare managed to exploit the whole syndrome of epigram and amatory epigram, of salt and sweet, now setting the two modes off against each other, now displaying them as parts of an interlocking whole. Of English poets, he most deeply penetrates the whole problem of sonneteering, even into the theory of the sonnet, testing out now one, now another, now yet another implication of the form, the vocabulary, and the theory of sonnets; expressing, with an extraordinary richness of resource, the whole range of ideas involved in sonnet-theory. This is not to say that Shakespeare, for instance, "knew" Scaliger (though he very well may have) or another such formulating author of Renaissance critical orthodoxy, but simply that his powers of analysis, apparently called into play naturally whenever he dealt with a body of literary material, somehow permitted him exceptional insight into the fundamental problems of that material, perfectly well-known to contemporaries who did not have to look up all the theory on the subject.

Sonnets were "like" epigrams but, as we shall see in the discussions that follow, they were also very different from epigrams. What the two genres shared Shakespeare set himself to understand. The significance of this pairing and opposing of sweet and salt, of sonnet and epigram, may well give us pause, in this case. Obviously, Shakespeare wrote, as his contemporaries and subsequent commentators have observed, markedly "sweet" verse, but he also wrote some of the most incisive satirical sonnets in any love-sequence. Patrick Cruttwell has suggested that he found the materials of the voguish sonnet too thin, too conventionalized for his uses, and that he therefore altered the convention to demonstrate its cliché overuse.[58] Very possibly: but also, Shakespeare's "sweet," "sour," "eisel," occurring as they do in contexts of highly personal emotional expressiveness, cannot be *only* the result of exercise or of conventional decoration. They are also, I think, signals of a poetic contrast radically new, though deeply inherent, in sonnet sequences, a poetic contrast adumbrated and formulated in literary theory. These words are, most of all, the marks of Shakespeare's effort to press the sonnet-sequence into areas of style and of feeling which the genre had, in English anyway, thitherto never attempted: his highly professional, highly literary exploitation of the orthodox possibilities of his chosen form.

III. *Mel* and *Sal*: Shakespeare's Sonnets to the Friend

Edward Hubler's remark that "sweet" was Shakespeare's favorite epithet[59] is in good part true—certainly his contemporaries found his poetry so. Weever, in his *Epigrammes*, remarked on "honie-tong'd Shakespeare," Meres on the parallel between "mellifluous and hony-tongued Shakespeare" and Ovid, Barnfield on his "hony-flowing Vaine."[60] Of course, some of this reference to sweetness merely meant that Shakespeare wrote amorous poetry, the "sugred *Sonnets*" specifically mentioned by Meres, as well as *Venus and Adonis* and *Lucrece*, officially "melic" and thereby, by a false etymology, "honeyed." "Sugared" is an epithet applied to lyric poets other than Shakespeare, as we have seen; and we know nowadays, thanks to Yvor Winters' polarization of sixteenth-century lyric styles, that a certain tension can be read into lyric writing of the period between poetry of a fancier sort and poetry of a plainer sort. Winters' terms are anachronistic in precisely the way Claudio Guillén deplores:[61] metaphysical, baroque, mannerist are terms Guillén finds anti-historical and obscuran-

---

58 Cruttwell, p. 19.

59 Edward Hubler, *The Sense of Shakespeare's Sonnets*, p. 79.

60 Weever, *Epigrammes*, p. 75; Francis Meres, *Palladis Tamia*, in *Elizabethan Critical Essays*, II, 317; Richard Barnfield, *Poems in Divers Humours, An English Garner*, XIV, 120.

61 Guillén, p. 50.

tist, and so do I. In spite of the superposition of twentieth-century theory on Renaissance practice, one can recognize that there were alternative styles available; and that, for the Renaissance poet, "ornament" tended to go with mellifluousness of sound and with sweetness (pejoratively, sentiment) of sense; "sugared" often meant no more than highly decorated with rhetorical and poetical figures.[62] In Shakespeare's context, Hubler's comment is well taken. The incidence of the word "sweet" in his sonnets *is* high, and images involving sweetness—of flowers, perfume, honey, springtime, and so on—are significant too. The young man is "sweet love," "sweet self," potentially a "sweet husband," who should "make sweet some vial," so that his "sweet issue" his "sweet form should bear" after he himself has gone gray and become dust. It is the young man, too, who calls forth from the poet the figures of sweetness—not, as in the customary formula, the poet's mistress.

What do we make of this, of a young man presented to the world invested in the magnificent decorative imagery characteristically used to celebrate a beloved woman?[63] What is the poet up to, so radically inverting a well-known convention—*the* well-known convention, as far as sonnets were concerned? Given the language of these sonnets, no wonder there have been such recurrent speculations into the actual identity of the young man and, by extension, into Shakespeare's personality as well: the apparent definiteness in the praise of the young man's family and rank (as well as his roundabout admiration of the mother's beauty), invites investigation into the roster of possible patrons in Shakespeare's young manhood; the intensity of the address itself raises questions of "Willie Hughes."[64] When we look at the

[62] In showing some of the complexities involved in too sharp a division into ornamental and plain styles (or, for that matter, into golden and drab), Douglas Peterson has clarified a great deal; see his *English Lyric*, esp. pp. 212-18.

[63] For petrarchan imagery in general, see Leonard Foster, *The Icy Fire* (Cambridge, 1969); Janet Scott, *Les Sonnets élisabethains* (Paris, 1929); Lisle C. John, *The Elizabethan Sonnet* (repr. New York, 1964).

[64] Cf. Lever, p. 165. I do not want to deal with the identity of either friend or mistress; even if Shakespeare was so dependent upon literal experience to transcribe into quatorzains his relations with friend, mistress, and rival poet, that information does not help us much with the plot and language of his *Sonnets*, and not at all with the skills involved in writing them. Further, the homosexuality issue seems to me made clear in the poems themselves: if at

long tradition of sonnets to men (Petrarca to Colonna and Sen-
nuccio; Mambo and Della Casa to their heroic patrons and colleagues; Tasso's poems to the dead Antonio Soranzo; the Pléiade
poets to their patrons and to one another), we find that the conventional sonnet addressed to a man is rather heroic, satirical, or
literary-critical than amatory. Some sonnets to men are not quite
so public as the list given just now, such as Michelangelo's occasional sonnets, notable for their intensity; but Michelangelo wrote
no concerted sequence, and it is difficult to extract any cogent
theory of love from his poems, passionately as critics have tried
to do just that.[65] Richard Barnfield's poems (some of them sonnets) to Ganimede, which have often been compared to Shakespeare's, do indeed form a kind of developmental cycle of praising
and wooing. Barnfield's poet-persona addresses the young shepherd Ganimede in poems of outspoken male love, but Barnfield
himself later dissociated his own personality from the passions
expressed in the Ganimede poems, asserting that he was simply
following the implications of his model, Vergil's second Eclogue,
to describe a love permissible and decorous in the pastoral milieu.

Nothing in the tradition of sonnets-to-men offers any significant analogue to what Shakespeare's sequence, in which unquestionably the language to the young man is that of petrarchan
sentiment and praise, habitually used about a lady typically
sweet in all the ways that Shakespeare's young man is sweet,
chary as he is, cold as he is, arbitrary as he is, elevated as he is.[66]

---

a deep layer of his psyche, Shakespeare may have been writing of a symbolic
homosexual love, in which two men share one woman between them, then
one can only say that in classical epigrams, this was a common theme—the
topos turns up in the exchange between Von Rauffenstein and de Boeildieu
in Jean Renoir's *La Grande Illusion*, as in many other places. Considering
the care with which the poet demonstrates his friend to be heterosexual and
his own physical love for his mistress to be "normal," I think we may for the
moment ignore the possible biographical revelations hidden in these poems
and concentrate on their literary significances.

65 Critics, such as J. B. Leishman and Robert Clements, who have dealt
with Michelangelo's sonnets and other short poems have not, I think, taken
into account the extraordinarily occasional nature of his poems and verses:
to extract a consistent platonic or other theory of love (or of art) seems to
me to do violence to the nature of the poems themselves.

66 Again, it is worth noting that although some of the language addressed
to patrons by poets calls into question the humanity of the patron addressed,
Shakespeare's patron is personally fickle in a way that abstracted, preoccupied

What is odd about this young man's coldness to the poet is, I think, largely a matter of mental set: young men in sonnets (who are, of course, more likely to appear in the poet's *persona* than in the beloved's) are not supposed to play Adonis and flee from love, but "should" embrace their love and, in some cases, their loves. This sonnet-friend's chilliness is "like" the lady's conventional icy detachment, but much more mysterious than hers. Seen against the background of literary type, decorum, and genre, the lack of ardency attributed to the young man is as "original"— which is to say, as literarily unexpected—as is the "sweet" petrarchan vocabulary applied to him—with which it is all of a piece.

The poet, then, transposes roles in his sequence, addressing a man in woman's language, though by no means giving him a woman's part, for the maleness of the youth is several times stressed. What makes it seem that the man is cast in the woman's part is largely a matter of readers' literary conditioning, since the poet maintains a traditional role of distanced, unselfish devotion for the person addressed in the poem, and the style is unquestionably that of the petrarchan situation. But to what end does the poet write so? Never does he suggest physical desire for the young man, as Barnfield's pastoral *persona* so clearly does for Ganimede; somehow, in spite of the honeyed language to this sweet love, Shakespeare manages to keep physicality quite out of his own feelings and expectations in the case. He does so partly by the "plot," which makes plain that the poet thinks of the friend as apt for women's love, and, in the triangle with the mistress and the friend, that he *is* apt for woman's love; partly by the decorum of the poet so clearly "patronized," conscious of the friend's superior rank, interests different from the poet's own, and obligations, social and institutional, in an entirely different sphere of activity; partly by the exclusive male camaraderie of, for instance, Sonnet 20, "A woman's face, with Nature's own hand painted."

This sequence has the power it has not by any merely mechanical shakeup of traditional sonnet conventions. The intensity of the poet's feeling—intensity extreme even for a genre analyzing and exploiting poets' inward feelings—comes through, the more

---

patrons in public places were not, customarily: this attitude attributed to the young man is consistent with the behavior of sonnet-mistresses.

powerful for its mysterious object, a young man now aloof, dignified, and chilly, now wayward, dissolute, and cruel, who has become a focus for the forces of the poet's strong idealism and his
poignant self-revelations. Nonetheless, the upside-downing of this
sequence is worth some attention, even at its simplest. For instance, it is not surprising that the sonneteer importunes his subject to an active love, for sonneteers habitually implore their
cool mistresses to yield to their inward ardency; in this case,
though, the sonneteer importunes his subject to *marry*. Marriage
is not a normal condition in the sonnet-world: Spenser's *Amoretti*
broke with tradition, the final *Epithalamion* turning the whole
sequence toward (if not into) a concerted narrative of successful
courtship. Shakespeare's notion moves past Spenser's—the argument to the young man to marry is clever, unexpected, and even
up to date, in the genre employed.[67] It is less unconventional,
though, in another genre, the ode, where such exhortation, based
on a feeling for institutional family continuity, is quite in keeping; nor is it entirely uncommon in that ode-aspiring subgenre
of the sonnet, the heroic sonnet, dealing in public address to
public men, treating the events of their private lives as public
events—which, in the case of men of rank, is what their private
doings really were.[68] In this sequence, which so flaunts its place
in the official sonnet-lineage by its scrupulous deployment of
conventional celebratory language, the invocation to marriage
has a certain playfulness about it. Not that it is unserious—the
powerful language of conception, birth, and growth precludes
such judgment—but merely that it has its own panache, its own
expansive gesture of outdoing and overgoing, its own manner of
putting down those sonneteers of love with whom the poet is in
competition. Another way of saying this is that there is a literary
detachment, in addition to the felt separateness of poet and
friend, which the poet exploits in many ways.

These sonnets' hyperbolical language of praise has often been
remarked on, sometimes interpreted as autobiographical revelation, sometimes called in witness to the extraordinary, even

---

[67] Variorum *Sonnets*, II, 123: Rollins cites Pooler, who asserts that the poet
in Barnfield's sequence exhorts the beautiful young man to marry; for the
life of me, I cannot find evidence to support this much-repeated comment.

[68] Prince, *Poems*, pp. 21-31, on the patron; Mrs. Tucker is preparing a
study of what she calls the "aspiring" characteristics of sonnets, among them
the sonnet's aspiration to the ode, or its celebration in a grand style of important public personages and events.

philosophical, depth of the poet's feeling for friendship, for love, and for human personality.[69] If we may without impropriety look upon the sonnets as exercises—deeply felt, but nonetheless self-conscious in craft—in the sonnet-tradition, and in particular in sonnet-limitations, an exercise which at once presses past the conventional barriers of sonneteering and examines the bases of the sonnet-conventions, then it is easier to see at once how inventive the poet was with the literary materials available to him and within the mental set the (overworked) genre presupposed. Because the young man is addressed in the lady's language, hyperbole in praise of him comes to seem very hyperbolical indeed, much more so than when the same conceit is used about a lady. What is even more interesting in this series than its hyperbole, though, is the use of restraining devices modifying the hyperbole. One such is the checking of magniloquence in a poem, as well as the checking of readers' emotional response, by means of figures of thought. Again and again, we are blocked from full emotional response called forth, to work through the tricks of syntax and inflection, the movements of wit, that the sonnets abound in. Particularly in the couplets, such play occurs—"unus'd" set against "use," "use" against "usury," as in Sonnet 4, so that the reader must pause over the stoic, epicurean, and financial associations of the words; day-daily, night-nightly, breath-breathe in Sonnet 28; "lives this" and "this gives life" in Sonnet 18. Another way of saying this is that Shakespeare's sonnets, as sonnets should, have "point," and the point they make is often linguistically within the epigrammatic style.

But it is with sweetness, not point or sharpness, that I wish to begin:

> The forward violet thus did I chide:
> Sweet thief, whence didst thou steal thy sweet that smells,
> If not from my love's breath? The purple pride
> Which on thy soft cheek for complexion dwells
> In my love's veins thou hast too grossly dy'd.
> The lily I condemned for thy hand,
> And buds of marjoram had stol'n thy hair;
> The roses fearfully on thorns did stand,
> One blushing shame, another white despair;

[69] J. B. Leishman, *Themes and Variations in Shakespeare's Sonnets* (repr., New York, 1966), pp. 27-91; Hubler, pp. 11-37.

A third, nor red nor white, had stol'n of both,
And to his robb'ry had annex'd thy breath;
But, for his theft, in pride of all his growth
A vengeful canker eat him up to death.
    More flowers I noted, yet I none could see
    But sweet or colour it had stol'n from thee.   (99)

Conventional enough, this invocation of flowers, substitute-attributes for beautiful parts of the beloved body—the violet for the grain in complexion and the sweet smell of the beloved, the lily for the whiteness of the beloved's hands, the marjoram for the sweetness and fairness of the beloved's hair, the roses for the beloved's sweet smell and lovely colour, conceits used over and over again in the amatory repertory, particularly in sonnets, to "explain" feminine beauty. Henry Constable's Diana was also "like" all these flowers, save for Shakespeare's use of the impressively scented marjoram in place of Constable's far sharper marigold:[70]

In brief. All flowers from her their virtue take;
    From her sweet breath, their sweet smells do proceed;
    The living heat which her eyebeams doth make
    Warmeth the ground, and quickeneth the seed.
The rain, wherewith she watereth the flowers,
Falls from mine eyes, which she dissolves in showers.

Shakespeare may have been writing variations on this very sonnet, but whatever he was doing, he worked directly in the "sweet" images fundamental to his genre. As it stands, his poem has no pronouns to indicate the gender of the particular addressee, and if the sonnet stood alone, we would without question assume its address to a mistress. In its conventional order, though, the poem is unmistakably a part of the set to the young man, whose affection and attention have, as the neighboring sonnets tell, removed from the poet to another, whose language and associations please the friend more. In the series, then, the conceits, addressed to a man, make the poem seem even more hyperbolical, more extreme, the expression of greater besottedness, than its analogues to ladies. When we consider what sort of figure was cut in the epigram by such a sweet-smelling, beautiful male, Shakespeare's daring is even more pronounced: in the epigrammatic world, the perfumed young man was typed at once and

[70] Henry Constable, *Diana*, ix, in *Elizabethan Sonnets*, ed. Lee, II, 83.

could count on the epigrammatist's contempt. Yet never does the poet suggest such a feeling about the young man in these sonnets —in Sonnet 20, for instance, he laughs away the implied delicacy of the young man's good looks by stressing his insistent masculinity.

I want to look at the language of sweetness in different settings in the sequence, first in the early sonnets addressed to the "sweet boy," then in a sonnet about poetry, and finally in the psychomachia of sweetness with sharpness, of *mel* with *sal*. In the early sonnets, most of them urging "increase" upon the young man, full of "sweet" imagery, several stand out for their use of the *word* "sweet."[71] Of these, I want to look especially at Sonnet 13:

> O that you were yourself! But, love, you are
> No longer yours than you your self here live.
> Against this coming end you should prepare,
> And your sweet semblance to some other give.

The first quatrain merely restates a common thought in the early sonnets and in verse generally, that time and death bear all away, and that the beloved is not his own, not even fully "himself," since death has an inalienable claim upon him.

> So should that beauty which you hold in lease
> Find no determination; then you were
> Your self again, after your self's decease,
> When your sweet issue your sweet form should bear.

The repetition is tricky—so much sweetness suggests parody, much as Sidney's Sonnet 79, "Sweete kisse, thy sweets I faine would sweetly indite," parodies the sonnet tendency toward sugared language.[72] Apparently, though, Shakespeare was parodying neither the traditional *suavitas* of the mode nor his own constant use of the word, for the same language is intensified in other poems, in an image of intensified sweetness, that is, of distillation. Sonnets 5 and 6 deal with time the destroyer, in seasonal language:

[71] For some sonnets using the word "sweet" and related words, see *Elizabethan Sonnets*, ed. Lee, II: pp. 144, 168, 271, 272, 273, 283, 303.

[72] Sir Philip Sidney, *Astrophil and Stella*, in *Poems*, ed. William A. Ringler (Oxford, 1962), p. 206.

> For never-resting time leads summer on
> To hideous winter, and confounds him there

but provides in metaphor a way to keep, to preserve summer's essence:

> Then, were not summer's distillation left
> A liquid prisoner pent in walls of glass,
> Beauty's effect with beauty were bereft,
> Nor it, nor no remembrance what it was. . . .

Sonnet 5 ends on an appropriate couplet, one which, severed from its poem, would make a perfect epigrammatic distich:

> But flowers distill'd, though they with winter meet,
> Leese but their show: their substance still lives sweet.

Sonnet 6 carried on the notion and the image, this time applying the distillation conceit to the beloved himself, urged to procreate as a perfumer—"Make sweet some vial"—before his sweetness, like the flowers', must yield to time.

In a poem placed later in the series, amid a cluster of sonnets dealing with the recession and resurgence of love and relating to poems on problems of love's expression, the notion of immortality has been transposed from its human, or "real," application of issue, to the less wordly, though equally "real" in poetical terms, language of poetic immortality. The "distillation" notion occurs again, in Sonnet 54, this time not in relation to organic living and giving life, but in relation to verse.

> O, how much more doth beauty beauteous seem
> By that sweet ornament which truth doth give!
> The rose looks fair, but fairer we it deem
> For that sweet odour which doth in it live.
> The canker-blooms have full as deep a dye
> As the perfumed tincture of the roses,
> Hang on such thorns, and play as wantonly
> When summer's breath their masked buds discloses;
> But for their virtue only is their show,
> They live unwoo'd, and unrespected fade;
> Die to themselves. Sweet roses do not so;
> Of their sweet deaths are sweetest odours made.
> > And so of you, beauteous and lovely youth,
> > When that shall vade, by verse distills your truth.

This poem is "about" a great many things, or, better, calls up associations of many different kinds, with different topics. The first, clearly, is the "subject," the situation it celebrates, the poet's writing to his friend, here unmistakably addressed as a young man. The poem touches on the problematics of beauty, in poetry and in life: the canker-bloom is as beautiful as the healthy ("sweet" in another sense) rose, but its essence is not, its capacity for beauty beyond appearances, in the perfume which, distilled from the roses, retains that sweetness in abstracted form: such is the sweetness of the youth. But lying behind this considerable compliment is the notion of poetry's function, with a hint of the question of style, dealt with more directly in another cluster of sonnets dealing with "style," with "ornament," and with "truth," but *not* with "sweetness." The sweet language in this poem is justified by its identity with the sweetness of the subject, particularly in a pair of reverberating lines:

> O, how much more doth beauty beauteous seem
> By that sweet ornament which truth doth give!

That is, the metaphor of perfume, conceited though it may seem, is reduced to mere literalness as it transcribes the remarkable sweetness of this particular "beauteous and lovely youth." As the rose lives on, essence of sweetness, so does poetry, the distillation of the sweetness of its incomparable subject, and the poetry in turn *is* the perfume, the prolonger of that sweetness. The poet reaches toward something else, toward finding an illustration in English of the metaphor implied in the critical use of *mel*, the sweet preservative of "sugred Sonnets." The poem runs the risk of too much sweetness—a risk which, in his Sonnet 79, Sidney turned into plain fun, half-joking with the reader over "What may words say, or what may words not say,/ Where truth it selfe must speake like flatterie?"[73] Shakespeare faced the risk and examined it, in this poem, demonstrating in the course of its writing the logic of his dominant image. By examining the risk in terms of the sonnet-decorum itself, the poet turns it into a minor but elegant strategic triumph.

[73] Sidney, p. 182. Indeed, Sidney's masterly handling of many problems of celebratory expression, with his whimsical self-referential examination of sonnet-conventions in particular, may have relieved Shakespeare of the need to explore this question in his own work.

In Sonnet 35, the poet plays on some of the common oppositions of sonnet-language, the contradictions of the petrarchan heritage:[74]

> No more be griev'd at that which thou hast done:
> Roses have thorns, and silver fountains mud;
> Clouds and eclipses strain both moon and sun,
> And loathsome canker lives in sweetest bud.

The first quatrain simply states the poetic formula; now for the application, the translation of metaphor into "fact," the matching of the image to its subject:

> All men make faults, and even I in this,
> Authorizing thy trespass with compare,

—that is, comparing, so conventionally, the youth's "trespass" to thorns, mud, clouds, eclipses, and cankers—

> My self corrupting, salving thy amiss,
> Excusing thy sins more than thy sins are. . . .

The second quatrain reaches out into an entirely different realm of discourse in its notably plain language, the images cut short ("salving thy amiss") or dispensed with altogether—the poet examines his fused poetic and emotional behavior and presents without concealment the results of that examination. "All men make faults" picks up the undefined "that which thou hast done" of the first line, and implies a continued apology for that fault— but instead, the poet shifts direction altogether, to turn the generalization back on himself, criticizing exactly what *he* is doing, criticizing, in short, both his emotional evasions and the poetic "compare" which is his rationalization of pain. "All men make faults" is, then, the covering law for the friend's "fault" as well as his own—"Excusing thy sins more than thy sins are," or, letting the hyperbolical language raise in degree of seriousness "that which thou hast done," letting it aggrandize lyric relations into dramatic ones. By complicated steps, the third quatrain moves on to the psychological drama of *odi et amo*, that petrarchist

---

[74] Cf. Spenser, *Amoretti*, xxvi, for a similar exercise in sweet-and-sour conceit. Shakespeare's sonnet has been much commented upon: Peterson, pp. 238-40; L. C. Knights, "Shakespeare's Sonnets," reprinted in *Elizabethan Poetry. Modern Essays in Criticism*, ed. Paul J. Alpers (New York, 1967), pp. 282-84. Cf. Booth, 3-8, 58-59, for some excellent remarks on this sonnet.

state of mind commonly communicated by oppositional imagery such as roses-thorns, fountains-mud, sun, moon-clouds, eclipses:

> For to thy sensual fault I bring in sense—
> Thy adverse party is thy advocate—
> And 'gainst myself a lawful plea commence;
> Such civil war is in my love and hate
> > That I an accessory needs must be
> > To that sweet thief which sourly robs from me.

There is a great deal here that is in the epigrammatic tradition, such as the plays upon sensual-sense, adverse-advocate, plea-accessory, to say nothing of sweet-sourly, so handy for our particular purposes; the sort of oxymoron commonly in sonnets suddenly flattens out to a more concerted opposition, borne in figures of thought, opposites united in the poet's own self, as he implicates himself in the young man's fault and finally condemns himself rather than accuse his friend. Poetry switches around. The poet leaves off writing in one decorum to write in another—or he stops writing one kind of poem and begins (or ends) another. Various sorts of split are pointed up by this poem: the split between poet and friend, the split in the poet's own feelings, and the stylistic and tonal split between the two parts of the poem.

Perhaps as well as any of the *Sonnets*, this poem makes patent the problem of matching language to form, language and form to content. By its self-referential operation, this poem destroys the validity of such terms, moreover: it says what it does, it is what it says, or does. Even "ornament" is intrinsic here, so that Winters' theory can be felt to break down. At this point, *mel* and *sal* are seen to interpenetrate: *sal* almost seems to be "sense," as the poet perceives what he is up to, sees its emotional falsity, and corrects by what is (in one realm) manifest falsity—that is, by conceits: thematic opposites become interdependent, finally become single, singular.

In the "slander" cluster of poems, in which the poet laments the youth's bad company and takes note of the gossip against him, there is much talk of the sourness, the bitterness, the unpleasantness of detraction, in a vocabulary commonly associated with literary satire and satirical epigram, where tongues are "sharp" by prescription, and linguistic bitterness is supposed to act as a purge. Sonnet 35 remarkably fuses poet and friend, but for all the implication of the poet in the friend's faulty condition, whatever it is the friend has done remains a hard if unidentified fact. The poet does not excuse him, even if he turns the accusations back on himself. The detractors enjoy slander, even if the poet does not. In Sonnet 69, they

> look into the beauty of thy mind,
> And that, in guess, they measure by thy deeds;
> Then, churls, their thoughts, although their eyes were kind,
> To thy fair flower add the rank smell of weeds.

The couplet, in multiple puns, gives the "explanation" for both the young man's misdeeds and the detractors' remarks, maintaining the dominant image the while:

> But why thy odour matcheth not thy show,
> The soil is this—that thou dost common grow.

Sonnet 70 develops the notion that the young man is innocent of whatever slander imputes to him: in a sharp psycho-social analysis of slander itself, the poet "proves" the friend's grace:

> That thou art blam'd shall not be thy defect,
> For slander's mark was ever yet the fair;
> The ornament of beauty is suspect,
> A crow that flies in heaven's sweetest air.
> So thou be good, slander doth but approve
> Thy worth the greater, being woo'd of time;
> For canker vice the sweetest buds doth love,
> And thou present'st a pure unstained prime.
> Thou hast pass'd by the ambush of young days,
> Either not assail'd, or victor being charg'd;
> Yet this thy praise cannot be so thy praise
> To tie up envy, evermore enlarg'd.
>> If some suspect of ill mask'd not thy show,
>> Then thou alone kingdoms of hearts shouldst owe.

In each of the first two quatrains, it is to slander that "ornament" is assigned—"A crow," and "canker vice"; the words about the friend which the poet in his own *persona* uses come very close to being pure statement. In the third quatrain, a brief morality-scene is postulated, the young man "pass'd by the ambush" of his own youth, "not assail'd" or "victor" over whatever dangers lurk where he passes. Envy, however, is "evermore enlarg'd" at his very success in evading danger, and turns out in the couplet to be a blessing in disguise.

In Sonnet 95, quite a different attitude to the young man is displayed; here, the poet criticizes the young man directly, without the help of others' slanderous tongues to echo or adumbrate his own message. This poem modulates from the language of the first phrase, "sweet and lovely," to images chosen for sharpness, "hardest knife," "ill-us'd," "edge," and somehow accommodates them in one microcosmic discourse. Though the poet does not criticize the friend's misdeeds directly, neither does he argue them away: they are unmistakably what they are—

O, in what sweets dost thou thy *sins* enclose!

O, what a mansion have those *vices* got
Which for their habitation chose out thee . . . ,

—but he cannot bring himself to blame the young man, for in spite of his shame, his sins, his sport, "all things turn to fair that eyes can see" in him. In this poem, as in the one previously discussed, even dispraise becomes a kind of praise. The balance is remarkable: in the first line, sweet-lovely-shame; in the second, canker-rose; in the third, spot-beauty-budding; in the fourth, sweets-sins, and onward to dispraise-praise, blesses-ill, vices-beauty's veil-blot-fair; so that when the epigrammatic couplet, with its epigrammatic vocabulary, sums up problem and poem, we are at once shocked and unsurprised by its hard language:

Take heed, dear heart, of this large privilege;
The hardest knife ill-us'd doth lose his edge.

Not for nothing had Richard Carew[75] likened Shakespeare to Catullus: the unmitigated praise is there, in the twelfth line— "And all things turn to fair, that eyes can see!"—as well as the stern moral accuracy of the last line, pointed with a personal vengeance.

Sonnet 94, "They that have power to hurt and will do none," has been endlessly explicated;[76] it remains, at its core, profoundly enigmatic, its figurative language pulling against the statement it seems to be making:

[75] Richard Carew, *The Excellency of the English Tongue*, in *Elizabethan Critical Essays*, II, 293.
[76] Booth, pp. 152-67, and the literature there cited.

> They that have power to hurt and will do none,
> That do not do the thing they most do show,
> Who, moving others, are themselves as stone,
> Unmoved, cold, and to temptation slow—

is mixed praise. That these persons "will" do no hurt is greatly in their favor; but to move others while remaining stone is less than compliment. "To temptation slow" is certainly better than being quickly moved to temptation, but leaves open the possibility of temptation; "unmoved" and "cold" certainly make the subject seem calculating, aloof, unresponsive, unemotional. He does not do that which he most "shows"—apparently the wickedness attributed to him by his slanderers; the poet acknowledges, throughout, that the friend's behavior is problematical. He is being praised, evidently, for the cool hypocrisy of a man unwarmed by ordinary human fires. Whatever the imagery may whisper, the initial statement is, however, unequivocal:

> They rightly do inherit Heaven's graces,
> And husband nature's riches from expense;
> They are the lords and owners of their faces,
> Others but stewards of their excellence.

Standing alone, this sonnet is difficult enough; in the series, which begins with an exhortation to a certain kind of self-expenditure, or self-gift, a kind of "excess," and an invitation to the young man to share himself, these lines seem even more difficult than when the poem is seen singly. It is good to be lord of one's self, but to be "owner" is odd; and to be lord and owner of one's *face* does not seem a condition worthy of such morally expressed praise, although *um des Reimes willen* the poet may have had little choice. The third quatrain goes on to praise essential goodness, barring from consideration the social inter-relations explicitly called up in the first quatrain and suggested in the second; it does so in what may be called the primary sonnet-language:

> The summer's flow'r is to the summer sweet
> Though to itself it only live and die;
> But if that flow'r with base infection meet,
> The basest weed outbraves his dignity.

"Base infection" and "basest weed" belong to the mixed world of society, and remind us, willy nilly, of the sonnets about the young man's low company; to be pure, the summer's flower *should* live only to himself, as is explained in the perfect epigram of the couplet:

> For sweetest things turn sourest by their deeds:
> Lilies that fester smell far worse than weeds.

To see what Shakespeare has done with a commonplace, one can turn to Barnfield's lilies-conceit:[77]

> Yea what more noysomer unto the smell
> Than Lilies are? what's sweeter than the Sage?
> Yet for pure white the Lilly beares the Bell
> Till it be faded through decaying Age. . . .

Shakespeare keeps us from thinking that a lily in bloom, displaying its perfect whiteness, might have an ugly smell; it is only those perfect lilies that later *fester*, from some mysterious corruption, which become evil-smelling, falling off from their brave show to be worth less than the (fresher smelling) weeds about them.

This sonnet, with its impeccable epigrammatic closure and its well-made epigrammatic point, returns us to consider Shakespeare's manipulations of the sweet sonnet-language, in his preparations so often and so elegantly flavored with the salt and vinegar of another vocabulary, another rhetorical tone and poetic attitude; with another area of feeling and response to personality and society. Standard sonnet-language opposed sweet and sour—the words themselves as well as the conceits involving things sweet and things sour, good and bad, pleasurable and painful; opposed them in image and conceit as well as in unconcealed, squared grammatical opposition: frequently, use of the words "sweet" and "sour" or "sweet" and "salt" points directly to the generic areas recognizable in Harington's "Comparison," calling up the profounder opposition of melic and epigrammatic modes of writing and perception. In his sequence, among so much else that he does, Shakespeare works between these extremes of generic tone and language, making them work together and against each other, so that his sequence is varied as no other sonnet-sequence (even Du Bellay's) is, in the range of emotions it expresses and calls up. Sonnet 70, its praise strong but equivo-

[77] Barnfield, p. 18.

cal in spite of its apparently plain moral and its unconcealed
superlatives, embodies in its clarity and its complexity, its directness and its indirections, its praise and its qualifications of praise,
the fundamental qualities of both sonnet and epigram.

IV. *Mel, Sal,* and *Fel*: The Mistress

One way to invert a convention is to parody it: Shakespeare's
Sonnet 130 is a straight parody of petrarchan praise, certainly—

> My mistress' eyes are nothing like the sun;
> Coral is far more red than her lips' red;
> If snow be white, why then her breasts are dun;
> If hairs be wires, black wires grow on her head.
> I have seen roses damask'd, red and white,
> But no such roses see I in her cheeks;
> And in some perfumes there is more delight
> Than in the breath which from my mistress reeks.
> I love to hear her speak, yet well I know
> That music hath a far more pleasing sound;
> I grant I never saw a goddess go—
> My mistress when she walks treads on the ground.
> > And yet, by heaven, I think my love as rare
> > As any she belied with false compare.

Berni's model has already been cited, a low-style analogue; in
English, Lodge's Sonnet 22, to Phyllis, Griffin's Sonnet 39, to
Fidessa; and Linche's Sonnet 31, to Diella, all offer parallels in
the traditional high style,[78] inviting a better poet to mockery.
Griffin's affords an interesting parallel to Shakespeare's poem:[79]

> My Lady's hair is threads of beaten gold.
> > Her front, the purest, crystal eye hath seen.
> Her eyes, the brightest stars the heavens hold.
> > Her cheeks, red roses, such as seld have been.
> Her pretty lips, of red vermillion die.
> > Her hand, of ivory the purest white.
> Her blush, AURORA of the morning sky.
> > Her breast displays two silver fountains bright.

[78] *Elizabethan Sonnets*, II, 6, 284, 317.
[79] Ibid., II, 284.

The spheres, her voice; her grace, the Graces three.
　Her body is the saint that I adore.
Her feet, fair Thetis praiseth evermore!
But ah! the worst and last is yet behind!
For of a griffon she doth bear the mind!

Leaving aside the poet's coy self-reference, the last line entirely reverses the thrust of Griffin's sonnet, revealing that the lady's highest attribute is of rather low quality. Shakespeare also reverses the direction of his sonnet, but does not turn to an opposite hyperbole, an overstatement of the lady's beauty, to prove his point. Rather, he "brings in sense," even here: "I grant I never saw a goddess go" breaks with the traditional anterotic petrarchan poem,[80] like Berni's, of mere and therefore monotone parody. The poem begins in one groove of anti-petrarchan sentiment and language and shifts to an entirely different one, personal, idiosyncratic, informal—in a word, original. The mistress—described in the "gulling" vocabulary of epigrammatic and satiric commentary on women as sexual objects, "dun," "wires," "reeks"—on the one hand makes mock of the traditional hyperbolical style, on the other of the emptiness, impersonality, and thinness of the official sonnet-mistress. Like Davies' Gulling Sonnets, Joseph Hall's Satire VIII is a useful gloss on Shakespeare's famous palinode. In Hall's poem, the sonneteer pours forth "in patched Sonettings/ His love, his lust, and loathsome flatterings":[81]

Then can he terme his durtie ill-fac'd bride
Lady and Queene, and virgin deifide:
Be shee all sootie-blacke, or bery-browne,
Shees white as morrows milk, or flaks new blowne.

Then, Jodelle's final poem in his short series, *Contr'amours*, speaks bitterly, not just of the poet's enforced obedience to the conventions of praise, but reminds his readers too that, however artificial his love-language may be, the poet suffers from love's pangs like any other lover:[82]

[80] Berni's poem is the model for the type; but see Giordano Bruno, *De'gli eroici furori*, ed. Michel, pp. 91-93. See also Jorg Ulrich Fechner, *Der Antipetrarkismus. Studien zur Liebessatire im Barocker Lyrik* (Heidelberg, 1966), and Schaar, *Elizabethan Sonnet Themes and the Dating*, pp. 23-24.
[81] Joseph Hall, *Poems*, ed. Arnold Davenport (Liverpool, 1949), p. 18.
[82] *Poètes du XVIᵉ siècle*, ed. A. M. Schmidt (Paris, 1953), p. 733.

Combien de fois mes vers ont ils doré
Ces cheveux noirs dignes d'une Méduse?
Combien de fois ce teint noir qui m'amuse,
Ay-je de lis et roses coloré?
   Combien ce front de rides labouré
Ay-je applani? et quel a fait ma Muse
Ce gros sourcil, où folle elle s'abuse,
Ayant sur luy l'arc d'Amour figuré?
   Quel ay-je fait son oeil renfonçant?
Quel ay-je fait son grand nez rougissant?
Quelle sa bouche? et ses noires dents quelles?
   Quel ay-je fait le reste de ce corps?
Qui, me sentant endurer mille morts,
Vivoit heureux de mes peines mortelles.

Like Jodelle's lady, Shakespeare's walks on the ground: from hyperbole denied, we are to read her specific reality. She is only "as rare as"—no rarer than—other ladies more conventionally praised; but precisely because of his refusal to overstate her rarity, the poet presents his love for her as "rare." Mistresses praised by images of rarity are, with the poets who praise them so, far too common.

As we have seen, the kind of "sweet" compliment normally paid to the sonnet-mistress Shakespeare pays to a young man; to the young man's idealized qualities the dark mistress is opposed —and, indeed, the dramatic plot of this sequence forces the two types into confrontation. The mistress is entirely different from the developed sonnet-lady in ways other than her appearance; she is, simply, a "mistress," not a distant lady to be wooed incessantly and by whom to be spurned. Neither is she a lady in the *dolce stil*, drawing her lover ever higher on the metaphysical scale, to God or to the true Love of Beauty, nor is she a respectable woman, like Elizabeth Boyle, to be courted to wife. She is not invited to pluck the poet's day—she can be trusted to do that by her own nature, if trusted in little else. Even when she is cold to the poet, she is never a cold woman; there is no talk in her case of heavenly raptures, Christian, platonic, or otherwise. She treads on the ground; she goes to bed, with the poet and with others.

Although extreme compliments are paid to ladies conventionally cold as ice, that does not mean that in writing of his willing mistress, a poet was required to be rude; nor *is* Shakespeare rude in this poem. His compliment is the greater for its arranged naturalness: he loves this woman for what she is, not for what others say of her looks, or even of her character (Sonnets 127, 131). He loves her, then, not in a mode of literature, but in the mode of actuality. There is a counterpart to this poem in the series to the young man, Sonnet 21:

> So is it not with me as with that Muse,
> Stirr'd by a painted beauty to his verse;
> Who heaven itself for ornament doth use,
> And every fair with his fair doth rehearse,
> Making a couplement of proud compare
> With sun and moon, with earth and sea's rich gems,
> With April's first-born flowers, and all things rare
> That heaven's air in this huge rondure hems.
> O, let me, true in love, but truly write,
> And then believe me, my love is as fair
> As any mother's child, though not so bright
> As those gold candles fix'd in heaven's air.
>   Let them say more that like of hearsay well:
>   I will not praise that purpose not to sell.

Of course the Sidneian trick is obvious: the poet has praised his friend in just the language he here rejects; but we find it easier to obey the "believe me" when we know that the poet knows how conventionally empty such ornamental compliment can be; we accept the beauty of this "mother's child" as of a real person. The couplet raises a question the quatrains had entirely screened out: the last thing we are led to think of, in the context of this poem and its neighbors, is the poet's "selling" of love. But the couplet says more to the critical commonplace about high-flown figures than to the notion of selling, either of love or of a lover. Harington has an epigram, "A comfort for poore Poets," which touches on the same topic:[83]

> Poets hereafter for pensions need not care,
> Who calls you beggars, you may call them lyars,
> Verses are grown such merchantable ware,
> That now for Sonnets sellers are and buyers.

[83] Sir John Harington, *The Most Elegant and Wittie Epigrams* (London, 1633), p. 40.

115

In Shakespeare's sonnet of ornamental compliment which denies its ornament to scrutinize the truth of poetry, the poet turns in the couplet, as often before, to the linguistic resources of epigram—but withal manages to maintain the notion that this beloved is exceptionally beautiful, exceptionally valuable, and exceptionally loved. He takes a less conventionally complimentary view of the dark, antiromantic mistress: she is made to seem so unattractive that one suspects a certain perverse counter-suggestion, a fascination with unfashionable *laideur* for its own sake— a fascination which, as the series develops, we find is not exclusive to the poet. The mistress-series stresses, as the friend-series does not, the sensuality of the beloved and thus of the poet who loves her; these poems, albeit without prurience, have something of the obscenity of epigram, the *foeditas* which Scaliger deplored.

Again, Shakespeare is far milder in this respect than Martial or even Catullus; he never dwells on sexually perverse acts, and nothing in his poetry need be left untranslated (as the Loeb edition leaves untranslated some of Catullus' poems). But he has his entirely loose, casual moments; in the series to the friend, he touched, lightheartedly enough, on the obscenity characteristically barred from petrarchan sonnets, as in Sonnet 20, where he delineated the friend's attractiveness:

> A woman's face, with Nature's own hand painted,
> Hast thou, the Master Mistress of my passion;
> A woman's gentle heart, but not acquainted
> With shifting change, as is false woman's fashion;
> An eye more bright than theirs, less false in rolling,
> Gilding the object whereupon it gazeth;
> A man in hue all hues in his controlling,
> Which steals men's eyes and women's souls amazeth.
> And for a woman wert thou first created;
> Till Nature, as she wrought thee, fell a-doting,
> And by addition me of thee defeated
> By adding one thing to my purpose nothing.
> > But since she prick'd thee out for women's pleasure,
> > Mine be thy love, and thy love's use their treasure.

"Nothing" and "prick'd" in this poem make game of the androgynous suggestions of the poems as a whole; they make a game of love, too, but without prurience, gloating, or doting. The man

116

is like a woman, but more beautiful in his kind—and he is, unmistakably, masculine. At this point it might be well to note that in the series to the friend, Shakespeare's exhortation to the young man to marry is not odd in the convention of sonnet-sequences; it is also a considerable elevation of the common epigrammatic exhortation to effeminate men to the proper "use" of their bodies.

There is far greater affinity with epigrammatic *foeditas* in the series to the mistress: the "nothing" pun,[84] common in English of the period, is played on in the poems to the woman, too. In the sexual sense, the word is quite frankly obscene, but in Shakespeare's handling of it, it is thoroughly good-humored as well. He says to his lady, in a riddling, argumentative poem:

> Among a number one is reckon'd none.
> Then in the number let me pass untold,
> Though in thy store's account I one must be;
> For nothing hold me, so it please thee hold
> That nothing me, a something sweet to thee. . . .
>
> (136)

There is more here to remind us of both Greek and Latin epigrams on prostitutes: the quantification (usually linked with payment, but here with lovers); the assumption that the lady is a person to keep accounts; the circumlocution for the pudenda. Further, the poet has no qualms, in this poem, about the lady's sexuality: if she will accept him as a lover, that is enough. He plays in the same carnal way on his Christian name—the lady's "will" is at once her sexuality and her poet:

> Whoever hath her wish, thou hast thy Will,
> And Will to boot, and Will in over-plus. . . .
>
> .   .   .   .
>
> So thou, being rich in Will, add to thy Will
> One will of mine, to make thy large Will more.
>   Let no unkind, no fair beseechers kill;
>   Think all but one, and me in that one Will.   (135)

In this poem, there is a decided hint of the physical geography of Martial's amatory epigrams. The lady's voracious sexuality is

---

[84] See Paul A. Jorgenson, "Much Ado about *Nothing*," *SQ*, v (1954), 287-95; Thomas Pyles, "Ophelia's Nothing," *MLN*, XLIV (1949), 322-23.

implied, but his own is acknowledged too, and (though less compelling than hers) his will is enthusiastic in accommodating to her will:

> Wilt thou, whose will is large and spacious,
> Not once vouchsafe to hide my will in thine?

Sonnet 151 plays games with higher-minded images of love. Love is too young to recognize conscience, but conscience is born of love. The soul instructs the body to love, with the result that the poet's body dutifully obeys, in the most bodily way possible: he finds that his body, "rising at thy name, doth point out thee/ As his triumphant prize," is content to "stand in thy affairs, fall by thy side." The couplet's concluding epigrammatically gives point to an already sufficiently pointed poem; it could, equally, stand alone as a sexual epigram:

> No want of conscience hold it that I call
> Her "love" for whose dear love I rise and fall.

The epigrammatic aspects of the mistress-poems do not lie in the final couplets alone, although a great many of the poems end on what could very well be independent epigrams (134, 135, 136, 137, 138, 141, 148, 150, 151); these poems are frankly given over to the study less of love, the ostensible subject of sonnet-lovers, than of obsession[85]—and, without equivocation, of lust. The poet begins with the unfashionableness of his mistress' beauty, and his apparent perverseness in choosing such an unbeautiful beauty. The lady is "black," or dark, the brunette officially less attractive than blondes.[86] This lady's blackness is so compelling that the poet must call it "fair" (127, 131), and is willing for her sake to swear that beauty herself is black and blondes all foul (132, 147). She is, however, black in more than complexion, as the poet comes to realize:

> In nothing art thou black save in thy deeds,
> And thence this slander, as I think, proceeds.   (131)

---

[85] Prince, *Poems*, p. 32.

[86] *Variorum Sonnets*, II, 755, for some other dark ladies (who, incidentally, owe their blackness and much of their beauty to Canticles). Martial, Marullo, Michelangelo, and Jamyn all admired dark ladies; and one of Ronsard's sonnet-ladies had chestnut hair.

For I have sworn thee fair, and thought thee bright,
Who art as black as hell, as dark as night.   (147)

   For I have sworn thee fair—more perjur'd I,
   To swear against the truth so foul a lie!   (152)

This is the satirist's language, choked with spleen, outrage, and rage; this is gall. In Sonnet 137, which begins with a trope entirely within the love-tradition, the rest of the poem goes on to use the language of epigram quite forbidden the sonnet-milieu:

   Thou blind fool, Love, what dost thou to mine eyes
   That they behold, and see not what they see?

Love is traditionally blind; but this lover is not inexperienced:

     They know what beauty is, see where it lies,
     Yet what the best is take the worst to be.

In the next quatrain, a commonplace gains intense new life:

   If eyes, corrupt by over-partial looks,
   Be anchor'd in the bay where all men ride,
   Why of eyes' falsehood hast thou forged hooks,
   Whereto the judgment of my heart is tied?
   Why should my heart think that a several plot,
   Which my heart knows the wide world's common place?
   Or mine eyes, seeing this, say this is not,
   To put fair truth upon so foul a face?
     In things right true my heart and eyes have erred,
     And to this false plague are they now transferred.

                             (137)

The eyes are corrupt and false; in addition they have corrupted the heart. All this is proper neoplatonic love-doctrine—by which Love enters by the eye and takes control of the lover's whole body, his whole self, his whole soul—but that love-doctrine turned upside down. The conceit of the lover-as-ship (a commonplace from the *Anthology* and elsewhere) underlines the bitter line "Be anchor'd in the bay where all men ride": both "bay" and "ride" carry connotations sexually repugnant. The poet's judgment is not free, but "tied" by (beautiful pun!) "forged hooks," so that the poet-lover cannot, as the metaphor might imply, sail off at will. The lady is "the wide world's common place"; her face is (what could be plainer?) foul. What is interesting about this poem, I think, is that it is not just "epigrammatic" in its denunciation, drawing upon the vocabulary and the tropes of disrespect for its subject; it lies also well within the petrarchan range—with its poet, his eyes blinded by the love-god, who remembers the norms of amorous feeling and expression. As in other poems in this set, the poet states his double awareness, of the intensity of his loving and of the unworthiness of that love's object; he condones, though he cannot approve, the painful double-knowledge of truths qualitatively so opposed.

In Sonnet 131, although we think as we read the quatrains that the poet has accepted his sonneteer's task of suffering for a lady's sake, and is ready to endure her arbitrariness however exerted, the *clausula* effectively turns against the poem to make clear that she is, existentially, as black as she seems: "In nothing art thou black save in thy deeds." What is all this complaint about? Conventionally, of course, the sonneteer's business is to suffer, and the poet records his proper suffering, his compliance with the lady's arbitrariness and to the friend's. And certainly, sonnet-cycles were in part developed to explore, define, and display the intricacies of tangled feeling that every lover (in the western tradition, at least) feels or is supposed to feel. The rhetoric of oxymoron meant that opposites were ever yoked together in sonnets, as the poet relied on these rhetorical means to express the turmoil within him. "Heaven" and "hell" recur in the conventional assignment of love's ups and downs, and are usually metaphorical *topoi*, understood as such, to indicate emotional condition.

Without sacrificing the charged meaning of such usage, Shakespeare manages at the same time (largely through his plainer language, I think) to divest his mistress-sonnets of their conventional implications even as he moves away from conventional norms. We know that heaven and hell are usually metaphorical, and in verse contexts generally indicate regions in a poet's mind; it takes a deeply disillusioned idealist (which is to say, a satirist) to tell us that "Beneath is all the fiend's." In the *Sonnets*, Shakespeare never says any such thing. Whatever his traumas, in the course of the sonnets he never denies the values of generation, even the value of coupling; never abandons his convictions of social worth. At the same time, his "hell" is no mere stylized pause on the way to true love's celestial redemption; his hell, here, has something of the absoluteness of Christian fate. The poet recognizes, in short, something fixed about his love-alliance, something fixed, for better or worse, in aspects of his own character.

In a much-commented sonnet, 129, I want to look at the various reminders of the epigrammatic mode which the poet uses to come to terms with his love for the mistress. Neither petrarchan sonnet nor epigram could supply him with the language he needed to express his good man's love for a woman flighty at best (and, he implies, far worse than that), but his denunciation of his own love has affinities with the satirical language of railing against concupiscence. Further, this sonnet has its point at its center (at the sixth and seventh lines), in the manner of the Continental epigram; and it has a smashing *clausula* as well, of heaven and hell. Throughout its vocabulary is notably bare, abstracted, and unornamental:

> Th'expense of spirit in a waste of shame
> Is lust in action; and till action, lust
> Is perjur'd, murd'rous, bloody, full of blame,
> Savage, extreme, rude, cruel, not to trust;
> Enjoy'd no sooner but despised straight;
> Past reason hunted, and, no sooner had,
> Past reason hated, as a swallowed bait,
> On purpose laid to make the taker mad—
> Mad in pursuit, and in possession so;
> Had, having, and in quest to have, extreme;
> A bliss in proof, and prov'd, a very woe;
> Before, a joy propos'd; behind, a dream.
>   All this the world well knows; yet none knows well
>   To shun that heaven that leads men to this hell.

(129)

The poet is not talking about mere lust, a beastliness which is, though beastly in reasonable creatures, after all natural; this poem is about obsession, a mental condition peculiar to humans from which, as the couplet despairingly acknowledges, there is no relief, for which no reason can be found, least of all in rhyme. The art of language here is very different from what we should expect, the rough lines demanding extra stresses ("Savage, extreme, rude, cruel, not to trust"; "Had, having, and in quest to have, extreme") as emotions are cramped into the iambic pentameter. Tenses and verb forms are schematic but carefully observed—

> Had, having, and in quest to have, extreme;
> A bliss in proof, and prov'd, a very woe;
> Before, a joy propos'd; behind, a dream. . . .

The phrases fragment the experience, at the same time the sound reinforces its likeness to the experience of love. The harsh repetitions of "had" and "mad"—had-mad-mad-had-having-have—hammer home the violent feeling without any respite or change. The variation of long and short syllables in the sequence hated-bait-laid-taker holds the disjointed, syllabic poem together. The proposition at the beginning—"Th'expense of spirit . . . is lust in action."—appears to proceed rigorously, until a string of bitter adjectives, barely sufficient to contain the poet's outrage, overwhelms the neat consecutive syntax and meter in a whirl of approximating descriptive words, at first metrically regular ("Is perjur'd, murd'rous, bloody, full of blame") but rougher in the second, and with a desperate rhyme for the couplet. This is a definition-poem,[87] among other things, but hardly undertaken in systematic inquiry: from the string of adjectives, the definitions shift to phrases in precarious balance—"Enjoy'd no sooner but despised straight"; "Past reason hunted . . . , Past reason hated"; "in pursuit . . . in possession"; "A bliss in proof, and prov'd a very woe"; "Before, a joy . . . Behind, a dream"—which culminate in the "heaven" and "hell" of the couplet.

An unqualified condemnation of lust, a fierce attack of self-hatred, magnificently condensed—and yet, the couplet alters the poem entirely. Without mitigating either the pain or the shame, the couplet comforts by universalizing the condition, by allowing consideration of "the world" as intermediary between heaven and hell and thus making the psychomachia, the emotional civil war, simply a normal part of being human.

Structurally, this sonnet is much like another poem of disillusionment, in the friend-series, Sonnet 66, "Tir'd with all these, for restful death I cry." In that poem, the poet makes his statement of *contemptus mundi* in a list of what "these" are, social

---

[87] Rosemond Tuve, *Elizabethan and Metaphysical Imagery* (Chicago, 1947), pp. 302-304.

and moral disorders arranged in eleven lines, of which ten begin with the word "And." Whatever else it is, Sonnet 66 is a daring experiment in sameness, of grammar and of content. In that poem, too, the couplet turns the whole thing around; instead of a *clausula* summing up for restful death, we get a statement of the counterbalancing worth of private affection:

> Tir'd with all these, from these I would be gone,
> Save that, to die, I leave my love alone.

The subject of this poem, world-weariness, has nothing of the vividness (Martial's wording, Ep. xi, xlii, important in Renaissance epigrammatic theory) of Sonnet 129, a headlong, desperate attempt to define and therefore to understand what "this hell" is. The poem is almost not a love-sonnet; its oppositions have been so heightened that it is nearly anterotic, a study of the kind of love shunned, outgrown, or rejected by the idealistic petrarchan sonnet-language.

Although the governing tone of the mistress-poems is very different from that of the friend-series, some poems in each group seem to ask for comparison and contrast. From the two poems just discussed, it might be safe to draw the conclusion that the friend-poems are on the whole gentler, less intense, far less self-disgusted; that they incline more to nostalgia, reflections in tranquility, and sessions of sweet silent thought than do the intimate, immediate, passionate mistress-poems. But the poet's relation to both is much the same: the mistress is not admired by the poet's friends (131, 148, 150), and the friend is slandered too (69, 70); in both cases, the poet affirms his commitment to love and to the beloved. The terms of commitment differ markedly, of course: the poet's involvement with the friend is idealistically expressed, with the woman, realistically. The commitment to the friend is made to seem a victory of the poet's reason and faith over jealousy, detraction, and carelessness; to the woman, the commitment is preserved as his obstinate obsession conquers the poet himself. Psychomachia and emotional civil war, self-analysis, self-absorption, and self-definition were all written into sonnet-sequences from Dante and Petrarca on. It is no surprise that Shakespeare wrote about his "civil war," about the "mortal war" between his eye and heart, about his separation from the beloved and thus from himself; nor that he poignantly lays bare the self-doubts and self-reproaches of a lover, despising himself as much for the justifiable rancor he feels as for his beloved's neglect of him. In Sonnet 35, as we have seen, he becomes an accessory to the friend's fault merely by reproaching him for it; in Sonnets 89 and 90, he undertakes to bear the friend's fault (of which he knows himself innocent) himself, and the fault of their estrangement from each other. Though certainly it was the role of the sonnet-lover to appear humble before his elevated beloved, Shakespeare manages a style of humility and humiliation transcendent only in the power of his imagination, which makes his debasement hyperbolically low:

> Say that thou didst forsake me for some fault,
> And I will comment upon that offence;
> Speak of my lameness, and I straight will halt;
> Against thy reasons making no defence.
> Thou canst not, love, disgrace me half so ill,
> To set a form upon desired change,
> As I'll myself disgrace, knowing thy will . . .
>
> . . . .
>
> For thee, against myself I'll vow debate,
> For I must ne'er love him whom thou dost hate.
>
> (89)

That to the friend; this to the lady:

> Canst thou, O cruel! say I love thee not,
> When I against myself with thee partake?
> Do I not think on thee when I forgot
> Am of myself, all tyrant for thy sake?
> Who hateth thee that I do call my friend?
> On whom frown'st thou that I do fawn upon?
> Nay, if thou lour'st on me, do I not spend
> Revenge upon myself with present moan?
> What merit do I in myself respect
> That is so proud thy service to despise,
> When all my best doth worship thy defect,
> Commanded by the motion of thine eyes?
>   But, love, hate on, for now I know thy mind:
>   Those that can see thou lov'st, and I am blind.
>
> (149)

When he was absent from his friend, the poet was restless and unhappy; Sonnets 28 and 29 record his uneasiness by day and night, and the journey poems show gnawing loneliness. But in Sonnet 147, to the lady, his reason abandons him "frantic mad with evermore unrest" because of her cruelty; his suffering from her treatment of him is far more painful than the suffering caused by the friend. By both, of course, he is shut out; part of the power of the two sets of poems stems from the poet's detached attempt to understand how things have come about, in these two uneasy associations. The melancholy cast of the first relates to the poet's separation from his friend, in rank, in function, in absence, in disgrace. In the case of the lady, he seems to find her door barred against him, as (in traditional epigrammatic fashion) she entertains others within.

An extraordinary *trouvaille* was the poet's decision to make a triangle of these two loves, to make the man and woman come together,[88] by their conjunction closing out the poet from all his solace, to torture him with imagining their mutuality. Characteristically, he was easier on the friend than on the lady. In Sonnet 41, he forgives the friend—"when a woman woos, what woman's son/ Will sourly leave her till she have prevailed"— though he allows that "a twofold truth" has been broken:

> Hers, by thy beauty tempting her to thee,
> Thine, by thy beauty being false to me.

This sonnet has one of those phrases that, in the poet's own words, "almost tells his name": instead of writing "what man," he wrote "what woman's son," invoking the mother's role in her son's response to women, drawing upon every manchild's first relation with a woman. The friend's lapse from friendship is forgiven, in a conceit that nowadays has considerable significance:

> That thou hast her, it is not all my grief,
> And yet it may be said I lov'd her dearly;
> That she hath thee is of my wailing chief,
> A loss in love that touches me more nearly.

[88] As noted above, this is an epigrammatic convention, where the mistress of poet and friend was often shared; but she was usually, in such a case, not a metaphorical but a professional prostitute. See also Catullus, *Carmina*, xci, where poet and friend share a mistress.

Loving offenders, thus I will excuse ye:
Thou dost love her because thou know'st I love her,
And for my sake even so doth she abuse me,
Suff'ring my friend for my sake to approve her.
If I lose thee, my loss is my love's gain,
And, losing her, my friend hath found that loss;
Both find each other, and I lose both twain,
And both for my sake lay on me this cross.
  But here's the joy: my friend and I are one;
  Sweet flattery! then she loves but me alone.   (42)

But resignation to the woman has no such rationalizing comfort
to it:

Him I have lost; thou hast both him and me;
He pays the whole, and yet I am not free.   (134)

In Sonnet 144, resignation is not even reached. In a morality-
conceit, the man and woman are assigned roles in his mind:

The better angel is a man right fair,
The worser spirit a woman colour'd ill.

Further, "my female evil/ Tempteth my better angel from my
side" and, not content with that, "would corrupt my saint to be
a devil," to turn fiend with her:

But being both from me, both to each friend,
I guess one angel in another's hell.
  Yet this shall I ne'er know, but live in doubt,
  Till my bad angel fire the good one out.

The dark woman is a devil; for the man, excuses can still be
found.
  This sonnet abstracts internal struggle but keeps it dramatic
in the psychomachic image of the two angels; Sonnet 146, "Poor
soul, the centre of my sinful earth," sets off the body and soul
against each other, till soul triumphs over the body's fading
mansion and the poet can, in his couplet, come to a Pauline
epigrammatic solution.[89] Again, heart and eye, which struggled

---

89 Cf. Pierre de Ronsard, *Œuvres complètes*, ed. G. Cohen (Paris, 1965), I,
7: this Pauline trope seems to have been adapted naturally into sonnet-tradition.

in the friend-sonnet 46, struggle again, in Sonnet 148, over the lady. Internal struggle and awareness of it take very new forms in Shakespeare's sequence, in spite of the conventionality of many of the devices he used to express it. One means is the dramatization of the conflict into flesh-and-blood characters, analogous to what we have already marked him doing in the Rival Poet series; another is his astonishing use of the resources of different styles, with their evoked emotions of reference. Sonnets 92 and 93 make clear that the poet knows the friend's inconstancy and, in spite of the pain it causes him, is prepared to put up with it. The couplet of 92 puts all into the governing perspective:

> But what's so blessed-fair that fears no blot?
> Thou mayst be false, and yet I know it not.

Sonnet 93 begins with accepted adjustment to the friend's betrayal:

> So shall I live, supposing thou art true,
> Like a deceived husband; so love's face
> May still seem love to me, though alter'd new—
> Thy looks with me, thy heart in other place.

As the couplet suggests—

> How like Eve's apple doth thy beauty grow,
> If thy sweet virtue answer not thy show!

—the poet knows that his self-deception may from time to time have to be strengthened against further pain from the friend; he is honest enough to know that in his choice of attachment there can be no security whatsoever. In this poem, he makes his choice on idealistic grounds, but does not forfeit his realistic sense of its dangers. In the same situation with the mistress, whose infidelity he knows full well, he makes the same choice without the bulwark built into the friend-series, of idealism insisted upon against all odds. Sonnet 138 is one of Shakespeare's most open poems, a poem of magnificently exact statement about a baffling if common emotional condition:

> When my love swears that she is made of truth,
> I do believe her, though I know she lies,
> That she might think me some untutor'd youth,
> Unlearned in the world's false subtleties.

Thus vainly thinking that she thinks me young,
Although she knows my days are past the best,
Simply I credit her false-speaking tongue;
On both sides thus is simple truth suppress'd.
But wherefore says she not she is unjust?
And wherefore say not I that I am old?
O, love's best habit is in seeming trust,
And age in love loves not to have years told.
    Therefore I lie with her, and she with me,
    And in our faults by lies we flattered be.

Here, to his sensual fault the poet brings in sense, a sense of balance and confidence in the kindly meant, generous if untruthful response. The solution, verbally reached by the *équivoque* of the couplet,[90] is expressed with a love that seems the realer for its disillusionment. *"Therefore* I lie with her, and she with me"— their love is too powerful, and too pleasant, for either to give up. Here, as in other poems, the poet settles for his own sensuality, accepts it as part of himself—"I am that I am," as he had said in Sonnet 121. He has learned to live with the pleasures and the pains, as well as with the pleasures of those very pains inflicted by his nature, attendant inevitably upon his personality. Sonnet 110 offers another version of his self-acceptance, without excuse or apology:

Alas, 'tis true I have gone here and there
And made myself a motley to the view,
Gor'd mine own thoughts, sold cheap what is most dear,
Made old offences of affections new.
Most true it is that I have look'd on truth
Askance and strangely; but by all above,

90 The English word "lie" is a handy source of puns in this connection. Cf. Davies, *Scourge*, pp. 32-33, "Epig. 68. Against Lawrentia's Lying":

In lying lyeth all Lawrentiaes grace,
Who to, and with men lyes, in Deede and word:
She paints her selfe: so, lyeth in her face:
Then gut'rall *Lauds* she doth her knaves affoord;
So, in her throat she lyes: and in her Heart
She needs must lye, when, for an abiect fee,
She love pretends to Swaines of no desert:
So shee, in summe, lies all, as all may see:
    Then sith still thus she lyes, twere good for her
    Still to be shipt, to make her still to stirre.

> These blenches gave my heart another youth,
> And worse essays prov'd thee my best of love.
> Now all is done, have what shall have no end;
> Mine appetite I never more will grind
> On newer proof, to try an older friend. . . .

In Sonnet 142, the poet can accept the fact that his mistress has "Robb'd others' beds' revenues of their rents," in a phrasing recalling the involved cutthroat world of the Roman prostitute; from accepting his own sensuality, he has learned to accept hers:

> O, but with mine compare thou thine own state,
> And thou shalt find it merits not reproving;
> Or, if it do, not from those lips of thine,
> That have profan'd their scarlet ornaments,
> And seal'd false bonds of love as oft as mine. . . .

"Let me excuse thee," he says to her in Sonnet 139. In Sonnet 141, a palinode-sonnet too, he alters the terms of dispraise away from sonnet-formula to something much closer to epigram-formula:

> In faith, I do not love thee with mine eyes,
> For they in thee a thousand errors note. . . .

As the two sonnets also affirm, the poet stresses not just her lack of beauty but her misdeeds in love as well:

> But 'tis my heart that loves what they despise,
> Who in despite of view is pleas'd to dote.
> Nor are mine ears with thy tongue's tune delighted.

(another dramatic fact documented in the sonnets just preceding)

> Nor tender feeling to base touches prone,
> Nor taste nor smell desire to be invited
> To any sensual feast with thee alone;

until the turning, with its confirmed commitment:

> But my five wits nor my five senses can
> Dissuade one foolish heart from serving thee,
> Who leaves unsway'd the likeness of a man,
> Thy proud heart's slave and vassal wretch to be.
>> Only my plague thus far I count my gain,
>> That she that makes me sin awards me pain.

Hardly an address possible to Laura, or to Hélène, or to Elizabeth Boyle—hardly an address possible to the young man, either, despite his "sensual fault" so painful to the poet's senses. Nonetheless this is, in the forced decorum of the poet's relation with this mistress, of experienced man with experienced woman, a complimentary poem. An odd poem, sneaking the courtly-love language into the twelfth line, after speaking largely in the language of the disillusioned libertine, yet denying sheerly libertine values while affirming the lady's sensuous appeal, and ending on a couplet extolling a witty emotional economy: the sonnet combines the values of irony with those of generosity.

In the friend-series, Sonnet 115 develops a standard sonnet-*topos*, the poet's task in expressing a love inexpressibly greater than it had been before:

> Those lines that I before have writ do lie;
> Even those that said I could not love you dearer. . . .
> Alas, why, fearing of Time's tyranny,
> Might I not then say, "Now I love you best"
> When I was certain o'er incertainty,
> Crowning the present, doubting of the rest?
> > Love is a babe; then might I not say so,
> > To give full growth to that which still doth grow?

Sonnet 150 handles the same problem, but far more immediately, and with the incidental drama conferred by the poet's ambivalence toward this love of his:

> O, from what pow'r hast thou this pow'rful might
> With insufficiency my heart to sway?
> To make me give the lie to my true sight,
> And swear that brightness doth not grace the day?
> Whence hast thou this becoming of things ill,
> That in the very refuse of thy deeds
> There is such strength and warrantise of skill
> That in my mind thy worst all best exceeds?
> Who taught thee how to make me love thee more,
> The more I hear and see just cause of hate?
> O, though I love what others do abhor,
> With others thou shouldst not abhor my state;
> > If thy unworthiness rais'd love in me,
> > More worthy I to be belov'd of thee.

That his wife might be as this mistress is, Othello could not even endure to think, although he did believe it; such an idea of love was simply insufferable for him. Antony learned the rewards of such a limited human love, and accepted with it the ruin such love brought upon him. So the poet here, writing about the opposite of sonnet-love, literally makes the best of bitterness.

For such adjustment to sensual love, the poet had been taught by his experience with the young man. There, he had renewed himself by drinking "potions of eisel," to outdo and suppress emotional pain:

> No bitterness that I will bitter think,
> No double penance, to correct correction.   (111)

His artist's eye had accepted the deformity of vision forced on him by his love for the young man (113); in his turn, he deformed everything to his preferred image, making "of monsters and things indigest/ Such cherubins as your sweet self resemble" (114). Full of the young man's "ne'er-cloying sweetness," the poet framed his feeding, as he says, "To bitter sauces" (118). In Sonnet 119, the epigrammatic vocabulary of *fel* manages nonetheless to affirm the triumphs of his difficult love:

> What potions have I drunk of Siren tears,
> Distill'd from limbecks foul as hell within,
> Applying fears to hopes, and hopes to fears,
> Still losing when I saw my self to win!
> What wretched errors hath my heart committed,
> Whilst it hath thought it self so blessed never!
> How have mine eyes out of their spheres been fitted
> In the distraction of this madding fever!
> O benefit of ill! Now I find true
> That better is by evil still made better;
> And ruin'd love, when it is built anew,
> Grows fairer than at first, more strong, far greater.
> So I return, rebuk'd to my content,
> And gain by ill thrice more than I have spent.

The "benefit of ill," then, is what he has learned and uses to cope with his feelings for his mistress; his nerves, proved in the contests with his friend not to be "brass or hammered steel," are tempered for the mistress' trials on them. The potions of eisel and the Siren tears permitted him, after all the raging and railing at his mistress' misdeeds, to accept her with all her sins upon her. Even in his bitterness over her broken bed-vow, the poet sees his own faultiness and complicity with her:

> But why of two oaths' breach do I accuse thee,
> When I break twenty?   (152)

In Sonnet 119, "What potions have I drunk of Siren tears," the poet forces us to recognize, in the very bitter-sweet imagery, what the generic clichés signify in emotional fact: after the tragical, satirical misery, he can still experience, inexplicably, "that better is by evil still made better." From the bitter passages of his life great sweetness can grow. In Sonnet 152, the oath-breaking sonnet, he plays with the Liar-paradox: his oaths, sworn to qualities his lady did not possess, were true precisely because they were false, and in their falseness matched her intrinsic falseness in love.

Such poems display an extraordinary honesty, a willingness to deal with the motives and actions of dishonesty, to understand and to judge—and to put up with them. For all the intensity of their satirical vituperation, the effect of these sonnets is of fundamental acceptance and good humor in spite of the lady's irregular response, the world's disapproval of her, her carryings-on with the friend, and the poet's own self-dislike and self-disgust. As compared to the friend series, these poems show far more anger and less strained solutions to the anger: they give the illusion, at least, of maturing self-acceptance and acquiescence in qualified satisfactions of love. Again, this ending is decidedly *not* canonical in sonnet-sequences, where behavior like the friend's or the mistress' properly sends the sonnet-lover up the ladder of love at a great pace, away from merely human, fallible objects of love toward some metaphysical ideal. In this sequence, the poet's sexuality is kindled by the lady's, his self-esteem set at hazard by his love—and he knows it all perfectly well. In sonnet-sequences, furthermore, to settle for sensuality, one's own, one's mistress', and one's friend's, and to learn to condone deceit on everyone's part is no orthodox purification by love, but a settlement for human values, human possibilities, human limitation. The broken, irregular, patched-up sonnet-sequence Shakespeare left us dramatizes the poet's experience of his own humanity—and of other people's as well.

Characteristically, the sonnet-sequence presents a closed world, a world inhabited by lover and beloved, with other people shadowy against its drawn curtains; a world internalized in the poet-lover's private musings. Shakespeare's sequence relinquishes none of this privacy—indeed, his self-probings are conspicuously honest and analytical; but the private action takes place on a scene open to the world. In the poems to the friend, the poet never postulates an imaginative world in which he and the friend might close out society's impingements. For one thing, the friend's rank and occupation, whatever it literally was, precluded any such idyllic enterprise; but in the poet's assumptions, also, there is no expectation of absorbing the friend's whole emotional life. Rather the opposite: the poet's relation to his friend takes place against the world's audible comment, comment which praises the young man and blames him too, comment which mocks the poet. His affair with the mistress takes place, too, in an acknowledged social context. She is known to his friends, whom he then gives up because they disapprove of her. In other words, this *liaison* is freely discussed by some ambivalent *losengeours* who evidently have the poet's welfare at heart.

Still more important, as the poems are traditionally arranged, the poet is never really alone with either beloved, though the lady and the friend appear to have found sporadic solitude with one another. The imaginative situation is so constructed as to be, minimally but crucially, social. Even the triadic connection of poet with friend and mistress is depicted as exceptionally shared: their experiences interlock, and each is too knowing not to know that each one knows too much about the others. The poet's self-explorations are set against social attitudes—approval, disapproval, business, multiple preoccupation and obligation—to open the sequence upon the worldly scene—again, not as the sonnet customarily does, but as the epigram does. Here, compromises are enforced that are unthinkable in the typical love-sequences, compromises with the world, compromises with the significantly inter-inanimating cast of characters in the sequence.

It is an oversimplification to suggest that one path to this extraordinary achievement was, simply, generic: that the epigram, traditionally an encapsulation of social attitudes and social modes, the interpreter of private quirkiness against society's assumed norms, contributed to the poet's accomplishment by permitting him a language to deal with a kind of love ordinarily beyond the sonneteer's franchise. That language was almost totally opposed to the sonneteer's characteristic stress, and permitted modulations into a social reality which, in general, the sonneteer chose to reject. But here, as in Sonnet 130, the languages serve reality: against the background of proud artifice provided by sonnet-vocabulary and sonnet-trope, plain-spoken love comes to seem real as it could not without some point of comparison. Equally, against the cynical licentiousness of epigrammatic "fact" and language, the ideals of sonnet-love are immediately reinforced. Indeed, having gone this far, I must go farther, to say that in his friend and his mistress, Shakespeare animated lyric and epigrammatic styles, gave concentrated personality to *mel* and *sal*, worked out in human terms the implications of their separate decorums. Out of the styles, twinned and opposed, linked and contrasted, of epigram and amatory epigram, he constructed his triangle of active figures, with himself as poet responding to the demands of both friends, coming to terms with their requirements of him, and through their means coming to terms with love and with himself as lover. Both the banquet of *agape* and the sensual feast were heightened and refined, to this poet's taste anyway, by the pinch of salt.

3

Othello
and the Problematics of Love

IT WAS NOT ALTOGETHER easy to make a tragedy of a love story, traditionally the stuff of comedy. We are so accustomed to *Romeo and Juliet*, for instance, and to *Othello* and *Antony and Cleopatra*, that we tend to forget that there were technical problems for the playwright in making sufficiently serious as tragedies the domestic problems of love. "Love" existed in the Renaissance in important literary shapes, but on the whole these were not tragic —indeed, if anything, the conjunctive powers of love were regarded, in drama, as suited rather to comic solutions than to high tragic decisiveness. Further, love itself is an unstable element: it is flighty, and as such a proper subject for farce, not for tragedy— at best, romantic comedy, ending in beautiful conciliations, offered a proper generic habitat for tales of love.

Outside of drama, literary love tended to take two major shapes,[1] one of them, the romance, was closely related to comedy, its organization owing much to comic conventions and feeding back into Renaissance comic formulations. The other, the love-lyric, presents quite a different world of love: from Dante's forceful presentation onward, love in lyric form seemed to be of a higher sort than the love presented in either comedy or romance, a private experience in a world—as opposed to the world of comedy or romance—sparsely populated, with a few figures all enjoying notably intense emotions.[2] In the lyric poetry of love, poets

[1] Though there are many more than those I cite, some studies of "literary love" have been very useful to me: John Bayley, *The Characters of Love* (London, 1961), especially Chapter 3, on *Othello*; Maurice Valency, *In Praise of Love* (New York, 1961), for the "courtly" background, as well as C. S. Lewis' classic (and classically-disputed) *Allegory of Love* (Oxford, 1936). For *Romeo and Juliet*, see H. A. Mason, *Shakespeare's Tragedies of Love* (London, 1970), Chapters One to Three, as well as Karl-Heinz Wenkel, *Sonettstrukturen in Shakespeares Dramen*, *Linguistica et Litteraria*, 1 (1968); Inge Leimburg, *Shakespeares Romeo und Julia*, Beihefte zu *Poetica*, IV (1968), stresses the "romance" associations of the play.

[2] For the development of sonnets and sonnet-theory, see Moench, *Das Sonett*; for petrarchanism, Forster, *Icy Fire*; and Mrs. Tucker's forthcoming work.

began all kinds of explorations into themselves, so that in literature if not in life, psychological self-exploration and self-description were normally practised, and a vast reservoir of *topoi* of
self-inspection became the inheritance of the great Renaissance
writers of songs and sonnets.

In particular, the sonnet cycle offered possibilities for developing the lyric themes of love.[3] Dante set the tone and Petrarca confirmed it, to influence writers of lyric cycles and sonnet cycles
throughout the long Renaissance, who in turn added their own
variations and contributed their own insights to a genre elevated
by those Italian models to something far beyond the ordinary
love-lyric. By the time Shakespeare tried his hand at a love-tragedy, he had already worked in several of the major literary love-
forms of the Renaissance. His sonnets are a major document in
the lyric tradition, and several early comedies served him as preparations for his major love-tragedies, *Romeo and Juliet* and
Othello: *Two Gentlemen of Verona* offered one kind of pre-study
for *Romeo and Juliet, Much Ado* is in part a comic dress-rehearsal
for *Othello*. Without *Romeo and Juliet*, I think, Shakespeare
would have had greater difficulties with the problems raised by
Othello.

It is, then, with that early play that I wish to deal first. With
Romeo and Juliet, its plot deriving from a sad and rather sordid
novella, Shakespeare attempted his first love-tragedy. How did an
ambitious and experimental author go about this task? First of all,
he drew upon types officially "comic,"[4] types which had already
colonized the prose narratives of the Renaissance. He peopled his
play in a perfectly familiar way, with figures from the comic cast:
the young girl; her suitor (*adulescens amans*), whom her father
does not favor; another *adulescens* (County Paris), whom the
father approves; a father, *senex*, who becomes, naturally, *senex
iratus* when crossed by his daughter; a nurse, not only the customary *nutrix* but a particular subtype, *nutrix garrula*. Our hero
is accompanied by a friend, indeed by two friends, Benvolio and
Mercutio; in a comedy, for symmetry, presumably Juliet would
have had two school-fellows with her, to be disposed of at the

---

[3] Evidently, the sonnet-sequence was particularly important in the development of self-preoccupation and introspection, and was its main literary vehicle, as Mrs. Tucker's work makes plain.

[4] Comic personages are discussed in Scaliger, *Poetices*, pp. 20-22; and see
John Vyvyan, *Shakespeare and the Rose of Love* (London, 1960).

play's end to the two young men. Here, though, she is unaccompanied; and because the play is a tragedy, Mercutio can be killed off and Benvolio fall out of the play without our wondering why or lamenting the absence of appropriate girls to be given away to Romeo's "extra" friends.

Comedies take place in cities; this tragedy is very city-bound; even Friar Lawrence's cell is within walking distance of the famous two houses. When Romeo flees Verona, he does not take to the woods, as a proper romance-hero might have been expected to do (and as Orlando does), but settles in nearby Mantua, to outwait, as he hopes, his troubles. As befits a comic city-scene, we have splendid servants of different sorts, baiting each other and irritating as well as serving their betters, providing relief for what turns out to be a very grim sequence of actions.

So far, so good; but how to turn the play into a tragedy of love? What language, for example, to use? From the first spoken words of *Romeo and Juliet*, the Chorus' speech in sonnet-form, we are directed to a major source for the play's language, the sonnet tradition, from which, as we see at once, Romeo had drunk deep; like the young men at Navarre's court, Romeo knew the literary modes of the Renaissance young gentleman. Critics of the play speak again and again of the sonnets in the play itself,[5] sometimes even a full fourteen lines spoken by a speaker alone or by two speakers in consort—the great sonnet exchange between Romeo and Juliet at their meeting is a sign both of their rhetorical sophistication and of their union with one another. Some of the sonnets have an extra quatrain or even sestet; once an octave stands alone, several times a sestet stands alone. All this sonnet-formality must draw our attention to what the playwright was up to—that is, his deepening of events by a language habitually associated with a particular kind of high-minded and devoted love. By his borrowing of devices and language from another genre for his tragedy, he cues us to the kind of love involved in his play. Of all the lyric forms, indeed of all the literary forms, of love, the sonnet-sequence honors the profound seriousness of the emotion: love is central to the life and existence of the sonnet-persona, who gives himself over to the delicious exigencies of his condition, which he celebrates with all the force of his soul and of his

---

[5] See Nicholas Brooke's excellent *Shakespeare's Early Tragedies* (London, 1968), pp. 80-106 (on sonnets and sonnet-likeness, especially pp. 87-88); and Calderwood, *Shakespearean Metadrama*, Chapter Four.

poetical powers. As more transitory love-lyrics do not, the sonnet-sequence also provides opportunities for deep and faceted
self-examination, as the sonneteer considers and reconsiders his
ever-changing emotional state, recording as carefully as possible
his perceptions of his own shifting progress and regress along his
path.[6]

We are introduced to Romeo, typed as a melancholy lover before he appears onstage, who enters speaking "distractedly" in the
proper Petrarchan rhetoric of oxymoron. He runs through the
rhetorical exercises of the love-poet with extraordinary facility.
He sets his own text—"Here's much to do with hate, but more
with love" (I.i.173)—and amplifies it:

> Why then, O brawling love! O loving hate!
> O anything, of nothing first create!
> O heavy lightness! serious vanity!
> Mis-shapen chaos of well-seeming forms!
> Feather of lead, bright smoke, cold fire, sick health!
> Still-waking sleep, that is not what it is!
> This love feel I, that feel no love in this.   (I.i.174-80)

Shortly after this comical though splendid display of his reading
in Petrarchan figure, Romeo defines love, in the manner, says one
French theorist, of the *blason*, or (as English critics tended to say)
of the definition:[7]

> Love is a smoke rais'd with the fume of sighs;
> Being purg'd, a fire sparkling in lovers' eyes;
> Being vex'd, a sea nourish'd with loving tears.
> What is it else? A madness most discreet,
> A choking gall, and a preserving sweet.   (I.i.188-92)

He runs through the repertory—the oxymora, so casually tossed
off, the variations upon a hundred sonnets in the official mode.
His *epideixis* is clear—"Why then," and "What is it else?" intro-
duce a spate of words in the right key, uttered by an energetic
youth creating his own role according to the best literary models.

Romeo's Rosaline, always invisible to us, is made up of whole
cloth, the texture of which is classical reference:

---

[6] See above, pp. 127-34.

[7] Note also Romeo's reference to *fel* and *mel* here, repeated at I.v.90; and
the adverse criticism of Romeo as a poet in Joseph Chiang, "The Language
of Paradox in *Romeo and Juliet*," *S. Stud.*, III (1967), 22-42.

> she'll not be hit
> With Cupid's arrow. She hath Dian's wit,
> And in strong proof of chastity well arm'd,
> From Love's weak childish bow she lives unharm'd.
> She will not stay the siege of loving terms,
> Nor bide th'encounter of assailing eyes,
> Nor ope her lap to saint-seducing gold.
> O she is rich in beauty; only poor
> That, when she dies, with beauty dies her store.
>
> (i.i.206-14)

Romeo's clichés play upon the Epicurean argument for love, using the themes of *carpe diem* and productivity so familiar from love-lyrics (and the second familiar from Shakespeare's own remarkable sequence of sonnets). Romeo continues in language remarkably close to those sonnets:

> For beauty, starv'd with her severity,
> Cuts beauty off from all posterity.
>
> (i.i.217-18)

The next couplet points to its own artificiality, with its ostentatious opposition of bliss and despair, again a sonnet-cliché. That couplet then leads to a familiar paradox:

> She is too fair, too wise, wisely too fair,
> To merit bliss by making me despair.
> She hath forsworn to love, and in that vow
> Do I live dead that live to tell it now.
>
> (i.i.219-22)

Even in the familiar self-denial of the sonneteer, self-critical and self-indulgent at once, Romeo the lover maintains decorum.[8]

Decorum or no, what we are asked to see in this Romeo is the lover by the book, the lover *too* decorous, who adopts the Petrarchan role and lives it to the utmost—in his rhyme, in his solitary nightlife, in the moping melancholy that so worries his mother. And Romeo sticks to the rules of his loving: when Benvolio urges him to Capulet's feast, hoping that he will there find another lady to fall in love with, Romeo is shocked—but in a sestet:

[8] For some discussion of this, see *Paradoxia*, Chapter Two; and Cynthia Grant Tucker's sonnet-study (unpublished dissertation, University of Iowa, 1966).

> When the devout religion of mine eye
> Maintains such falsehood, then turn tears to fires;
> And these, who, often drown'd, could never die,
> Transparent heretics, be burnt for liars!
> One fairer than my love! The all-seeing sun
> Ne'er saw her match since first the world begun.
>
> (I.ii.88-93)

Romeo's hyperbolical fidelity leaves much to be desired, since he falls in love with Juliet the instant he claps eye on her and rhymes his new love at once, in familiar language most beautifully disposed:

> O, she doth teach the torches to burn bright!
> It seems she hangs upon the cheek of night
> As a rich jewel in an Ethiop's ear . . .

and on and on, to

> Did my heart love till now? Forswear it, sight;
> For I ne'er saw true beauty till this night.
>
> (I.v.42-44, 50-51)

Both Romeo and Juliet are quick at this kind of language: their sonnet, with its "extra" quatrain at the end, spoken in turn by the two of them, is a marvelous sublimation of the witty exchange of young people meeting and trying each other out. Romeo speaks the first quatrain, Juliet the second; they divide the sestet, Juliet setting the rhyme and Romeo matching it. As Juliet notes, Romeo knows the rules of love—"You kiss by the book"—and so does she, certainly, for she is capable of very conventional wit in terms of love, as, it turns out later, she is also capable of conventional comment on hate.

Mercutio offers a critical voice against Romeo's softer one: as the young men go to the dance, Mercutio teases Romeo, challenging him to exchanges of wit much like those to which Benvolio had earlier challenged Romeo. All three young men knew their rhetorical alternatives and chose their styles freely: Mercutio mocks Romeo in terms of his love-learned language:

> Romeo! humours! madman! passion! lover!
> Appear thou in the likeness of a sigh;
> Speak but one rhyme and I am satisfied;
> Cry but "Ay me!" pronounce but "love" and "dove" . . . ,
>
> (II.i.7-10)

to pass on to a wonderfully punning salaciousness about the true purpose of loving. Mercutio provides at these points an Ovidian voice, that of the high-spirited libertine whose awareness of the physical delights of love balance the sweetness, the near-namby-pambyness of the Petrarchan traditional language. In his later exchange with Mercutio, Romeo answers in kind, thereby convincing his friend that he is once more "sociable," which is to say, out of love and a sane man again. Romeo has altered his decorum, as Mercutio notes—"Thy wit is a very bitter sweeting; it is a most sharp sauce"—from his melancholy sonneteering to the man-about-town, man-among-men style of the epigrammatist; he sharpens Mercutio's Ovidian voice to something nearer Martial's tone. And this of course is what fools Mercutio into believing that his friend has fallen out of love, for no man in the lover's pose can make the jests of II.iv. about sexuality. We of course know better: Romeo is finally and at last in love—and, dutiful to convention, has fallen in at first sight. This prescription of love's proper origin is written into the action, given reality, unmetaphored, in the scene at the feast: both young people recognize, too, what is happening to them, though they obey the rules of courteous word-play, which detonates their passion, as well as observing the rules of courtly loving.

Romeo by no means abandons sonnet-language because he has in fact fallen truly in love—again and again in his speeches to and about Juliet, conventional sonnet-topics turn up. To his new love, seen at her window, he offers the conventional likeness of eyes to stars:

> Two of the fairest stars in all the heaven,
> Having some business, do entreat her eyes
> To twinkle in their spheres till they return.
> What if her eyes were there, they in her head?
> The brightness of her cheek would shame those stars,
> As daylight doth a lamp; her eyes in heaven
> Would through the airy region stream so bright
> That birds would sing, and think it were not night.
>
> (II.ii.15-22)

Which is to say, her eyes are not like stars, but like suns; Romeo is a conceited poet, who draws out his conceits to utter hyperbole —as we shall see, his Juliet can do the same. He borrows other stock-elements from the sonneteer; in the orchard he wishes to be a glove on her hand to feel her cheek leaning against that hand, in Mantua he wishes to be a mouse, the humblest beast about the house, so as to catch sight of Juliet in Verona. Again, he combines two common sonnet-images, that of the lover as skipper and that of the lady as merchandise, in three pretty lines:

> I am no pilot; yet, wert thou as far
> As that vast shore wash'd with the farthest sea,
> I should adventure for such merchandise.
>
> (II.ii.82-84)

As critics are fond of saying, Juliet's language is less artificial than Romeo's, which seems to point to her greater simplicity in love than his, to her greater realism about their situation than his.[9] But she too has had her training in the love-rhetoric: her Romeo will "lie upon the wings of night/ Whiter than new snow on the raven's back" (III.ii.18-19). She too can pursue a conceit to its ultimate, absurd conclusions:

> when he shall die,
> Take him and cut him out in little stars,
> And he will make the face of heaven so fine
> That all the world will be in love with night,
> And pay no worship to the garish sun.
>
> (III.ii.21-25)

It is worth noting that Juliet's metaphoric daring is greater than Romeo's: she solves the sun-stars problem firmly and defiantly in favor of her image, while his imagery was less committed, less precise, and less extreme: he speaks, more than she, by the book. Her conceit of "little stars," which shall translate Romeo to classical immortality in a constellation, sends us back to his likeness of her to the sun. Her language honors the darkness in which her love is conceived, and its ugliest, most forceful image ("cut him out in little stars") forebodes that love's violent end.

When the Nurse comes in with the news of Tybalt's death at Romeo's hands, Juliet bursts into oxymoron, violently denouncing her lover in a passage as rhetorically extreme as anything Romeo had uttered in his period of self-persuaded, false love:

---

[9] Harry Levin, "Form and Formality in *Romeo and Juliet*," *SQ*, XI (1961), 3-11; Calderwood, pp. 87ff.

O serpent heart, hid with a flow'ring face!
Did ever dragon keep so fair a cave?
Beautiful tyrant! fiend angelical!
Dove-feather'd raven! wolfish-ravening lamb!
Despised substance of divinest show!

(III.ii.73-77)

On she goes, in this language, until her reason returns to remind her that of the two, she would far rather have lost Tybalt than Romeo. With that realization, she returns to the simpler poetry more characteristic of her utterance. It may be, as Levin has suggested, that Juliet's linguistic extravagance marks her estrangement from Romeo—certainly it marks her loss of herself in passionate outrage; on the other hand, the images she uses in this passage are linked both to those she had earlier used to try to express her large love for Romeo, and to those he used of her. Even here, the conjunction between the lovers is maintained in their language.

As we look back over the lovers' utterance, we can see very plainly the problem of expression: petrarchan language, *the* vehicle for amorous emotion, can be used merely as the cliché which Mercutio and Benvolio criticize; or, it can be earned by a lover's experience of the profound oppositions to which that rhetoric of oxymoron points. When Romeo and Juliet seek to express their feelings' force, they return constantly to petrarchanisms hallowed with use—but, having watched their development as lovers, an audience can accept as valid the language upon which they must fall back. When Romeo readies himself to die, he does so in the proper sonnet-imagery, to which he has earlier had recourse—

Thou desperate pilot, now at once run on
The dashing rocks thy sea-sick weary bark.

(V.iii.117-18)

After this crisis and the acknowledgment that ends it, the love of Romeo and Juliet resumes its course, to express itself in the familiar dawn-song of medieval tradition, a song which the lovers speak in dialogue. At this point, one might note a general feature of this play, of which the *aubade* is a splendid example: it is full of set-pieces of different kinds. Lady Capulet and the Nurse speak a duet about the County Paris's charms; at Juliet's supposed

143

death, Lord and Lady Capulet, the Nurse, and Paris utter a quartet. There are many double exchanges—Juliet's sonnet-exchange with Romeo at the dance, Romeo's exchanges with Benvolio and Mercutio, Juliet's stichomythy with Paris at Friar Lawrence's cell. Arias as well: Juliet's great prothalamic invocation to night, with its Ovidian echoes, "Gallop apace, you fiery-footed steeds"; her schematic meditation on death and the charnel-house just before she takes the drug; Mercutio's inventions on the subject of dreams. The effect of these passages is greatly to draw our attention to the poetry of this play, to the evocativeness of its language, but also to do something else, risky in a play though ideal in a lyric, to arrest the action for the sake of poetic display.

When we look at the play from some distance and in terms of fairly stock rhetorical patterns, we can see how formalized, how static, much of its organization is, how dependent upon tableaux and set-pieces. The Chorus begins the play with his sonnet, then one party enters, then the other (from, we presume, "houses" demarcated in the stage-architecture). The two parties engage in a mock-version of the vendetta which, with Tybalt's entrance onstage, quickly transforms the action into real violence, and ends with the Prince's order for the maintenance of peace. At the play's end, one party enters to lament the death of a child, then the other, lamenting the death of the other child; both parties stand to hear Friar Lawrence's unraveling of the plot and the Prince's strictures. Each bereaved father promises the other, appropriately, a sepulchral statue of his child in commemoration of child, of love, and of the ultimate sad settlement of the long feud.[10] With a final moralizing sestet, the Prince, a dignified *deus ex machina*, ends the action altogether. The lyric interludes, so important to the tone and psychology of the whole play, are of a piece with the pageant-like dramaturgy. Though they reveal the conditions of the speaker's mind, they do so in language rather dictated by the situation than obedient to the complexity of the plot, character, or action. The language loosens itself in many ways from the sonnet-substance from which it draws so much, but in *Romeo and Juliet* it is never so free as in *Othello*, where the

[10] For something of this "fixing" at a work's end, see Francis Berry, *The Shakespearean Inset* (London, 1965); and Murray Krieger, "The Ekphrastic Principle and the Still Movement of Poetry," in *The Play and Place of Criticism* (Baltimore, 1967).

same body of conventional language is managed to fit the characters' and the plots' needs without drawing undue attention to itself.

Romeo and Juliet is in many ways an apprentice-play: there the poet first met the real problems involved in turning lyrical love into tragedy. The Chorus must tell us at the outset that these lovers are star-crossed, and, in case we should forget that this is so, Romeo says later, rather awkwardly, "my mind misgives / Some consequence, yet hanging in the stars, / Shall bitterly begin his fearful date / With this night's revels" (I.iv.106-109). Friar Lawrence's *sententiae* reinforce the notion of rash haste, but they do not increase our sense of tempo—rather, in the way of *sententiae*, they do just the opposite. Rash haste and star-crossing are the rigid *donnée* of the action, which we are not invited to question or to consider. Love is unhappy, deeply-felt, beautifully expressed; youth is wasted at the behest of irrational old age, but the involvements of tragic behavior have not found their language in this play, although the spectacular oppositions of the petrarchan rhetoric have been enlarged into plot, as well as into the emotional and social structure of the play.

All the same, *Romeo and Juliet* makes some marvelous technical manipulations. One of the most pleasurable, for me, of Shakespeare's many talents is his "unmetaphoring" of literary devices, his sinking of the conventions back into what, he somehow persuades us, is "reality," his trick of making a verbal convention part of the scene, the action, or the psychology of the play itself. Love-at-first-sight is here made to seem entirely natural, set against the artificiality and unreality of Romeo's self-made love for Rosaline; its conventionality is forgotten as it is unmetaphored by action. Again, the *aubade* is indeed a dawn-song sung after a night of love, when the lovers must part, but a dawn-song of peculiar poignancy and relevance because of the way in which these lovers must part on this particular day. Another brilliant, natural unmetaphoring is the *hortus conclusus*, which by metaphoric convention a virgin is, and where also pure love naturally dwells, according to the Song of Songs and a host of subsequent poems and romances. Juliet's balcony simply opens upon such an orchard, a garden enclosed, into which Romeo finds out the way. The virgin is, and is in, a walled garden: the walls of that garden are to be breached by a true lover, as Romeo leaps into the orchard.

Still more important is the much-noticed manipulation of light and dark in the play; for Romeo and Juliet, ordinary life is reversed, with darkness the only safe time, when love between them is really possible. They meet at night, their marriage lasts one night, until light parts them. When they finally come together, it is at night in a tomb, which becomes their tomb in actuality. Their second night together is *nox perpetua una dormienda*. A conventional figurative setting in lyric tradition becomes the "real" setting, carrying with it a specific symbolic significance for the play.

The common juxtaposition and contrast of love and war are also involved in *Romeo and Juliet*, though not as simile merely. In Verona, love emerges as involved with warfare: the love of Romeo and Juliet is set in contrast to brawling and feud, but its poignancy comes from the bitterness of the unexplained vendetta. In their lives the lovers speak for peace and reconciliation and at their death are turned into symbols of that reconciliation, into sepulchral statues. Love and war are both real enough, but they do not and cannot coexist in this play's world: the one destroys the other. The conjunction of love and death, commonly linked in the metaphors of lyrical tradition, make this play unmistakably non-comic; death is the link between the love-theme and the war-theme, the irreversible piece of action that stamps the play as tragic. Still, Romeo and Juliet die as much by accident as Pyramus and Thisbe do, to whose story the narrative of their death owes much. Indeed, the lovers are preserved in a nearly Ovidian way, not as plants, but in an *ecphrasis*, as memorial statues exemplifying a specific lesson to future generations.

By the time he came to write *Othello*, Shakespeare had learned to cope with some of the problems still open in *Romeo and Juliet*, and could do so without losing any advantages of his working out in the earlier play a wonderfully heightened language of love. *Othello* is a remarkably integrated play, its action compressed, its imagery consistent, its language profoundly connected with the personalities of the various characters, as well as subservient to the needs of plot, action, and theme.[11] In *Othello*, it seems, the different aspects of the play have been deeply driven into one another, to be separated by some narrow critic only at grave

[11] The major studies of *Othello* are Robert B. Heilman's *Magic in the Web*; and G. R. Elliott's *The Flaming Minister* (Durham, N.C., 1953).

danger to the play as a whole. I know that this is so, and since my way of working in this exercise necessarily stresses certain elements at the expense of others, I shall try to strike my subject as lightly as I can and, wherever possible, to indicate the connection of my stress-points to other parts of the play.

Othello is a play about love and its relation to the rest of life. *Antony and Cleopatra* aside, it is difficult to find another major English Renaissance tragedy in which love is so frankly central, so stripped and so exposed. In this play, the lovers are not star-crossed, but crossed by their own personalities, by their own natures, so excellently fine, and by the peculiarities of the small, intimate society in which they carry on their lives. Like *Romeo and Juliet*, this play makes use of a situation and of characters habitually associated with the classical comic tradition.[12] From a slightly different perspective, the play's elements can be seen to be those of the city comedy. An elderly man, a blackamoor even, marries a young wife and is jealous of his young assistant. We do not commonly think of *Othello* as a tale of January and May, though Iago and Othello are quick enough to accept such an interpretation of the situation. Actually, Shakespeare has turned that triangle of *senex, puella*, and *adulescens* upside down. Desdemona loves the *senex* with unqualified devotion, and though Cassio certainly admires Desdemona, and his language to and about her is in the classic courtly tradition, his affections are clearly occupied elsewhere. Othello fears that he is mocked by the public for being a January deceived by May; in fact, the public admires him the more for his achievement of so lovely a wife. The stock characters in the play are not at all what we might expect, either: the prostitute Bianca, for instance, stationed on an island where transient military and naval men are always ready for her favors, turns out to love Cassio "really," far beyond her rights as a stock figure.

With the major characters Shakespeare performs splendid tricks. Othello is a Moor, by stage convention expected to be both lecherous and violent, as well as servile; so Moors appear on the English stage, one of them, Aaron, cast by Shakespeare himself as

---

[12] Robert A. Watts, "The Comic Scenes in *Othello*," *SQ*, XVIII (1967), 349-54; Barbara H. C. de Mondoça, "*Othello*: a Tragedy Built on Comic Structure," *SS*, XXI (1968), 31-38. See also the important remarks by K. M. Lea in *Italian Popular Comedy*, II, 378-79; and Allan Gilbert, *The Principles and Practice of Criticism* (Detroit, 1959), pp. 27-45. For material on this subject, I am indebted to June Fellows.

a typical eastern villain.[13] What has happened in this play is that at the outset the Moor is introduced to the audience in terms of such extraordinary nobility as to erase the stereotype from the audience's mind. Later we are forced to discover that it is just the stereotyped qualities of emotionalism, volatility, and gullibility from which Shakespeare finally derives Othello's tragic breaking—after he has bred us away from expecting them in such a hero. By these means, as so often elsewhere, Shakespeare gets it both ways: he breaks the traditional presentation and exploits it at its most conventional points, after having quite cleaned the situation of stereotypical implications. Othello *is* noble, but in his nature reside those qualities of which he is most afraid, exactly the violence, the trickery, the gullibility of the stock-Moor. As was his custom in the great tragedies, Shakespeare chose heroes of startling eccentricity—Hamlet, a thoughtful prince cast as revenger; Lear, an old madman, conspicuously foolish and unjust; Macbeth, corrupted early in the play, whose corruption plays itself out during the action; Antony, proud, careless, and sensual, linked to a cheating, trivial, sensual partner both with him and against him; Coriolanus, cold, proud, passionate, and unreasonable. Not the least daring was Othello, a Moor in Venice, a warrior turned lover, a primitive more civilized than the super-subtle Venetians.

In *Othello* there is much unmetaphoring, largely in relation to medieval and Renaissance romance and lyric traditions; I want to deal especially, though not exclusively, with Shakespeare's use in this play of the sonnet-tradition. First of all, the appearance of hero and heroine: traditionally, the lady-love is fair, both in coloring and in spirit; golden hair and white skin are so typical for the role of beloved that Sidney made the point that his individuated Stella's eyes were black, and Shakespeare could appear original in loving a brunette. Desdemona is fair, within and without. The less fair, less spiritually refined qualities attributed to the standard courtly lover-poet have in fact been written into Othello's background and appearance. He *is* black, and, when pressed, the Venetians remind him of it. Though we are led to expect the opposite, Othello's external blackness turns out to match one segment of his inner life, as well of course as his external behavior to his wife. By taking literally conventional fairness and darkness, Shake-

13 Eldred Jones, *Othello's Countrymen* (Oxford, 1965).

speare has given a new dimension to an artificial arrangement so trite as to appear meaningless: part of the shock involved in this marriage relies upon literary as well as upon social conventions. The relations of lover and beloved conventional in romance and lyric—she morally superior to him—have also been deepened to mean in this play something more than a traditional compliment to a lady. Mere *compliment* is indeed irrelevant: in *Othello* the conventions have been translated into consequential moral fact.

As in *Romeo and Juliet*, in *Othello* much is made of the difference between light and dark, between night and day, here tightly connected to the emblematic fairness and darkness of heroine and hero. As in *Romeo and Juliet*, crucial scenes in *Othello* are night-pieces. The abrupt and brilliant beginning, when Othello's bridal night is interrupted by the news of the Turk; a second interrupted bridal night on Cyprus; the sacrificial murder—each has its language of light and dark reinforcing the conjunction of fair heroine and dark hero, of moral clarity and psychological darkness. Other kinds of contrast occur, one of which has not received its notice due—the more remarkable because it is so obvious. Recently, much has been made of "Venice" as a way of life, in this play as in *The Merchant of Venice*.[14] We know, perhaps even better than the Elizabethan audience did, how appropriate Venice is as the setting for this sort of scene. We know why the merit-system worked to Othello's benefit and to Iago's annoyance, why strangers were in Venice at all, and why strangers, however favored, had difficulty in coming to terms with their difference in the city. We know the social exclusiveness of the class from which Desdemona came, and why Venetian patricians were willing to pay so much to keep war at a distance from their lives ("Why this is Venice; my house is not a grange"). Othello's usefulness to the state, in protecting it from warfare on its shores, was sufficient to override even a patrician's rights in his daughter's marriage. The source aside, which made clear that the story was a Venetian one, Shakespeare made excellent use of his locus, contrasting the comfort and materialism of the great trading city with the intangible values of Othello's courage and Desdemona's purity.

[14] See Alvin Kernan, Introduction to the Signet *Othello* (New York, 1963), xxv-xxx; Allan Bloom, "Cosmopolitan Man and the Political Community: an Interpretation of *Othello*," *ASPR*, LIV (1960), 139-58; with Sigurd Burckhardt's rejoinder, ibid., 158-66; and the further discussions by these authors (ibid., 457-64, 465-71, 474-93).

Another way of saying all this is that Shakespeare contrasted materialist Venetian ways with those of love—or, to take love's most obvious location, Venetian with Cyprian ways. In spite of its distance from Venice, the island of Cyprus was, like Rhodes, crucial to the strategic defense of the city against the Turk. In realistic terms, Cyprus was a familiar name on the Venetian tongue. Othello and Iago had seen action there before the events of the play began; the Venetians murmur about Cyprus and Rhodes before the danger is made "certain then for Cyprus." Once Othello and Desdemona arrive on the island, all the action of the play takes place there, and appropriately, when we consider that the rites of Venus, with actual and metaphorical sacrifices, were centered on that island.[15] For Cassio, Cyprus is "this worthy isle"; for Iago, "this warlike isle," and "this fair island." It is peopled by "generous islanders," for whom on their deliverance and his wedding-night Othello is glad to proclaim holiday. Cinthio's story had established Cyprus as the cite of the complicated murder of a Venetian wife by a Moor and a machiavel, but Cinthio made no particular reference to the symbolism implicit in the site. Shakespeare deepens the references to Cyprus, drawing out the island's latent power as the primary locus of love, the island to which, after her birth from the sea-foam, Aphrodite was wafted on her pearly shell. In Cassio's approach to Desdemona coming ashore on the island, the significance of the place is made plain: his heralding of her, "our great captain's captain," turns into a welcoming benediction of the lady, "The divine Desdemona" (II.i.73), coming like the goddess from the sea. *O dea certe*:

> O, behold,
> The riches of the ship is come ashore!
> Ye men of Cyprus, let her have your knees:
> Hail to thee, lady! and the grace of heaven,
> Before, behind thee, and on every hand,
> Enwheel thee round!   (II.i.82-87)

That the island is sacred to love, Cassio had made clear a few lines earlier in his invocation for Othello's protection at sea:

---

15 For standard redactions of relevant material, see Natalis Comes [or Conti], *Mythologiae* (Venice, 1581), Lib. iii, cap. xiii, pp. 251-52; Vincenzo Cartari, *Le Imagini de gli Dei degli Antichi* (Venice, 1609), pp. 387-92.

> Great Jove, Othello guard,
> And swell his sail with thine own powerful breath,
> That he may bless this bay with his tall ship,
> And swiftly come to Desdemona's arms,
> Give renew'd fire to our extincted spirits,
> And bring all Cyprus comfort. . . .   (II.i.77-82)

Quite without Iago's suggestiveness, Cassio simply celebrates the ritual love proper to the occasion, the characters, and the island; in his turn, Othello disembarks with love's rites on his mind, speaking to his wife in a speech of marvelous hyperbole, interrupted by his memory of his duty as commander, and by his courteous greeting of his "old acquaintance of the isle."

Love is rarely simple, and only at first blush does Aphrodite appear to provide uncomplicated satisfactions. The island dedicated to her is not, as the play makes clear, so well-fortified as Rhodes; Othello, we are told, knew "the fortitude of the place" from his stays on the island earlier. Actually, in its metaphoric sense, "the fortitude of the place" is what Othello did *not* know—the enormous secret strength of Aphrodite was what overthrew him, his sexual jealousy (in the existence of which he could not believe) coming to dominate his mind and finally his personality. All the references to Cyprus—and there are many more, some of Iago's with considerable *double-entendre*—make perfectly good superficial sense within the literal arrangements of the play; taken with their undertone of symbolic reference, their meaning is even more deeply sunk into the central preoccupation of *Othello*, the problematics of what is called "real" love.

The island is almost magically restored from the threat of war to peace, but it remains ringed about by war and rumors of war. As Ovid put it, war is a proper metaphor, even the proper habitat, for love:

> Militat omnis amans, et habet sua castra cupido;
> Attice, crede mihi, militat omnis amans.
>
> (*Amores* I.ix)

In that poem, the extended metaphor is of love and war, lover and warrior. Both soldier and lover keep vigil, both lie upon the ground, both do great feats in the line of duty, both lay siege to defended places, both find it practical to attack while the enemy sleeps. Donne's version of Ovid's elegy, "Loves Warre," outdoes Ovid in complicating the extended metaphor, outdoes him so readily because the image had such good use in the centuries between Ovid and Donne. In Donne's poem, love and war are not merely paired in metaphor; they are also deeply intermixed by argument so as to seem entirely interdependent conditions. Othello's greeting to Desdemona as he comes ashore at Cyprus— "O my fair warrior"—and Cassio's "Our great captain's captain," as well as Iago's harsher "Our general's wife is now the general," all honor one Petrarchan formula, "O dolce mia guerrera!" by which the lady becomes her lover's commander, his "domina," "donna," his lady as the feudal lord was his master. Again and again the theme runs in the sonnets; Spenser's *Amoretti* LVII, "Sweet warriour, when shall I have peace with you?" is but one of many examples. In *Romeo and Juliet*, love and war co-existed but were always held in rigorous contrast to each other. Throughout *Antony and Cleopatra* and *Troilus and Cressida*, the interrelations of love and war are explored: Helena parries with Parolles on the subject; Adonis wars with his boar instead of frolicking with his goddess.

In *Othello*, as in Donne's elegy, the war-world invades the love-world to make the metaphor not a far-fetched stylization but the literal truth; in this play, love is inconceivable without war. Not that this is really so surprising—Venus, of whom I have spoken much, classically played out her great love-affair with the god of war; indeed, she has much of the stock character of comedy about her. Matched with an elderly and un-beautiful husband, she took a lusty young warlike lover. Vulcan turned his shame to advantage, forging in his miraculous fire a net of gold so strong that from it his wife (*puella*) and her *adulescens* could not escape being hauled off to Olympus and displayed to divine ridicule. Love and war are matched throughout western literature; love began the war that destroyed civilization in the *Iliad*; in medieval romance, the knight was characteristically ennobled and elevated by his love, to become more puissant in war for his lady's dominant sake.

Sometimes a lover was unmanned by Venus: a test of his consistency was his capacity to resist ladies, even the ladies he loved, lying naked as needles beside him. Caught in uxoriousness, Erec felt his manhood threatened, as did also Romeo after Mercutio's death. Like Erec, who went on an immense errand, taking on all comers in his own proof, Romeo turned to fighting and managed to dispose of Mercutio's killer. Something of this tradition lies behind the exchange before the Duke over Desdemona's desire to accompany her husband to his wars. Acceding to his wife's request, Othello takes care to clear himself of the imputation of effeminate preoccupation with love:

> I therefore beg it not
> To please the palate of my appetite,
> Nor to comply with heat, the young affects
> In me defunct, and proper satisfaction,
> But to be free and bounteous of her mind;
> And heaven defend your good souls that you think
> I will your serious and great business scant,
> For she is with me. . . .   (I.iii.261-68)

There is much in this speech to betray Othello's self-deception, his apparent ignorance of the body's proper sway in love. Suffice it simply to note that Othello *is*, or says he is, aware that love can overwhelm a man, turning him in a direction other than the one his occupation dictates. The speech goes on to insist upon Othello's capacity to regulate his own weakness:

> no, when light-wing'd toys,
> And feather'd Cupid, foils with wanton dullness
> My speculative and active instruments,
> That my disports corrupt and taint my business,
> Let housewives make a skillet of my helm,
> And all indign and base adversities
> Make head against my reputation!   (I.iii.268-74)

The conjunction of "light wing'd toys," "feather'd Cupid," and "a skillet of my helm" suggests a common Ovidian source, again and again portrayed in the visual arts, of Venus resting complacently beside an exhausted Mars, reduced almost to coma by his encounter with her. Venus' troop of *amorini* often make game of the war-god's armor; in Botticelli's picture now in London, Mars' huge helmet quite covers the imp trying it on.

As in *Romeo and Juliet*, there are many uses made of "medieval" romance conventions—the fatal handkerchief is a common guerdon exchanged between lady and knight; Iago's crude reference to Cassio and Desdemona in bed together raises one standard test of control in courtly romance, "naked abed, and not mean any harm!" Iago himself is a figure of many literary origins; as Mr. Spivack laboriously demonstrates,[16] he is a type of morality Vice closely connected with the devil himself; he is another old Nick, the stage-machiavel; he is the presenter of the interlude, as well as the manipulating parasite of Roman comedy. He is, also, an Ovidian or libertine voice,[17] speaking to undermine true love, which has its medieval parallel in the figure of the *losengeour*, the voyeuristic deceiver and liar about lovers' relations with one another.

In Iago's exchange with Cassio about Desdemona, one can see two love-rhetorics in conflict, the *losengeour's* derogation of the whole business, and the plain man's acceptance of honest love:

> *Iago*: . . . our general cast us thus early for the love of his Desdemona, who let us not therefore blame: he hath not yet made wanton the night with her; and she is sport for Jove.
> *Cass*.: She is a most exquisite lady.
> *Iago*: And I'll warrant her full of game.
> *Cass*.: Indeed she is a most fresh and delicate creature.
> *Iago*: What an eye she has! methinks it sounds a parley of provocation.
> *Cass*.: An inviting eye, and yet methinks right modest.
> *Iago*: And when she speaks, 'tis an alarm to love.
> *Cass*.: It is indeed perfection.
>
> (II.iii.14-25)

Iago uses images commonly applied to sexuality—of the hunt ("full of game") and of war ("parley of provocation," "alarm to love")—in his attempt to lead Cassio into indelicacy about Desdemona; but Cassio rejects the invitation to lewdness, continuing to praise Desdemona in fairly abstract terms—"a most exquisite lady," "a most fresh and delicate creature," "methinks right modest," "indeed perfection."

Cassio does not speak in petrarchan, or petrarchistic, hyperbole here; his attitude to his general's wife is respectful and affection-

---

[16] Spivack, *Shakespeare and the Allegory of Evil*; G. N. Murphy, "A Note on Iago's Name," *Literature and Society*, ed. Bernice Slote (Lincoln, 1964), pp. 38-43; S. L. Bethell, "Shakespeare's Imagery: the Diabolic Images in *Othello*," *SS*, v (1952), 62-79.

[17] For "voice" in this sense, see Maynard Mack, "The Jacobean Shakespeare," *Stratford-upon-Avon Studies*, I (London, 1960).

ate, but generalized and never passionate. It is Othello who speaks of and to Desdemona with the magniloquence of the sonnet-lover; Othello who, disclaiming rhetorical control, displays the powerful effects of his rhetoric whenever he comes to Venice. This trick is worth noting—it is the disclaimer of Ronsard, of Sidney, of Shakespeare himself, who in their sonnets deny literary eloquence precisely while most self-consciously exploiting its resources.[18] Compared to *Romeo and Juliet*, where the sonnet-language is highly stylized, even over-audible, the sonnet-language of *Othello* is muted, does not draw attention to itself, but is nonetheless very important indeed, not only in shaping our reactions to these lovers and this love, but also in opening upon their attitudes to each other and their love for each other. The two scenes where sonnet-language is most telling are those between Othello and Desdemona at Othello's disembarkation, and just before the murder. Into the first incident, there has been an interpolation by Shakespeare of an element absent from Cinthio's narrative, the detail of the storm separating the lovers' ships on their way to the island. That storm has many analogues in Renaissance love-poetry. Wyatt, for instance, has a beautiful storm:[19]

> After great stormes the cawme retornes,
> And pleasanter it is thereby . . . ;

Petrarca:[20]

> Non d'atra e tempestosa onda marina
> fuggio in porta gia mai stanco nocchiero,
> com'io dal fosco e torbido pensero
> fugge ove 'l gran desio mi sprona e 'inchina.

We have noted Cassio's beautiful language about the storm and the safe haven of the ship that carries Othello to Desdemona's arms, again an unmetaphoring, the realization in fictional "fact" of a conventional image.

Within the context of the play's action, Othello's address to Desdemona, filled with the imminence of their bitter future, reverses the usual poetic procedure: instead of making up an imag-

[18] *Paradoxia*, Chapter Two.
[19] Thomas Wyatt, *Collected Poems*, ed. Kenneth Muir (London, 1949), p. 63.
[20] Francesco Petrarca, *Canzoniere*, ed. G. Contini and D. Ponchiroli (Torino, 1964), p. 207 (cli); Spenser, *Amoretti* lxiii.

inary storm, a metaphor for a psychological stage of love, Othello associates the real storm to his condition:

> O my soul's joy,
> If after every tempest come such calms,
> May the winds blow, till they have waken'd death,
> And let the labouring bark climb hills of seas,
> Olympus-high, and duck again as low
> As hell's from heaven.　　　　　　　　　(ii.i.184-89)

At the play's end, the sea-imagery flows back with peculiar force, as Othello realizes the enormity of his mistake, to know what his own end must be, the distance of hell from heaven. Over Desdemona's body he says,

> Here is my journey's end, here is my butt,
> And very sea-mark of my utmost sail. . . .
> 　　　　　　　　　　　　　　(v.ii.268-69)

"O my fair warrior" echoes Petrarca's "dolce mia guerrera," picked up by so many sonneteers: Ronsard to Cassandre, "ma guerrière Cassandre," Sidney to Stella, "dear Captainesse." Cyprus has been spoken of, its meaning as Venus' isle deepening Othello's greeting to his wife, "Honey, you shall be well desir'd in Cyprus." Of sonnets more is made in this play: Petrarca and Ronsard particularly refer to Venus as the Cyprian, calling their ladies Cyprians and Venusses too. Ronsard's "Vœu à Venus. Pour garder Cypre contre l'armée du Turc" has particular poignancy in relation to this play, though of course no direct connection with it:[21]

> Idalienne, Amathonte, Erycine,
> Garde des Turcs Cypre, ton beau séjour;
> Baise ton Mars, et tes bras à l'entour
> De son col plie, et serre sa poitrine.
>
> Ne permets point qu'un barbare Seigneur
> Perde ton isle et souille ton honneur;
> De ton berceau chasse autre part la guerre.

21 Ronsard, *Œuvres complètes*, I, 298; cf. Philippe Desportes, *Amours de Diane*, ed. Victor Grahame (Geneva, 1959), II, 211; and Joachim du Bellay, *Œuvres*, (Rouen, 1592), p. 76 (*Olive*, civ).

Surrey's poem about Cyprus makes clear the island's power, as well as the power of love in general:[22]

> In Cypres springes, wheras dame Venus dwelt,
> A well so hote that who so tastes the same,
> Were he of stone, as thawed yse should melt,
> And kindled fynde his brest with secret flame;
> Whose moist poison dissolved hath my hate.
> This creping fier my cold lymms so oprest
> That in the hart that harbred fredom late
> Endles dispaire long thraldom hath imprest.
> One eke so cold in froson snow is found,
> Whose chilling venume of repugnaunt kind
> The fervent heath doth quench of Cupides wound,
> And with the spote of change infects the mynd;
>   Whereof my deer hath tasted to my payne.
>   My service thus is growne into disdayne.

Of this darker side of love, Othello has no inkling. His exalted idea of himself, in view of his relations with Desdemona, so much more conventional than her view of the same connection, took into account only his "perfection" as warrior and noble soul, ignoring the potential seriousness of love's disruption. In Othello's imagery, much is presaged in just his speech of welcome on Cyprus:

>   If it were now to die,
> 'Twere now to be most happy, for I fear
> My soul hath her content so absolute,
> That not another comfort, like to this
> Succeeds in unknown fate.   (II.i.189-93)

As in so many love-poems, the rhetoric of supreme happiness in life turns poets' minds to its opposite, annihilation in death, in this passage so clearly expressed. Immediately after this imagery of joy and death, Othello turns to musical metaphors, kissing Desdemona and saying,

> And this, and this, the greatest discord be
> That e'er our hearts shall make!   (II.i.199-200)

[22] Henry Howard, Earl of Surrey, *Poems*, ed. Emrys Jones (Oxford, 1964), p. 3.

Iago picks up the metaphor at once, making discord of their harmony, in an image active and manipulative like himself:

> O, you are well tun'd now,
> But I'll set down the pegs that make this music,
> As honest as I am.   (II.i.200-202)

The image of harmony, so important in love-poetry from Dante on, stems from Plato's image of cosmic harmony, traditionally instituted by love's ordering of chaos. Though the image is a commonplace in literature as in thought,[23] the sonneteers made the most of it, their love creating harmony when it was happy, reducing all things to chaos when it was not. As Othello looks after his wife, departing from him for a moment, he speaks of chaos in terms that remind us that he had, at the peak of his contentment, used the imagery of heaven and hell in his great passage about the storm:

> Excellent wretch, perdition catch my soul,
> But I do love thee, and when I love thee not,
> Chaos is come again.   (III.iii.91-93)

Interestingly enough, this speech, sandwiched between Iago's insinuations, is the last spoken out of Othello's conviction of his own invulnerability, the last with the ever-so-slightly megalomaniac overtones of a man invincible in his content—as if *his* love, like the deity's or the sonneteer's, could order chaos! Ronsard's lines, set in the context of the lover's declaration, provide an instructive parallel to Othello's:[24]

> Or, s'il te plaist, fay moy languir en peine,
> Tant que la mort me de-nerve et de-veine,
> Je seray tien. Et plus-tôt le Chaos
>   Se troublera de sa noise ancienne,
> Qu'autre beauté, qu'autre amour que la tienne,
> Sous autre joug me captive le dos.

[23] See, e.g., *Elizabethan Sonnets*, ed. Lee, II, 159 (*Zepheria*, Canzon 4), 4 (Lodge, *Phillis*, III); Scève, *Délie*, p. 103; Ronsard, I, 23 (*Amours de Cassandre*, lii). For the associations of heaven and hell see (beside Shakespeare's own famous sonnet) Constable, *Diana*, vii dec. (*Elizabethan Sonnets*, ed. Lee, II, 106). The standard critical commentary is Leo Spitzer's *Classical and Christian Ideas of World Harmony* (Baltimore, 1963).

[24] Ronsard, I, 24 (*Amours de Cassandre*, liii); cf. also 25 (*Cassandre*, lvi).

In Ronsard's poem, chaos is entirely conventional—the fact that the poet considers another beauty, another love, as possible, makes probable the defection so hyperbolically denied. His Cassandre, one knows even in this poem, is one mistress in a series. Othello's language admits no quarter; it points directly to his actual future within the play's plot, his life and his world dependent upon his love.

Other echoes of the hyperbole of literary love-traditions sound in Othello's language. "My life upon her faith" is conventional enough, but in a less committed, or a more experienced, lover need not have led so absolutely to its fulfillment as in Othello's case, who took the words at their literal value. His emphasis on Desdemona's lovely smell,[25] his likening of her to a rose, are all familiar enough from the sonnet-tradition—and, incidentally, serve to stress for us not only the enormous physical appeal Desdemona's person had for her husband, but also his very conventional view of what love ought to be. Yet more: these references underline Othello's self-deception, his pleasure in the sense-experiences which he himself tries to argue away. "Thou smell'st so sweet, that the senses ache at thee," he cried out in the midst of his diatribe against Desdemona. At the end of the play, the traditional image of *carpe diem*, the rose, comes with an awful exactitude. Othello does pluck the day and the rose with it:

> when I have pluck'd the rose,
> I cannot give it vital growth again,
> It must needs wither; I'll smell it on the tree,
> A balmy breath. . . . (v.ii.13-16)

So lightheartedly gathered, from the Greek Anthology on, the rose of love tended to lose specificity, in the common usage it was accorded; in Othello's speech, the familiar metaphor alters into something actual, into something far more charged than it usually is. Abruptly, all the implications of the image, folded into the rose-petals, unfold again—once plucked, *all* roses wither. Indeed, all roses wither anyway, even if left unplucked upon the tree. Once destroyed, nor roses, nor light, nor love, nor life can be "relum'd." Ronsard's[26]

[25] Cf. *Amoretti*, lxiv; Petrarca, *Canzoniere*, lxxi, clxxxv, cccxxxvii; Scève, *Délie*, pp. 65, 166, 372.
[26] Ronsard, I, 41 (*Cassandre*, xcvi).

> Pren ceste rose aimable comme toy
> Qui sers de rose aux roses les plus belles,
> Qui sers de fleur aux fleurs les plus nouvelles,
> Dont la senteur ma ravist tout de moy. . . .

ends on the flower's death. In another poem, he describes the marvelously seductive odor of the opening rose, dying after so brief a blooming:[27]

> La grace dans sa feuille, et l'amour se repose
> Embasmant les jardins et les arbres d'odeur;
> Mais batue ou de pluye, ou d'excessive ardeur,
> Languissante elle meurt, feuille à feuille declose . . .
> Pour obsèques reçoy mes larmes et mes pleurs. . . .

The extraordinary sweetness of the rose often mingles with other images for marvelous sweetness—the phoenix and its sweet-smelling locus, Arabia; or Laura's sweetness, greater than all the nards of the East; other sonnet-ladies' sweetness, then, outdoing Laura's. At Desdemona's death, Othello becomes such an eastern tree; his

> subdued eyes,
> Albeit unused to the melting mood,
> Drop tears as fast as the Arabian trees
> Their medicinal gum. . . .   (v.ii.349-52)

Another sort of imagery, that of jewels, was also standard in the description of beloved ladies, as of Juliet, "like a rich jewel in an Ethiop's ear." There are several jewel-references to Desdemona, beginning with Brabantio's terrible leave-taking:

> for your sake (jewel),
> I am glad at soul I have no other child. . . .
> (i.iii.195-96)

and ending on Othello's far more terrible description of himself as Desdemona's killer:

> one whose hand,
> Like the base Indian, threw a pearl away,
> Richer than all his tribe. . . .   (v.ii.347-49)

The jewels come from cases of conventional compliment; but Othello's word "tribe" reminds us of the difficulties in his own

[27] Ronsard, I, 184-85 ("Sur la mort de Marie," iv).

life, and the way in which, so bitterly, he turns out to manifest just the passions attributed to that "tribe," which he had so long, and apparently so successfully, struggled to suppress in himself. Petrarca's sonnet 51, furthermore, offers the image-cluster of jewel, old man, and Moroccan darkness: the lady is the changeless precious stone. So Desdemona's value can be measured by that "one entire and perfect chrysolite," with all its cosmic radiance, for which her husband would not have sold her.[28]

Other themes in Othello's last speeches offer commentary on the customary languages of literary love. Traditionally, ladies are "cold," as diamonds, as the springs of Helicon, as snow, as ice. Beatrice and Laura were both chilly; even Ronsard's willing ladies were occasionally "froides." Desdemona, we know, was not cold in her lifetime, but only in her death:

> cold, cold, my girl,
> Even like thy chastity.   (v.ii.276-77)

Once more, the metaphor is made real, thrust back into brutal actuality: Desdemona is at last made "cold."

The imagery of light and dark, playing in many contexts, comes to its climax in the great speech before Desdemona's murder. By her marriage, Desdemona had evidently come to terms with Othello's blackness, as her explanation of her unfilial behavior makes plain. But Othello, it turns out, had not, whatever he may have thought. As Iago's insinuations bore into him, Othello seeks reasons why Desdemona should not love him:

> Haply, for I am black,
> And have not those soft parts of conversation
> That chamberers have, or for I am declin'd
> Into the vale of years,   (III.iii.267-70)

he says, pathetically and ambiguously explaining things to himself. And a bit later, in a rage:

> my name, that was as fresh
> As Dian's visage, is now begrim'd, and black
> As mine own face. . . .   (III.iii.392-94)

[28] For the meanings of chrysolite, see Lawrence J. Ross, "World and Chrysolite in *Othello*," *MLN*, LXXVI (1961), 683-92; for "pearl," see John E. Seaman, "Othello's Pearl," *SQ*, XIX (1968), 81-85.

Desdemona had spoken for herself when she said, "I saw Othello's visage in his mind"; but as events turn out, his mind can be "begrim'd" and black as his face.

Robert Heilman and others have studied the ways in which Othello's grandiloquence falls into the extravagant, passionate, fragmentary, derogatory language that shares more and more with Iago's choice of syntax and vocabulary.[29] It is interesting to note that even in this degeneration, there are traces of literary love-conventions. Othello ceases to see Desdemona whole: as she loses her integrity for him, he sees her only in parts—and, far more important, his rage is such that he wishes to tear her into bits. It is the passionate rage that strikes us, as it ought, with most force, so that Othello's abusive "Noses, ears, and lips" does not obviously make mock of the catalogue of mistress' separate features so dear to writers of blasons and sonnets. Such literary elements are by the by, of course: they do not insist upon themselves, and we do not insist upon them. What we are to notice is the realistic use by the playwright of this kind of reference, as the disjunction of the parts of Desdemona's face is seen to match the disruption in Othello's mind and feelings about her.

Believing himself wronged, Othello reverses the light-dark imagery, calling Desdemona "thou black weed"—although her fairness never ceases to move him deeply, even at that terrible moment. As he readies himself to take her life, Othello speaks in an image-cluster gathering up all the themes of fairness, coldness, hardness, and death:

> I'll not shed her blood,
> Nor scar that whiter skin of hers than snow,
> And smooth, as monumental alabaster. . . .
>
> (v.ii.3-5)

The notion of a tomb, made so concrete in *Romeo and Juliet*, is only glanced at here, its power the greater for its obliqueness. A few lines after these, the rose comes in, to make the contrast between cold and warmth, colorlessness and intensity, death and life. A literary parallel might be Petrarca's sonnet 131, where the rose blooms against the snow and, after its brief life, cannot be revived. To hunt among Petrarca's poems for parallels is reliably rewarding, even precisely to the combinations of light and dark

---

[29] Heilman, *passim*; and Matthew N. Proser, *The Heroic Image in Five Shakespearean Plays* (Princeton, 1965), Chapter Three.

that best fit this play. In Laura, of course, light and fairness combine in exceptional radiance; in her imperfect lover, especially imperfect when absent from his lady, darkness prevails—and, one notes, the very darkest sort of darkness, Petrarca tells us: Moroccan or Moorish darkness.

Other love-poets rang changes on Petrarca's oxymora and oppositions, his freezings in fire, his burnings in ice, his poverty in riches, his "dolce ire," "dolcezza amara," "dolce errore," his love that brightens night, darkens day, embitters honey and sweetens vinegar, his peace unfound after armistice, and so on. Oxymoron and contradiction became official figures, expressing in figural shorthand the internal conflicts surfaced by love's intensity. Worked by generations of lyricists, the figure of oxymoron tended to stretch into longer syntactical forms, sentences expressing contradictoriness and paradox. Othello speaks in such contradictions —"O thou black weed, why art so lovely fair?" is his *odi et amo*, a highly condensed version of the conflicting emotions Shakespeare had far more fully worked out in his own sonnets of obsession.[30] Finally, in the soliloquy before Desdemona's death:

> So sweet was ne'er so fatal: I must weep,
> But they are cruel tears; this sorrow's heavenly,
> It strikes when it does love . . . ,　　　(v.ii.20-22)

the confusions and contradictions of the language bespeak the degree of his suffering. Paradox takes hold at the end, when Othello is beyond restitution and beyond honor, in an echo from the love-poetry, and, more poignantly, from his own disembarkation speech: "Then in my sense 'tis happiness to die." This time, "dying" fulfills great crimes and great grief, not the overwhelming happiness he had experienced at reunion with Desdemona. Like Romeo, Othello himself dies as the sonnet-lover should, upon a kiss:

> I kiss'd thee ere I kill'd thee, no way but this,
> Killing myself, to die upon a kiss.　　(v.ii.-359-60)

The metaphor is gone, but its echo remains, to remind us, as it reminds Othello, of what is gone with the loss of that love, with the loss of that lady's life.

What all this language does in *Othello* is what it does in *Romeo and Juliet*: it reminds us of what love-lyrics exist to proclaim, that

---

[30] See above, pp. 121-26.

through all the misunderstandings, the violence, the betrayals
and self-betrayals, love is at base the most beautiful of human
experiences, its satisfactions so great that loss of love can bring
incomparable results. It reminds us that in spite of their fictions,
poets can be right—that whatever else happens in a man's life, it
is his love which most reveals and strips him, which makes his
private life sufficiently important to outweigh his public life. In
Romeo and Juliet the lovers try to live privately, in a social situation which permits no such privacy; their sonnet-language is
properly self-important and self-referential, overriding all other
considerations as long as love can. The lyrical language of that
play, beautiful and buoyant, is at the same time a very obvious
language, as befits the subject and the energies of a youthful play
about youth; the lyrical element in *Othello* is so understated, so
absorbed into the whole play so that we hardly realize all that
it does.

When we do, at last, realize that even the plot of *Othello* is in
fact the unmetaphoring of typical sonnet-narrative, it comes both
as a surprise and as a revelation. Nonetheless, that is just what it
is: the sonnet-sequence plot has been animated into dramatic
action. Fair bride and darker lover achieve, after initial difficulties, perfection of happiness, only to have jealousy break in,
which in sonnet-narratives may indeed result in love's death, but
at most a metaphorical death. The lovers in sonnets generally
survive, either to achieve a deeper love after the clearing-up of
misunderstanding, or to free the lover from an unworthy obsession. In life, of course, such endings are rare: real misprision, real
jealousy, real irrationality sicken love past revival. In ordinary
life, the ends of such affairs, even between great spirits, are not
heroic and are rarely tragic, merely wasteful and sad. In this play,
one conventional sonnet-ending is reached, with the metaphorical death in fact unmetaphored. Love literally dies, then; that act
is irreversible, Desdemona and love cannot be revived or recalled.
But through all the misunderstanding, a kind of reconciliation
is reached: the hero learns that his lady is true and his notion of
her false. He recognizes the consistent virtue of his wife, and, by
reason of his new understanding, can take the terrible consequences of his error. We accept Othello's heroism in part because
of the speed and sureness with which he reaffirms his original
judgment of Desdemona and of his love for her; after his praise
of her steady goodness, he ends his life as judge and executioner

of his own criminal self. It is not life-like, perhaps: but the love-fiction has, at Desdemona's death, come to take its consequences, to move onto another moral plane, to become, as tragedy must be, a fiction of responsibility.

In Othello's psychology, too, the *schemata* of official romantic love have left their deep mark. Because his view of love was so stereotyped, he could not see his wife as she actually was, but was fooled into taking her at Iago's fictional assessment. She was in fact generous, frank, and devoted, more openly so than the coy mistress of sonnet-prescription. Her very deviation from romantic type made it easier for Othello to accept Iago's explanation of her, to accept, then, a familiar literary stereotype in place of the (remarkable, it is true) real person. Part of the extraordinary irony of this play is that in one sense, Othello's acceptance of Iago's story is a version of realism, as the world, or the literary world, sees realism. Desdemona's behavior was so romantic, so ideal, that it could indeed seem very unlikely. Iago's interpretation of the world, cheap and cynical though it is, is the version the world tends to take for real—or, Iago's interpretation most persuasively presents the stereotype of realism. Just as with Edmund, whose bastardy speech makes us at first entertain some sympathy for him, but whose behavior reveals, by his own account too, his fundamental lawlessness, so with Iago: the conventions of cynicism, usually protected by fears of romanticism within us, are ultimately revealed as the shoddy things they are. Altogether, we find the problematics of love—the psychology, the language, the behavior of love and its twinned opposite, jealousy—can ultimately be restudied through its expressive stereotypes.

Stereotypes themselves are a problem, because they are at once shoddy and valuable. Their thinness attenuates meaning; their commonplaceness and cliché reiteration make them seem automatic and trivial. All the same, though, stereotypes are developed in the first place because they answer in some measure fundamental needs, either as a simplified version of reality or to give shape to our deep hope that reality can be reinterpreted in some simple way. Artists and writers working with the stereotypes and schemata of their craft must maneuver delicately through the problems so raised, attempting not to say something everyone knows or expects to hear, and yet to speak in terms that everyone can understand.

Shakespeare managed miraculously to bring off his tragic exercise in dramatic sonnetry: by springing the sonnet-plot back into what seems to be reality, he made the effects of love suddenly more patent, more critical, more crucial than they seem to be in their usual habitat, the protected and enclosed garden of love-lyrics. By exploiting the self-examination and self-expression of the lyric lover, especially the sonnet-lover, he made such private feelings seem suddenly almost heroic. By allowing private to move into public life, the profound inwardness of love to work in heroic personalities and thus to open upon tragic possibilities, he raises a lyric plot to tragic scope. Another way of saying this is that the playwright took the literary love-conventions seriously, and by making various literary conventions seem elements in a real situation shows us the power and grievousness of the love they represent.

From literary conventions, he took part of his fable and much of his language. Without the literary conventions at his disposal—and without having practised them in his own earlier works—Shakespeare would have had a hard time convincing us of the importance, especially the tragic importance, of a story so trivial and so sordid as Cinthio's novella. At this play's heart lies a critique of the artificiality built into stylized language and the behavior which that language permits and even encourages. In *Romeo and Juliet*, there is plenty of criticism of the love-language—Mercutio's comments on the numbers that Petrarca and others "flowed in" tell us much—but this criticism never points to the morality beneath the conventions. There, the language points toward emotional condition, but does not reveal its nearly inexpressible complexities. In a fairly standard way, too, the sonnet-ethos is affirmed unquestioned. Juliet, with her language more "real" than her lover's, is to be taken as the nobler, or more mature, character of the two—indeed, in the simplifying of his language, we are to read Romeo's growth through his new love. Desdemona's language is even more direct than Juliet's, both in a comparison between the two women's utterances and within the contexts of the two plays. As a result, Desdemona is obviously less rhetorical, even less poetic, than her husband; her verbal directness displays, we think, the plain "truth" of her nature. Othello's language displays something quite other: it shows us that his concepts of love are less grounded in psychological reality, are far more stereotyped, than those of his wife. Othello, after all, wooed an admitted prize among women; Desdemona studied her husband and chose him at considerable expense to herself. Othello's vulnerabilities show in his enormous pride, to warn us, if not him, of the delicate balance of his personality, especially when it is subjected to peculiar and unfamiliar stress. Less fearful of her senses and fearless of appearing sensual, Desdemona finds it easier to behave with absolute loyalty to Othello than he to her—a loyalty rare in what is called real life. She dies, indeed, upon an act of generosity, trying to clear her husband of the imputation of crime. By convention, the lady is of finer stuff than her lover; by convention, her excellence raises his moral level. Desdemona is fair; she has, in Spenser's words, "The trew fayre, that is the gentle wit,/ and vertuous mind . . . ,"[31] and thereby raises the moral level of her lover, at a cost, however, incommensurate with the gain. Love is not a thing to be taken lightly, nor can it be interpreted along conventional lines, even when, as in *Othello*, its conventions turn out to be true. In criticizing the artificiality he at the same time exploits in his play, Shakespeare manages in *Othello* to reassess and to reanimate the moral system and the psychological truths at the core of the literary love-tradition, to reveal its problematics and to reaffirm in a fresh and momentous context the beauty of its impossible ideals.

[31] *Amoretti*, lxxix.

4

Antony and Cleopatra:
The Significance of Style

I

LIKE EARLIER CHAPTERS, this one is concerned with a particular manifestation of Shakespeare's control over style and styles. By definition, Shakespeare was a very stylish writer indeed, conscious of the range of stylistic alternatives available to him, concerned to honor the particular decorums of style and to extend (even to subverting those official decorums) the possibilities of expressive style. We have looked at his analytic prodigality in *Love's Labour's Lost*, as well as his counterpointing of epigrammatic and sonnet styles in his *Sonnets*: we have seen both how closely style is tied up with topic, subject, and moral tone, and how far away from these it can pull. In *Othello*, the charged passages in sonnet-language owe their impact to Shakespeare's significant control over the resources of that "language," his ability to make *topos*, epithet, and cliché resound with the generic meanings of a whole tradition of sonneteering. *Antony and Cleopatra* relies on that language too—a whole piece could be written on its unmetaphoring of standard love-conventions—but it is with another stylistic paradigm that I am concerned here. As in the sonnets, where Shakespeare exploited the *ping* and *pong*[1] of two different short-form genres, in *Antony and Cleopatra* he transposed the *ping* and *pong* of another literary paradigm rejuvenated in the Renaissance; and once again, his penetrating literary eye, fixed on the implications of a stylistic cliché, reopened the whole question of appropriate style in tragedy.

This time, the paradigm so examined was an ancient antithesis brought into contemporary prominence in the argument over expository prose styles, that is, the polemic over the "Attic" and "Asiatic" styles which, as an offshoot of the polemic over strict Ciceronianism, preoccupied such men as Lipsius, Muret, Montaigne, Bacon, Browne, and even Robert Burton. In *Antony and Cleopatra*, I think, Shakespeare subjected to scrutiny the personal,

[1] See E. H. Gombrich, *Art and Illusion*, pp. 370, 381.

psychological, and cultural meanings implicit in that polemic, dealing with the very stereotypes of moral life that had, long before when Greeks confronted Persians, given rise to the terms in the first place—and, typically, examined those styles in the lives of his hero and his heroine.[2]

Obviously, Shakespeare was skilled in constructing dramatic characters who speak in what seems "personal" styles—one thinks at once of such confrontations as that of Hal with Falstaff, or of Hotspur with Glendower; of Hamlet with Polonius, Hamlet with the Gravedigger; of Iago with Othello—or even of Iago with Cassio; of Kent with Cornwall, of Cordelia with her sisters, of Lear with his Fool. The list of such episodes, in which with the greatest economy so much is revealed about character, class, and motivation, is very long.

In *Love's Labour's Lost*, as we have seen, the playwright translated something else, the degrees of social hierarchy and occupation, into linguistic styles, managing therewith to mock the pretensions both of hierarchy and of occupations.

Underneath the nonsense with words in *Love's Labour's Lost*, a point of considerable importance is being made: that words' artifice does not reflect the real behavior of men and women. Well within the comic mode, the gaps are opened between *res* and *verbum*, between pathos and its expression, even between personality and life-style, and shown to be traps where individual preferences, drives, and even personalities can be lost. Language is played with, criticized, and praised, but all in terms of comedy —although the comedy in which these questions are raised rejects the standard comic solution. The play moves within, at, and beyond the limits of conventional language, nonetheless always celebrating the resources of the language it sometimes chastises. We are shown the predestination in language, and its flexibility as well, but no one is by these means predestined to suffer forever,

[2] My chapter owes much to earlier studies of the play, especially to Maurice Charney's *Shakespeare's Roman Plays*, chapters 1 and 4. My hypothesis states, more overtly and probably more pedantically than Charney's, that Shakespeare deliberately animated a stylistic paradigm in this play, a paradigm polemically discussed in his lifetime and of which he was aware, in order to re-examine interchangeable relations of verbal style to style in living and (far more important) to cultural style. See also Benjamin T. Spencer, "*Antony and Cleopatra* and the Paradoxical Metaphor," *SQ*, IX (1958), 373-78; Proser, *The Heroic Image in Five Shakespearean Plays*; Madeleine Doran, *The Endeavors of Art* (Madison, 1954), pp. 245-50; and Burckhardt, *Shakespearean Meanings*.

as at the play's end languages are readjusted lightheartedly to fit the characters' new understanding of society and of themselves.

In other plays quite unlike *Love's Labour's Lost,* we hear language used in contexts where *language* itself is crucial:[3] even in what used to be called "interpolations," such as the Porter's speech in *Macbeth,* or the Gravedigger's exchange with Hamlet, we now hear thematic supports for central events and tendencies in the plays. Kent's linguistic disguises, manifestly "garments" the man chose to put on, nonetheless display an honesty which Cornwall, Oswald, and the wicked sisters, all speaking in their own persons, cannot call up. Lear's great speeches demonstrate, as Edgar said, "reason in madness";[4] Coriolanus' inarticulate utterances portray with great purity the struggle of polity with pride. In *Julius Caesar* (as to some extent in *Coriolanus* as well) critics have seen in the spare language the playwright's effort to match his style to his austere subject, to achieve a peculiarly "Roman" style.[5] And in both plays, *la questione della lingua,* or at least *dello stile,* is written deeply into the plot: action turns on *how* men speak as well as what they say, appropriately enough, in plays about Roman political life.

The high point of *Julius Caesar* and its greatest set-piece is a rhetorical contest, in which two considerable orators compete for public favor in the matter of Caesar's death. Brutus was a stoic—except for Monteverdi's Seneca, the most attractive stoic ever staged—whose mode of speech is properly "plain." He tries, as the stoic rhetoric urged, to represent "himself" in his words and his syntax.[6] In the case at hand, such self-representation is of prime importance, since on the authority of Brutus' integrity the conspirators' justification can be said to rest. Although in the source Shakespeare used, Plutarch tells us a great deal about Mark Antony's speech at Caesar's funeral, he attempts no version of that speech itself—its invention was Shakespeare's own, who did not flinch from the task; and Brutus' speech is entirely Shakespeare's interpolation into the story. Brutus' reputation as an

[3] See chapter 1, above.

[4] Sheldon P. Zitner, *"King Lear* and its Language" (*Some Facets*); "Shakespeare's Secret Language" (unpublished paper).

[5] See, in particular, Charney, chapter 5; and James L. Calderwood, "*Coriolanus*: Wordless Meanings and Meaningless Words," *SEL,* vi (1966), 211-24.

[6] For the theory behind this concept of "matching," see Gombrich, *Art and Illusion,* pp. 29, 73, 116-18, 188-89.

Atticist—thus, as a plain speaker and proponent of a rhetorical style designed to match the directness of the person using it— was well-known; so was Antony's predilection for Asianism, recorded so fully by Plutarch.[7] By picking up hints from Plutarch and the rhetoric-books, Shakespeare could treat Brutus and Antony as the living exemplars of what might otherwise have been mere *topoi*: he could make them live the styles in which they chose to speak.

At the same time, he glanced at aspects of the current controversy over prose-style which reanimated an ancient polarity. Greeks had, naturally enough, characterized Persians and others to the east of Athens as "Asiatic," meaning sensuous, sybaritic, self-indulgent, rich, materialist, decorated, soft. According to the paradigm, Asiatics lived a life of ease, delicacy, even of sloth, surrounded by ornate works of art and elaborate amusements for body and spirit. Gradually, the moral disapproval leveled at their eastern neighbors came to be applied to a style of oratory conceived as "like" Persian life, a style formally complex, ornate, decorated, and elaborate. Naturally, a simple, direct, relatively plain style was "Attic."[8] Needless to say, what was Attic and what was Asiatic varied considerably according to context, period, and generation: a given style can always be seen as plainer or more ornate than some other, and what was Attic to one generation sometimes seemed Asiatic to the next. In Rome, the debate recurred, centered on Cicero's style or styles, which to one generation (Cicero's own) appeared clear, intelligible, and direct, matching style to matter—and thus Attic; but to the next generation, which sought to reform it, elaborate, overly-wrought, untruthfully formal—thus artificial and Asiatic.[9] In late humanism,

---

[7] Plutarch, *The Lives of the Noble Grecians and Romanes*, tr. Thomas North (London, 1595), p. 969.

[8] M. von Wilamowitz-Möllendorf, "Asianismus und Atticismus," *Hermes*, XXXV (1900), 1-52; Eduard Norden, *Die antike Kunstprosa* (Leipzig, 1915-1918); G. L. Hendrickson, "The Original Meaning of the Ancient Characters of Style," *American Journal of Philology*, XXVI (1905), 248-90; C. N. Smiley, "Seneca and the Stoic Theory of Literary Style," *Wisconsin Studies in Language and Literature*, III (1919), 50-61; A. D. Leeman, *Orationis Ratio: the Stylistic Theories and Practice of the Orators, Historians, and Philosophers* (Amsterdam, 1963); F. Quadlbauer, *Die antike Theorie der genera dicendi* (Vienna, 1958).

[9] Cicero himself exemplifies this process: see *Tusc. Disp.*, II, i; *Brutus*, xiii, 51; lxxxii, 284-lxxiv, 291; *Orator*, viii, 27-31; xxiii, 76-xxvi, 90.

the terms of the debate were revived, this time appropriately over "Ciceronianism," the formally correct style established by precedents in Cicero's works, that instrument by which humanists sought to purify their Latin of scholastic barbarisms. Morris Croll and others[10] have presented valuable analyses and hypotheses of this prose-*agon* of the late Renaissance, and upon their writings I lean with gratitude. Not all Croll's normative statements are acceptable now without qualification. Even his hypothesis has borne considerable rethinking; but his paradigm of Attic and Asiatic is of immense use, and illuminates much not only about prose-styles but also about the range of poetic styles in that highly rhetorical period, when writers, trained from boyhood on rhetorical exercises, practised with immense control their vernacular skills. What the notions of "Attic" and "Asiatic" do for us, then, is to provide us with a *ping* and *pong*, a range of comparison, for Renaissance styles.[11] By comparing one passage with another, one style with another, we can get some sense of what seemed "plain" and what "ornate" to contemporary readers interested in such matters.

The decisive oratorical contest in *Julius Caesar* is a case in point: we know that Shakespeare recognized in the two orators representatives of the two styles. In the competition between Brutus and Mark Antony for the people's approbation, the playwright used styles as marks of characterization for both personality and motive. The obvious difference between Brutus' style and Antony's points directly to the differences in their characters. In the play, Brutus speaks first, in prose, a device designed to show his relative directness and sincerity. If we examine that plain prose of his, though, we see it not simply as an expression of his naked personality (such as Attic theorists advocated for their style), for from his style we can read how sophisticated Brutus was, how studied in the rhetoric of the schools:

> Romans, countrymen, and lovers, hear me for my cause, and
> be silent, that you may hear. Believe me for mine honour, and

---

[10] Morris W. Croll, in essays now conveniently collected in *Style, Rhetoric, and Rhythm* (Princeton, 1966); see also George Williamson, *The Senecan Amble* (Chicago, 1951); Brian Vickers, *Francis Bacon and Renaissance Prose* (Cambridge, 1968); and E. R. Curtius, *European Literature and the Latin Middle Ages*, pp. 67-68.

[11] Gombrich's ping-pong paradigm perforce alters the moral intention of Winters' division of poetic styles into plain and ornate.

have respect to mine honour, that you may believe. Censure me in your wisdom, and awake your senses, that you may the better judge.

It sounds straight: it is too often circular.

> As Caesar loved me, I weep for him; as he was fortunate, I rejoice at it; as he was valiant, I honour him; but, as he was ambitious, I slew him. There is tears, for his love; joy, for his fortune; honour, for his valour; and death, for his ambition. Who is here so base, that would be a bondman? If any, speak; for him have I offended. Who is here so rude, that would not be a Roman? Who is here so vile, that will not love his country? If any, speak; for him have I offended.
>
> (III.ii.13-17, 25-34)

Syntactical regularity of this sort is not accidental; Brutus was an orator, who knew his craft: his particular job this time was to demonstrate in his speech, and thus in his person, that his motives in a complicated situation were above reproach. The speech certainly exploits directness—"I slew him" is an admirably uncompromising statement of responsibility assumed. All the same, that frankness is elaborated in beautiful polysyndeta, zeugma, and parison, all going to show that even the plain-speaking Brutus knew in his bones how to make speeches and had, long before Julius Caesar's death, submitted his natural, unretouched personality to the finish of the rhetorical schools.

Brutus was an honorable man: when Mark Antony enters the Forum with Caesar's body, Brutus leaves the platform to him, enjoining the crowd to listen to whatever Antony has to say. What that was, is too well-known to warrant quotation: Mark Antony wins over the people in a long oration several times broken by applause and by the speaker's own display of emotion. In Antony's words, "I am no orator, as Brutus is,/ But (as you know me all) a plain blunt man" (III.ii.219-20), an Attic appeal apparently entirely untutored, we can read truth and trickery. Antony was, as he said, no orator—officially; but he had studied the rhetorical arts in Athens, where he had been drawn to Asianism, as Plutarch tells us. What he displays is a style more intimate, more moving—and far more demagogic than Brutus'. Of course, by his false modesty, Antony means to imply that he has no skill in rhetoric and that his speech, therefore, cannot be expected to move the crowd, which had no need to be on guard against his wiles. In that implication, of course, Antony lies.

Shakespeare's confronting of these two styles is highly complex: he does not rely on a simplistic or moralistic paradigm, that "simple" is honest ("kersey noes") and "fancy" deceitful— but manages rather to show the limitations in the characters of both men, at once displayed and concealed by the styles they use. In the simplest ways, the two speeches are set in opposition: Brutus speaks prose, Antony verse. Since verse is by definition more decorated than prose, to that extent Antony's is the more decorated speech. Brutus' speech, though, is *syntactically* more formal by far—in other words, more structured, more Ciceronian —and has a firm structural consistency which Antony's by design lacks. Antony's flexible oration shifts from the formality of its beginning—"I come to bury Caesar, not to praise him"; "If it were so, it was a grievous fault,/ And grievously hath Caesar answer'd it"—to an astonishing frankness and intimacy at its end:

> Good friends, sweet friends, let me not stir you up
> To such a sudden flood of mutiny.
> They that have done this deed are honourable.
> What private griefs they have, alas, I know not,
> That made them do it. . . .
> For I have neither wit, nor words, nor worth,
> Action, nor utterance, nor the power of speech
> To stir men's blood; I only speak right on.
>
> (III.ii.211-16; 223-25)

In this artful and insidious speech, the grammatical members are plain but varied, more "naturally" disposed than those in the oration of the stoical Brutus. In one sense, signalized by shifting syntax and broken tone, Antony's language is "plainer," answers more honestly to his mood, and is thus more "Attic" than Brutus'. Brutus' syntax is elaborate, carefully-constructed, balanced, but his *tone* is consistent and direct and his whole oration markedly economical. Antony's tone fluctuates and shifts as the refrain "And Brutus is an honourable man" measures its altering direction. Again and again that refrain returns us to the tonic, showing Antony's remarkable way with words—and with his words, his way with his hearers' emotions. In sum, in their oratory we can hear the differences between the two men: Brutus' innocence shines out compared with Antony's guile; Brutus' self-deception is plain beside Antony's manifest scheming.

Mark Antony had indeed "studied eloquence": his rhetoric is active, emotional, moving, and ultimately victorious over the relatively more neutral, more correct rhetoric of his opponent. The tricks of irony and sensationalism in Antony's repertory win over the fickle, casual populace, with important political results. But we must realize how *political* both men are, how they both use forensic oratory as a political weapon. Brutus seeking to damp down, Antony to stoke, the potential fires of popular wrath, both men address themselves in entirely different styles to their different tasks. Underneath Brutus' sincerity, we are aware of how consciously he plays upon that sincerity; in Antony's speech, we come to realize equally the man's love for Caesar and the artfulness of his own political intent.

Mark Antony's style, too, fits his character as given in the play. He makes no high pretensions to virtue; we see him temporizing with the conspirators after the murder, and we are early told that for all his talents Mark Antony is a dissolute young man. From his speech we sense his political acumen and, perhaps, his ambition—and the fluidity of his temperament as well: no one attending to his rhetoric alone would judge his personal rectitude to be higher than Brutus'. In *Julius Caesar*, Shakespeare dealt in the problems of politics, as of character and motive; nothing is simple here—not even the rhetoric officially designated as "plain." Caesar was and was not a tyrant; Brutus was a good man seduced with lamentable ease; Antony a clever and expedient man, at the same time more loyal than would conventionally be supposed from his casual behavior and his slippery rhetoric. In the play's stylistic *paragone*, all this is implicit: Brutus' honesty and self-deception, Antony's loyalty and his political skills, the cloudy ethics of the whole matter, the deep chasm separating the self-centered patricians from the unstable populace on whose favor their authority so peculiarly rested. Among so much that he has done, Shakespeare has here examined not only the motives of political men engaged by enormous power, but the problematics of public utterance as well, by means of which such motives were traditionally displayed—and concealed.

II

In *Antony and Cleopatra*, the problem of style, although equally telling, is set entirely differently. Oratory and public speaking are not at issue in this play, are not the plot-elements they are in both *Julius Caesar* and *Coriolanus*. Nor is style displayed at the outer surface of the play, as in *Love's Labour's Lost* styles are animated into personality. Nonetheless, its peculiar language is a major force in the play, as critics from Dr. Johnson to Maurice Charney have pointed out; in comparison to the plainer speech of the other Roman plays, the verbal richness of *Antony and Cleopatra* demands attention not only for its spectacular imagery but also as a function of the play's subject. As in *Julius Caesar*, where the economical style seems properly mated to its severe subject, so in *Antony and Cleopatra* the abundance of the language seems to match the richness of its subject, the fertility of the Egyptian setting, the emotional largesse of hero and heroine. The play's language bursts with energy and vigor; figures abound; of figures, as Charney so cleverly shows,[12] hyperbole is particularly common, that overreacher of the figures of speech. Indeed, the figures are so numerous and so rich that at times they seem almost to crowd out other meanings, to stop the action and the plot, to force attention to their resonances alone. Enobarbus' speech on Cleopatra is one example, the most famous of the play's set-pieces; Cleopatra's memories of the absent Antony, her paean to Dolabella, Antony's evaluations of his own emotional and worldly situations raise speech above the movement of plot.

Magniloquence fascinates both hearers and speakers. Antony's "normal" decisions to undertake his Roman responsibilities as triumvir and husband vanish in the hue and cry raised by his emotions and expressed immediately in the language he uses. More markedly, Enobarbus' famous detachment gives way before his recognition of Cleopatra's sources of power. In his great comment on her qualities his magniloquence rolls out to contrast with the plainness and irony of his previous speeches about her. In that speech, Enobarbus abandons himself to Cleopatra, and thereby gives himself away: from his response to her, apparently so out of character, we feel the force of her enchantment. Indeed, Enobarbus' giving way to grandiloquence seems an almost sexual

---

[12] Charney, pp. 79ff.

abandon before her; the cynical and experienced Roman soldier, suspicious of Egypt and its ways, cannot and will not contain his climactic praise of the Queen.

Though the language seems at times to crowd out action and judgment, it does not crowd out meaning, for much of the meaning of this play, as one critic has argued, resides in the characters' attitudes to the language they use.[13] The stated, plotted action of the play is in itself grand enough to require no rival in language: the range of the play is epic, over the whole Mediterranean world which was, in the Roman context, the whole world altogether. Action and scene oscillate[14] between the poles of Rome and Egypt. From the beginning, in Philo's first speech, Rome and Egypt are set off against one another, in the shapes of Caesar and Octavia on the one side, Cleopatra on the other. The two locales, with their properly representative *dramatis personae*, seem to struggle for domination over Mark Antony's spirit and will. Like his great ancestor, the god Hercules, Antony stood at the crossroads of duty and sensuality, of self-denial and self-indulgence. Rome is duty, obligation, austerity, politics, warfare, and honor: Rome is public life. Egypt is comfort, pleasure, softness, seduction, sensuousness (if not sensuality also), variety, and sport: Egypt promises her children rich, languorous pleasures and satisfactions. Rome is business, Egypt is foison; Rome is warfare, Egypt is love. Egypt is "the East," where the beds are soft— and what "beds" can mean is never scanted in this play. To keep us aware of Cleopatra's power, the Romans, in their own eyes contemptuous of her life, show themselves as fascinated by Cleopatra's reputation as a bedfellow as Antony is by the actuality. Egypt is florid, decorated, deceitful, artful, opulent, sensual, idle; is "inflatus," "solutus," "tumens," "superfluens," "redundans,"

---

[13] Charney, *Roman Plays*, pp. 93ff; and see John Danby, "The Shakespearean Dialectic: An aspect of *Antony and Cleopatra*," in *Poets on Fortune's Hill* (London, 1952); William Rosen, *Shakespeare and the Craft of Tragedy* (Cambridge, Mass., 1960); Robert Ornstein, "The Ethic [*sic*] of Imagination: Love and Art in *Antony and Cleopatra*," *The Later Shakespeare, Stratford-upon-Avon Studies*, VIII (1966); Maynard Mack, Introduction to *Antony and Cleopatra* (Pelican Shakespeare, Baltimore, 1960), p. 19.

[14] "Oscillate" is Danby's word; see also Northrop Frye, *Fools of Time* (Toronto, 1967), pp. 70-71; Mack, Introduction, pp. 19-20; Ernest Schanzer, *The Problem Plays of Shakespeare* (New York, 1965), pp. 138-39; Charney, pp. 93ff.; Dipak Nandy, "The Realism of *Antony and Cleopatra*," in *Shakespeare in a Changing World*, ed. Arnold Kettle (London, 1964), pp. 172-94.

"enervis," "inanus."[15] I took this list of Latin adjectives from various critiques, not of the fleshpots of Egypt, but of the Asiatic style; these epithets can, within the frame of this play, be transferred to the loose, ungirt life in Alexandria, the life to which, according to the source, Antony was inclined by temperament and which, in the end, he chooses as his own.

The question at issue is another dimension of style from those already discussed: not style as garment, or as chosen rhetoric or self-presentation, not style as manipulative instrument, but style as fundamental morality, style as life. Style of speech necessarily reveals personality, values, and ethics: one recognizes both the rectitude and the chilliness of Octavia, the silliness of Lepidus, the policy of Dolabella, from the way they speak as well as from what they say. In the speeches of Antony, Cleopatra, Octavius, Enobarbus, we recognize not just the varying moods of the speakers but their complex inner natures as well. How otherwise, indeed, could we ever assume anything about dramatic characters? Language must act to indicate quality and character, but here it does more: by reaching to the heart of the moral problems faced by Antony and Cleopatra, the language of their play makes us realize anew the ingrained connection between speech and style of life. The "square" of Roman speech and Roman life has its values, which we recognize the more easily as we see those values betrayed by Romans;[16] the "foison" of Egypt, both its fertility and its corruption, find expression in the *agon*. If one felt that the play were only an essay in style as life-style, then one might draw back from it as superficial and trivial; but *Antony and Cleopatra* seems to be more than a presentation-play of theatrical and unpersoned types, more also than the *psychomachia* to which it is occasionally reduced.[17] One thing that makes the play so compelling is that it *is* all these things—show, morality, exercise of power; it *is* a study in cheapness as well as in extravagance and costliness. Its chief characters are undisguisedly selfish and often trivial; in what lies its force? The language is one indicator, again, for the very style, with its grandioseness and hyperbolical explosions, finally points to the real problem: the

---

15 Leeman, pp. 140-41.

16 The point is made by many critics; see Julian Markels, *The Pillar of the World* (Columbus, 1968), pp. 35, 41-43.

17 See, e.g., J. Leeds Barroll, "Enobarbus' Description of Cleopatra," *Texas Studies in Language and Literature* (1958), pp. 61-68.

efforts of two powerful, wilful, commanding personalities to bring their styles of living, their ingrained alien habits, into line with one another, for no reason other than love.

In a sense quite different from that of the morality-play, *Antony and Cleopatra* is about morality, about *mores* and ways of life—not by any means just about sexual morality, although problems of sexuality are not ignored—but about lives lived in moral terms. "Style" is—especially in the Attic-Asiatic polarity—a moral indicator, but here displayed as deeply thrust into the psychological and cultural roots of those ways of life. In this play, a given style is never merely an alternative way of expressing something: rather, styles arise from cultural sources beyond a character's choice or control.[18]

At the beginning of the play, this does not seem to be the case: Antony doffs and dons Egyptian and Roman styles, of speech and of life, apparently at will and at need. By the play's end, he has settled for a manner of speech and behavior proved by his decisive final actions to be the signature of his inmost nature. That is to say, his style can be seen not only to express his deepest sense of self, but also to relate to the consequences of his life-choices.[19] It is possible—indeed, it was the classical view, which Plutarch tried hard to present—to see Mark Antony's life as ruined by Cleopatra, to see the play, then, as a struggle between *virtus* and *voluptas*[20] in which Antony fails to live up to his ancestor Hercules' example *in bivio*. But as Plutarch takes pains to tell us, and as Shakespeare in *Julius Caesar* lets us know clearly enough, there was much in Antony's temperament, bred though it was in Rome, to explain why the pull of Egypt was so strong upon him, and from Enobarbus we know how strong that pull

[18] I do not here speak of Antony's self-deception, of which Proser and Markels write so well, so much as of the *cultural* force of his language, with its sources in Roman ideas of magnanimity and greatness as well as in Roman ideas of duty and service. There is, also, a major literary source for Antony's speech and self-presentation, in the *Aeneid*—though Antony, as his references to Aeneas and Dido indicate, did not choose (like Aeneas) to subdue his passions to his mission: Antony is, in this sense, a reviser of the story. For this, as for much else, I am indebted to discussions with Roger Hornsby.

[19] See Arnold Stein, "The Image of Antony: Lyric and Tragic Imagination," reprinted in *Essays in Shakespearean Criticism*, ed. James L. Calderwood and Harold E. Toliver (Englewood Cliffs, 1970), pp. 560-75.

[20] Barroll, *passim*; Schanzer, p. 155. This notion is qualified in the work of Barbara Bono (still unpublished) and of Raymond Waddington: see below, footnote 34.

was on anyone. Though there is a structural and thematic contrast in the play between Rome and Egypt, the scenes alternating to give us that strong sense of oscillation between these poles, the play is not so simple as a straight contest between their different values.

Seen from one perspective, Rome dominates the play: Rome's wide arch covers the epic scene, Roman policy decides the order of events and the order therefore of these important private lives. The play begins and ends with expressions of the Roman point of view; by Roman standards, Antony perishes for his failure as a Roman. But seen from another angle, Egypt commands the play, where the action begins and ends and where all the major episodes take place. In this respect, the oscillation between the two localities makes it difficult to identify a single and certain source of power. Further, the two areas are not really kept polar: Rome and Egypt interpenetrate each other, just as past history continually penetrates the play's present. Rome's impact on Egypt has helped make Cleopatra what she is; and Antony's Roman-ness flaws his pleasure in Egypt, even as his Egyptian experience dulls his Roman arrangements. Together and apart, Antony and Cleopatra recall their own and each other's past; Octavius speaks of Antony's and his shared past; Pompey takes the action he does because of events long over before the play begins. We see Antony unwillingly come to accept the fact that his present has been shaped by his past behavior, or that his "Rome" can never be an unqualified value again. Cleopatra dies as a Roman, or so she thinks—but does so in a *décor* undeniably Egyptian, and by a means particularly local. Her attributes, the iconographical details she chooses for her last tableau, are entirely Egyptian, but her suicide is itself the final Roman gesture consciously chosen.

Nor is the mixture of Rome and Egypt in her accidental: deep in her experience lay the same Julius Caesar who had such a marked effect on both Mark Antony and Octavius Caesar. Before the play's beginning, Cleopatra and her Egypt had been Romanized; by its end, she is once more Romanized, and her Egypt has finally fallen to Roman rule. Indeed, throughout the play, Egypt is constantly open to Rome: Cleopatra's relation to Julius Caesar, to Pompey, to Antony, even her efforts to charm Octavius, are symbolic of her country's dependency upon Rome's dominion. The presence at her court (a court "hers" only by the conqueror's grace) of so many Romans, full of what she calls with distaste "Roman thoughts," assures that the force of Rome upon Egypt is never unfelt, even at the height of Egyptian wassail.

However he may think of himself, Antony is a Roman soldier; Roman soldiers are always with him, even at the moment of his death. When he is away from Egypt, Roman messengers bring Cleopatra news of him and of affairs in Rome. He himself was sent to Egypt as a political administrator; he is succeeded at the play's end by Caesar himself, the last of a series of Romans proclaiming the dominion of the empire, Thidias, Dolabella, Proculeius. People die *à la romaine*: Enobarbus, Eros, Antony, Cleopatra, Charmian, Iras. Antony is borne to die his long-drawn-out death after the high Roman fashion; Cleopatra promises a like death, in which she shall be "marble constant" at the end of a life lived, publicly and privately, in significantly "infinite variety." There is no altering Roman historical destiny, however captivating Egypt and the Egyptian way of life may be.

As the play begins, we are instructed to take Roman virtues for granted as the measure from which Antony has fallen off, but as it develops, we are shown more and more to criticize in Rome.[21] No one could be sillier than Lepidus, one of the triple pillars of the world, grosser and more clownish than any Egyptian; nor more opportunistic than Menas, whose master regrets only that Menas forced him to veto his schemes. Octavius calculates ever; Pompey seeks his own ambitious ends; Octavius' relation to Roman polity is hardly self-subordinating. Further and most important, when he is "Roman," Antony is at his least attractive—in his relations to his Roman wives, Fulvia and Octavia, both dismissed in his mind's economy as terms of political function. As the play advances, the notion of Rome becomes more and more tarnished, particularly in the great orgy-scene in which even Octavius' tongue "splits what it speaks," and Lepidus is carried drunk to bed (a scene unmatched in the play by the "sensual" Egyptians so constantly criticized by these same Roman tongues). In that scene, the grossness of Rome is unequivocally displayed in the unbending ambitions of Caesar, the jealousy of the triumvirs, the thinness of Pompey's honor, Menas' crude hankering after power, the heroes' dancing to their roundsong. Into such hands the world has been delivered. Of course "Egypt"

---

[21] Again, most critics comment on this: see Markels, pp. 35, 41-43; Ornstein, p. 393, for especially interesting comments.

offers no moral improvement over this—Cleopatra lies from first to last, to others and to herself. We are never in doubt of her duplicity, but its naturalness comes to seem worthy in comparison to the slyness of Octavius and of the "trustworthy" Proculeius. Cleopatra's is a consistent and therefore honest duplicity: her policy is innocence itself compared to the masterful and automatic deceptions of the politic Octavius. More: life in its natural spontaneity is set against machination, as Cleopatra faces Octavius symbolically and in fact. Against such an opposition, all the more obviously can Cleopatra be seen to satisfy a universal human need: though she makes hungry where most she satisfies, both hunger and satisfaction are natural enough. The Roman hunger for power can never be filled; in it there is always something barren, inhuman, and perverse—but Cleopatra can allay, even as she rekindles, one Roman's hunger for the satisfactions of love.

III

The question at issue is not so much the value of Rome set against the value of Egypt, clear as these are, as it is the private relation between Antony and Cleopatra, a relation always colored by their different backgrounds and local loyalties. Normally speaking, it is not considered admirable, nor even sensible, for a man of public position to jeopardize his career for a woman. When the man is Antony, well-married in Rome and well-supplied elsewhere, and the woman Cleopatra, full of experience and of years, it is easy enough to see the matter with Roman eyes as a dissolute business between middle-aged sensualists having a last fling while they can, sinking into sloth and indolence and letting the affairs of empire go hang. Further, there is opportunism even in this love affair—that Cleopatra's political position was immensely strengthened by Antony's presence in Egypt, Caesar's sharp observations make plain. The suspicion certainly exists that she loves Antony for what he can do for her as well as for what he is to her.

The play begins with a Roman inductor, who takes the worst for granted. Philo (what a name for him!) evaluates the major characters according to accepted Roman standards; his critical speech breaks off as Antony and Cleopatra enter to act out what he has just, so degradingly, described as their typical behavior:

Nay, but this dotage of our general's
O'erflows the measure: those his goodly eyes,
That o'er the files and musters of the war
Have glow'd like plated Mars, now bend, now turn
The office and devotion of their view
Upon a tawny front: his captain's heart,
Which in the scuffles of great fights hath burst
The buckles on his breast, reneges all temper
And is become the bellows and the fan
To cool a gipsy's lust.
                         Look, where they come:
Take but good note, and you shall see in him
The triple pillar of the world transform'd
Into a strumpet's fool: behold and see.   (I.i.1-13)

The hero and heroine then enter, to act out their tableau of mutual absorption. They behave with freedom towards each other
—perhaps with abandon, indeed—but *not* as strumpet and fool.
Their language, that of lovers bent on ideal expression, is thus
quite counter to Philo's assessment of them:

Cleo.:   If it be love indeed, tell me how much.
Ant.:   There's beggary in love that can be reckon'd.
Cleo.:   I'll set a bourn how far to be belov'd.
Ant.:   Then must thou needs find out new heaven, new earth.
                                                (I.i.14-17)

The inflation of their language may strike us, but hardly as exceptional in any pair of lovers mutually absorbed. Rather, theirs
is the common rhetoric of love, unspecified and generalized, seeking to express inexpressible heights and depths of feeling. Cosmic analogies are habitually called up by lovers less involved
than these in the "real" world; the fact that Antony and Cleopatra are so deeply involved in the factual political world lends
poignancy, irony, and a kind of accuracy to their occupational
hyperbole. The "new heaven, new earth" of their love, created
by them for themselves alone, must substitute for the real geography around them, the Mediterranean world over which their
influence and the play's action range. Symbolic geography is invoked, with its real referents: Rome, Alexandria, Athens, Sicily,
Sardinia, Parthia, Judea, Media, Mesopotamia, Syria, Armenia,

Cyprus, Lydia, Cilicia, Phoenicia, Libya, Cappadocia, Paphlagonia, Thrace, Arabia, Pontus all testify to the reach of Rome, whose "universal peace," proclaimed by Caesar, was endangered by Antony's withdrawal from the world-scene in wilful, careless, selfish pursuit of private satisfactions.

All this real world, then, was insufficient for these two—but more important than that, it was also too much for them. To keep their love safe, they must shut out the actual world in hopes of finding a new space for themselves small enough[22] to exclude occupations other than love, large enough to contain their exalted imaginations. In this play, the common literary metaphor of lovers' giving up the world for love is taken as the literal *donnée*: meaning pours back to give substance to the cliché, as the play teaches something of the human cost involved in neglecting the serious public world, the glories and woes of war and administration, for love of one woman.

Antony and Cleopatra speak "excessively" from the beginning, in an idiom familiar enough in love-poetry.[23] But it is worth noting that they are not alone in this habit of overstatement: Philo's initial speech is wholly cast in terms of excess. He degrades the amorous exploits of his commander with Egypt's queen, certainly: his account of that commander's military accomplishments is as excessive as his contumelious commentary on Antony's amatory achievements. Antony's eyes in war "glow'd like plated Mars"; "his captain's heart . . . burst the buckles on his breast." Caesar's speech too follows the pattern of overstatement: he makes the same kind of contrast of Antony's "lascivious wassails" and "tumblings on the bed of Ptolemy" to his astonishing endurance at Modena and on the Alps (I.iv.55-71). Whatever Antony does, it seems, "o'erflows the measure"—but the Romans can *recognize* excess only in Antony's un-Roman acts: the heroic rest is, to them, natural in a Roman. Excess, then, is culturally conditioned: men recognize as excessive only what they regard as "too much," so that Romans who valued military extravagance as much as Cleopatra valued extravagant pleasures could find in

22 On world-imagery, see Charney, pp. 82-93, an extremely perceptive analysis.

23 See Stein, *passim*; though their language relies on expression conventionally assigned to lovers, Antony's and Cleopatra's speech, with its curiously generalized, unspecified imagery, suggests an enlarged range of love. Theirs is, in language as in life, an *extreme* love, fully human but at the edge of human capacity.

her Antony much to praise. When Octavius denounces Antony's self-indulgence, he calls him "A man who is the abstract of all faults/ That all men follow." Who could be more than this, an epitome of ill? Taking exception to Octavius' statement, Lepidus casts his comments in terms equally hyperbolical:

> I must not think there are
> Evils enow to darken all his goodness:
> His faults in him, seem as the spots of heaven,
> More fiery by night's blackness.   (I.iv.10-13)

What are we to make of Antony, then? What are we to make of his present love-experience, judged by Philo as tawdry and low, judged by the lovers as quite past the reach of expression? In fact, what do Antony and Cleopatra *do*? We are told (by Romans) how they pass their time, in behavior characterized as "Asiatic" in the extreme. Egypt is, certainly, "the East," regularly so designated in the play. As queen, Cleopatra is often addressed by her country's name; when she dies, she is called "the eastern star," that is, the planet Venus. What Antony and Cleopatra do, evidently, is live by the attributes of the Asiatic style; they act out, they and the Romans tell us, a life-style gaudy, loose, ungirt, decorated, artful, contrived, and deceitful. The Egyptian court is an idle, opulent, sensual, Asiatic place, where men are effeminate and women bold. Mardian the eunuch exists to remind us of what can happen to a man in such an environment, and we see Antony unmanned in various symbolic ways. Normal decorum is constantly breached by this general, this queen. Drunk, Antony will not hear his messages from Rome; playing with Cleopatra, he relinquishes his armor to her and dresses in her "tires and mantles." She takes his sword away, and though she returns it before their battle, she disarms him entirely in the midst of a real battle, by more critical means. Publicly she ignores him, however preoccupied with him privately. Nor is she manly, for all the dressing in armor and proclaiming herself a man's equal before the last battle. At Actium she flees out of fear, and retires in the last pitch as well: when Antony is dying before her eyes, she will not emerge from her monument, nor even open its doors that he may easily be brought in to her—because, she says, she is afraid.

In Egypt men feast and sleep. "The beds in the East are soft" in many ways. Both defeat and victory are celebrated in Egypt

185

by one other gaudy night, and Caesar seems to acknowledge this Egyptian need for self-indulgence when, to reassure the captive Cleopatra, he urges her to "Feed and sleep." Though the meanings of "sleep" deepen radically by the end of the play, at the beginning and for the most part, "sleep" is a sign of Egyptian indolence and womanishness. Festivities are unmanly too; Caesar says of his great competitor:

> From Alexandria
> This is the news: he fishes, drinks, and wastes
> The lamps of night in revel; is not more manlike
> Than Cleopatra; nor the queen of Ptolemy
> More womanly than he.   (I.iv.3-7)

His last comment may indicate Caesar's limitations as a judge of human character, but it also sums up the Roman attitude to Egypt, a place merely of "lascivious wassails." The way most Romans think of Cleopatra, it is no wonder that she shrinks, at the end, from being carried through Rome to see "some squeaking Cleopatra boy my greatness/I' the posture of a whore." She knows how she is named in Rome, because in his rage Antony tells her:

> I found you as a morsel, cold upon
> Dead Caesar's trencher; nay, you were a fragment
> Of Gnaeus Pompey's, besides what hotter hours,
> Unregister'd in vulgar fame, you have
> Luxuriously pick'd out.   (III.xiii.116-20)

Again and again, "appetite" is a word used to cover all satisfactions. Feasting and love (or, better, sex) are equated, as in the passage just quoted. Cleopatra is often reduced to food—by Enobarbus, speaking of Antony, "He will to his Egyptian dish again"; by herself, in her youth "a morsel for a monarch," although those were, as she says, her "salad days," when she was both greener and colder than she later became.[24] Pompey speaks man-to-man to Antony of "your fine Egyptian cookery" (II.vii.63-65) and, later, of the "cloyless sauce" that Egypt proves for Antony.

Unquestionably the preoccupation with sex and with the shared sexuality of Antony and Cleopatra runs as an undercur-

---

24 Charney, pp. 102-104.

rent through the play. The difference between Egyptian and Roman talk of sex is instructive: Charmian and the Soothsayer, Cleopatra and the Eunuch, speak playfully and naturally; Enobarbus speaks cynically to and about Antony, on "death," on horses and mares; and the other Romans show their prurience and crudity when they speak, as they compulsively do, about the subject. The imagery too carries its sexual meanings: Cleopatra's "sweating labour" joins with the imagery of bearing and of weight to remind us of the woman's part in the act of love. This language in turn conjoins with the marvelous and varied horse-imagery[25] which reaches its peak as she imagines the absent Antony on horseback: "O happy horse, to bear the weight of Antony!" Such language assumes sexuality to be a normal part of life; the Nile-imagery, with its "quickenings" and "foison" references, suggests procreation and creation as part of a natural cycle. Nature provides reproductive images for sexuality, and war another sort. The constant reference to swords, in fact as in image, keeps manliness ever at the forefront of our awareness, as it is at the forefront of the dramatic characters' awareness, too.[26]

There is more than the suggestion, then, that love is no more than appetite or a drive; if that were all there was to love, the Roman view of this affair would be correct, Cleopatra simply a whore and Antony besotted, "ne'er lust-wearied." But can a man remain "ne'er lust-wearied" by the same woman, however infinite her variety, if she is merely a whore, however aristocratic her birth?[27] Enobarbus, in so many ways faithful to Antony and Cleopatra in spite of his disapproval of their behavior, sees something more in her and tries to say what that "more" is. Once again, significantly, he speaks in terms of food—"Other women cloy/ The appetites they feed, but she makes hungry,/ Where most she satisfies." Mere sexuality, strong sexual love, idealized love: however it is described, the emotions shared by Antony and Cleopatra challenge the heroic world of Roman military organization.

This miracle of love (or whatever it is) we do not see acted out onstage. Indeed, we never see Antony and Cleopatra alone, as

[25] G. Wilson Knight, *The Imperial Theme* (repr. London, 1965), pp. 212, 213, collects the imagery of horses in this play, and comments on the different associations it calls up.

[26] Charney, pp. 127-29.

[27] For this, see Markels, especially p. 150.

we do Romeo and Juliet, Desdemona and Othello. What we see is something quite different: a man and a woman playing, quarreling, making up; a woman sulking, pretending to anger, flying into real rages, running away from danger, flirting even in deep disgrace and danger. Except on Roman tongues, there is little that can be called shameless or lascivious in Cleopatra's or Antony's utterances about love: her language on this preoccupying subject is remarkably clean—which is not the case with Roman commentators on these spectacular lovers.

To make so commonplace, so vulgar a mixture into a woman worth losing the world for is a considerable task for any playwright. Our playwright accomplishes it by fairly simple, even domestic, means. His Cleopatra has, among other things, a girlish, hoydenish companionability. She is obviously amusing company; she will try anything once. She has a lovely imagination and considerable command of language. She tries to rise to occasions, and sometimes she does. We hear much of Cleopatra's whoredom, and we see Antony blundering after her, twice fatally; we hear him speak of the less pleasant side of his love, of the "Egyptian fetters" which tie him in Alexandria, of his "dotage," and later, when he misses her in Rome, of his "pleasure" with Cleopatra. There is every reason to think very little of Cleopatra—although, to balance her crudities (as when she had a salt-fish attached to Antony's line), we are made to see that even in her breaches of decorum, her riggishness, her foolish middle age, she is delightful. She is earthy, and down-to-earth;[28] her sudden accessions of realism puncture both the romanticizing of the lovers and Antony's simplistic view of love and Cleopatra as satisfaction to his appetite. This woman is something more:

> Sir, you and I must part . . .
> Sir, you and I have lov'd. . . .   (I.iii.87-88)

> In praising Antony, I have disprais'd Caesar . . .
> I am paid for't now.   (II.v.107-109)

> Think you there was, or might be such a man
> As this I dreamt of?   (v.ii.93-94)

---

[28] This in spite of the fact that she is "all air and fire": the elements, earth, water, air, and fire, are all used in connection with Cleopatra, a world in herself.

> Antony
> Shall be brought drunken forth, and I shall see
> Some squeaking Cleopatra boy my greatness
> I' the posture of a whore.   (v.ii.218-20)

When her ironical common sense pierces her own theatricals, her charm is irresistible: though she rarely acts on that knowledge, we see that at moments she knows herself and the precarious, politicking world she lives in. It is this side of her, the practical, real woman, that is picked up in Charmian's farewell epithet: to "a *lass* unparallel'd." Age, apparently, could not wither her, nor a rakish life, nor child-bearing.

But in her first parting from Antony, as in her exchange with Dolabella after Antony's death and just before her own, Cleopatra's common sense rises to something greater:

> Sir, you and I must part, but that's not it:
> Sir, you and I have lov'd, but there's not it. . . .

The facts are clear enough—but they do not provide Cleopatra with an explanation for the pressure of her feelings, that this love for Antony is unduly significant, that parting from him must radically diminish her. Her sentence loses its direction as she seeks to express the "more" of her feeling for him:

> That you know well, something it is I would,—
> O, my oblivion is a very Antony,
> And I am all forgotten!   (i.iii.89-91)

As she later says, she wants to sleep out "the great gap of time" that Antony is away from her; in his absence, even by herself, she is, imaginatively, "forgotten" and therefore does not exist. Both Antony and Cleopatra speak feelingly and movingly about their sense of identity lost. Part of their tragedy lies in Antony's feeling himself dissolve when he is with her, and Cleopatra's feeling her "nothingness" when he is not with her.

Cleopatra makes clear that her love for Antony is fully sexual; but, as has been noted,[29] this emphasis comes in reverie, not in lascivious action or exchange. What is significant, surely, is that in a life given to sexual conquest and enjoyment, her relation to Antony means more to her than anything else. It is not that

[29] Ornstein, p. 391.

Cleopatra does not want to be reminded of her old connection with Caesar; it is that she knows its qualitative difference from the connection with Antony. Certainly Cleopatra does not shirk the facts of her sexual past; however giddy and irresponsible her behavior with Antony, though, she knows that for him, she has quit being a rake. For her, sexuality is never just the "pleasure" that Antony implies early in the play it is for him. It has (at last, one has the impression) risen above itself to become love of a sort that defies definition in psychological ways, not just in "literary" ways.[30] Indeed, in literary ways, the lovers' extreme preoccupation with one another is almost *too* resonant to the conventional language of love: as in *Othello*, but in an entirely different context, the petrarchan mixture of love and war has here been actualized in the necessary conditions, unmetaphored into actuality, of everyday life for this general and this queen. But the love-poet's transcendent aim is the same as theirs: how to express the indefinable love they share, a love that to unsympathetic onlookers seems ordinary enough, vulgar enough, but to the lover experiencing it inexpressibly glorious and valuable. Their language is pitched at the familiar literary goal, to make the "new heaven, new earth" of lovers' cliché into a universe for their exclusive dwelling. Their *folie à deux* is in part a matter of language, manipulated to record heightened experience and to displace both conventional and particular renditions of their experience by others.

Cleopatra's imagination particularly works at this task: if sex is the reality and imagination the fantasy of love, then the two fuse in Cleopatra's speech in Antony's absence from her, when she imagines him as he at that very moment actually *is*:

> Stands he, or sits he?
> Or does he walk? or is he on his horse?

> (I.v.19-20)

Her sexual memories crowd into the single line, "O happy horse, to bear the weight of Antony!" Her images of weight, realistic enough in any woman's experience of love, come to their culmination in the terrible scene of Antony's death, as she draws him into her monument:

---

30 One way in which Caesar is made to seem young, inexperienced, and closed to human experience is that he is completely unaware of this aspect of either Antony or Cleopatra.

How heavy weighs my lord!
Our strength is all gone into heaviness,
That makes the weight.   (IV.xv.32-34)

The reality is there, although not displayed to us, of the children
she has borne him; "the lap of Egypt's widow," as Pompey so
rudely said, has actually held Antony and known what it was to
do so. Finally, to her "demi-Atlas" she attributes more weight
than any man can carry; she turns her love into an even more
colossal personage than the world will recognize or can, in the
person of Dolabella, accept.

IV

In this habit of stretching expression, of trying to say more
than words or figures habitually allow, lies some clue to the effect on each other of these lovers. They make each other feel that
age is no bar to living fully; they make each other feel, not still
alive, but more than usually alive, a feeling, however illusory,
which can exercise curious power over a man and a woman
more than commonly experienced. The connection between
them, obviously, is quite different from other experiences they
have had; Cleopatra knows this from the beginning of the play,
and we witness Antony coming to know it too.[31] It is precisely his
marriage to Octavia, with all its chilly merits, that teaches him
what Cleopatra is to him. In their view of each other, Antony
and Cleopatra are more than lifesize. So Cleopatra speaks truth
in her great speech of hyperbole about Antony:

I dreamt there was an Emperor Antony.
O such another sleep, that I might see
But such another man! . . .
His face was as the heavens, and therein stuck
A sun and moon, which kept their course, and lighted
The little O, the earth. . . .
His legs bestrid the ocean, his rear'd arm
Crested the world: his voice was propertied
As all the tuned spheres, and that to friends:
But when he meant to quail, and shake the orb,
He was as rattling thunder. For his bounty,

[31] Again, Mr. Markels seems to me the critic who preeminently expresses
both the universally human and the particular, specific experience of love depicted in this play.

> There was no winter in 't: an autumn 'twas
> That grew the more by reaping: his delights
> Were dolphin-like, they show'd his back above
> The element they liv'd in: in his livery
> Walk'd crowns and crownets: realms and islands were
> As plates dropp'd from his pocket. (v.ii.76-92)

Antony has then finally turned into that "new heaven, new earth" he had told Cleopatra in the first scene she must find as the appropriate bound of their love. Microcosm and macrocosm change places: the earth is smaller than this man, as the common cosmic metaphor expands into all space and more-than-time in the images of ever-ripe autumn and a creature, the dolphin, transcending his natural element.[32] Correspondence imagery involving worlds in different scales—the cosmos, however thought of; macrocosm and microcosm; stars and eyes—is so common in sixteenth- and seventeenth-century poetry as to be mere cliché, and certainly at one level, all Cleopatra is doing in this magnificent speech is making more extravagant a notion already hyperbolical at its base. But in this particular case of lovers, the standard hyperbole has its peculiar reality to "match" this particular psychological and political situation. In the imagery, the larger world has been contracted into the limits of Antony's body (normally a microcosm), and Antony's body in turn enlarged encompasses and surpasses the macrocosm to which originally it had been likened. In fact, this is what happened to these lovers: "the world," in this case half or a third of the civilized world which was under their control, was rejected in favor of the "little world," quite literally, of man. "Bodies" are very important in the play, and although Antony and Cleopatra speak with remarkable delicacy about each other's bodies and their own bodily sensations in love, this speech gives the literary justification for that physical love. Hyperbolic metaphor that it is, this speech at the same time unmetaphors its literary content by making plain the crucial importance to these lovers of their finite, particular, well-worn bodies.

[32] Another "philosophical" suggestion of Antony's being more than a man lies in the implications of this simile, in which a creature "transcends" its element: so he, a man, becomes (at least in Cleopatra's imagination) a god. See also Ruth Nevo, "The Masque of Greatness," *S. Stud.*, III (1967), 111-28, for the "gigantism" of the play, and the "cosmic contrived into a pageant."

Cleopatra does not linger on the fantasy, but asks Dolabella, with the realism characteristic of her:

> Think you there was, or might be such a man
> As this I dreamt of? (v.ii.93-94)

To that, Roman Dolabella can only respond, "Gentle madam, no"—which serves to arouse Cleopatra to still more immense reaches of imagery, to language rejecting anything nature can offer as fit comparison to the wonder that Antony was. This time momentary realism touched off, as it habitually does not, the reassertion of hyperbole's value. Hyperbole becomes "true"— and yet even that hyperbolical language is not "enough" for the intense feelings between these two overreachers of life. In the references within the play, they are always more than merely human, more than triumvir and queen: Cleopatra was, we hear, more beautiful than the most beautiful picture of Venus. Art cannot render her, nor can nature's works render Antony. In her eulogy of him, Cleopatra never denies his manhood—"My man of men," she says, and she should know—but the manhood she attributes to him no ordinary mortal can aspire to. His bounty was endless—and his treatment of Enobarbus suggests that this is so—his delights transcendent. His empire was to be prodigal of imperial power—"as plates dropp'd from his pocket." Compare that magnificence with Caesar's careful accounting of Mark Antony's distribution of empire in iii.vi: for Caesar, these political entities which Mark Antony gave away were no mere "plates" but the extended possessions of Rome, to be protected, at cost, for Rome's sake.

Cleopatra's imagination is as bountiful as Antony's generosity. Her language is rich as her habitat, and she is, as both detractors and admirers point out, histrionic to a degree. She stages herself at Cydnus; she stages herself as dead for Antony; she stages herself for her death. She speaks and is spoken of in theatrical terms of scene, act, and stage; she is a creature of impulse and whim, which she tries out on her audiences, acting to Dolabella, to Caesar, to Antony, acting even with her familiar maids. That habit of acting stands her in good stead in her determination to outwit Caesar at the end. Reversing Marx's famous quip, this play first acts out in farce what becomes tragedy a second time through. Cleopatra pretends to be dead—trivially, but with horrible results for Antony—before she dies in earnest. The theme of death echoes throughout the play—the lovers know, long before the crisis, the cost of their choice. Enobarbus plays on the slang term, "death," for sexual intercourse, when Antony first tells him he must be gone; his cynicism can seem justified to an audience which sees Cleopatra feign illness and death. Her coquetry, charming within the domestic protections of her court, is fatal on the battlefield. It is worth noting that for the deceit which cost him his life, Mark Antony never reproaches her; instead, he promises to be "A bridegroom in my death, and run into 't/As to a lover's bed." She too equates love and death: "The stroke of death is as a lover's pinch,/Which hurts, and is desir'd." She dies to join Mark Antony—"Husband, I come"—as his wife, taking for granted the meaning of a simple social act which could never take place in the Roman world during their lives. Put in the simplest terms, the word "death" is gradually ennobled by what happens in the play—but not before its seamier implications have all been laid before us.

So the play begins to live up to itself. As Philo's crudity is submerged under the lovers' flood of words, again and again the nasty turns out to have its noble aspect too, the Gorgon indeed becomes Mars. Because the playwright never shirks the unpleasantness, the triviality, even the occasional brutality of the lovers, because he always allows them to recognize and to reveal the compulsiveness of their love, its literal extremity, that love's peculiar force begins to take its confirmation from the radical action and the extreme language. As we watch the hyperbole coming true, we recognize a maturing of emotions more than lifesize to begin with, commanding a space of their own making, relying on their mutual respect for their own worth. The simplicity, singleheartedness, and intensity of this faulty human love, magnificent in spite of the lovers' politics and duplicity, in spite of the inevitable deceits of their world, come to seem a far greater achievement, against greater odds, than the successful Roman quest for power.

And for this, as we shall see, there is theoretical precedent in Longinus' defense of the style Antony and his acquaintances used, a style designed to express generosity, magnitude, magnanimity; a style, as he put it, "with the true ring of a noble mind."[33] Though Shakespeare does not slight the cultural structure and

---

[33] Longinus, *On the Sublime* (LCL), pp. 144-45.

construction of any style—Roman, Egyptian here, Navarrese else-where—he is concerned in this play with the significance of a personal style within the cultural matrix, with what Longinus called "μεγαλοφροσύνη." Though we know, from Philo's initial speech, of Antony's capacity for greatness and perceive, in his dealings with Enobarbus and Cleopatra, his magnanimity in the face of terrible losses, he still has to live up to the nobility of his soul and to the elevation of his speech. Still more Cleopatra, unused to Roman gestures of magnanimity: from riggish, rakish queen who plays tricks with a man's honor and his life, she must grow into the moral capacities her hyperbole seems to make light of.

The risks are great—how does a man, how can a woman, leave off grandiose and bombastic play-acting, even to the roles of god and goddess, to die as heroes? The lovers set their sights high from the start: chose as their models superhuman figures from Roman mythology—Antony in the play's first speech is likened to Mars, Cleopatra unmistakably to Venus.[34] They act out that archetypal coupling throughout their lives, even to receiving mockery like the gods of Venus and Mars. Cleopatra is a goddess of love in her disguises, both the Roman Venus and the Egyptian Isis: she celebrated her greatest political triumph, over Antony and by his means over Rome, dressed "in the habiliments of the goddess Isis," as Caesar in outrage reports. Isis was also a moon-goddess, whose variability, reflected in the feminine psychology, is made much of in the play; her "habiliments," as Plutarch tells us in another place, are varicolored, to show her involvement with all nature—with light as well as dark, fire as well as water, life as well as death, beginning as well as ending. These robes are singularly appropriate to Cleopatra: they symbolize all matter and "afford many disclosures of themselves, and opportunities to view them as they are changed about in various ways."[35] Cleopatra is too much

[34] I have been greatly helped in the matter of the mythographic element of this play by the published work of Raymond B. Waddington, "Antony and Cleopatra: 'What Venus Did with Mars,'" S. Stud., II (1966); and of Harold Fisch, "Antony and Cleopatra: the Limits of Mythology," SS, XXIII (1970), 59-68 (whose argument seems to me too fine-spun, particularly in his reliance on Christian myth); and by the unpublished work of Barbara Bono, which reaches very subtle and illuminating conclusions about the play. See also Adrien Bonjour, "From Shakespeare's Venus to Cleopatra's Cupids," S.Stud., XVI (1963), 73-80.

[35] Plutarch, Isis and Osiris, Moralia, v; see Michael Lloyd, "Cleopatra as Isis," S.Stud., XII (1959).

a woman, variable and faulty, to "be" either Venus or Isis, but she takes the part of both of them; posing as these goddesses, she occasionally takes on some of their meanings, as Antony on occasion takes on some of the meanings attributed to Mars and Hercules.[36] In addition, this pair is too intermingled in one another for such an interpretation: whatever their natural attributes making them godlike, Antony and Cleopatra are a man and a woman to each other and to the world.[37]

Although it is as a man that she most values him, Cleopatra symbolically and actually unmans Antony. We hear of her dressing him in her clothes, as Omphale did Hercules.[38] His decline from perfect manhood to something less than that is part of Antony's tragedy. In this play, however, the facts of the Roman idea of manhood are examined again and again and found wanting, particularly in respect to the very quality Antony so lavishly displays, magnanimity. He was a generous, a prodigal man, but always a man large of spirit. Largesse is his attribute, in all senses. He gave away his goods to his soldiers in defeat; his graciousness drove the defected Enobarbus to his shamefast death. To Antony's naturally great character Octavius stands in cheerless contrast; and no one in Rome, ever, is shown as rising to Antony's heights of grace. Again and again we are brought up against the hard realization that if to be a Roman is to be so narrow and calculating as Octavius, so vulgar as Pompey, so divided as Enobarbus, then Antony has surely chosen the better part. Octavius speaks beautifully of Antony's death:

> The breaking of so great a thing should make
> A greater crack. The round world
> Should have shook lions into civil streets,
> And citizens to their dens. The death of Antony
> Is not a single doom; in the name lay
> A moiety of the world.   (v.i.14-19)

[36] Eugene M. Waith, Jr., *The Herculean Hero in Marlowe, Chapman, Shakespeare, and Dryden* (New York, 1962), discusses this aspect of Antony's character and behavior; see also Plutarch, *Lives*, p. 913, for Antony's self-comparison to Hercules, and p. 921 for Cleopatra as Venus. It is important to note that Shakespeare excises from his play Plutarch's many references to Antony as Bacchus; mention of Bacchus, in the Roman orgy, is made in specifically Roman associations. See J. Leeds Barroll, "Shakespeare and the Art of Character," *S. Stud.*, III (1967), 159-235.

[37] Cf. Markels, and Barbara Bono's unpublished work.

[38] Waith, p. 113; Schanzer, p. 158.

Beautiful words indeed to eulogize a dead colleague and opponent—but Caesar cannot help calculating the man's worth: "A
moiety of the world."[39] That coveted demi-monde is at last his;
the reckoning is over, the world brought under Caesar's universal
landlordism. The "boy" has become, as Cleopatra names him,
"Sole sir of the world." After the briefest respite in honor of his
dead "mate in empire," Caesar turns back to the business of the
world and lays his plans for the future. To such a man, it is
difficult not to prefer the prodigal old ruffian, who can assert, and
mean it, "There's beggary in love that can be reckon'd," who can
risk and lose his moiety (or his third) of the world for something
which, however flawed, he valued above himself.

For Antony is no standard Roman, as the Romans testify. Men
speak of his greatness of character and action, his stature in virtue
and in vice. Men *act* to honor those qualities: his soldiers love
him; his servant kills himself rather than stab his master; Enobarbus dies of having betrayed him. Philo can speak of him only
in hyperbolical terms; so, in spite of themselves, can Caesar and
Lepidus. In everyone's mind, this man was aggrandized and enlarged above the commonalty of men. Like his ancestor Hercules,
Antony does things no other man can do, on a scale on which no
other man can do them. It is not Cleopatra alone who feels this,
but everyone who knows him. When we compare this Antony
with the man duped twice by Cleopatra, or with the man causing
Caesar's messenger to be beaten, or the man feasting, joking, and
making love with Cleopatra, we see the range of the problem
Shakespeare set himself—and we must suspect that some of this
hyperbole is merely bombast. But when his imagination is fired by
Cleopatra, Antony *can* do great deeds at arms. He conquered the
entire East and redistributed its countries (without consulting
Rome) among Cleopatra and her children. When she arms him,
he defeats the Romans at odds, and returns to tell her his "gests"
that day. At his death, when an ordinary man might well have
nagged, he looks to an Elysium in which he and she shall outdo
Aeneas and Dido; he warns her to look after her safety and, like
the great lover he is, dies on a kiss. No trace remains of his rage
at her, no trace of reproach for her false message: with his own
life he was prodigal; with hers, he was generous.

These are the gestures to match an hyperbolical style, the be-

---

[39] On this point, see Terence Eagleton, *Shakespeare and Society* (New York.
1967), p. 127.

havior so admired by Longinus: the gestures of the overreaching man whose imagination is larger than the stage it must act upon. For Antony, the two "stand up peerless"; Cleopatra remembers that

> Eternity was in our lips, and eyes,
> Bliss in our brow's bent; none our parts so poor,
> But was a race of heaven.   (I.iii.35-37)

For her he was, finally, truly Herculean, a "demi-Atlas," a colossus whose "legs bestrid the ocean"; he was greater than the arch of empire itself: he was her world. For him, she could make herself into Venus and Isis, could "be" ageless and infinitely desirable, immortal, more than human. They read their stature from their mutual view of one another. Their ideas of themselves and of each other may have been unrealistic, vain, self-flattering, and self-deceitful, but they reflected what can never be readily explained, the peculiar sense of well-being and power a man and woman in love can give each other. So their clumsy games, their open love-making and open quarreling, their flirtations, their drinking, their mockery, turn somehow from nonsense and bombast into legitimate hyperbole, into a language forever on the stretch to express what had not been expressed before. Far from ideal lovers, Antony and Cleopatra demand a language for their love which rejects conventional hyperbole and invents and creates new over-statements, new forms of overstatement. In the language itself, we can read the insatiability of their love, as the language seems to make hungry, too, where most it satisfies. Nothing is enough for these two, not even the most extravagant figures of speech.

The language Antony and Cleopatra use, the language others use about them, is stretched at its upper and lower limits, to express their high and low gestures as bigger than lifesize. It is interesting that Antony and Cleopatra do not bewitch others' imaginations only by their charismatic presence; their great qualities are praised, described, referred to, and criticized mostly in their absence. These two are watched by a world fascinated even when disapproving; they are staged in a play of their own making, with the world as their willing audience. But they do not really play for that audience: their imaginative acting is all for each other, and in their mutual absorption they do not care who happens to look on at the spectacle. Of course the Romans cannot keep their eyes off them; beneath the language of official disapproval, one can see

Roman fascination with this un-Roman style of life, with this abundant, prodigal, excessive manner of doing things. Their bounty knows no winter but is, in Antony's word, always "foison."

V

Ripeness, overripeness: certainly the images of fertility, in particular the Nile-imagery, stresses life-giving, fecundity, creation; and, with these good qualities, also corruption and rotting. Action can corrupt; so can inaction. In Caesar's image for the variable Roman people, the famous "vagabond flag" passage, we read of one kind of rotting; in Antony's inaction we see another. The flag is dissolved in the stream's current; "solutus," dissolved, was one word of disapprobation applied to the Asiatic style, and (as Charney points out) images of dissolution and deliquescence abound in the play.[40] We see things dissolve and resolve—the liaison with Cleopatra, the marriage with Octavia. Antony vacillates between his Roman alliances and his Egyptian delights, choosing now the one, now the other. The tide is against him, literally at Actium, figuratively on land as well. And yet one is not surprised at this particular literalization of water-images of dissolution, for the metaphor has gained power through the play until, in Antony's great speech about himself, we see that he thinks of himself as formless, his shape lost. The metaphor of dissolution is overtly made use of through the play—"Let Rome in Tiber melt," Antony cries at the beginning; "Authority melts from me," he says near the end of his life. Cleopatra too speaks in this image: "Melt Egypt into Nile." If she should ever play him false, then "dissolve my life." Both use the neologism "discandy," Cleopatra in a hyperbolical assertion of love, Antony in connection with his melting authority:

> The hearts
> That spaniel'd me at heels, to whom I gave
> Their wishes, do discandy, melt their sweets
> On blossoming Caesar.   (IV.xii.20-23)

The most important of the dissolution-passages is Antony's speech about himself as a cloud in which shapes continually shift, dissolve, and reform until "The rack dislimns, and makes it indis-

---

[40] Charney, pp. 18-19; 137-40; Danby, p. 131.

tinct,/ As water is in water." When he finds his Roman form again and dies "a Roman, by a Roman/ Valiantly vanquish'd," Cleopatra says of him, "The crown o' the earth doth melt," into a nothingness she feels as palpable. To mark Cleopatra's death, Charmian calls for cosmic dissolution, "Dissolve, thick cloud, and rain, that I may say/ The gods themselves do weep" (v.ii.298-99).

Peculiarly enough, other words characteristically applied in denigration to the Asiatic style are picked up and openly developed in the powerful imagery of this play. "Enervis" is such a word—Antony and Cleopatra taunt each other with idleness (i.ii.113-14, 127; iii.xiii.90-92), and Antony accuses himself of "slackness" (iii.vii.27). The notion of effeminacy is related to the notion of idleness and, in Enobarbus' last speech to Antony, is explicitly connected with melting. Enobarbus weeps ("I, an ass, am onion-eyed"), and asks Antony to stop talking—"for shame/ Transform us not to women" (iv.ii.35-36). "Inanis," empty, is another word played in the imagery: "vacancy" occurs, in connection with voluptuousness (i.iv.26), and in Enobarbus' attempt to praise Cleopatra (ii.vi.216). By all odds the most significant use in the play of such a term is the imagery and the practice of enlargement, of blowing up. The Asiatic style was "inflatus": we have seen how Cleopatra continually enlarged her idea of Antony, until in her paean to Dolabella of Antony's greatness she outdid her hyperbolical habits of rhetoric. There is, too, much about inflation in the play's language. In the first speech of Philo, in which so much of the play's implications, sexual and other, lie coiled, Antony is said to have "become the bellows and the fan/ To cool a gipsy's lust." Primarily, the bellows blows up, the fan cools: but *both* can actually blow up and both can cool. On her barge, Cleopatra has magical fans, apparently, also both blowing and cooling: the "winds did seem/ To glow the delicate cheeks which they did cool,/ And what they undid did." (ii.ii.203-205). Breathless, Cleopatra breathes forth her power; in her, Enobarbus assures his hearers, defect becomes perfection. Antony and Cleopatra, then, "inflate" each other—or, to put the same thing more gracefully, they inspirit each other. For those Atticists who polemicized against the Asiatic style, such "inflation" was bad because it was untrue to nature and gave false impressions of fact. Now, Antony and Cleopatra may have had, and have fostered, false impressions about themselves and each other; but they were trying to do something else, something highly respectable and highly poetic: to give utterance to their own convictions and sensations of being larger than life, which in turn demanded a style of expression more spacious than that used by the ruck of mankind. By means of the style, ever on the reach for an undefined "more," the infinite longings of these figures can be understood: but, furthermore, by means of this twice-heightened speech, the play examines not only the values of an enriched style, but the values of the life it seeks to match. The play is a study in richness and ripeness, necessarily also a study in overripeness as well, a study even of corruption. But never may we conclude, in morality vein, that these last qualities are valueless, that the people who speak so are simply megalomaniac and self-deluded. Indeed, what emerges from the play is something quite different, the affirmation of the values, qualified by an awareness of its dangers, of such a way of life.

As one works through the play, several things become clearer: at the beginning, Antony speaks hyperbolically, bombastically: his honest heartfelt emotions, mingled with an ironic self-criticism, are reserved for his realization of Fulvia's death. It is Cleopatra who checks his overstatement, questions the sincerity of his hyperbole ("Excellent falsehood"; "Hear the ambassadors"). Mocking him, she is still besotted with him; no less than Antony is she manipulable by her love. Both Antony and Cleopatra suffer from self-surpassing rages, she at the messenger, he at her apparent and real betrayals of him; hyperbole operates there in both language and gesture. By the third act, something has begun to happen which demonstrates the identity of the lovers: the hyperbolical style with which Antony began the play now issues from Cleopatra's mouth:

> Ah, dear, if I be so,
> From my cold heart let heaven engender hail,
> And poison it in the source, and the first stone
> Drop in my neck: as it determines, so
> Dissolve my life; the next Caesarion smite
> Till by degrees the memory of my womb,
> Together with my brave Egyptians all,
> By the discandying of this pelleted storm,
> Lie graveless, till the flies and gnats of Nile
> Have buried them for prey!   (III.xiii.158-67)

It is Antony now who says, "I am satisfied," evidently needing that assurance to go on with the "chronicle" of which he feels himself to be a part. Early in the play, Antony and Cleopatra are separately hyperbolical; as their unity grows, they adapt to each other's modes of speech. These lovers are in many ways temperamentally alike, and they become more so as their meaning for each other becomes more conscious and more motivating in their lives. In the third act, as they pitch their lives together once more, their most hyperbolical speeches of love are signs of their deepening unity with one another, the more poignant for their violent and frequent misunderstandings.

To speak as they do, so grandly, so magnificently, so frankly in hyperbole, is in Antony's and Cleopatra's nature. They are true to one aspect of the Attic (or "Senecan") prescription, after all, in that they express "themselves" truly in their language—this is to say, then, that their style *must* in honesty be bombastic, which according to Attic prescription should mean that their style matches the variability and shoddiness of their characters, discovers beneath their bluster and shouting mere fustian cheapness, secondhand emotions, and sleazy intentions. Longinus was fully aware of how close the elevated style was to bombast: it is almost as if Shakespeare set himself to examine Longinus' problem fully in this play, to test out against human actions and human speech the human aspiration for sublimity.

Antony's habits of speech reach toward and respond to the fundamental grandeur of his nature, as his actions increasingly confirm the propriety and integrity of his grand style. That Enobarbus adopts the hyperbolical mode—that Plutarch adopts it, indeed—to render Cleopatra's magnificence, tells us much about the "real" application of an inflated and hyperbolical style. In Enobarbus' mouth we are invited to recognize things as they are: Enobarbus knows *ping* from *pong*, Rome from Egypt. For better and for worse, Enobarbus is a Roman, speaks as a Roman, acts as a Roman. Yet to this man is given the great speech about Cleopatra, its figures stretching farther and farther as the speech goes on and as he realizes the difficulties involved in making anyone who has not experienced her charm understand what this woman is. Like his master, vacillating between Rome and Egypt in his own life, Enobarbus seems to opt for Rome against Egypt. At his end he chooses neither place, but rather chooses a man, a human being involved with both symbolic places and, for him, transcending both. From his relation to Mark Antony, Enobarbus took his final definition, to die with his betrayed master's name

on his lips. By the pull of hyperbole, of overstatement, of inflation, and of magnanimity on such a man, we can measure the
power of Antony for Cleopatra—and, just because of his greatness, can measure her power for him. The two lovers confirm
each other and themselves—so much we might expect. Enobarbus,
with his excursions beyond his habitual style and behavior, not
wanting to do so, nonetheless confirms them from outside themselves.

In his set-speech on Cleopatra, Enobarbus had called upon a
natural miracle to attest to her power:

> Antony
> Enthron'd i' the market-place, did sit alone,
> Whistling to the air; which, but for vacancy,
> Had gone to gaze on Cleopatra too,
> And made a gap in nature.   (ii.ii.214-18)

Even in figure, though, this miracle cannot take place: there is
no gap in nature, nor in this play, however crowded things are by
the space Antony and Cleopatra take up, by the bruit of their
presence, the bustle of their companionship. To stretch the metaphor, the play's dominant style is not one of vanity, although
there are vanities enough blatantly set forth in the protagonists'
characters. They are self-centered and self-indulgent—but they
are not self-satisfied. They look to each other forever for more;
they criticize each other and themselves. In their lives, however
lived out in the Asiatic style, in dissoluteness, inflation, swelling,
enervation, slackness, effeminacy, and idleness, these two do *not*
decay. Their satisfactions breed hunger; their desire neither stales
nor cloys, not even at the moments in which they die. Finally,
their desire can be seen to be a particular kind of love, a kind of
love rarely made romantic, firmly based in shared sexual experience. Out of such love, each can think only of the other at the
time of death.

Even when they are idle, Antony and Cleopatra make a stir in
the world. This is perhaps part of the tragedy (though not in
Renaissance terms): that public figures cannot afford private
joys.[41] In the modern jargon, there is no solution to their problems either of aspiring temperament or of historical situation.
They could not do without each other and, their world being

41 See Markels, chapter 2.

what it was, they could not live comfortably with each other. But imagine alternative solutions: suppose Antony *had* gone back to live in Rome with Octavia and their daughters (present in Plutarch but excised from the play); the political struggle with Caesar could hardly have failed to come to a head, for Caesar, if not Antony, had to find opportunity for quarrel. Suppose Cleopatra had gone back to her philanderings with eastern potentates and Roman ambassadors: could she have restrained herself from political troublemaking, out of boredom if nothing else? Or, turning the matter about still more, how could Antony have lived among Romans whose view of Cleopatra was as extreme as his own, though at quite the other end of the scale? Could he have endured the silliness of Lepidus, the calculations of Octavius, the prurience of Menas and the rest, their eagerness to vulgarize personal experiences beyond their capacities to imagine? Character has something to do with "fate"—the struggle with Caesar would have come in the end, without the satisfaction for Antony of having chosen for Cleopatra, without the heroics at his death which, self-deceiving or not, eased him into Elysium with the conviction that his life had been worth its trouble and pain, and that his final disgrace was canceled by his grandiose final gestures of love.

This is a curious play, resting on an ambivalent concept of love impossible to sum up, to categorize, or to define. We learn throughout that desire can remain insatiable, that vacillation breeds corruption, that rewards in one sphere exact penalties in another. Cleopatra's fans heated where they cooled, what they undid, did. So Cleopatra: she undid Antony, but also she made of him not so much what she wanted him to be—indeed, in that she failed—as what *he* wanted to be. Certainly one cannot draw as a general conclusion from this play that an intense connection between a man and a woman justifies all else, justifies all the neglect, the idleness, the betrayals, the prodigality of lives and honor. Shakespeare shows us, unmistakably, that it does not, by the play's eternal balancing of one thing against another, its long vacillation between the bombastic and the sublime, its constant qualification of virtue by fault, of vice by virtue. But on balance, it is obvious that those experiences, from whatever source, which can elevate human beings are judged more favorably than those which do not; that those human beings who can be elevated are nobler than those whose nature is too small to permit such enlargement. With all its qualifications and all its defects admitted, proclaimed, displayed, the love of Antony and Cleopatra is nonetheless affirmed, the strumpet and the strumpet's fool grow into the imaginative warrior and the theatrical queen. There is no denying their excesses, which are examined, studied, and reassessed both by the speakers within the play and by the audience watching the excesses demonstrated onstage. We learn that in such excess, life itself can reside. Though it threatens to rot, and seems at times to have corrupted the lovers, their style of living affirms their life—and that despite the deaths of the proceedings.

Indeed, in the deaths we see the value of the lives. Antony says that he dies as a Roman, but he bungled his death all the same, both by letting Eros die before him, and by not killing himself outright. However significant the "elevation" of Antony into Cleopatra's tomb, it is an awkward business;[42] the queen's failure to open the tomb lays stress, just at the worst moment, on the weakest side of her nature. Antony's dying skirts bombast the while, and we may assume that his failure to die efficiently in the Roman style is one mark Egypt laid upon him.

His beauty of character, though, emerges clearly through this uncomfortable death-scene: in spite of the clumsiness, what we remember is Antony's magnanimity and Cleopatra's high poetry. Antony affirms in his manner of dying both the Roman and the eastern sides of his nature; Cleopatra too comes to accept Roman ways, even to embrace them in her own death. Her contemptuous fear of "Roman thoughts" in the first act gives way before her desire to emulate Antony and to die, like him, "in the high Roman fashion." Her suicide, though, cannot be said to be pure Roman: she had done research into painless ways to die; she chose the Nile worm as a suitable weapon; she arranged the spectacle of her death with a care and love inappropriate to Roman suicide. In both suicides, a Roman pattern has been expanded and enriched by Egyptian opulence and Egyptian decoration, not least in the ornate style in which both Antony and Cleopatra take leave of their world. The actual world has shrunk away from them; in expectation of Elysium in each other's company, they affirm the larger world of their fantastic and extravagant imagination, which their love had brought into being. The play's language affirms that determination to enlarge life: even at the end, Cleopatra speaks as woman, lover, and mother. After all, it is only by Roman

---

[42] Charney, pp. 134-36, is valuable on Antony's "elevation."

tongues that the hero and heroine are spoken of as mere voluptu-
aries, softened and weakened by self-indulgence and excess. Antony's and Cleopatra's speech is consistently vigorous, various,
copious, vivid, liveliest in those remarkable passages where excessive behavior, excessive sensation, excessive emotions are given
their due.

Even though it threatens to do so, this hyperbolical play does
not get out of hand: its images are as closely controlled as those
of the other late tragedies. Further, the richness and decoration of
the language, in passages of passionate disgust as in passages of
grandiloquent elevation, match the richness of temperament
which confers upon their characters the privilege of an equal
elevation. What at first sounds like bombast in Antony's speech is
naturalized in the course of the play, until his way of speaking
becomes a standard against which other men are judged. Of effeminacy, slackness, or idleness, Antony's behavior may sometimes be accused—but never his language, nor Cleopatra's. From
first to last what emerges is its affirmation of activity, of creativity,
of unending and unendingly interesting emotional process. Till
their very last breaths, these persons change and develop, to involve the audience in that development toward greatness. During
the course of the play, then, Antony and Cleopatra grow into their
rhetorical measure. At the play's start, Philo had called a spade a
spade, or even a shovel; in contrast, Antony and Cleopatra spoke
in love's arrogant, idealized overstatements. By the end of the play,
Philo's linguistic practice is blocked out by Antony's hyperbole
coming true, until we too believe that "the nobleness of life" is for
such lovers to embrace. Until the very end, we are never quite sure
of Cleopatra, such is the oscillation of the play and the woman between extremes, from rejection to reunion, from reviling to re-
affirmation, from lie to truth, from denigration to encomium.

By their manner of dying, these figures are known: the Roman
world, with all its real space, could not house the love of Antony
for Cleopatra. That Antony lost his place in the real world, lost
that world altogether, is made to seem unimportant beside the
imaginative satisfactions of his emotional life. What Antony and
Cleopatra do and say represents them: for all their own vacillation and oscillation, they turn out to be true in their ultimate
commitment to each other. Antony dies with energy and (oddly
enough) enthusiasm; Cleopatra looks to her last moment and beyond it, both on earth and in Elysium—she remains alive, feeling,

imagining, to her last breath. Both catch and express their visions of the new heaven, new earth, seen always in terms of each other and of being with each other. They die as they had lived, beyond definition, in expectation of more. It is the strength, the vividness, the vigor of excess which this play presents, examines, criticizes, and ultimately, with full understanding, confirms, in a language of hyperbole built to match the size and scope of the subject. In the *ping* and *pong* of plain and grandiloquent styles, now one seeming to lead and now the other, Shakespeare manages to show us the problem and the problematics, in moral as in literary terms, at the heart of style. By sinking the notions associated with the Asiatic style back into life itself, in the play's dramatic action he can examine and assess both the style and the style of life in terms of each other, and to see them as one. He can demonstrate, then, by the peculiarly literary device of a stylistic *agon*, the moral problematics of dimension, can manage to make acceptable—more, to make admirable and comprehensible—the values of an honestly ostentatious style.

5

Hamlet:
Reflections on an Anatomy of Melancholy

I

As WE KNOW FROM THE PLAY itself, from the many commentaries on it, and now from Bridget Lyons' careful and sane book, Prince Hamlet was melancholy.[1] At the risk of turning the play *Hamlet* into a museum-piece, which it so clearly has proved itself not to be, I want to explore some of the analytic and symbolic uses Shakespeare made in the play of the various syndromes of melancholy. In the work of Fritz Saxl and Erwin Panofsky, now modernized and Englished by Raymond Klibansky,[2] as well as in Lawrence Babb's valuable study of Elizabethan melancholies,[3] we can see how the extremely varied symptoms of melancholy had been made formulaic in medical practice, and how deeply the psychology of the melancholic was related during the Renaissance to

[1] Bridget Gellert Lyons, *Voices of Melancholy* (London, 1971). The text I have used is the Norton Critical Edition of *Hamlet*, ed. Cyrus Hoy (New York, 1963). Though this essay certainly deals with Hamlet's "character," it is with his literary character, with character-*building*, that I am concerned, not with the Prince conceived as an actual person, either in the manner of A. C. Bradley or in the manner of G. Wilson Knight (*The Wheel of Fire*, London, 1948). Nor do I think, with O. J. Campbell ("What's the Matter with Hamlet?" *Yale Review*, XXXIII, 1942), that Hamlet was a classic manic-depressive; nor, with Ernest Jones (*Hamlet and Oedipus*, London, 1949), that Hamlet suffered simply from an Oedipus complex, although that was certainly one component of his problem. Certainly, it is not new for me to say that Hamlet is melancholy: with the exception of Lily Bess Campbell, from Bradley on this diagnosis has been taken for granted. This essay is concerned with Shakespeare's use of the forms of melancholy in a particularly significant literary way. I am particularly indebted to Bridget G. Lyons' book and, even more, to discussions of the play with her.

[2] Panofsky and Saxl, *Dürers' Melencolia I, Studien der Bibliothek Warburg*, 1923, now translated and expanded, with the help of Raymond Klibansky, as *Saturn and Melancholy* (New York, 1964).

[3] Lawrence Babb, *The Elizabethan Malady* (East Lansing, 1951); see also John W. Draper, *The Hamlet of Shakespeare's Audience* (Durham, N.C., 1938), pp. 175-79; and J. Dover Wilson, *What Happens in Hamlet* (Cambridge, 1935).

the notion of intellectual greatness.[4] Literary schemata had been developed from the medical formulas of melancholy: melancholics and malcontents, noble and ignoble, were presented over and over again in literature and in art.[5] Before *Hamlet* and after, Shakespeare drew on the repertory of melancholy types—Jaques, for instance, the philosopher of *lacrimae rerum*, manages to play a role in *As You Like It* as problematic as the disease from which he suffers. In *Twelfth Night* Malvolio dons the disguise of melancholy lover, a part Romeo played in quite a different mode. Iago has much of the malcontent, and Thersites the railer expresses a bitterness excessive even by the standards of the sordid scenes on which he comments. Timon's disappointments in his friends tips him over into melancholy madness; Antonio's joylessness and inertia mark him as suffering from yet another version of this multitudinous disease. From Aaron in *Titus Andronicus* to Prospero, Shakespeare exploited different canonical versions of melancholy.

But clearly Prince Hamlet is something else again[6]—and by ex-

[4] For comments on Hamlet's philosophical range, see Maynard Mack, "The World of Hamlet," *Yale Review*, XLI (1959), 502-23; Harry Levin, *The Question of Hamlet* (New York, 1959); D. G. James, *Shakespeare and the Dream of Learning* (Oxford, 1951); Hiram Haydn, *The Counter-Renaissance* (New York, 1950); Robert Ornstein, *The Moral Vision of Jacobean Tragedy* (Madison, 1960); Theodore Spencer, *Shakespeare and the Nature of Man* (New York, 1952); Geoffrey Bush, *Shakespeare and the Natural Condition* (Cambridge, Mass., 1956); Ruth M. Levitsky, "Rightly to be Great," *S. Stud.*, I (1965), 142-57. Nicholas Brooke, in *Shakespeare's Early Tragedies* (London, 1968), pp. 165-66, makes some extremely perceptive remarks on Hamlet's "thinking."

[5] See Timothie Bright, *A Treatise of Melancholie* (London, 1586), p. 126; Andreas Laurentius, *Discourse of the Preservation of the Sight: of Melancholike Diseases* (London, 1599), tr. Richard Surphlet, pp. 82, 85-86. For creative melancholy, see Panofsky-Saxl, pp. 15-42, 241-74, esp. pp. 254-74; Marsilio Ficino, *Opera Omnia* (Basel, 1576), I, 731-32. See also Seneca, *De tranquillitate animi*, XVII, 10-12 (LCL, II, 285); and Rudolf and Margot Wittkower, *Born under Saturn* (London, 1963), esp. pp. 98-113. Many figures in Medieval and Renaissance art hold skulls: the melancholy figure with a skull is more often a woman than a man. Of pictures of men with skulls, Lucas van Leyden's is particularly apt (see Lyons, frontispiece; and Max J. Friedlaender, *Lucas van Leyden*, 1924, pl. 174; and also G. J. Woogewerff, *De Noord-Nederlandsche Schilderkunst*, The Hague, 1939, III, fig. 287; and F.K.J. Rezniček, *Hendrick Goltzius*, Utrecht, 1961, II, fig. 11). I owe these last two references to Professor C. Richard Judson of Smith College.

[6] Mack, Levin, and James (with others, of course) have commented on Hamlet's multiplicity and profundity; see also Peter Alexander, *Hamlet, Father and Son* (Oxford, 1955), pp. 183-85; John Holloway, *The Story of the Night* (Lincoln, 1961), p. 21; and L. C. Knights, *An Approach to "Hamlet"* (London,

amining Shakespeare's means of making him so different from these melancholy characters, all acting according to a single melancholy stereotype, we can recognize how simply so complex a dramatic character as Hamlet could be built. For Hamlet exhibits not one but many kinds of melancholy, plays on and with his melancholy in such a way as to implicate the audience in his doubts and despairs, as well as in the elevations and intellectual investigations melancholy could and did induce in him. As we look sharply at Hamlet's developing and alternating behavior, we can see that in him Shakespeare combined many of the disparate and even contradictory aspects of the melancholy syndrome, thereby making the problematics of the disease a reliable resource from which to draw for the problematics exhibited in the play. In the attribution of contemplation to a melancholic lies much of Hamlet's acceptable tendency toward thought and thinking. As, for instance, Faustus is not, Hamlet is persuasive as an intellectual hero partly because of the widespread acceptance of melancholy stereotypes of contemplative thinkers. But of course Hamlet is not just a contemplative melancholic; his melancholy is no single stable stereotype. When he first appears onstage, Hamlet is shown as suffering from an acceptable, traditional, entirely explicable form of melancholy caused by the sudden death of his father. This loss is aggravated for him by the frustration of his legitimate hopes for succession in Denmark. Embarrassing though Hamlet's melancholy was in the context of marriage and a new reign, it was in no sense personally aberrant—his mother, for instance, minds the *prolongation* of Hamlet's grief, not its existence.[7]

Subsequently we hear from Ophelia of Hamlet's love-melancholy, so canonically described that we can hardly blame Polonius for his diagnosis of love-madness. The arranged confrontation be-

---

1960), p. 11. I must take exception to Levin's wording (though not, I suspect, to his meaning) that at the beginning of the play, Hamlet is "single-minded, all of a piece, all melancholia: *then* he puts on his mask and plays the antic" (*Question*, p. 51; italics mine), since in my view—and that of most Renaissance men who knew anything about this well-known subject—melancholy also involves antic, hysterical, and clownish behavior, as well as gloomy, aloof, downcast behavior. A connection might also be drawn between some aspects of Hamlet's melancholy and Prospero's contemplative and manipulative stances. Both heroes are concerned with role-playing, with "directing" things, as well as with thinking through their problems.

[7] Bright is particularly full on melancholy induced by loss of a person dear to the patient.

tween Hamlet and Ophelia demonstrates clearly enough to Claudius that Hamlet's affections do not tend toward love, as the King hears in the Prince's railing the sources of his deeper distress. The railing is of course a melancholy symptom; so is Hamlet's histrionism, real or assumed.[8] His antic behavior is, surely, partly under his own control, but his wildness after the Mousetrap play forces Horatio to call him back to more reasonable behavior ("Half a share"; "You might have rhymed"). After his return from his sea-voyage, Hamlet displays in the graveyard the manners and mores of the noble melancholic,[9] but his sudden competitive histrionics in Ophelia's grave demonstrate clearly enough how far he had to go to achieve the real thing, the final stability reached before the duel.

What we *can* see—and what an Elizabethan audience could see even more clearly—is that Hamlet was made to seem many-faceted simply by endowing him with many of the facets of the total melancholy syndrome. Further, Hamlet himself develops and exploits aspects of melancholy, from the first exchange with his mother over the difference between his "customary suits of solemn black" and the pressures of his inward woe, through the powerful soliloquies of *addubitatio*,[10] on suicide, death, and his own role-playing. In Hamlet's phrase, "actions that a man might play" (1.ii.84), the first tone strikes of what is throughout a major theme, worked elaborately into the imagery and into the very plot and symbolic action of the play, of acting as playing, as acting-out, and as action. The play itself becomes highly self-reflexive in that "playing" becomes one of its major considerations, a plot-element as well as a theme. The play itself comes to stand for the relation between acting and action.[11]

[8] For more on railing, or the satiric melancholy type, see O. J. Campbell, *"Comicall Satyre" and Shakespeare's Troilus and Cressida* (San Marino, Calif., 1938); Alvin B. Kernan, *The Cankered Muse* (New Haven, 1959); and Lyons, *Voices*, esp. chapters 2 and 3. For Thersites, see below, chapter 8. Bright gives good commentary on histrionism.

[9] Giordano Bruno's *Gli eroici furori* offers a classic example of the elevations of melancholy; see also Juan Huarte, *Examen de ingenios*, tr. R. C. (London, 1596), p. 59: " . . . whatsoever notable men for learning, have lived in the world (saith *Aristotle*) they were all melancholike"; and Burton, *passim*.

[10] Bright, p. 126; Levin, p. 48; Leon Howard, *The Logic of Hamlet's Soliloquies* (Lone Pine Press, 1964); James, *Dream*, p. 48. See also Levinus Lemnius, *The Touchstone of Complexions*, tr. Thomas Newton (London, 1576), p. 143.

[11] Everyone writing on *Hamlet*, from Goethe on, has at least touched on the drama's display of the problems of appearance and reality. Of recent crit-

But the theme of appearance and reality, of acting and action, is not left in some unattached symbolic layer of language alone; in their peculiar stresses, the problems of acting and action are dovetailed into the naturalistic needs of the play. Hamlet, for instance, sees a ghost—and with that ghost, the audience, like the protagonist, becomes involved in epistemology itself, in the reasons for a melancholic's legitimate doubting, in the demonstration of Hamlet as an intellectual and discriminating hero who looks critically at expressions of character and morality. First of all, it must be established whether or not the ghost is a true ghost, whether or not it acts from the motives it claims. Since one of the major symptoms of melancholy was hallucination, and the commonest hallucination was of ghosts, and, of ghosts so hallucinated, the commonest manifestation was of a dead person dear to the hallucinator, it is difficult to know at once the status of this particular ghost. Two commonsensical men-at-arms have seen it more than once. Horatio sees but does not trust it. Gertrude does not see it at all, rather sees her son "bend [his] eye on vacancy" and speak with "th' incorporal air."[12]

Among the questions[13] Hamlet asks the ghost is "Be thou a spirit . . . or goblin damned?" The Mousetrap is his skeptic's test of the ghost's credibility. With the ghost, with the Mousetrap, and with other complications of the plot, we can see at work in Hamlet's melancholy one of the disease's major intractabilities, which caused Robert Burton, some twenty years after *Hamlet* was put on the stage, to call into question the whole intellectual status of the disease and thus of the humoral psychology.[14] Apparently the ghost helps his son out of the original depression, toward some action of the traditional revenge laid upon him. At first, then, the ghost seems to offer a cure for the original melancholy by providing the energies and purpose Hamlet had so consciously

---

ics, Holloway, *Story of Night*; R. A. Foakes, "Character and Speech in *Hamlet*" (*Hamlet*, ed. J. R. Brown and Bernard Harris, New York, 1966, p. 148-62) and Mack, "The World of Hamlet," have been most useful to me. See also Anne Righter, *The Idea of the Play*, as well as forthcoming work by Jackson I. Cope and my colleague John W. Erwin, on metatheatrical devices in this play.

12 For material on Elizabethan stage ghosts, I am greatly indebted to Dr. Eva Latif, of San Fernando State College.

13 For background to this, see Mack and Levin.

14 For a discussion of Burton's brilliant mixtures and overlappings of the concepts of cause, symptom, and cure of melancholy, see *Paradoxia*, p. 431; and Lyons, *Voices*.

lacked in the earlier stage of his suffering. In the perverse way that melancholy tends to work, however, the ghost's "cure" turns out to be a further cause for another and deeper kind of melancholy, in which Hamlet questions his relation to other people and to his own personality, even to his own life. At this point, the disease in the play becomes problematical, as cure and cause intertwine to increase Hamlet's confusion and our own.

Other "cures" are applied to Hamlet's malady. Ophelia, for instance, is used by her manipulative father, first withdrawn from the Prince and later reapplied like some inert dosage.[15] Rosencrantz and Guildenstern are offered to Hamlet as a cure, though as instruments of Claudius their friendship itself becomes deeply threatening to him. One cannot help noting, too, that their parts in the manipulation were hardly good for them: Rosencrantz and Guildenstern are destroyed by Hamlet's direct action, and Ophelia dies in reaction to Hamlet's killing of her father. The players too are conceived as a cure, a Galenical antidote to the Prince's sadness; an interesting sequence of cause and effect ensues as a result of the players' arrival. The potential cure they offer is turned by Hamlet against his uncle, who then in turn offers the solace of a sea-voyage and a change of air, normal antidote to melancholy[16] this time designed to destroy the patient—who then turns *that* experience around into an opportunity for mortal action. On his return to Denmark, Hamlet has accepted responsibility for his conscious doings at sea, only to find himself faced with the terrible consequences of his accidental killing of Polonius.

Not all Hamlet's melancholies are as swerving, as various, and as unstable as this description of events would suggest. In his great soliloquies, remarkable speculative speeches in themselves, Hamlet consistently shows another psychological plane of melancholy, therewith another level of dramaturgy. By tradition, actors present their deepest "selves" in soliloquies; by convention, we are disposed to believe in Hamlet's turning his inward self outward to our view.[17] But *what* self is displayed in them? How many sides

[15] See Lemnius, p. 138: in the company of "amorous and beautifull Damosells, they [melancholics] set cocke on hoope, and shake away from them al their former grimnes, and wayward maners, and become as merry as the meryest," a description offering some "reason" for Hamlet's antic behavior during and after the Mousetrap play.

[16] Laurentius, p. 123, cites a change of air as the best cure for love-melancholy, and see Burton on air generally.

[17] For perceptive comments on this subject, see Sheldon P. Zitner's still un-

of this man's self must we take account of? These soliloquies are more than conventional touchstones for dramatic motive; they are also Hamlet's conscious efforts at self-definition, as his "self" alters with heightened experience, designed not to satisfy an audience only, but to concentrate himself as well.[18] The soliloquies show him donning, doffing, struggling with the roles he chooses or feels forced upon him, and offer as well a reason for his postponements of decisive action; the roles themselves absorb a great deal of his emotional intention.

Because the soliloquies present Hamlet in such different states of mind, engaged in such courageous self-analysis, they force an audience into realizing how complex this literary hero's personality is. His introspection, undertaken in intellectualist and even in epistemological terms, is different from the pressure to know himself set on any tragic hero: "knowing" by itself is, for Shakespeare's protagonists, a problem only for Hamlet. In both major speeches, "To be, or not to be," and "O, what a rogue and peasant slave am I," Hamlet takes several positions within the soliloquy itself, looks at himself and his situation from different angles of vision. This perspectivism keeps an audience fully alert to the magnitude of Hamlet's problems both of action and of knowing how to act; but at the same time, the soliloquies speak two languages, letting us know how Hamlet feels and at the same time moving *him* beyond the state of melancholy *we* are asked to accept. For Hamlet works through his problems, and at the same time plays with them: in the suicide-speech, for instance, he works through the temptation to kill himself by talking it out, by acting it out in his imagination.[19] The speech itself carries him away

---

published paper, "Shakespeare's Secret Language," delivered at the University of Iowa Renaissance Conference, spring, 1965. See also G. K. Hunter's valuable "The Heroism of Hamlet," in *Hamlet*, ed. Brown and Harris, pp. 103-106; J. B. Walker, "The Structure of *Hamlet*," ibid., pp. 60-68; and Patricia S. Gourlay, "Guilty Creatures Sitting at a Play," *Ren. Q.*, XXIV (1971), 221-25.

[18] Peter Ure, "Character and Role from *Richard III* to *Hamlet*," in *Hamlet*, ed. Brown and Harris, p. 27; Mark Rose, "*Hamlet* and the Shape of Revenge," *ELR*, I (1971), 132-43; Stephen Booth, "On the Value of *Hamlet*," in *Reinterpretations of Elizabethan Drama*, ed. Norman Rabkin (New York, 1969), pp. 152-55.

[19] For a good discussion of the suicide problem see Wittkower, pp. 133-49 ("Suicides of Artists"), and S. E. Sprott, *The English Debate on Suicide* (La Salle, 1961). Eleanor Prosser's *Hamlet and Revenge* (Stanford, 1967) deals with important points, though she vastly simplifies Hamlet's problem to a conflict

from suicide's quietus; his intellect could protect him, as Ophelia's could not, from the pull toward self-destruction. For this kind of man, a real intellectual, thinking through his problems was as much action as, say, killing is an action. For us, audience and readers, the soliloquies externalize the inward action by which the overt action is governed and directed.

For there is much overt action in the play, in spite of all the commentary on Hamlet's dawdling and indecision. He acts in the world, to put on the Mousetrap play, to kill the eavesdropper who turns out to be Polonius, from whose irrevocable death Hamlet can never look back. Returning from the sea-voyage, he must discover the further effects of his killing of Polonius in Ophelia's "maim'd rites," must discover that though it may be "not now," yet the end will come. In spite of all the destruction he causes, however, Hamlet is not, as Iago, Bosola, and De Flores all were, a temperamental malcontent seeking to ruin everything about him.[20] A major irony in this heavily ironical play is that Hamlet produces a malcontent's destruction by acting like such a malcontent. In real life, he has to learn, roles have consequences.

And for consequences there are responsibilities to be borne: roles are not, as Hamlet learns again and again, real defenses against responsibility. Sometimes Hamlet seems to choose a pose meant to conceal his inward thoughts from his stage auditory—in the arras scene, in the antic disposition episodes. At other times, his pose may somehow liberate him from himself (dangerously, perhaps, as at the end of the Mousetrap); again, it may force a behavioral shift upon him, altering his mood, his rhetoric, and his style.[21] Only by the play's end, with the extraordinary cleansing of ignoble by noble melancholy, do Hamlet's lesser symptoms, real and feigned, fall away, to leave both him and his audience in no doubt about his resolution: "If it be now, 'tis not to come; if it be not to come, it will be now; if it be not now, yet it will come." Manipulation is over, too: "The readiness is all."

Only at the end is melancholy over, then—and so are plot, plotting, and the play. With the end of the melancholy symptoms

---

between honor and Christian theology. On this point, see the masterly article of Sheldon P. Zitner, "Hamlet: Duellist," *UTQ*, xxxix (1969), 1-18.

[20] E. E. Stoll, "Shakespeare and the Malcontent Type," *MP*, ii (1906).

[21] At this point, rather late in the game, I want to pay tribute to Maurice Charney's invaluable *Style in* Hamlet (Princeton, 1969), which has helped me immeasurably with difficulties in this play.

we can perceive how inevitably they are involved in plot and plotting, how remarkably Shakespeare has exploited the disease to make intelligible a truly intellectual hero. The daring of casting such a man as the enforced revenger is the more obvious[22] as we recognize that this skeptical, stoical prince, struggling not to be passion's slave though in the grip of inexorable passions, is the last man a reasonable playwright would choose as a revenge-hero. The forms of melancholy have been exploited in counterpoint to an archaic theatrical plot-convention. They call into question the values of tribal heroic life, and present the spectacle of a man thinking this terrible problem through. A set of medical formulas dictating thoughtfulness, doubt, and contemplation has been literarized, to give us a chance to think about character, society, knowing—and even the writing of plays.

To treat this play, so extraordinarily about a character in search of his own character, as an exercise in a dramatist's ingenuity may seem to demean its emotional significance and to detract from its hero's moving self-conquest. For me, though, the playwright's achievement is the more remarkable because he could construct, out of the types and commonplaces of an obsolescent psychology, a character who so classically conveys the excruciations of living with himself, as well as the commoner (and lesser) pains of living with imperfect companions in an imperfect world. Shakespeare's good eye for life and living selected the problems of melancholy to dramatize the epistemological questions at the core of *Hamlet*. Melancholy works as a medium for the character's own confusions and solutions, his visions and revisions. It works further as an idiom which to some extent takes for granted the imbalance, the relativism, the insecurities implicit in any judgment. As perspectives shift, the chief character shifts, and so does the audience, sharing the protagonist's difficult perspectivism. Quite incidentally, Shakespeare has also made his comment on the inadequacy of the systematics of humoral psychology, with its separate categories, its "characters" and stereotypes too static to express the

---

[22] For revenge-tragedy, see Fredson Bowers, *The Elizabethan Revenge Tragedy* (Princeton, 1940); Levin's comments in *Question*, pp. 8-9; and Dame Helen Gardner's in *The Business of Criticism* (Oxford, 1959), pp. 59-61. Philip Edwards, in *Thomas Kyd and Early Elizabethan Revenge Tragedy* (London, 1966), makes incisive remarks about revenge-tragedies in general, as well as about Kyd's critical play; David L. Frost, *The School of Shakespeare* (Cambridge, 1968), pp. 167-208, studies the influence of *Hamlet* on later revenge-plays.

complications of a human being conscientiously trying to become what he can be, against the dictates of what he must do. Nor does Shakespeare permit us, any more than Hamlet permits Rosencrantz and Guildenstern, to pluck the heart out of his mystery. Rather, we come to recognize and experience, as Hamlet recognizes from experiencing, the limitless mysteries of the thoughtful man's heart.

II

Hamlet in the graveyard, contemplating the skull, contemplates himself and his death, in that emblematic scene reflecting upon the life of all men as well as his own, upon all men's and his own death. We have seen how much the meditative and melancholy traditions rely on self-absorption and self-reference: among much else, that scene presents us with one of the fundamental self-references in the play, in which Hamlet reflects upon himself, observes himself as in a mirror, takes external, objective, separate elements as mirrors in which to observe himself. Technically as well as substantively, the play is full of such reflections, which match its theme of intellectual reflection and thus reinforce in various ways the play's central preoccupation with problems of epistemology. This section deals with some of the ways in which the constellation of ideas and themes around "noble melancholy" are transferred into literary and dramatic terms.

One reason for the successful emergence of the concept of noble melancholy in the Renaissance was its association with the ideal of intellectual talent and creativity, attributed in greater measure to those born under Saturn than to men born under other planets. A more covert reason for the exaltation of this sort of melancholy may have been that its symptoms supported a general exaltation of mind which, in this very period, resulted in a striking philosophical shift of emphasis from metaphysics to epistemology. Of all the alterations made in intellectual patterns during the Renaissance, this one seems to me the most crucial, as well as the chief justification for the notion that in the Renaissance, creative thinking was principally concerned with "man" rather than with the universe, or with deity, or with hierarchy, or with larger abstract patterns of one sort or another.

Of the belle-lettristic documents for Renaissance interest in epistemology, surely *Hamlet* is a major text, since in this play the epistemological theme is worked into its least likely literary context, that of revenge tragedy. Not only does the hero explore and examine himself, his examination essential to his pursuit of duty and role—essential, then, to the plot of the play he is in—but also he knows that he does so, and sets about doing so consciously, even programmatically. Hamlet tries to understand what he thinks and knows, and how he thinks and knows what he thinks and knows. Shakespeare had made us magnificently conscious of Hamlet's peculiarly intellectual and critical self-searching by ways other than simply *depicting* that process, although he certainly depicts it with great skill and sensitivity.

In Hamlet's great soliloquies, where the Prince can be seen to go through the painful process of self-examination and self-criticism, we recognize that "epistemology" is being played out for us: this man thinks about what he thinks and the ways he thinks. This man is threatened by the infinite regress involved in the very process by which, by means of the mind's operation, one tries to determine the mind's operations. In self-examination the thinker must be his own reference, must hold up himself as a mirror to himself; no wonder this process is called "reflection" and "speculation," terms which record our recognition that epistemology is a mirror-process with all the limitations, as well as the limitlessness, that such a process implies.

In this play, as in many other Renaissance plays less concerned with epistemological process, there is an emblematic episode for such recessive mirror-action: the play-within-the-play.[23] At once a tautological and an active element in the plot, the Chinese-boxing play-within-the-play has contradictory simultaneous effects upon the audience. Neatly packed within demarcated limits, it seems precise and exact, to "fit" as it should; but the self-reference of the

[23] For a discussion of plays within plays, see Anne Righter, *Shakespeare and the Idea of the Play* (London, 1962); Thomas Stroup, *Microcosmos, the Shape of the Elizabethan Play* (Lexington, 1965); Robert J. Nelson, *Play within a Play* (New Haven, 1958); Charles R. Forker, "Shakespeare's Theatrical Symbolism and its Function in *Hamlet*," *SQ*, XIV (1963), 215-29; G. C. Thayer, "*Hamlet*: Drama as Discovery and Metaphor," *Studia Neophilologia* XXVIII (1956), 118-29. See also Lionel Abel, *Metatheater* (New York, 1963), esp. pp. 46-48, with whose interpretation mine is at variance; and Jackson I. Cope, "The Rediscovery of Anti-Form in the Renaissance," *Comparative Drama*, II (1968), 155-71. I have had much help from James L. Calderwood, whose study of Shakespeare's early plays, *Shakespearean Metadrama* (Minneapolis, 1971), has been a considerable support. Nigel Alexander's *Poison, Play, and the Duel* (London, 1971) deals with the play as a series of stratagems—in this case, stratagems *about* stratagems.

container and the thing contained, as well as the levels of reality on which it calls at once, also suggest an infinite process. Any play-within-a-play, or picture-within-a-picture, raises questions of perspective illusion, of "frame," of imitation and invention, of aesthetic scale and value. A play-within-a-play which mirrors the plot, or part of the plot, of the play in which it is embedded, offers a dramatic analogy to the mirror mirrored, infinitely reflecting itself. In a play like *Hamlet*, so overtly concerned with questions of knowing and unknowing, and of moral reality and illusion, the Mousetrap offers an acted image for "speculation" and "reflection." Indeed, in *Hamlet*, the whole device of allowing actors to be part of the *dramatis personae* offers another reinforcement of the same theme: the professional actors stand as a measuring rod for the amateur actors, to emphasize the idea of role and of playing so crucial to plot, imagery, and theme of this play. The actors' professional functions, so honestly carried out, stand against the many role-players of the play: Claudius, assuming a role not properly his; Polonius, pretending to wisdom; Rosencrantz and Guildenstern, duplicitous but bumbling, bad actors in every sense; Ophelia, a puppet in her father's hands; Laertes, a puppet in Claudius'; Hamlet, role-playing throughout the play; even Gertrude, invited to assume a virtue if she have it not. The players offer a living metaphor, a device within the play to illustrate what the abstracted theme is. At surface-level, the whole idea of "playing" fits naturally into the courtly and the medical milieu into which the play is cast. For Hamlet's illness, the players might have offered a specific cure, since comedy was regarded as the purge for heavy thoughts: so Rosencrantz and Guildenstern thought of the players, sent to cure the Prince diagnosed as in the dumps. These players are not comedians, however, but "the tragedians of the city"; they come with another kind of play, one which ought to have deepened Hamlet's melancholy. As things turn out in the topsy-turvy world of Elsinore and melancholy, though, they provide the right therapy in spite of expectation: Hamlet's malady is so contradictory that he can derive some comfort from their Italian murder-play.

In their professional occupation, these players mirror Hamlet's mood and his problem; the play they present, ostensibly to cheer the Prince up, mirrors the Danish situation with only a slight distortion. So they provide us, who watch the play, with an example of infinite regress: Hamlet, the histrionic melancholic, plays the part of a melancholic, sick of a different sort of melancholy from the one from which he really suffers, watches his own situation as in a mirror, in the play-within-the-play. Hamlet is slightly distorted from what he is by what he is believed to be; the play-within-the-play also presents a distorted version of the real situation. There is more to it than this, of course—with the coming of the players Hamlet turns playwright (or, acts the playwright) constructing a play intended as a mirror-image of the situation in his family and also as an experimental device, an "assay of bias" to test the ghost, himself, and the new king's conscience. The actors act out the situation in which Hamlet believes himself to be; by objectifying it for him, they help him to his independent action. As impresario of their play, Hamlet manages to shift the plane of his own behavior from psychological acting-out to chosen action—action which is, appropriately enough, "playing," the one activity in which acting-out and action can be combined.[24]

A play-within-a-play is an old device to give a sense of depth to meaning, since it can provide simultaneously different planes of psychological behavior and different perspectives of awareness. It can be, equally, a device to induce confusion in an audience, a device to raise questions of truth, rarely answered by the device itself. In *Hamlet* the audience is presented with a plot, the *donnée*, in which much role-playing goes on: the persons of the drama (like any persons in any drama) are roles assigned to "real" people, that is to actors—to Burbage, Kemp, Gielgud, Olivier— some of whom, in this case, are cast as men whose roles in the play demand that they play roles (Claudius, Hamlet, the Ghost). Into this play comes a troupe of actors, that is, of actors playing the roles of actors; these in turn act out another play—or, actors play actors who in turn act the parts of king, queen, and poisoner. The play so acted out is an emblem of the situation of the "real" play, the host-play—but an emblem unreadable to the actors in it or to the courtly audience witnessing it, intelligible only to Hamlet (and perhaps Horatio) within the play, and to the audience or readership entirely outside. What can be understood by everyone is that actors playing actors who play at being a king, a queen, a

---

24 For playing, see the classic work by Johan Huizinga, *Homo ludens* (London, 1949), as well as the considerable literature about literature as play which has come out in the last ten years: e.g., Jacques Ehrmann, "Homo ludens Revisited," *YFS* XLI (1968), 31-57; and the various works of Roger Caillois.

poisoner, are watched by a king, a queen, and others at Elsinore. There, Hamlet is that play's inscrutable commentator ("You are as good as a chorus, my lord") as well as its director. Like the courtiers around him, Hamlet watches the play and watches the watchers as well—and all these are watched, from the outermost rim of this ptolemaic illusion, by a real audience.

So concentration is focused on the play-within-the-play which, bad though it is in literary terms, becomes for a time the pivot on which the "real" play turns. However contrived its artifice, the play-within-the-play is dramaturgically and dramatically "correct": after the Mousetrap, Hamlet's and Claudius' relations to each other are radically altered, which means that the real play's action is altered. Also (perhaps even more important), the Mousetrap acts as a metaplay, reflecting in small the life-situation at the Danish court, making that situation, in its moral magnitude so overwhelming for Hamlet, manageable for him; reflecting also, in its own reflection of the real situation, the epistemological process itself, with its self-regard, self-criticism, its infinite regress, its mirroring. In turn, the play-within-the-play has its reflection in the dumbshow, the short interlude providing, in yet another dimension, a representation of the deed at the outer play's center. In the dumbshow, the miming states the deed in its crudest simplicity, without even words to smooth over any of its brutality and calculation. In the play-within-the-play, as Gertrude perceives, words are already instruments of deception, while the dumbshow moves a stage back so that mere gesture can be seen to carry as much duplicity and deceit.[25]

Mirroring the play *Hamlet*, the Mousetrap underscores Hamlet's curious concern for epistemology, and besides offering that thematic stress, also alters the action, by acting upon it. Since the Mousetrap is organized at the center of the host-play, the play-within-the-play can indeed be seen as important; as a metaphor, then, it suggests that Hamlet's self-reflections may not forever stand in the way of action.

[25] See William Empson, "*Hamlet* when New," in *Discussions of Hamlet*, ed. J. C. Levinson (Boston, 1960), esp. pp. 100-101, for comments on the playwright's use of technical self-reference in the play, and his manipulation of audience reactions; and D. J. Palmer, "Stage Spectators in *Hamlet*," *English Studies*, XLVII (1966), 423-30. Muriel Bradbrook, *Shakespeare the Craftsman* (London, 1969), pp. 122-32, writes succinctly on Hamlet's remarkable recapitulation of English dramatic history. See also Righter, *Idea of the Play*.

The play-within-the-play also alerts us to what, in another way, Hamlet's skeptical utterances stress, that human knowing is always dependent upon point of view and "set," both of which can shift and by shifting demonstrate how much all human knowledge is subject to qualification and context. Simply as a device, the crude play-within-the-play helps to objectify the problems involved in Hamlet's thinking-process, since it is at once a *product* of those processes as well as a *mirror* of them.

There is a good deal of mirroring in the conceptual background of the play, too. A fundamental assumption underlying the humoral psychology involves a kind of mirroring, since in that scheme of thought the literal correspondence of man to earth and universe is taken for granted. The four humors and the four elements are similarly distributed in the physical makeup of all three natural "worlds," man, his habitat, the planet Earth, and the cosmos. Implied in this view of correspondence is that human speculation, even about external nature, must be to some extent self-referential; the contemplative melancholic, who thinks about the world, is therefore engaged in an ultimate self-reference, since the world also reflects him and he the world. Because he is in a particularly "conscious" symbiosis with his world, that correspondence presents special difficulties in his self-assessment and the assessment of any objective truth. "Give me a place to stand, and I will know the world": the doctrine of correspondence precludes an external reference-point from which to measure one's contemplative object. At best, paradox results from such a situation, at worst, solipsism.[26]

In the device of the players, some aspects of this intellectual problem are actually illustrated onstage. There, one actor plays the part of a king, another the part of an actor playing the part of a king: suddenly we are offered the usual metaphor of the whole problematical matter of kingship. Is "kingship" ever more than a rôle, the result of chance or of particular fortitude? The play reiterates the theme of player-king: Claudius mimics his brother's rightful role; Polonius had played Julius Caesar (a man who refused to take on the role of king in fact, but who died because others thought he nonetheless played the king); Hamlet waits in the wings of a kingship rightfully his, and polishes off his school-fellows by playing a king, with his father's seal signing their death-warrant; Fortinbras exercises in preparation for a rule

26 See *Paradoxia*, chapter 16.

he confidently expects to achieve; Laertes hopes for the election after he invades the palace, expecting to kill the King there; one of the players plays a player-king, another the usurper of that king's kingship.[27] The written roles reinforce the theme, in a way that we have been taught to expect imagery to do rather than the actions of a play. Since also the written roles are so often of pseudo-kings rather than real kings, the status of the theme itself becomes problematical in the play.

By other means than these, too, reflection is underscored, particularly in the overt mirror-imagery. Most notably, the players are commanded to "hold the mirror up to nature" in their acting-style. Shakespeare permits himself some critical commentary on acting-methods by means of his critical prince; the play selected for performance and its dumbshow mirror the situation in the actual play.[28] Ophelia calls Hamlet "the glass of fashion," a mirror for courtiers, as the central figure of any court ought to be the model in whom all lesser courtiers see themselves and who sees himself in turn reflected in the courtiers around him.[29] In her closet, Hamlet threatens his mother with having had some part in his father's death, promising to "set you up a glass/ Where you may see the inmost part of you." Of Laertes, Hamlet says in a sophist tautology outdoing Osric's popinjay rhetoric, "his semblable is his mirror."

Another and more complicated reflection, itself often multiple, is the device of the mirror mirrored. Hamlet has the impression that he is mirrored in the characters around him; this device is an unmetaphoring into the play's "life" of the common relation assumed between prince and courtiers. The mirror of a prince is, ideally, his perfect court, as Castiglione classically presents it; in such a perfect environment, good men see themselves mirrored wherever they look. Elsinore is quite different, of course; as a court, it is the ideal parodied, travestied—and yet in spite of

[27] Anne Righter makes most of these points; see also Cope, "Rediscovery"; and Harry Berger, Jr., "Miraculous Harp: a Reading of Shakespeare's *Tempest*," *S. Stud.*, v (1971), 253-83.

[28] Richard Leighton Green is preparing a paper on the thematic significance of the dumbshow in the play's plot (the dumbshow as charivari); for charivaris, see Natalie Zemon Davis, "The Reasons of Misrule," *Past and Present*, Number 50 (1971), 41-75. The classic work on dumbshows is Dieter Mehl's *The Elizabethan Dumbshow* (London, 1965).

[29] See Baldessare Castiglione, *The Boke of the Courtier*, tr. Sir Thomas Hoby (Everyman, 1937).

that, blurred and distorted as he feels himself to be, Hamlet in some way rightly sees himself reflected in the distorted courtiers about him. In the player who weeps for Hecuba, he sees himself; and in Hamlet's judgment, the advantage goes to the player, more committed to the demands of his profession than he himself to the demands of his duty. He sees himself also in Fortinbras, "a delicate and tender prince," who at the beginning of the play is prevented by the diplomacy of old men from avenging his father; in Laertes, as he says: "by the image of my cause I see/ The portraiture of his." All three young men, Hamlet, Fortinbras, Laertes, have a father killed, whom they variously attempt to avenge. The Player's speech, which had so moved Hamlet in the speaking, reinforces the same theme, since it is about Pyrrhus, Achilles' son, seeking revenge for his father upon Priam and upon Troy, for a moment unaccountably paralyzed before striking down the Trojan king. In Ophelia, too, Hamlet is mirrored, though he never perceives the likeness between them, left to the audience to recognize. Even in the equivocating grave-digger there is an echo of the antic Hamlet, who returned such enigmatic and equivocal answers to Polonius and Claudius. That absolute knave deals with Hamlet as Hamlet dealt with counselor and king—and, we note, Hamlet is annoyed, for equivocation is a game that pleases only one player. By the time he reaches the graveyard scene, Hamlet has passed beyond the defensive or offensive uses of language to regard it as a true instrument of psychological conviction. As Bridget Lyons has shown us, one sign of Hamlet's acceptance of the flawed social world around him is his abandonment of equivocation.[30] Always just outside Elsinore until the kingdom falls to him, Fortinbras exists in a subplot to mirror Hamlet's situation and to offer, much as Hotspur offers Hal, an alternative solution to the kind of difficulties under which Hamlet labors. Warlike and active, Fortinbras is the model strong-armed man: the election will light on him, since his is so suited to the rough realities of up-to-date princely politics.[31] Fortinbras, evidently unquestioning of its ideal, embraces in more modern terms the active heroic life which both young princes attribute to their fathers. Fortinbras marches here and

[30] For material on this, see Lyons, *Voices*; and Foakes, "Character and Role," pp. 156-57.

[31] See Zitner, "Hamlet: Duellist" and for this point generally, Maurice Charney, *Style in* Hamlet.

there for honor's sake, challenging great kings and kingdoms. Like Pyrrhus in the player's speech, Fortinbras does not hesitate to act on his dead father's behalf, though like Pyrrhus and like Hamlet, he too is long thwarted in his pursuit of his aims.[32]

Behind the machiavellian rhetoric of Claudius and the sophisticated intellectualism of Hamlet, we hear the sounds of a lost heroic age in which, for example, kings hazarded their kingdoms in single combat. A rhetorical parallel to this distinction between generations is the stylistic archaism, both of the player's speech and of the Mousetrap play, written in an idiom older than that of their host-play. From the references to Troy, in language much like that of earlier English translations of classical epic, and the rhymed couplets like those of English Senecan tragedy, we recall that there had been an age of heroes, now well past, and realize that a more equivocating—in many ways, a more taxing—rhetoric and age have been entered upon.[33] By the standards of heroism, the time is out of joint. In terms of dramatic styles, simply, the players' language offers another comment on the chronological and generational theme of the play.

III

For *Hamlet* is a play very much about generations, a play, in spite of everything, on the side of youth, against the old men who scheme their children out of their inheritance, out of their rights, out of their very lives. Hamlet, Horatio, Rosencrantz, Guildenstern, are all students; Laertes sows wild oats in France; Fortinbras is at practice for the kingship (*his* canny uncle is alive, but bedridden); Ophelia is a girl on the edge of marriage—all conditions normally youthful and promising, except in this play, where youth is darkened by the situation into which it has been born. This play turns out to illustrate that, willy nilly, youth must end. In *Hamlet*, young people actually die, in good numbers: Rosencrantz, Guildenstern, Laertes, Hamlet, Ophelia do not live to grow up fully; and all, save (in a way) Ophelia, die by violence. Fortinbras lives to rule in Denmark, Horatio at least long enough to tell Hamlet's story, but both must live gravely thereafter under the burden of their responsibilities and

---

[32] See Levin, *Question*, pp. 141-47.

[33] Eugene M. Waith makes some of these points in his *Herculean Hero*. I am indebted to Mr. Waith for illuminating conversations on this subject.

of the past: the ebullience of youth is over for both of them. In the curious theatrical details, the relation of generations is underlined by the "little eyases" who have elbowed out the mature actors, "usurping" their place and thereby endangering their own futures as they put the adult theater out of fashion. Significantly, it is Hamlet who perceives the theater-war as a succession question in which the children, with no profession to grow into, commit a kind of suicide by their usurpation.

In this play, youth is not gilded, affords no protection against danger. Nor does second childhood bring relief from tension, as in Folly's description in the *Encomion*: second childhood does not protect Polonius from his death. The sons grow up menaced by the mistakes of their elders and burdened by the meaning of their fathers, forced to bear weights imposed on them by older generations. The sons feel themselves somehow born "to set it right," or to die in the attempt.

The theme of youth and its transience is borne out in part by a familiar language of imagery, that of flowers. Around Ophelia this flower-imagery clusters, in strong contrast to the vegetable rankness and rottenness used, chiefly by Hamlet, to describe the Danish court. By the flowers, Ophelia's freshness and innocence, as well as her unprotectedness in the unweeded garden that Elsinore is, comes through clearly; the flowers suggest something else, far less attractive, the *vanitas*-motif, in which flowers are the major emblems of beauty's transience. In such references, there is always the warning that destruction will come:

> The canker galls the infants of the spring
> Too oft before their buttons be disclosed,
> And in the morn and liquid dew of youth
> Contagious blastments are most imminent.
>
> (I.iii. 39-42)

As Laertes speaks to his sister thus, he warns her against the importunities of Hamlet's desire: the educated segment of the audience hears the inversion of the usual *carpe diem* theme, here twisted to support the argument for economical chastity. Laertes, it is clear, is his father's son, with his father's gift for misapplying conventional language to conventional sentiments. The flowers associated with Ophelia have many meanings—the first and last flower used in reference to her is the violet, shy and faithful flower of spring, to whose brief blooming Laertes scornfully likens Hamlet's "love" for his sister and which, at her death, he hopes may spring "from her fair and unpolluted flesh" to shame the "churlish priest" refusing her full burial rites. The first violet is an image of fragility and transience, the last of sweetness and natural purity. Just as here the violets are used to refer to opposed qualities, the flowers in general refer to opposed ceremonies. Joining marriage and funeral, indirectly reminding us of her own too-quick juncture of those ceremonies, Gertrude says at Ophelia's grave,

> I thought thy bride-bed to have decked, sweet maid,
> And not have strewed thy grave. (v.i.221-22)

In other connections, flowers are unambiguous images for perfection. Ophelia calls Hamlet, before his declension into lunacy and abuse, the "rose of this fair state"—evidently blooming while Hamlet's father lived; Laertes, seeing his sister similarly declined into madness, calls her "the rose of May." Transience and roses are images for perfection rudely marred. In a simpler time, Hamlet might have looked to a bride-bed with Ophelia, but their love did not blossom, and "contagious blastments," of a kind different from those Laertes feared, contrived to kill it. For Ophelia, the violets all withered when her father died, so unaccountably, at Hamlet's hands. Ophelia's "document in madness," her distribution of emblematic flowers at a funeral, looks forward to her own funeral, when flowers are sprinkled upon her; and those flowers show, as Laertes says, how "a young maid's wits/ Should be as mortal as an old man's life." In her gesture of distributing flowers, Ophelia may also be doing something quite different from what at first she seems to do: she may also be acting out the sexual implications of her balladry, like Flora who offered flowers as images of and in prelude to the offering of her own body.[34] Ophelia dies garlanded, not this time by domestic plants, the rosemary, rue, violets, and pansies of her posie; she dies crowned with weeds—crowflowers, nettles, dead-men's-fingers—the rank growth of the garden. From the contradictory use of the flower-imagery applied to her, the contradictoriness and instability of Ophelia's divided mind can be read, a mind less violent, less passionate, but no less dangerous to herself than Hamlet's self-division was for him.

[34] Julius S. Held, "Flora, Goddess and Courtesan," *Essays in Honour of Erwin Panofsky* (New York, 1961), pp. 201-18.

The modes of connection afforded by imagery seem to point toward difference and distortion, rather than toward true reflection. On a larger scale, reflections are distorted, too. Ophelia partly reflects Hamlet, but to an important degree she does not; she dies deprived of her wits, quite without insight into her situation, whereas when he dies, he is finally in control of wit and will. As for Hamlet's reflection in Laertes, though *he* sees his situation in Laertes', the audience knows very well the radical difference between the two young men. Such slant reflections as these work two ways at once, to bind elements of the play together and to offer criteria for distinction between the elements so bound. Hamlet's self-knowledge for a long time remains distorted too, so that when he sees himself mirrored in the player, in Fortinbras, in Laertes, he entirely fails to recognize significant differences between himself and others, save for the grossest sort. From beginning to end of the play, Hamlet fails to apprehend the temperamental affinity between himself and Ophelia, so breakable on the turning wheel of others' fortunes. Ophelia was actually the victim of others' mistakes, as Hamlet so long regarded himself.

At the end, Hamlet understands himself the better for what has happened to Ophelia: perceiving the disastrous in her situation, he comes to terms with his own. His hysterics at Ophelia's grave is the crux of Hamlet's temperamental dilemma. Till then, he perceived the separation between the visible world and his action in it, for all his efforts to align them with one another. Thereafter, he could suit his word to his action, his action to his word. His behavior at the grave, after all, resulted from another mirroring: in Laertes' histrionics, Hamlet recognized his own and could see to what they had led. Though Laertes failed to gain insight into himself from that confrontation or any other, and thus continued to play his deceitful role, Hamlet therewith gave up his role-playing to become himself, "I, Hamlet the Dane," after the painful and purgative graveside scuffle.

In the "readiness" finally achieved, we perceive Hamlet's true mirror, his model and his reflective reflection—Horatio. For Hamlet, this fellow-student, bred like him to a life of reason, devoted to skeptical testing and persuaded of stoical values, represented the self-sufficiency and balance he himself hoped to achieve. Much earlier, Hamlet characterized Horatio in stoic terms of praise: "Thou has been/ As one in suffering all that suffers nothing." Horatio is one of those "blest"

> Whose blood and judgment are so well commeddled
> That they are not a pipe for Fortune's finger
> To sound what stop she please . . .   (III.ii.57-58, 61-63)

—he is, indeed, the perfect stoic man. Hamlet's words, "fortune" and "pipe," in this passage point to his use of both terms in addressing the time-serving friends, and thus make a contrast of Horatio's consistent, loyal behavior to their deviousness and carelessness. In a splendid compliment, Hamlet says to Horatio,

> Give me that man
> That is not passion's slave, and I will wear him
> In my heart's core, ay, in my heart of heart,
> As I do thee.   (III.ii.63-66)

Through the play, Horatio provides ballast for Hamlet's whirligig lightness—"These are but wild and whirling words, my lord"; "Half a share"; "You might have rhymed"—as well as steady support. Horatio first apprized Hamlet of the ghost, and kept counsel thereafter; Horatio was privy to the Mousetrap experiment and to Hamlet's jubilation after its apparent success; Horatio was Hamlet's chosen confidant and his first point of contact with Elsinore after the sea-voyage; Horatio companioned Hamlet to the duel and would have companioned him, had he had his way, to death as well. In the graveyard, Horatio listens to Hamlet's philosophizing; at the end, he is enjoined to poetry:

> Absent thee from felicity awhile,
> And in this harsh world draw thy breath in pain,
> To tell my story.   (v.ii.332-34)

Just before the duel, we recognize from a remarkably compressed speech that Hamlet has come to live by Horatio's steady stoicism, tempered by a subtle awareness and acceptance of unknowing: both stoic and skeptic, comfortably domiciled at last in Hamlet's mind, speak in the passage,

> There is special providence in the fall of a sparrow.
> If it be now, 'tis not to come; if it be not to
> come, it will be now; if it be not now, yet it
> will come. The readiness is all. Since no man of
> aught he leaves knows, what is't to leave betimes?
> (v.ii.199-202)

This passage, echoing the *topoi* of the two philosophical positions Hamlet has sought to conjoin through the play and which Horatio had, evidently, satisfactorily reconciled, knits up Hamlet's intellectual resolution to a simple confidence from which he can act without damage to his integrity. The speech records something else as well, the achievement of the philosophical stance which Hamlet had, without proper self-examination, believed himself at the play's outset to hold. As he had to learn from watching his own unaccountable behavior, he was quite wrong about himself: he had by no means managed to translate his philosophy into his natural behavior. By the play's end, though, Hamlet has arrived where he thought he was at the beginning, come roundabout through labyrinthine confusion and deceit, self-reference and self-criticism, through his own confusing tentatives toward truth. A way of saying the same thing, far more simply, is that by the play's end Hamlet has grown and grown up, to "readiness" for life at its extremity. In Hamlet's "readiness" and Edgar's "ripeness" we have translations of the same stoic commonplace; the variation in the noun measures some of the thematic difference between *Hamlet* and *King Lear*. Where Edgar's word "ripeness" designates natural process, Hamlet's "readiness" points to a condition of the human will, a context of decisiveness and action. He finally becomes "a man that is not passion's slave," after having labored under that very slavery for the better part of the play, to prove upon his own will passion's positive and negative powers.

IV

As well as thematic character-mirrorings, there are other kinds of mirror-action. Language overlaps with theme (as the flower-imagery indicates); by its repeating, echoing, quoting, the language shows differences and likenesses between characters and between situations. The play is full of echoes, for example, to "the primal eldest curse," the murder of brother by brother which motivates the plot. The elder Hamlet, slain by his brother, has also slain a brother-king in the primitive single combat which seemed so heroic to their sons. "Cain" is everywhere, from Claudius' "first corse," in his very first speech to Hamlet, to the graveyard, where Hamlet sees, in one skull turned up, "Cain's jawbone, that did the first murder." Brother hurts brother: Hamlet says to Laertes, "I have shot my arrow o'er the house/ And hit my brother." Hamlet calls his duel with Laertes "this brother's wager," which, for us, knowing the unfamilial resentments with which this play is so full, is an omen of what is to come. As *Hamlet* and *King Lear*, together with most Greek tragedy, demonstrate, the bitterest hatreds are those aroused by the fundamental and inevitable abrasions of family life. In "a brother's wager" can lie frightful hazard.

Brother's death, father's death: the elder Fortinbras, the elder Hamlet, Polonius, all propel their sons to some assertion of birthright and identity, all motivate revenge. The Mousetrap reflects the Danish situation, with an important difference: in the staged play, the murderer is a nephew, killing his uncle, evidently without cause; Hamlet's transposition of brother-murder to uncle-murder gives some warning of his intentions.

The Hercules and Caesar references in the play also relate different thematic aspects. Hamlet refers to Hercules, a major stoical hero,[35] in his character of reformer; the "Nemean lion's nerve" reminds us that Hercules was "born to set it right" and, furthermore, that he did so, accepting his lot in cleaning up the entire Mediterranean world. A reference to Hercules' supporting the world on his shoulders makes one kind of point about heroic burden-bearing, but, occurring as it does in a theatrical context, it is at the same time a self-reference, another mirroring, this time of the actual locus of the play, the Globe Theater, on whose sign was painted Hercules holding the world. Finally, in Hamlet's resigned jingle as he leaves Ophelia's grave, the heroism of Hercules is submerged beneath the commonplace trifles of everyday life.

The pattern of Caesar-references is much the same: first, the murdered ruler is invoked in a scholarly context by Horatio, seeking comfort from authority against the sudden apparition of figures in whom he does not believe. The ghost in question turns out to be, like Caesar, who also appeared as a ghost, a murdered ruler. Next, Polonius speaks of Caesar and Brutus, remembering his own histrionic past, in comic counterpoint to the king-killing theme—though the comedy turns dark when Polonius, standing in for the King, is in fact killed by mistake. By extension, the

[35] Waith, *Herculean Hero*, gives a good account of Hercules in Renaissance English literature; see also Erwin Panofsky, *Hercules am Scheidewege, Studien der Bibliothek Warburg*, 1930; and Lyons, *Voices*, pp. 107-109.

thoughtful Brutus becomes Hamlet—an actor playing Brutus had once killed Polonius playing Julius Caesar; now a man bedeviled (like Brutus) kills Polonius and lives (like Brutus) to regret the murder. Finally, in the graveyard scene, Hamlet refers to Caesar, gone like all men down to dust; from this reference, we realize that the Prince has absorbed the fact of his father's death and can face the expectation of his own.

Thematically, both Hercules and Caesar cast their long shadows across the play: Hercules was a hero who reformed the ancient world, who made hard choices readily—and, indeed, who was killed through the unwitting treachery of his wife, desired by another. Hercules was also, notoriously *in bivio*, a man who met the challenge of decision and chose correctly. Caesar was a ruler slain by a younger man whom he had treated as his spiritual son (and who, the gossip ran, may have been his son in fact). In Shakespeare's version of that story, finished not long before *Hamlet*, Brutus' inward struggle, to bring himself to kill an older man in some sense his father, has much in common with Hamlet's. Neither Brutus nor Hamlet knew what was right; both had to rationalize their behavior, the one an action too quickly taken, the other his delays on the way to action.

Other ties help to connect disparate parts of this play: friendship imagery, so differently handled by Polonius and by Hamlet, and painting imagery, active on many moral levels. Giving his son advice which, at first hearing, seems to be of the purest stoical sort, Polonius actually teaches Laertes policy and expediency. For all their circumspection, though, both Polonius and his son are willing tools of the machiavellian Claudius, each lending himself to the plans of the monarch simply because he is a monarch; both thereby instrumental in their own destruction. In Polonius' farewell address to his son, stoic saws are debased to fit this view of human relationship. Although he is apparently quite unconscious of what he is up to, Polonius' moralism works as a cover for his efforts at advancement and honor. So those friends whose fidelity has been tried, he says, should be grappled to the soul with "hoops of steel"—both "grapple" and "steel" part of the language of mechanical contrivance (windlasses, springes) which reveals Polonius' instrumental view of the world. The stoic truism takes very different shape on Hamlet's tongue: "I will wear him/ In my heart's core, ay, in my heart of heart." For

232

him, friendship is organic integration, not mechanical connection.

As we have reason to know, Laertes is Polonius' son. The father's usual "springes to catch woodcocks," with which he dismisses Hamlet's intentions toward his daughter, turns up in Laertes' speech at his own death, in which he recognizes his own responsibility for what has happened to him—

> Why, as a woodcock to mine own springe, Osric.
> I am justly killed with mine own treachery.
>
> (v.ii.290-91)

Such verbal echoes are a shorthand designed to remind the audience of themes stressed earlier, to hold a remembered note. The man was father to the child: Laertes is easily duped, made a tool, in spite of his self-protective suspicion of other people's motives. And yet Laertes is not just like his father, who was always disguised to himself, who meddled in situations the seriousness of which was unknown to him, who died without realizing his own part in his fate. Bombastic, sententious, energetic, impulsive, machinating, stupid though he was, Laertes was not the moral imbecile his father was. He hesitated before stabbing Hamlet with his envenomed sword ("And yet it is almost against my conscience"); recognizing his own end near and recognizing it to be just, he reveals the tricks for Hamlet to punish in the ever-shortening interim of his life.

Even Hamlet is not entirely free of machination, or of the language of machinery and contraption. Polonius' "windlasses and assays of bias" search by indirection to find direction out: so Hamlet, with his Mousetrap. Hamlet knows a hawk from a handsaw; Hamlet has his weapon-references too: "hoist with their own petard," the "arrow" with which he figuratively wounded Laertes, as well as the axe he knew his uncle to be grinding for his death. The arrow links up with Claudius' arrow, a self-wounding stratagem to kill Hamlet which he had to reject, his axe with Claudius' "great axe" which must fall on Hamlet.

Many verbal connectives link Hamlet with his uncle, each intent on the other's destruction and linked therefore in pursuit of a single aim. Hamlet's imagery of rankness, infection, and blood, his preoccupation with the "shufflings" of inaction, all show up in Claudius' prayer. As Marcellus had said at the play's beginning, Denmark is diseased; Hamlet everlastingly repeats the sentiment, and Claudius—"Denmark"—admits his own illness, though he diagnoses it as "Hamlet," or, as his nephew's continued life. So Hamlet is for Claudius the "disease" in Denmark, the hectic in his blood which, when purged, will make the state as healthy as him again. From Hamlet's perspective, of course, the opposite seems to be the case: his uncle is the disease from which the state suffers, and rid of his uncle, the purged state can recover some of its purity. These formulations are important in the play, which *does* deal fundamentally in terms of disease. The audience knows that Denmark is diseased, knows also that Hamlet suffers from melancholy; it is logically possible to accept Claudius' formulation that Hamlet, obviously ill, is the disease from which society suffers.[36] After all, Hamlet *is* ill, the state is unbalanced and uneasy, its precariousness increased by Hamlet's peculiar killing of Polonius. Perhaps with Hamlet gone, the state could come to its balance again. Of course this is another instance of the illusionism, the pseudo-logic, of appearances. Denmark is in fact diseased. Hamlet is melancholy and is therefore ill, but his illness is sympathetic, corresponds to and stems from the illness in the state; it springs from outward, not inward, deformations. It is, then, a true illness, an honest illness. The more Claudius speaks of Hamlet as the source of ill health in Denmark, the more Hamlet's illness seems to afford a norm for proper reaction, and the "health" for which Claudius strives seems abnormal, even immoral.

In Hamlet's speeches, the commonplace of man as reasoning beast recurs in his efforts to understand a world of infected will; this formulation is displayed in many contexts, as Hamlet tries out the various situations in which he is placed. Claudius echoes the platitude when he sees Ophelia mad, though with a patness that denies the possibility of his understanding the seriousness either of her situation or of his own. For Claudius reveals himself always as a "reasoning beast"—a bestial man, predatory and violent, relying upon his reason to preserve him and to destroy whatever is in his way. As his self-revealing prayer makes plain, appetite is paramount with Claudius, his ambition stronger than his desire for peace of mind. Claudius is always at the ready—he does not have to learn, like Hamlet, that "readiness is all," since

36 This seems to be Wilson Knight's view (*Wheel of Fire*), but see Holloway, p. 30.

it could never occur to him, good machiavellian that he is, to let down his guard for a moment. He manipulates from moment to moment, seizing each moment as it comes, laying longer plans as he can, taking advantage of any respite to organize for his ends. At the graveside Claudius says to his wife,

> An hour of quiet shortly shall we see;
> Till then in patience our proceeding be.
>
> (v.i.276-77)

while the audience knows that he is going to use that "hour" to scheme her son's destruction. Hamlet's "It will be short; the interim is mine," records his awareness of how crucial the situation has become, and his resolution to make the best of it too. The two speeches contrast radically: Claudius has spoken to deceive, Hamlet simply to state his unconcealed resolution and patience.

With these connectives supporting the complicated personal interrelations of the plot, *Hamlet*, like *King Lear*, emerges as a play in which no man is free of any other. No one is free of responsibility, for one's self or toward other people. The playwright ties the characters together by the tricks of his craft: sometimes a device acts as thematic connective, as the Hercules and Caesar references do; sometimes it acts as a touchstone testing different reactions to the same subject, the same theme; sometimes it acts, as the echoing language does, to show the ways in which characters otherwise very different share qualities or life-situations with one another. In the case of Polonius and Laertes, we cannot be surprised at similarities, but in the case of Claudius and Hamlet, we come to recognize their shared qualities far more slowly and more painfully.

V

Insofar as the devices serve to mirror aspects of the play, they connect in another way, important structurally as well as thematically. *Hamlet* is one of the many Renaissance literary works constructed on the principle of reinforcement, its theme echoed in different categorical ranges, in this case, of action, character, imagery, style. The melancholy-idea, so handy in managing the problem of Hamlet's nature and personality, lends itself to the mode of reinforcement chosen, since its emphasis on "specula-

235

tion" and "reflection" can be translated into mirroring literary devices which serve to reflect the epistemological theme. Shakespeare never sacrifices naturalism to symbolism, though: none of these mirroring-devices calls undue attention to itself or fails to make sense within the data of the play. The players, for instance, are thoroughly integrated into the plot: only secondarily do we perceive that the actors are an episodic and thematic metaphor as well. Their very presence reinforces the problem and theme of role-playing, by which Hamlet interprets his world for a time, and which shades into the disguises and deceits of the various *dramatis personae*. Insofar as the characters in the play are presented as role-players, as actors, we have a commonplace illustrated, at one remove, in the whole action of the play: "all the world's a stage," then, "and all the men and women merely players." Quite different, the unspoken commonplace in this play, from Jaques' speech, or from Prospero's; quite different, the relation of the commonplace to the whole play in this play and in *A Midsummer Night's Dream*. Here, the commonplace is not discussed or debated; rather, it is absorbed into Hamlet's personality. The world itself is seen *sub specie dramatis* for a while, until finally that too seems to be an illusion, and Hamlet and we can take the world as it really "is."

The play-within-the-play functions as a plot-element as well as an emblematic presentation of the difficulties of assessing one's judgment of appearances, of Hamlet's self-study, of his thinking about thinking. The play-within-the-play translates epistemology into dramatic terms, providing the audience with a visual example of the problems involved in interpretation with which Hamlet is really faced. Another device involving "levels" of reality and of apprehension is the poisoning in the play: the ghost tells Hamlet that he was poisoned "in his orchard," by the serpent who now wears his crown. In the dumbshow the sleeping actor-king is killed as the elder Hamlet was killed, by poison poured into his ear. At the end, the King, Hamlet, and Laertes are all poisoned by the sword. So the poisoning moves out of narrative history into emblematic action and finally into the play's fact, such as it is. "Poison in the ear" is also a major theme expressed in another way, by the everlasting eavesdropping in the play. Polonius eavesdrops to his death; Rosencrantz and Guildenstern sent to "listen" to Hamlet—"at each ear a hearer," as he says of them; Claudius and Polonius eavesdrop on Hamlet. What is overheard is "poison," one way or another, painful truth or painful deceit. Yet real *listening* is rare: Reynaldo finds it hard to listen to Polonius' orders to spy on Laertes; Ophelia does not attend to Laertes; Rosencrantz and Guildenstern cannot hear what Hamlet really says to them. When he appears to Ophelia in her closet, Hamlet does not speak to her, nor does the ghost speak to the Queen in hers. Indeed, only Hamlet and Horatio seem capable of listening to others, or to another: Hamlet with his uncannily heightened perceptions attends to the ghost and hears what other people—except Ophelia—do not mean to imply; Horatio attends to Hamlet's words, direct and whirling, and is able in both cases to read the Prince's meaning.

Perhaps because the theme is so important, and because there is so much eavesdropping and so little listening in this play, we are given instances to study in the very first act, where people continually give each other advice: the King, the Queen, the ghost all advise Hamlet; Laertes and Polonius advise Ophelia; Polonius advises Laertes. By their styles of giving and taking advice, we come to know the personalities of this play; by comparing this giving and taking, we can discriminate among the moral personalities of the play.

The major translation of the idea of reflection into professional terms is the mirror-language and action itself.[37] Mirrors in the form of other characters are held up to Hamlet; in them, he sees aspects of his own nature, sometimes in true reflection, more often sadly distorted. In its turn, the language nets these connections with its echoes of mutual borrowing. Underneath these familiar methods of reinforcement, present in many other Shakespearean plays besides *Hamlet*, lies another crucial self-reference, peculiar to this play, summed up in the word *play*. In its most functional meaning, "play" involves practice for maturity, as when young animals play in the offensive-defensive gestures required for serious struggles in mature life. So Hamlet and Fortinbras practise for a struggle as inevitable for Renaissance princelings as for young animals: Fortinbras plays quite naturally at kingship; Hamlet's temperament leads him toward other habits, playful also, but with the play of intellect rather

[37] For mirrorings, see Francis Fergusson, *The Idea of the Theatre* (Princeton, 1949), a brilliant study of the play. David Bevington, Introduction to *Twentieth Century Interpretations of Hamlet* (Englewood Cliffs, 1968), p. 4, speaks well of the mirrors in the play.

than of body or power. Mad or sober, Hamlet's deliberate word-play[38] demonstrates his exceptional agility of mind, reminding us, in another way, that a man with talents like his is wasted by the assignment of revenge. To make himself do what he ought, Hamlet must play a role unnatural to him; to act that role properly, he must undertake other roles, learn to watch other people in their roles and to assess their motives and intentions. The theme is centrally important in its moral context, worked out and reinforced in purely literary ways. In *Hamlet,* "role" is never unambiguous: playing cannot be dismissed as mere recreation. The fact is that temperament does not always coincide with role— a topic Shakespeare had presented and explored in *Richard II,* for example—as Hamlet had to learn. Hamlet was in fact im-properly cast, by fate, by providence, by his playwright, as a re-venge-hero; eventually he faces the moral dilemma of revenge, although his temperament rejects the problem as long as possible. Hamlet's attempt to solve his problem by trying out various roles is, at one level, simply what all experimental young men do: play with life while making their way into life. But this experiment was more than just play: for Hamlet, caught in the limitations set by his position and his life, experimentation could not be the wonderful open-ended entry into maturity of other young men, but was both critical and crucial, literally a matter of life and death.

The final fencing match is the acted metaphor for this aspect of the game.[39] Fencing enforces rules: it is a game of mortal violence, a game which tries to subject destruction to the rules of a game. In that game both Laertes and Hamlet put themselves at hazard, agree to risk their lives. Fencing is both attack and defense. It leads men to risk eternal damnation, with its invitation to murder and to suicide. By acquiescence in the rules of that game, one's life and soul are hazarded forever: one way or another, suicide is written into fencing. The match in the play, apparently a courtly mock-battle between two young men, is in fact the *agon* in earnest, a design in deceit in this case. "The readiness is all": though we assume the phrase to refer to Hamlet's finally composed mind, it seems to refer also to something far more mundane. For once, Hamlet has exhibited foresight, practising in Laertes' absence.

[38] See M. M. Mahood, *Shakespeare's Word-play* (London, 1957), pp. 111-29.
[39] Zitner, "Hamlet: Duellist," and references cited therein.

In a fair fight, he expects to win. The fight is not fair; he wins nonetheless, though at the expense of his life. In the fencing match, "play" turns into tragedy, just as in the play-within-the-play and the real play, appearances turn into tragic truths.

Hamlet's duel with Laertes is a mock battle of sorts in another sense, for it is a single combat in which one of the adversaries is a surrogate for someone else. Laertes stands in for Claudius, as his father too had substituted for the King at his death; except for this substitution, the duel is entirely real. In the duel, too, much else is focused: for this semi-suicide, Hamlet saved himself from death by his own hand and from death in England. Seen in connection with what has gone before and what will come, the semi-suicide grades into the actual suicide of Ophelia and the promised suicide of Horatio; it grades into all the self-induced deaths of the play: Polonius', Hamlet's school-fellows', Claudius', Laertes', and Gertrude's, all of whom played with mortality just too long. Knowing and unknowing, they all connived at their own ends, as they had connived for their own ends. The imagery of engines, weapons, tools, and machines which turn back against their manipulators serves to underscore the danger involved in any potentially tragic situation, as well as the morality-lesson that no machinator can be sure of his machines or machinations. Simply being in a tragic situation, as Ophelia for instance was, involves self-destruction, an act in which suicide is one risk.

Suicide is a self-reference,[40] the most negative self-reference possible in any life, by which a man unmakes himself, cancels himself out. In its self-referential nature, the theme of suicide touches and reinforces the curious self-reference, often radically self-questioning, of epistemology. In epistemology, a man tries to define his thought and his thinking processes; in suicide, he defines—i.e., "finishes"—himself in another way, by determining his life by his own act of will, that is, by choosing his death. In tragedies, as in some philosophies, the paradox is often illustrated that in a man's death his life is realized, that to live is to learn how to die. A man's attitude to his life qualifies and guides the ways he leads, or tries to lead, his life. Suicide always entails some paradoxy, as epistemology does too: by means of these self-references, *Hamlet* manages to open inward on an immense vista of private meaning, of distancing possibilities, into complexities reflecting on com-

40 *Paradoxia*, chapter 16, deals with suicide as self-reference.

plexities, difficulty dissolving into difficulty, into puzzles turning back on themselves, and by these vistas to transfer to the audience the legitimate confusions of the hero.

Placed at the very center of the developing action, the play-within-the-play acts as a focus, saved (as Hamlet himself is saved) from solipsism because it is more than just self-comment, but is also an instrument of action within the real play. Because of the little Mousetrap play, so crudely presented, Hamlet and Claudius enter their *agon* in earnest. In this tricky play, about trickiness, one of the trickiest elements is the playwright's decision to link the crude and cliché structure of a revenge-plot to an intellectual protagonist, to present us with a stereotyped revenge-situation and a hero who examines that situation critically, who takes his time about acting the part assigned him. Hamlet proceeds, then, as a moral critic, analyzing and reviewing the problems of such a play and of such a situation; he behaves, too, as a literary critic, stands in for his playwright, acting out the criticisms the playwright makes of the schematics of revenge.

By using the various patterns of melancholy to make credible and sympathetic such a protagonist, the playwright solved some of his problems of presentation. By paralleling the mysteries of Hamlet's thoughtful character in technical devices stressing mystery, mirroring, self-reference, tautology, and relativism, the playwright has constructed a more complicated and more intellectual play than a revenge-tragedy has any right to be. Philosophies become translated into behavior, and behavior opens back into philosophy, as Hamlet's skepticism and stoicism direct his attempts to find assurances for his cause, for his undertaken actions. The Prince's elegant habits of mind find their images in other ranges of theatrical practice, in the peculiar mirroring-devices which Shakespeare so heightens, so develops for this play, increasing the peculiar illusion of indefiniteness and limitlessness which so strikes the reader throughout, endowing at the same time each slightest theatrical act with a sense of profounder significance, often undefined.

These devices support our conviction that Hamlet is a thinking man, making the play seem properly shifty and shifting, properly disjunctive and untidy, as Hamlet's mind, working on its intransigent problem, must also be. Though both play and mind turn out to be very tightly constructed indeed, part of the drama of this order is achieved because of the perspectivism, the puzzles, the disjunctions, and conspicuous disorders of most of the play. Since *Hamlet* is, among much else, also about what Anne Righter has called "the idea of the play" and Lionel Abel "metatheater," one can see the fundamental importance of the world-as-stage commonplace, though the peculiar "realities" of the trope's use in this play, in which the whole meaning of "playing" is examined as well as demonstrated, are beyond the decorative and emblematic function of the commonplace, even in other Shakespearean plays.

Like Hamlet the character, *Hamlet* the play experiments in self-reference; as Hamlet the character is self-referential and self-analytical, so is *Hamlet* the play. In the simplest terms, those of contemporary psychology, the metaphor of playing can be seen to be "true," though the playwright does not present its "truth" before he has examined its illusions and its deceits. The melancholy man saw all men and women as playing parts, all their lives long, himself included. So Hamlet, legitimately and illegitimately melancholy, playing his parts, sometimes for aggression, sometimes for defense, sometimes considerately, sometimes reflexively, sometimes for fun, sometimes in dead earnest. By choosing melancholy as a naturalistic locus, which permits and even encourages acting-out as part of action, the playwright was able to find many metaphors and devices, not only for presenting an intellectual protagonist as interesting and sympathetic—in itself a problem in a play—but also for dramatizing his own examination of the moral commitments of his craft. The playwright's self-reference is only a ghost behind the fulfilled demands of plot, but its shadowy presence serves to remind us that any moral self-examination, even of a play by a playwright, is a very difficult undertaking which can lead, directly indeed, to the extremities of a man's situation.

By translating the problems of playwrights into the language of tragedy, the playwright gives another dimension to his play; in *Hamlet*, life is examined and found to be worth living—and worth dying for as well. The relation of acting to acting out, the relation of both of these to action, are perceived and presented as alternatives to simple choice: they are taken seriously, not offered as inadequate simulacra of and substitutes for action. In Hamlet's own maturing, histrionics turns out to be not all bad; his playing protects him as much as it inhibits him, instructs him more than it disgraces him. Like any young animal, Hamlet learns to act by acting, learns to do by playing at doing. Playing permits him to cross the several abysses of his own perception—gulfs between appearance and reality, between opinion and fact, between intellect and will, between youth and maturity, between unpreparedness and readiness for life and for death. By raising a professional problem to a moral plane, the playwright was able to examine the nature of knowing, as well as the relation of knowing to acting; to examine the relation of opinion to fact and thereby to examine also the nature of fiction and fictions. He was able, then, to make us feel the immense distances between fiction and fact, and their unaccountable confluence in the symbolizing, analytical understanding. *Hamlet* presents us—slowly, painfully, like the experience itself—with a man experiencing what it is to "know," after trial and error, after revelation and denial, the truth of a human situation. In this play, the playwright has demonstrated what acknowledged fictions can do for imaginative knowledge, as the play's fiction proffers us some understanding of what "understanding" can mean.

6

Perspectives on Pastoral:
Romance, Comic and Tragic

I

By the end of the sixteenth century, the pastoral mode embraced many particular genres, offered rich options to writers interested in literary experimentation, particularly in mixed genres, and, furthermore, had become embroiled in one of the great literary quarrels which characterized Renaissance literary theory. The pastoral permitted and encouraged opportunities for mixing in one work "imitation" with "invention," art with artifice, the artless with the artful—and generated discussions of such mixes. Eclogues were the principal pastoral form, hallowed by antiquity, but other pastoral lyrics flourished: the love-lyric, the dialogue, the song. Pastoral episodes regularly offered relief in poems largely devoted to epic gests; an English poet wrote a heroic epic in prose entitled, in spite of its relatively scant preoccupation with shepherds, *Arcadia*, and set into this prose-epic a series of pastoral poems which are themselves a self-sufficient anthology of pastoral forms and themes. Following hints from Italian eclogue-writers and fulfilling medieval Latin literary traditions, Marot and Spenser presented unabashed models of Christian pastoral, enriching the imaginative possibilities for their successors; both poets also experimented successfully with satirical poems within the pastoral mode. Indeed, one can recognize anthologies of pastoral work— Sannazaro's *Arcadia* is one example; *The Shepheardes Calender* offers a survey of pastoral themes and topics, and Sidney's shepherds in the *Arcadia* offer a magnificent epideictic display of the eclogue's range of possibilities, formal and topical.[1]

[1] Thomas G. Rosenmeyer, *The Green Cabinet* (Berkeley, 1969), is the most valuable analysis of pastoral thematics I have seen; see also Alice Hulubei, *L'Églogue en France au xvi*^e *siècle* (Paris, 1938); Mia I. Gerhardt, *Essai d'analyse de la pastorale* (Assen, 1950); W. Leonard Grant, *Neo-Latin Literature and the Pastoral* (Durham, N.C., 1965); W. W. Greg, *Pastoral Poetry and Pastoral Drama* (London, 1906); E. K. Chambers, *English Pastorals* (London, 1895); Frank Kermode, ed., *English Pastoral Poetry* (London, 1952), Introduction; Jules Marsan, *La Pastorale dramatique en France* (Paris, 1905);

From *commedia dell' arte* and other popular forms to the grand productions of Tasso and Guarini, drama exploited pastoral scenes, pastoral characters, and what might be called (in the Renaissance anyway) the lyric pastoral *pathétique*.[2] The way in which the pastoral locale was taken as an official site for love-play and for love-poetry can be illustrated by a late anthology of pastoral lyrics published in 1600, *England's Helicon*; that an English Arcadian rhetoric and a mildly Arcadian logic were produced at the turn of the century shows how powerfully the literary notion of Arcadia had come to operate across the spectrum of literary possibility in England's green and pleasant land. From one end to the other of the social and literary scale, pastoral myths and patterns were available: in Whitsun pastorals, pastoral interludes, pastoral romances, in narrative books and on the stage, pastoral masques and (even more common) pastoral episodes within masques, spectators could take their pastoral experience. The ways of pastoral, then, were many and varied; the mixtures of forms, conventions, devices in pastoral allowed a very wide range of decorums.

The richness of the mixture is not really surprising: the literary critical quarrel over the pastoral as *the* mixed dramatic genre, thus as the official locus of tragicomedy,[3] broke out over Guarini's *Il pastor fido* and culminated in the establishment of the pastoral play as the official mixture of comedy with tragedy (sometimes with satire as well), exemplified in such devices as double-plotting, mixed styles, and even interludes from the non-literary arts, such as music, dancing, and the visual arts.[4] Wherever one looked, one could find pastoral—and once-found, twice-found, for the generous, nearly boundless forms of pastoral offered immense opportunities for craft and for imagination.

Enrico Carrara, *La poesia pastorale* (Milano, n.d.); Hallett Smith, *Elizabethan Poetry* (Cambridge, Mass., 1952).

[2] See Rosenmeyer, pp. 77-85, who offers a corrective to the view of Renato Poggioli as expressed in "The Pastoral of the Self," *Daedalus*, LXXXVIII (1959), 686-99; see also Bruno Snell, *The Discovery of the Mind*, tr. T. G. Rosenmeyer (New York, 1960), Chapter 13.

[3] For this, see F. H. Ristine, *English Tragi-comedy* (New York, 1910); Marvin T. Herrick, *Tragicomedy* (Urbana, 1962), esp. pp. 125-71; Madeleine Doran, *Endeavors of Art*, pp. 182-215; Karl S. Guthke, *Modern Tragicomedy* (New York, 1966), pp. 3-5, 45-92; Cyrus Hoy, *The Hyacinth Room*, pp. 270-73.

[4] Cf. Rosenmeyer on the "mix" of pastoral, pp. 145-67; and K. M. Lea, *Italian Popular Comedy*, I, 196, for *commedia dell' arte* mixtures.

From such a background, Shakespeare's sophisticated traffic with pastoral is hardly surprising; typically, he experimented with the mode in various ways, in both early and late plays. In *As You Like It*, a play with a remarkably tight thematic construction, he worked with many pastoral themes and motifs, to say nothing of pastoral types in the *dramatis personae*, in what is primarily a romantic love-story derived from a prose narrative. Although "romance" and its proper subject, love, dominate this play, with the shepherding and versifying rather its decoration than its psychological locus, nonetheless the skeletal structure of this romantic comedy *is* the standard dramatic pastoral pattern—a pattern of extrusion or exile, recreative sojourn in a natural setting, with ultimate return "homeward" from the exile, a return in moral strength reinforced by the country experience of kind and kindness.

As You Like It is, for once, about sheep, but this plot-form, from academic drama to *commedia dell' arte*, was so thoroughly identified with the pastoral that as a formula it could imply without overtly stating a great deal of standard pastoral thematics. Sheep, for instance, were often quite absent from such plays, which sometimes lacked even the pasture environment. But the *themes* associated with pastoral (court-country, art-nature, nature-nurture) could be counted on to inform plays with this plot-pattern. A plot on this plan, thus, was a recognizable vehicle for discourse on the pastoral themes, an abstraction designed to interpret problems of nature and nurture originally associated with more overtly pastoral topics.

Though it follows the pastoral dramatic plot and has to do with sheep and shepherds, *As You Like It* is by no means "officially" pastoral. It ignores, certainly, some of the major cruces of Italian pastoral dramatic theory: it has no double-plot, for instance, in the pure sense. Though the De Boys story is separate from the ducal story, nonetheless Orlando is early displayed at court, catching the attention of Rosalind; throughout, his situation is seen as a counterpart to hers. Although the country lovers overlap with their courtly parallel figures, they are in the play rather to round out the range of pastoral alternatives than to divert into a "plot" of their own. Nor are there radical shifts of locale and of genre in *As You Like It*: the ducal and gentlemanly affairs, so to speak, are conveniently focused in one place, the forest, by means of the exile-device; though the breath of tragedy blows through the forest, the dominant tone is always, through Duke Senior's and Rosalind's efforts, kept lucidly "comic."

Duke Senior, Rosalind, Orlando: all are exiled, and in their company come the spiritual exiles who will not part from them, Celia, Touchstone, the Duke's men, Adam. In the forest these exiles, valiantly seeking some cheer, meet that symbolic, alienated, self-exiled figure, the melancholy Jaques, already located in the wood. All these victims—Jaques too—of the world find renewal in the simple culture of the Forest of Arden, and all, save Jaques and Touchstone, return triumphantly to reconstruct the social world from which they had been driven out. Against this basic construction, the play is rich in additional pastoral themes and motifs, many of them ultimately Theocritan and Vergilian, reworked throughout the Latin Middle Ages, reconceived in the Renaissance.

The play makes much of the dialogue and dialectic which so inform pastoral: the love-debates of Silvius and Corin, Silvius and Phebe; the discussion of court and country between Corin and Touchstone; the styles of courtship of Orlando and Rosalind; the dialogue on nature and nurture between Orlando and Oliver; and, as in Spenser's wonderful array of pastoral debates, *The Shepheardes Calender*, the themes so dialectically handled provide an enriching counterpoint to one another. Both the pastoral *agon* (Corin-Silvius) and the pastoral *paragone* of real sheep-herding versus literary sheep-keeping (Corin-Touchstone) are part of the play's thematic structure. Among the many things this play is, it is a *comparative* work about competing life-styles, among these the competition of shepherdly lives, with real shepherds who dip their sheep and lambs, whose hands smell of tar and of the oil from the sheep's wool, and others who live "poetically." We are asked to measure the real and literary shepherds against each other, not once but several times. Behind the prating of the shepherd's life, important thematically as it is in the play, lies a grander anthropological conception, the (pastoral) myth of the Golden World, "the antique world" in which there was perfect commerce and mutual service among men naturally well-disposed to one another, the myth, then, of the Golden Age.[5] In antiquity, the pastoral life

[5] For this topic, see the classic work of A. O. Lovejoy and George Boas, *A Documentary History of Primitivism and Related Ideas in Antiquity* (Baltimore, 1935); Harry Levin, *The Myth of the Golden Age in the Renaissance* (Bloomington, 1969); Rosenmeyer, pp. 220-24; Mia I. Gerhardt, *Het Droom-*

had been assigned to the Age of Gold, when men lived in com-
mutual confidence and kept their flocks and herds together, their
natural characters attuned to the gentle world they inhabited,
their goods held comfortably and easily in common. Such a world
had no need for war and was therefore an ideologically pacifist
community; such discomfitures as men suffered were not caused
by human agency but by natural hazards (winter and rough
weather) and by creatures not yet enrolled in the peaceable kingdom (wolves and snakes, in ancient pastoral; snakes and lions in
As You Like It; metaphorical kites and wolves and real bears in
The Winter's Tale). Insofar as this ideal theme bears upon the
dialectic of pastoral, it implies the corruption of an imperfect
world of men—urbs, the court—against which its perfections
could be fully felt.

With the development of a pastoral pathétique by which men
identified with the gentler creatures and, in the Renaissance, allowed themselves the luxury of self-cultivation, even of emotional
self-exploitation,[6] love officially became the major pastoral occupation, taking precedence even over keeping sheep real or poetical. That is, the shepherd was naturally a poet in the pastoral
genres, but before long was also a poet-lover. At first, the pastoral
world was pleasant, natural, easy, and so was its love—although
the shepherd's complaint about his cold, coy, or faithless mistress
(with a corresponding saddening of his landscape to match his
emotional situation) was the celebration of another kind of love,
troublesome, upsetting, potentially destructive of the mutuality of
pastoral society. Gradually shepherds and, later, shepherdesses began to die of love—even the pastoral landscape was not always
sufficient to nourish the love-struck pastoralist through his emotional afflictions. Though the pastoral world with its celebration
of timelessness and harmony would seem to have been created
precisely to deny the efficacy of death, nevertheless death's shadow
lay across even its green perfections to chill its warm airs.[7]

---

beeld van de Gouden Eeuw (Utrecht, 1956); and E. H. Gombrich, "Renaissance and Golden Age," Norm and Form, pp. 29-34.

[6] See Renato Poggioli, "The Oaten Flute," Harvard Lib. Bull., XI (1957),
147-84; "Pastoral of the Self"; and Rosenmeyer, p. 223.

[7] The classic statement of this is Erwin Panofsky's " 'Et in Arcadia Ego,' " in
Philosophy and History, ed. R. Klibansky and H. J. Paton (Oxford, 1936); reprinted in Meaning in the Visual Arts (Anchor, 1955), pp. 295-320. Cf. Rosenmeyer, pp. 224-31.

The pastoral elegy offers a marvelous rationale for death, with its classic expression of the wonderful comforts and assuagements for personal loss; it provides the pattern for the pastoral relation of man to nature, of creation to inspiration: there, the shepherd-singer, the shepherd-maker, is gathered into the pastoral artifice of nature's eternity, these two fused into one. At one with this imaginative and nutritive nature, the dead shepherd-poet becomes a part of the inspiration he had himself once drawn from nature's store. In life poetically competitive—shepherd, goatherd, and cow-herd continually sang in *agon*, each praising his own particular life-style, ritualized into poetic activity—and in death tradition-preserving, the pastoralist invented a world of the imagination in which, depending on his temperament, he could live as he would. He might, then, live sparingly, in simple opposition to urban luxury, confident of nature's power to provide for him; or he might live richly, feasting from nature's endless store, recreating himself and his art thereby. Whichever "nature" he chose as his setting, that entity was expected to provide sufficiently for his aesthetic and emotional needs—in other words, to nurture him.[8]

Theocritus, with whom this all began,[9] was less concerned with the relative values of city and country than with the positive recreations of the country: what court-country *agon* we find in him, we bring with us from reading subsequent pastoral writers. Vergil, however, made overt the *paragone* of city and country life; certainly implied in his eclogues and subsequently in the pastoral psychology is the sense of relief from the pressure of daily concerns (*negotium*) in a "liberty" and "freedom" (*otium*) consciously contrasted to the workaday round, a praise of simplicity (and, therefore, of "nature") as contrasted with the artificiality of urban life.[10] As needs no reminder, the inventors and practitioners of literary pastoral were not professional shepherds, but highly sophisticated city-dwellers, whose country life of the imagination was quite different from that enjoyed by the inhabitants of the real Arcadia or, after erosion, of the real Sicily. Thomas Rosenmeyer has put it well: Theocritus' Sicily is not so much a geo-

[8] Cf. Lovejoy and Boas, *passim*; Poggioli, "Flute" and "Pastoral of the Self."

[9] Rosenmeyer's book deals primarily with the Theocritan elements of the pastoral lyric tradition; for Virgil, see Michael Putnam, *Virgil's Pastoral Art* (Princeton, 1970); and Kermode, Introduction, pp. 14-15, for the city-country transition to court-country.

[10] Rosenmeyer, pp. 65-97, 98-129; and Barber, *Festive Comedy*, chapter 2 and pp. 223-29.

graphical place as a cartographical fiction. Even the country of Vergil's *Eclogues* is a mixed scene, by no means the recognizable North Italian locality of the *Georgics*, for instance.[11] To call such a locale "Arcadia," Rosenmeyer tells us, is precisely to rob it of its "real" geographical implications, to insist that, as a natural spot, it is a mental artifact, a concept, an image in itself.

The encroachments of the city on the green world—of *negotium* upon *otium*—are destructive not only of a simpler form of society, but also of the psychological symbol the pastoral world is. For the literary pastoral celebrates the glorious unrealities of the imagination, its necessary furlough from its assignment of work, obligation, and duty.[12] The iron, or at best brazen, world is man's normal portion: as Sidney put it, "poets only deliver a golden." In the literature with which we have here to deal, the literary opposition between *urbs* and *rus* shifted to become in the Renaissance a *topos* in itself, but with a particular fit to Renaissance literature and socio-economic notions—that is, it shifted its formulation from "city" to "court," and the court-country paradigm became one major focus of pastoral organization.[13] The naturalness, freedom, delightfulness of the pastoral ethos often criticized, overtly or by implication, the self-seeking, self-aggrandizing materialistic artificiality of any court—"court" a synechdoche for any artificial, programed social organization. "Sicily" and "Arcadia" were not measured merely against (as Poggioli believed) the megalopolis, Alexandria, Rome, Paris, but against *any* strict program of social forms, formalities, polite fictions, or flatteries. At Versailles, later, queen and courtiers carried crooks and passed their time as shepherdesses and dairymaids; consciously or not, they acted out the extreme solipsism of the pastoral fiction, so delicately self-referential that only the most sophisticated can comprehend its significations. In the ambivalent symbiosis of court and country, at least in Renaissance pastoral writing, it was the courtier who came for instruction or confirmation to the

[11] Rosenmeyer on "place" p. 232; on chores, p. 25.

[12] Empson, *Versions of Pastoral*; Barber, *Festive Comedy*; Harry Berger, Jr., "The Ecology of the Mind," *Centennial Review*, VIII (1964), 409-34; "The Renaissance Imagination: Second World and Green World," *Cent. Rev.*, IX (1965), 36-78.

[13] An interesting instance of unawareness of generic traditions occurs in Charles Barber's discussion of *The Winter's Tale* in *Shakespeare in a Changing World*, ed. Arnold Kettle (London, 1964), pp. 233-52.

shepherd, from whom the courtier, an apprentice shepherd, could learn what natural "courtesy" was.

Since the poet's world could be reshaped according to the imagination, could reject conventional decorum to set queens in the dairy, eating bread and honey, poetic imagination could work what miracles it would with its pastoral situation. If queens are dairymaids, shepherdesses can just as well be queens, or at least princesses—and so they turned out to be, over and over again, in the wish-fulfilling satisfactions of pastoral myths. The "marvelous," that subject for endless discussion among Italian critics,[14] was commonplace in the pastoral environment, with social miracle one of pastoral's chief donations. Not least of these was the re-establishment in the pastoral environment of Golden Ageness ("poets only deliver a golden"), or (better) Golden Agelessness: in this generic country, there was no season's difference, in the forest no clock.[15] The landscape stood, at its best, at a perpetual spring, fruiting, and harvest; at worst, the season's round was characteristically benevolent. When the landscape was not at its rich mellowness, the pastoral *pathétique* was generally to blame—the landscape had fallen off to mirror its shepherd's disappointments or depression. In this fiction, then, a poet's triumph was complete: by its means, he could create a nature whose sole poetic obligation was to identify with his emotional state. Such a nature is entirely dependent upon imaginative art, is a nature openly, proudly artificial, a nature which inverts the usual system of imitation, by which art conventionally looks to nature as its model, to offer an art form on which nature might model itself for its own improvement. The pastoral, then, offered a paradigm for the creative imagination in which the doctrine of *mimesis* is questioned or rejected[16]—and so, really, is the idea of decorum. Not that the

---

14 Cf. Baxter Hathaway, *Marvels and Commonplaces* (New York, 1963), pp. 35-56.

15 For the timelessness trope, see Rosenmeyer, 86-88; and above, footnote 5.

16 Though the pastoral mode, utilizing the "low style," observed strict prescriptions of *mimesis* with respect to matching style to country matters and, in many cases, to primitive states of society, nonetheless (by the Renaissance anyway) part of its literary power lay in the ironies involved in portraying this kind of society for a courtly audience. With the development of a literary criticism centering on *maraviglia* (see Hathaway, op. cit., *passim*), as well as the theory of tragicomedy which accepted pastoral setting as requisite to the new genre, *mimesis* in the strict sense fell out of the debate, in spite of continued talk about decorum and "matching."

pastoral has not its own rules, conditions, and decorum—but its decorum is a conscious reversal of worldly decorus standards.

For these reasons, the art-nature question, another major critical topic of the period, was deeply tied to the pastoral mode, which became the debate's normal habitat. Poets played with the notion of pastoral nature, used as a stalking-horse against the artifices of another ethos—itself a magnificent, self-conscious artifact. From pastoral writing (often mixed with notions of education and cultivation generally classed as georgic),[17] men took a major metaphor, that of the "improvement" of natural things, especially the improvement of breeds by crossing or grafting. "Breeding," that most natural of procedures, became an area where art counted most. The question was delightfully debated: was a man entitled to use his wit to perfect nature, or did he, by interfering in natural processes ("The Mower against Gardens"), degrade and adulterate natural patterns and products?[18]

For agriculturalists as well as for poets speaking metaphorically, this is at once an aesthetic and a moral problem—involving, among other things, the rights of the arts (all the arts, not just poetry, certainly not just pastoral poetry) to do what art does: that is, to "improve" the nature it imitates. In the simplified and rigid scheme of styles and topics inherited by Renaissance theorists ("systematized" is surely the better word[19]), shepherds are honest people, as George Herbert put it: they speak in a simple, or low, style befitting the life they lead and the landscape in which they dwell. Should, then, kings and princesses masquerading as shepherds and shepherdesses undertake a simple style of life and of speech? What does such disguise do to a literary decorum based upon a hierarchy of values, with strict relations observed between social rank and level of style? Should those nobles who opt for the country learn, like Berowne, an uncourtly speech, doff, like Kent, the latinate orotundities of rank? Should they not, in short, suit their words to their new actions? Within the artifice of the pas-

---

[17] In his forthcoming work, Dr. Alarik Skarstrom will lay out some of the "georgic" aspects of pastoral.

[18] This question, a topic in Pliny and Seneca, is discussed in *"My Ecchoing Song,"* pp. 36-38; see Edward A. Tayler, *Nature and Art in Renaissance Literature* (New York, 1964), pp. 16-17; and Charles Barber, "The Winter's Tale and Jacobean Society," *Shakespeare in a Changing World.*

[19] See Fred J. Nicholls' excellent (though oddly-titled) article, "The Development of the Neo-Latin Theory of the Pastoral in the Sixteenth Century," *Humanistica Lovanensia,* XVIII (1969), 95-114.

toral frame, all this is made problematical, to be interestingly explored in many works. If, as countless Renaissance pastoralists demonstrate, the pastoral natural world is a complex imaginative artifice, why should not princes and princesses, with their sophisticated and fine-spun speech, be welcome in Arcadia, where their rhetorical finesse simply adds to the imaginative beauties in the pastoral ecology? And welcome they were—which meant that another mixture of decorums was made in this already most mixed of modes.

Such *genera mixta* bring their own contradictions. For instance, in this literary ethos so deceptively simple, the best of everything is selected: the best of genres, the best of styles, the best of solutions to human problems. No wonder then, when we seem to lose a major figure in Tasso's *Aminta* by suicide, we yet recover that figure alive by love's magic power and the accident of a convenient bush: Aminta is too valuable to be spared, and the landscape's marvels are sufficient to save even the most despairing shepherd. Art rescues men from the trials of their lives,[20] and the pastoral makes no bones about it. No wonder, then, that as Guarini laboriously insisted against his fierce opponents and as Fletcher so gracefully observed, comedy and tragedy came so easily to dwell together in the nurturing environment of literary pastoral. Fletcher's comment on his own *Faithful Shepherdess*, written after *As You Like It* and well after the major documents of the Guarini quarrel, states the plain case for the mixture of comic and tragic modes:[21]

A tragie-comedie is not so called in respect of mirth and killing, but in respect it wants deaths, which is inough to make it no tragedie, yet brings some neere it, which is inough to make it no comedie: which must be a representation of familier people with such kinde of trouble as no life be questiond, so that a God is as lawfull in this case as in a tragedie, and meane people as in a comedie.

Part of the reason for the tragicomic mix, then, is in the nature of the action; another reason lies in the mixture of ranks involved in most pastoral romances and plays, where disguise of great ones is a principal plot-device.

[20] See below, pp. 289-92.
[21] Cited in Eugene M. Waith's valuable book, *The Pattern of Tragicomedy in Beaumont and Fletcher* (New Haven, 1952), p. 44.

With these literary or generic and social mixes, comes also moral mixture, a mixture of ways of life set in actual or implied contradistinction or even contradiction.[22] Looking back to Theocritus, we can see that some cultural distinction underlies the agonistic presentation of pastoral eclogues, in the competitions between singers judged for their skill in singing—or, to say it another way, between singers judged for their success in defending their particular variant upon the pastoral life. Neatherd, goatherd, shepherd challenged one another, to be challenged in turn by fishermen and mowers, sometimes even by huntsmen[23]—and, given such a thoroughly country mixture, why not by a courtier as well, especially a courtier disguised as a countryman?[24] Of course, by the time we arrive at this particular elaboration of pastoral *agon*, a radical discharge of original pastoral democracy has been effected: when court invades country, rank, however understressed, intrudes upon such egalitarian commutuality as countrymen enjoy, alters the condition in which, as the Golden Age myth had it, social class was irrelevant. Once the mixture of class is accepted in the pastoral system, then alienation may become a conscious topic, too: perhaps this is Vergil's point in the First Eclogue. So the melancholy Jaques may not be all that out of place in the Forest of Arden, even though he is "Monsieur Traveler" and, it would seem, at the very least a university wit. He has, presumably, become disgusted and worn out by the conflicting sophistications he has seen and is, at least, true to the Arden he criticizes, when alone of the cast he declines to return to court. Celia's choice of pseudonym, Aliena, honors the reason for her voluntary exile and is one token of her courtier-status within the forest. The pastoral world is not for the disappointed and victimized alone, to relearn their integrity; it exists also for those more seriously estranged from society, as the early reference in *As You Like It* to Robin Hood suggests.

II

As You Like It[25] miraculously collects the major themes of the pastoral, manipulating and juxtaposing them so as to bring that

[22] See Rosenmeyer, pp. 68-70, 86-88.   [23] J. C. Scaliger, *Poetics*, ii, xcix.

[24] I.e., Florizel in *The Winter's Tale* fulfills the simple prescription, while the guileless Perdita's unconscious disguise as a shepherdess moves into the problematic realm. See Rosenmeyer, p. 103.

[25] See Edwin Greenlaw, "Shakespeare's Pastorals," *SP*, xiii (1916), 122-54;

rich mix under critical scrutiny. Not only is the classic pastoral dramatic pattern its basic fiction—exile from court; country restoration; triumphant return to court—but so also are the themes of nature and nurture, of art and nature, of art and artifice, of court and country debated in eclogue-like exchanges uttered by representatives of pastoral and non-pastoral (sometimes even anti-pastoral) positions. The "parallel and parody" of the play, so well analyzed by Jay Halio and others,[26] works beautifully to undermine doctrinaire attitudes, social, moral, or literary. The play's perspectivism is sufficient exposure of the implications of the *vie sentimentale* for which pastoral had come so masterfully to stand.

Even satire and folly, embodied in Jaques and Touchstone, in turn set into *agon*, come to challenge and to reinforce the values of this pastoral. The love at the center of the play is not a particularly pastoral love, save in that the playwright works toward eliminating the artificial and non-natural aspects and elements of love; but the pastoral tradition, with its exquisite concentrations upon the emotional nuances and values of love, offered a superb literary opportunity for examining the love-subject.

Nor is love the only topic so scrutinized: Corin speaks of his content in the life he leads, in open contrast to Touchstone's obvious dependency upon his ladies, yet we know from his own mouth that Corin is shepherd to another man and not, in Fletcher's sense, one of the true literary shepherds who are "owners of flockes and not hyerlings."[27] Corin qualifies his own position: so does Touchstone who, praising the court above the shepherd's life, by his witty chop-logic lays open the shabbiness of the court's customs. Shepherd and jester are brothers, after all, under the skin: Touchstone, remembering Jane Smile, recalls that early love in the generic language of the peasant Corin. The "country copu-

Mary Lascelles, "Shakespeare's Pastoral Comedy," *More Talking of Shakespeare*, ed. John Garrett (London, 1959), pp. 70-86; Helen Gardner, " 'As You Like It,' " ibid., 17-32; Peter G. Phialis, *Shakespeare's Romantic Comedies* (Durham, N.C., 1966), pp. 219-31; Harold Jenkins, " 'As You Like It,' " *S.Stud.*, VIII (1955), 40-51; R. P. Draper, "Shakespeare's Pastoral Comedy," *Études anglaises*, XI (1958), 1-17; Waith, *Pattern*, pp. 80-83; Sylvan Barnet, "Strange Events: Improbability in *As You Like It*," *S. Stud.*, IV (1968), 119-31; Marco Mincoff, "What Shakespeare did to *Rosalynde*," *Sh. Jhrb.*, XCVI (1960), 78-89.

26 Jay L. Halio, Introduction to *As You Like It: Twentieth Century Views* (Englewood Cliffs, 1968); and see Gardner, " 'As You Like It,' " pp. 61-62.

27 Waith, p. 44; Rosenmeyer, pp. 99-103.

latives" comment on each other, and on the courtiers: Orlando, courtly mock-shepherd genuinely disinherited, dotes on Rosalind; Silvius, a real shepherd who has learned his love-role as thoroughly as Orlando has his, dotes upon Phebe; Phebe, a real shepherdess struck by the *coup de foudre* prescribed by Marlowe (to whom they refer as "the dead shepherd," in pure literary idiom), dotes upon Ganymede; and Ganymede dotes, as he insists, upon no woman.

All of them, even the trim Ganymede, smugly apart from their encirclement, show some aspects of pastoral loving; all of them, in turn, have been called (like all fools) into a circle. Ganymede assumes with his disguise (Shakespeare's one-upmanship is manifest in this boy-actor-disguised-as-a-girl-disguised-as-a-boy-acting-the-part-of-a-girl) one proper pastoral love-attitude, that conventionally assigned the shepherdess, of coolness to the lover. Orlando may not have been given a gentleman's education by his hard-hearted brother, but he knows all the same that proper pastoral lovers hang poems on trees. Silvius loves his lady totally, as if she were perfectly beautiful, in spite of Rosalind's rebuke to Phebe; and Phebe illustrates, before our very eyes, how totally love can wipe out all other considerations, particularly those of common sense.

Yet all shall be changed: though in the beginning each loves the wrong person, we see Phebe settle for Silvius; we see Touchstone, clad in his courtly aura as well as in motley, win the goat-girl Audrey from the well-to-do rural William—win her, then, by his courtly "rank." We see Aliena paired with the repentant Oliver, both of them struck as finally as Phebe by Marlovian love at first sight. And we see, by a magic attributable to her forest-character, Ganymede-Rosalind claim her lover Orlando. Only Silvius and Phebe, of the whole crowd, are what they seem and no more: the others, one way or another, have been disguised from others and from themselves. And all of them, save Silvius and Phebe, must cope with the undisguising: Audrey must be either taken to the court by her fool or brutally abandoned: Aliena-become-Celia at once threatens her lover's recent vow of shepherd-hood, that sign of his reconciliation with kind nature; Orlando must learn what his beloved is to inherit.[28]

28 For the convention of disguise as written into pastoral drama and interlude, see Lea, I, 191. Also Walter R. Davis, "Masking in Arden," *SEL*, v (1965), 151-63. For love-in-a-circle, see Lea, I, 182.

Desengaño does not rob the pastoral of its sweetness in *As You Like It*. These considerations do not intrude upon the play itself, in which, however much pastoral love is mocked, its sweet fidelities are rewarded, too. By making fun of Orlando's language, Rosalind jokes him into ever-increasing avowals of his love for her. She may seem to mock all lovers, but at the news of Orlando's hurt by the lion faints like a green girl. Touchstone does not want to be in Arden and contrasts Corin's life unfavorably with what he had known at the court, but he makes the best of his forest opportunities, and his logic actually recoils on him, to endorse the simplicities Corin embodies. The melancholy-satiric Jaques comes to scoff at pastoral sentimentalism, but he is scoffed at in his turn—and for pastoral sentimentalism at that. The data of various literary modes are mocked and yet, through all the mockery, reaffirmed: questioned, teased, tested, found wanting— and found valuable in spite of manifest weaknesses.

In this way, perspectivism is built into this play; it is the play's method, but it relies on traditional implications within the mode, by developing an inherent dialectical tendency in pastoral eclogues to an astonishing degree. Many contests question the traditions which ultimately they endorse: the lovers' fourfold catch suggests the merry-go-round illusion of the experience of loving; Corin and Silvius speak not just about love, but about the kinds of love appropriate to the different ages of man, and Jaques deals with love as developmental folly in his far more total indictment of man's ages and the illusions of each age. Touchstone and Corin debate the life of court and country to demonstrate the limitations of both. Jaques marches through the play, in his melancholy isolation a challenge to everyone's social assumptions and conclusions: like Philisides, Sidney's name for his symbolic self in the *Arcadia*, Jaques has retired to the forest in disappointment with the world's offerings. Though established in Arden, Jaques is characterized as a traveler, a continentalized Englishman who (as the character-books assure us) can never find aught at home good again. He is also—a bit unexpectedly—the superpastoralist of the play, speaking out for the pathetic identification of creatural suffering with human unhappiness. He it is who criticizes the Robin Hood band of gentlemen around Duke Senior for their unbrotherly attacks upon the deer-commonwealth, whose "fat burghers" are slaughtered for men's whims and pleasure; but all this while he is also unpastorally melancholy, unpastorally anti-social. As we look at him more narrowly, of course, we see the social role his melancholy fulfills, and how consistently Jaques acts the part the Duke's men expect of him. It is he who recognizes a freedom even greater than that of the forest in his cry, "Motley's the only wear!" He knows how to call all fools into a circle; he, in short, reminds us by most unpastoral means that Arden is a pleasaunce, that for all its rough weather, the forest is also Cockayne, where all is upside down to be set aright. He knows what his fellow-fool recognizes at sight: "Ay, now I am in Arden; the more fool I; when I was at home I was in a better place; but travellers must be content." And yet Arden is his home, as he chooses to remain in the forest now solitary enough for his nature.

What the forest is, is never made entirely clear, although it *is* obvious that, even with the season's difference, the forest is a better place than the usurper's court. In the forest there is no need for "new news o' the new court"; fashionable gossip is irrelevant to the fundamental constants of courtesy, civility, and humanity. And yet, for all the talk of the golden world, Arden is never "really" that—Corin's master was of churlish disposition and inhospitable, ready to sell his sheepfarm for gold. Unprofessional cleric that he is, Sir Oliver Martext is nonetheless at home in Arden; Duke Senior's fellow exiles do not hesitate to comment on the bitter wind, painful to them if less "unkind" than man's ingratitude. The moral arrangements of the golden world are, come wind come weather, scrupulously observed, together with the pastoral delusions. The melancholy Jaques is courteously received, his idiosyncrasies are respected, enjoyed, and even admired;[29] when Orlando, assuming the role of salvage man, bursts in upon the *fête champêtre*, he is welcomed, not repulsed, in spite of his words and his sword; the country lovers ultimately accept each other with grace. The Duke lives, "the Robin Hood of England" to whom young gentlemen flock "every day, and fleet the time carelessly," so that such rank as he has is, like Robin Hood's, only first among equals. To the forest come Rosalind and Celia, Touchstone faithfully in attendance;

---

[29] For the combination of satire and pastoral see Waith, 81-85 (citing Donatus' confusion of satire with satyr); Rosenmeyer, p. 25; Greg, p. 411; Ralph Berry, "No Exit from Arden," *MLR*, LXVI (1971), 11-20; and James Smith, "*As You Like It*," *Scrutiny*, X (1932), comparing the satiric element with that of the tragedies.

to the forest comes Jaques; to the forest comes the outlawed Orlando, with old Adam on his back.[30] In the forest Oliver de Boys and Duke Frederick make their moral recoveries and find their various rewards. In the forest, the fairy-tale world rules: a serpent and a lion, hitherto inconceivable, threaten the only newcomer distinguished for his savagery: in token of his recognition of the beast within, Oliver had become a hairy man.[31] In Arden, an untaught innocent younger-brother-hero can save that newcomer from these creatures by the "kindness" of his "nature," which marks him as trueborn in spite of his deprivation of nurture. In the forest, whatever nature's natural drawbacks, nature makes written calendars irrelevant: there are no clocks in the forest, and there is time enough for everyone's inner and social needs: the forest, as C. L. Barber reassuringly claims, induces and confirms holiday humor.[32]

Time does not pass, theoretically at least, in the golden world —but this rule does not hold for our play, where we are endlessly made aware, both in earnest and in jest, of the passage of time: in the confrontation of generations (Silvius and Corin, dukes and daughters, Sir Rowland's sons and his aged servant Adam);[33] Orlando comes late to his appointments with Ganymede, who rates him for that—because she is a young girl in love, as she tells us in her psychological typology of time, time trots hard with her. A living emblem of the last age of man, the nearly dying Adam is brought in to emphasize Jaques' classic oration. In other words, this forest is at once ideal and real; the inhabitants of Arden insist that their life is unvaried, as in the Golden Age; but the play works in the rhythms of experience's human actuality. On one side, Arden *is* holiday, and thus timeless; it offers a chance for recovery and redemption, a parodic, exalted imitation of the real world, now corrected and purged. In Arden, fools are visibly in circles, men feast graciously on venison and wine—but time passes as they do so, as we are continually reminded, and men ripen and rot in spite of the lack of clocks.

30 For this as an emblem of *pietas*, deriving from the *Aeneid*, see Nancy R. Lindheim, *"King Lear* as Pastoral Tragedy," *Some Facets.*

31 See Richard Bernheimer, *Wild Men in the Middle Ages* (Cambridge, Mass., 1952).

32 Barber, *Festive Comedy*; Berger, "The Renaissance Imagination."

33 Jay L. Halio, " 'No Clock in the Forest,' " *SEL,* II (1962), 197-207; Frederick Turner, *Shakespeare and the Nature of Time* (Oxford, 1971), pp. 28-44.

What the forest offers is its liberties: love finds what it seeks; Jaques is allowed to criticize as he likes; Touchstone may mock, Corin may be threatened with impoverishment. But nothing untoward happens; the forest offers restitution to the dispossessed as well as the far more important imaginative freedom in which the natural spirits of men and women may expand. Duke Senior, Rosalind, and Orlando know that this forest is their goal; there they find a world where even real brothers can be brothers. For with the psychological flowering favored in Arden, we are reminded that all life is not so free: Cain and Abel patterns recur in the play, in each generation. Even in *that* pattern, indeed, one can find a pastoral analogue: the pastoral Abel is the contemplative man, Cain the cultivator, the active man, the man of violence prepared to defend the value of his way of life and its produce. In his underpopulated world, Cain felt he had to savage his brother, as Duke Frederick and Oliver seek to savage their brothers. When these romance-brothers enter the forest, however, reformation strikes at once; the virtuous maintain and corroborate their gentility and their gentleness, and the evil recover or discover the gentleness in themselves they had denied. Orlando's lapse into savagery, so clearly motivated by his concern for old Adam, is immediately reversed by the gentleness with which his threat of violence is received. As is usual in these discussions of pastoral nature, we find throughout the play the terms which form its structure: nature, natural, kind, kindness, civil, civility, gentle, and gentleness. For nature is kind, and kindness: a recognition of one's kind, a response designed to protect and to strengthen whatever is mutually human.

Against this background, Orlando's complaint against his unnatural nurture makes full sense. His brother owed him, as kin, to raise him as the gentleman he is, but chose instead to rob him of his rights and to cast him, if he could, as a type of Prodigal Son. Finally, Oliver even tried to kill the boy, in an unmotivated gesture of the supreme unkindness. Oliver is presented, as Iago was to be, as simply evil—"simply" evil. The question of nature and nurture running through so much of the play is nowhere debated outright, but from the start the debaters are given real parts in the play. In contrast to his brother, Orlando is, as his behavior consistently confirms, preternaturally "gentle," even though he is also preternaturally strong. Actually, as he and we come to recognize, he has no need of that mysterious education he laments, and grows into a symbolic portion far grander than his inheritance would have been. Orlando assumes responsibility for Adam, grown old in his father's service, to the extent that he violates his own nature by attempting to steal for his sake. He cannot pass by on the other side and let the lion attack his sleeping brother, for all that his brother has done against him. His natural qualities caused him to fall in love with Rosalind, and her to fall in love with him. He speaks of his own gentility ("Yet am I inland bred")[34] and recognizes the same "inland" quality in Ganymede's speech, anomalously cultured for the child of the forest he claims to be. Folk hero that he is, Orlando, the youngest of three sons, is eminently suited to take his place at the head of his family and to marry the Duke's daughter at the end of the play, to return with daughter and Duke to the court, confident of exhibiting the courtliness he has always naturally displayed.

The debate between nature and nurture overlaps the problem of nature and art: nurture is education, altering, improving, grafting, conventionally taken as "good." In Orlando's case, it turns out that the art of which he laments the lack is in fact superfluous. He is what he is "by nature"—and when he assumes various stylized, courtly poses, such as in his role of pastoral lover, Rosalind makes fun of his efforts. As often happens in Shakespeare's versions of pastoral, the nature-nurture debate is skewed and ultimately denied, as received dialectical opposites are shown to be fused in the person (Orlando, Perdita, Arviragus, Guiderius) whose gentle birth marches with his courteous nature. Nurture is not necessary for such as these: all the education in the world had failed to improve Oliver, until he experienced his brother's miraculous assertion of kindness. In Jaques, we see that education has even weakened his feelings for his kind. Rosalind is not the nutbrown boy she pretends she is; her cultivated ancestry of magicians is a fiction to account for the cultivation of her nature and her breeding. In her case, indeed, the disguise which makes it possible for her to take her place in Arden is a fiction in itself. Though she is spokeswoman for what is natural, real, and psychologically sincere, and persuades Orlando to natural and unstylized love, she is of course always neither simple nor boy.

[34] Madeleine Doran, "'Yet Am I Inland Bred,'" *Shakespeare 400*, pp. 99-114.

The forest, then, shelters a countersociety, idyllic and playful, offering a model of possibility to the real world,[35] a countersociety made up on the one hand by the fictions of a literary convention and on the other by the types of that convention, determined to express the goodness of their natures. The pastoral second chance offered by the Forest of Arden is not just a second chance for the people in the play; it is equally a second chance for the larger society of which the *dramatis personae* are representatives. As the procession troops courtward, men with antlers on their heads, girls dressed as country brother and sister, nut-brown from sun or dye, dukes and reconciled brothers, we believe in the escapade and in their unlikely return, believe in their capacity to maintain reform, because of the upright good sense they have demonstrated or learned in the forest, because of their natural courtesy, kindness, and radiant moral strength. But we believe in them also because the pastoral refuge has acknowledged the flawed realities of the workingday world; the holiday has recognized real experience. Touchstone is not the only character on whom the truth of experience can be proved: all of them try, assay, essay the pastoral myth, each from his own perspective, and all of them find at its heart the recreative values of nature, kind, and kindness promised by the tradition. The play's perspectivism insists also upon the convergence of all views at its central and controlling point, the symbolic, simple truth of this most artificial of literary constructs.

III

As You Like It's beautiful finish seems the greater achievement precisely because of the playwright's uncompromising insistence upon the problematical within pastoral thematics. The conventionally counterpointed themes (variant and at variance with one another) which he examines display their inconsistencies and insufficiencies for us, so that we are forced to attend to the tensions underlying even this most idealized of literary modes. In *The Winter's Tale*, the playwright turned to an entirely different aspect of the pastoral mode, to a particular version of pastoral become over the two decades preceding the play's composition one of the most controversial questions in Renaissance literary criticism. This is the matter of pastoral tragicomedy, a question

---

[35] For countersociety, see Berger, "The Renaissance Imagination."

which had aroused one of those decisive and bitter genre-quarrels of the *Cinquecento*, a period in which many questions of literary theory and criticism were debated with particular acrimony.[36] The publication of Guarini's *Il pastor fido* turned out to be polemical. Soon strict Aristotelian critics, chiefly Giason Denores, began to attack its mixed nature; Guarini, under a series of pseudonyms and in his own person, ably defended the development of a new genre, tragicomedy, a genre, as he saw it, within the pastoral mode. Guarini's defense of his play and his genre rested on grounds of classical authority as impeccable as his critics': like them, he was himself a believer in genres and genre-theory, seeking authority from Plautus, Euripides, and Aristotle himself to bolster his independent arguments for the acceptance of his new genre of drama.

W. W. Greg's account of the Guarini quarrel makes plain how natural it seemed, within the context of pastoral, to establish a genre so mixed as this; Bernard Weinberg's masterly presentation of *Cinquecento* criticism shows how this particular quarrel—the last, eventually, of those stirring critical polemics—showed both the inadequacy and the tenaciousness of the idea of genre in literary consciousness: the mixes already so important in the pastoral mode might anyway have been expected ultimately to emerge in an official mixture of the chief dramatic forms. It is noticeable, too, how thoroughly pastoral drama became identified with tragicomedy: although Guarini and defenders of his play and theory of drama cited all kinds of sources—Mercury's prologue to Plautus' *Amphitruo*, where the word *tragicomoedia* was first used, was one principal source, Euripides' *Cyclops* and Terence's *Andria* others—they insisted that the proper matter for tragicomedy lay in the pastoral mode, with pastoral fables. In this they were schoolmasters prescribing a strict new Renaissance genre; however new it was, their genre followed ancient models in excluding rival aspirants to the title. Cinthio's *tragedia di lieto fin* was not enough to make it a tragicomedy; Christian drama, and even Plautus' play itself, could not qualify as tragicomedy by Guarini's rules. Mercury's awareness of Aristotelian and Ciceronian distinctions among the dramatic genres underlies his com-

[36] Greg supplies a basic account and bibliography of the quarrel; for a fuller discussion, see Weinberg, *A History of Literary Criticism*, II, 656-79 and Chapter 21.

ment on *Amphitruo*, "tragicomic" partly because it mixed decorums by exposing gods, kings, and slaves on one stage and in one scene. Those English "mungrell tragi-comedies" that so provoked Sidney's annoyance, plays which ignored proper decorum, would not have passed muster with Guarini and his troop of acolytes either; mere mixture of decorums was not enough. Guarini's insistence on *kinds* of mixture—double plotting, in the social ranks of persons in the drama—set a standard for the new genre designed to exclude any old play loosely called "tragicomedy" simply because it did not quite conform to Aristotelian generic prescription.[37] (One amusing offshoot of Guarini's success was the spate of critical essays seeking to distinguish between "tragicomedia" and "comitragedia": Jesuit theorists were particularly interested in this problem.)

Though the long polemic over *Il pastor fido* is the major source for academic notions of pastoral tragicomedy before Shakespeare, for purposes of theoretical clarity, I want to linger over some of the works of the Bolognese Jesuit Mario Bettini, who seems to have profited from Jesuit definitions of tragicomedy and comitragedy in an interesting way. Bettini wrote several closet-dramas, all in Latin, in the most mixed forms imaginable; his *Rubenus* (1612, 1614) is about a Hebrew shepherd; the play's subtitle, *Hilarotragoedia Satyropastoralis*,[38] gives Bettini's game away. In a critical introduction to this literarily worthless but critically important text, Dionysius Ronsfert defends the play on many counts, citing Scaliger on rustic and rustic environments and associating *Rubenus* with the doctrines of "Baptista Quarinus." In other words, what one might guess from the play itself its own elaborate critical apparatus makes plain: this is a theoretical play, testing the limits of mixed genre in drama.

The author includes everything: in his address, "Amice lector," he assures that learned worthy that in this play he can read "Diverbia, Soliverbia, Monodiae, Canticae, Saltationes, & caeterae eiusmodi inscriptiones, quas in actibus leges, ideo factae, ut qui lecturus, seu daturus hoc drama, videat qua ratione recitandum sit." Most things must be done "cum gestu": the dances of the

---

[37] G. B. Guarini, *Compendio della Poesia Tragicomica Tratto dai due Verati* (Venice, 1601), pp. 32, 4-5, 21-23, 39, 52.

[38] Mario Bettini, *Rubenus, Hilarotragoedia Satyropastoralis* (Parma, 1614, 2nd ed.). I am indebted to Sears Jayne for a microfilm of this text.

chorus of shepherds without gestures, but with song, dance, and pipes; the "Saltationes pantomimicae" with gesticulation, song, dance, and pipes. The plot is entirely mixed: Rubenus, the hero, is a Hebrew shepherd accompanied by a chorus of shepherds; the place is Palestine, where, however, among the choruses of Levites, of shepherds, of hunters, there is also a chorus of satyrs.

There are extremely complex directions given for the scenes, including those wordless pantomimic dances in which satyrs mimic longnecked cranes; one direction, to the actor playing the dog Baal, instructs him to bark in meter; another scene is a complex exchange between Rubenus' servant (!), who sings to a chorus divided into three parts, supposed to be different kinds of birds: all sing various bird-languages in interesting metrical arrangements. Both the onomatopoeic wit and the metrics called forth Ronsfert's admiration in his long commentary on the merits of this witty, but highly programmatic, academic exercise in mixture. Ronsfert's awareness of current interest in such mixtures led him to draw up a catalogue of the *topoi* and forms on which Bettini had drawn: one term he uses (following Bettini) is *epico-drama*.

Ronsfert's defense of the form *hilarotragoedia* relies on earlier writing—Guarini, Scaliger, Patrizi—but insists that the real justification for this particular mixture is mimetic: the form imitates life, in which there is nothing unmixed. Later, Athenaeus and Suidas are cited as forerunners in the critical formation of this canon:[39] its chief value, finally, lies in its deliberate mixture of all the *genera dicendi*, all the *topoi*, and all the *genera*. Authority for Bettini's particular mix comes from Vitruvius, who had sanctioned "scena satyrica pastoralis." Bettini's play is, clearly, a *tour de force*, hardening into official *topoi* the elements and arrangements of the form so debated between 1588 and 1601. The rigidity of this exercise makes apparent the ideological intensity of the quarrel. The play is surely the extreme development— either entirely humorless or thoroughly tongue-in-cheek—of the mixed form in drama: every device possible is worked into the fabric of the play, for its own virtuoso, epideictic sake rather than for any intrinsic appropriateness either to story or to form. In *Rubenus'* subtitle, too, we are asked to recollect the satyr-play, with its associations of both *favola boscarecchia* and of satirical

---

[39] For more on such mixture, see my *Resources of Kind*, forthcoming from the University of California Press.

commentary: Jaques' presence in *As You Like It*'s forest may be more orthodox than it is sometimes taken to be.[40]

Bettini wrote other plays (two of them compliments to the French king) in mixed genre. *Ludovicus* (about Louis XIII) was called *Tragicum Sylviludium*, and *Clodoveus, Comitragedia*.[41] The point of all this is not to claim importance for these Latin exercises, amusing as they are; but rather to suggest that the reason they smell so of the lamp is relevant to the Guarini polemic over tragicomedy, here hardened into an anthological catalogue of possible devices, tricks, and gestures. Bettini's plays caricature the problems others handled more creatively; my suggestion is that Bettini's plays draw broadly upon a tradition of dramatic "mixture" with which Shakespeare's *Winter's Tale* more obliquely has to do. For *The Winter's Tale* is an astonishingly *timely* play, seen against Continental preoccupations: its examination of pastoral mix, utterly different from the concerns pursued in *As You Like It*, is cast in terms of the Guarini debate.

As You Like It, as we have seen, is an extremely "finished" play, its parts in a beautiful balance, its languages modulated into one another, even its plot well-made according to the sanctions of pastoral plot. Further, the complex interrelationship of characters, symbolic behavior and gesture, and symbolic language is always maintained at pitch, and the undercutting of pastoral values is never allowed to destroy their delicate significances, as perspectives throughout the play shift to show both the inexhaustible casuistry of the human condition and its simple communal wishes, hopes, and dreams.

IV

Compared to other plays by Shakespeare—and by any standards, indeed—*As You Like It* is extraordinarily well-made, its elements modulated and dovetailed to satisfaction. We are never tempted to say the same of Shakespeare's other major confrontation with pastoral materials, *The Winter's Tale*, a play in which

[40] See John L. Lievsay, "Italian *Favole Boscarecchie* and Jacobean Stage Pastoralism," *Essays on Shakespeare and Elizabethan Drama*, ed. Richard C. Hosley (Columbia, Mo., 1962).

[41] Mario Bettini, *Ludovicus, Tragicum Sylviludium* (Paris, 1624): and *Clodoveus, Comitragedia*, given at Parma in Latin in 1612, at Bologna in Italian in 1614; printed in Bettini, *Florilegium* (Bologna, 1632).

we miss not only the fundamental source of delight which the pastoral myth offers its believers, but also the structure of argument and demonstration so evenhandedly managed in *As You Like It*, where the possibilities of overprogramming are kept carefully in check by the spontaneity, lyricism, and specificity of the incidents, confrontations, and exchanges. The play works with other kinds of traditions, too (folkish, melancholy, satiric, romantic), to become far richer than any mere exercise in pastoral themes. It qualifies its pastoral thematics by counterpointing themes from other modes in the repertory. As so often in his workings-out and workings-into and workings-through of conventional literary syndromes, Shakespeare manages to get it both ways—to make us realize the limits of the pastoral artifice and at the same time to appreciate its enormous psychic promise and solace.

As You Like It questions pastoral assumptions, often by means of counterposing other pastoral assumptions, offers perspectives upon any of the conventional attitudes and actions associated within the pastoral decorum, and insists on a relativism normally denied within that decorum; but we feel throughout that the playwright knows where his questioning leads and where it will all come out. Not so *The Winter's Tale*, a play conspicuously ill-made, in which our attention is withdrawn from verisimilitude; in which motivations are not to be inquired into; in which the marvelous, the incredible, the impossible are so insisted upon (statue, bear, baby) that they force themselves to become subjects of critical consideration. In this late, mystifying play so deeply involved with the pastoral mode, the lovely ease of *As You Like It* has been replaced by an inconsiderate insistence upon the *invraisemblable*, a departure from mimesis and from reality so radical and so multiple as to send us back to reconsider what "possibility" and "probability" can mean as elements of a drama.

In *The Winter's Tale*, the playwright, having solved some pastoral problems to his own satisfaction, seems to have turned his attention to a wholly different range of problems in the pastoral mode, problems still unsolved (by him and by others): that is, those problems of genre and structure debated with such passion in the Italian polemic over Guarini's *Il pastor fido* and so amusingly and trivially demonstrated in Bettini's academic dramas.

In its own peculiar shorthand, *The Winter's Tale* is a truncated torso of a play. It pays no tribute to those demands for classical modulation between genres and modes that drove Guarini and his defenders so carefully to explain how to mix comic and tragic genres in one decorum. Shakespeare's play simply forces us to face what is "tragic" and what "comic" in life and in plays, forces questions of genre and decorum. The playwright makes no compromise with generic expectations or even with conventional verisimilitude: tragic and comic members of this body are not articulated, and the differences between them are not at all glossed over, but pointedly stressed.

In this respect, remembering the beautiful organization of *As You Like It* may help us: the playwright did not *have* to write this way; he obviously chose to conduct a frontal examination of the structural and thematic limits of modern pastoral drama, that is, of tragicomedy. Even the events of the play, so often considered unnecessarily bizarre or intelligible only because vaguely "allegorical"—the shipwreck, the bear, the fortuitous love of innocent teenagers, the statue—are conventional within the pastoral frame of marvel, artifice, and disguise. The themes of the play are quite as pastoral as those of *As You Like It*: the nature-nurture problem is for Perdita very like what it was for Orlando; the debates about sheepdip and civet are, after all, another version of the *paragone* of nature and art; Rosalind's smart answer to her father foreshadows Perdita's remarks on the democracy of sunshine. It is the naked, disillusioning dramaturgy[42] of *The Winter's Tale* that so separates it from *As You Like It*, not its themes and devices.

In as many ways as they are like each other, though, the plays differ. That there was no clock in the forest is belied by men's ripening there and rotting, but the importance of time is made clear by the subtitle of *The Winter's Tale*'s source: the timeless has been abandoned in favor of an ambivalent, ambiguous "triumph of time."[43] Leontes' early telling of time—"wishing clocks

[42] See Nevill Coghill, "Six Points of Stagecraft in *The Winter's Tale*," reprinted in *Casebook: The Winter's Tale*, ed. Kenneth Muir (London, 1968), pp. 198-213; Dennis Biggins, " 'Exit pursued by a Beare': a Problem in *The Winter's Tale*," *SQ*, XIII (1962); Charles Lloyd Holt, "Notes on the Dramaturgy of *The Winter's Tale*," *SQ*, XX (1969), 42-51. Since this chapter was completed, R. A. Foakes' *Shakespeare: The Dark Comedies to the Last Plays* (Charlottesville, 1971) appeared; see particularly pp. 2-4 and 118-44.

[43] See Fritz Saxl, " 'Veritas Filia Temporis,' " in *Philosophy and History*; Inga-Stina Ewbank, "The Triumph of Time in *The Winter's Tale*," *RES*, V (1964), 83-100; L. G. Salingar, "Time and Art in Shakespeare's Romances,"

more swift?/ Hours, minutes? noon, midnight?"—points to the importance of "moment" in consequential (and therefore tragic) lives; but the end of the drama presents time's triumph within an impeccably comic decorum. Nobles are disguised in both plays, but in the early one, the girls know that they are disguised and why that had to be; in the later play, the Princess believes herself to be the shepherdess she seems to Florizel and Polixenes to be in fact. But there is a difference, in quality and intensity, between the nature-art game in *As You Like It* and the peculiarly unnatural confluence of the two themes (nature and art, reality and its imitation) in the confrontation of Polixenes with Perdita, to say nothing of the dramatic conceit of Hermione's statue. In *The Winter's Tale*, genre is "forced" by the particularly unvarnished conjunction of tragedy with comedy, and so is generic dramatic device. The play begins entirely within the genre of tragedy, so that by the end of the third act all seems lost: Mamillius dead, Hermione stricken, Perdita exposed to die, Antigonus bizarrely slain. The audience is not let in upon the playwright's (and Paulina's secret, that Hermione lives after all, until the very end of the play. That revelation comes as a miracle for everyone onstage and for the audience.

At the same time, the throwaway death of Antigonus, with the astonishing (marvelous—and thus properly pastoral) stage-direction about the bear, suggests that in spite of its horror, the play is about to turn around to match in unpredictability Antigonus' unpredictable death. Certainly that death is just as sudden, causeless, and startling as the psychological violence Leontes has so fully displayed in the first two acts—but Antigonus' death is in an entirely different mode, that of romance. The bear is too much—the situation's very grotesqueness protects the audience from feeling the full terror of the bear's mauling the man, as Leontes' seizure, with its hideous consequences, had conspicuously failed to do. The absolute rejection of verisimilitude in this episode moves us away from tragic expectation to another mode, one which assumes as its own ground unreality, impossibility, and exaggeration. The horrible death, furthermore, is *told* in the shepherdly clown's rustic malapropisms—turned into a topic for laughter. Indeed, as we stand off from *The Winter's Tale*, the

RenD, IX (1966); G. F. Waller, "Romance and Shakespeare's Philosophy of Time in *The Winter's Tale*," *SQ*, IV (1970), 130-38; Foakes, pp. 130-31.

Antigonus episode comes to stand for a great deal in the play's technique, as the dramatist strips his presentation of the usual modes of dramatic persuasion to belief: in this schematic *sinopia* of a play, devices are forced beyond their own limits to point unequivocally at their thematic and technical significances, to remind us once again that any conventional literary device, however technically "fixed" it may seem, carries thematic implications. This is, then, a particularly problematical "problem play," as Ernest Schanzer has noted;[44] it is about the problems inherent in drama generally and those of the pastoral mode and tragicomic form specifically.

Perhaps because English drama, pastoral and other, was so mixed in form compared with Continental practice,[45] Shakespeare does not need to appeal in any polemical way to the Continental quarrel over pastoral drama, as Fletcher did appeal to it in introducing his *Faithful Shepherdess* or as Daniel, in *Hymen's Triumph*, seems to have done. In this play, Shakespeare was guileless: he simply starts his play in the tragic mode, offering us tragic figures in the grip of a characteristically tragic psychology, then works out their solution in terms conventionally comic.[46] After we have witnessed King Leontes invaded by inexplicable jealousy, willing under its sway to destroy his family altogether,

[44] Ernest Schanzer, "The Structural Pattern in *The Winter's Tale*," reprinted in *Casebook*, ed. Muir, pp. 87-97. Major studies of the play are: S. L. Bethell, *The Winter's Tale: a Study* (London, 1947); F. D. Hoeniger, "The Meaning of *The Winter's Tale*," *UTQ*, xx (1950); D. G. James, *Scepticism and Poetry* (London, 1937); Derek Traversi, *Shakespeare: the Last Phase* (2nd ed., New York, 1956); A.G.H. Bachrach, *Naar Het Hem Leek. . . .* (The Hague, 1957), pp. 168-249 (a book that decidedly deserves translation into English); Northrop Frye, *A Natural Perspective* (New York, 1965); A. P. Nuttall, *William Shakespeare: The Winter's Tale* (London, 1966); Fitzroy Pyle, *The Winter's Tale: A Commentary* (London, 1969); S. R. Maveety, "What Shakespeare Did to Pandosto," *Pacific Coast Studies in Shakespeare*, ed. Waldo F. McNeir and Thelma N. Greenfield (Eugene, 1966). See also E. C. Pettet, *Shakespeare and the Romance Tradition* (London, 1949); Carol Gesner, *Shakespeare and Greek Romance* (Lexington, 1970); Philip Edwards, "Shakespeare's Romances: 1900-1957," *SS*, 11 (1958), 1-18; and Stanley Wells, "Shakespeare and Romance," *The Later Shakespeare*, *Stratford-upon-Avon Studies*, VIII (1967), 49-79.

[45] For Sidney's complaints against mixed genre on the English stage, see *An Apologie for Poetry*, in *Elizabethan Critical Essays*, ed. G. G. Smith (Oxford, 1904), I, 175, 196-99.

[46] See William Blissett, " 'This Wide Gap of Time': *The Winter's Tale*," *ELR*, I (1971), 52-70.

as well as his court; after we have reached the nadir of this king's emotional and social career, we are abruptly confronted by an oracle (on which Hermione, perhaps conscious of her own genre-preferences, had insisted!), that standard device of pastoral romance. At first Leontes persists in prolonging the mode of tragedy: he exposes his baby daughter, he rejects the oracle altogether, and only when his son is reported dead does he submit to the romance conventions, accept the oracle at its received rate, and prepare to atone indefinitely.

Then, in utter flouting of verisimilitude, sixteen years intervene and we see, in another country, that the wench is not dead: the anti-courtly comedy begins. The Princess exposed as a baby has turned into a shepherdess, brought up ("bred," "nurtured") as sister to a clown who cannot read. Her beauty has attracted the attention of a hunting prince, who courts her in disguise; his courtship is challenged by his father, the King, Leontes' erstwhile victim now behaving as violently as his victimizer had done sixteen years before. Romance sequence: faced with separation, the young people resolve to flee together, on the advice of the exiled Sicilian Camillo, to Leontes' court, where they are greeted with such hospitality that the sharp-tongued Paulina, afraid of King Leontes' attraction to the young shepherdess-princess, seizes the moment to bring Sicilian affairs to their climax. She invites King and all into her gallery to view a statue of the late Queen, so life-like that the King, whose memory of his wife has been stimulated by the Princess' resemblance to Hermione, is overwhelmed by his sense of loss, overwhelmed by the "meaning," then, of the tragic half of the play that lay at his responsibility—at which point the statue steps down from its pedestal, flesh and blood, a creature alive and feeling.[47] The statue brings into the sharpest possible focus that element in pastoral that sets "art" (the statue) against "nature" (the forgiving, living woman); of this more below.

Other, far simpler pastoral themes surface in the play, in particular the dialogue between court and country. In this case, the "court" is far more deeply compromised than even Duke Frederick's court. In a further upside-downing, in *The Winter's Tale* the court bears the name of the never-never locale preeminently pastoral—Leontes rules in Sicily, is himself called "Sici-

---

[47] See Northrop Frye, "Recognition in *The Winter's Tale*," in *Fables of Identity* (New York, 1963); and *Natural Perspective*, pp. 112-17.

lia," is king and center of that pastoral island. In that land of
his, though he apparently spent an arcadian youth (he and
Prince Polixenes were "twinned lambs"), all is utterly antipastoral. We never hear of shepherding or poetry, and even courtliness is denied in Leontes' frenzy. The King is rude beyond measure to friend and guest, tyrannical to his councillors, and
monstrous to his kind—the best of that court must flee, or must
die, in trying to rectify the King's brutalities. Further, the court
is sick—Sicily's air is "infected"—Sicily's!—cleansed only after
Perdita returns from her pastoral oasis in Bohemia.[48]

Times and places are confused in the play. "A sad tale's best
for winter," says Mamillius in a prophecy of what is to come, for
him and for his family. Leontes' courtly family is utterly unlike
that Baucis-Philemon, Darby-and-Joan pair in Campion's song,
with its realistic pastoral set up against the anxious observances
of the court:[49]

> *Jacke* and *Jone*, they thinke no ill,
> But loving live, and merry still;
> Doe their weeke dayes worke, and pray
> Devotely on the holy day;
> Skip and trip it on the greene,
> And help to chuse the Summer Queene;
> Lash out, at a Country Feast,
> Their silver penny with the best.
> Well can they judge of nappy Ale,
> And tell at large a Winter tale. . . .
> *Tib* is all the fathers joy,
> And little *Tom* the mothers boy.
> All their pleasure is content,
> And care, to pay theire yearely rent.

Tib-Perdita is cast out, and Tom-Mamillius dies of sorrow at what
his father has done to his mother. Leontes' court does not permit
domestic content, and even exemplifies antipastoral and antiro-
mance. There is no hint in his country of the greening Sicilian
muse, who has, in a highly unliterary way, migrated to Bohemia.
Shakespeare has turned the pattern around, both from his source
and from the larger tradition, to endow an utterly unpastoral

[48] On this, see Turner, *Shakespeare and the Nature of Time*, pp. 162-74;
and David Grene, *Reality and the Heroic Pattern* (Chicago, 1967), pp. 68-86.
[49] Thomas Campion, *Works*, ed. Walter R. Davis (London, 1969), p. 80.

habitat with pastoral possibilities. But even this is problematical: "Bohemia" is dislocated too: it has the same mysteriousness, the same geographical neutrality, that Thomas Rosenmeyer attributes to all the names chosen as pastoral sites. Pastoral requires never-never qualities, and the common reader knows very well that Bohemia has no seacoast, nor was it a desert either, inhabited by bears and other predatory beasts.

For all its hospitality to Perdita, its harvest queens and sheep-shearings, pastoral-unpastoral Bohemia can match Sicily in pastoral unkindness: the ship that brought Perdita thither perishes (another unnecessary, exaggerated romance convention), and on Bohemian shores Antigonus is forthwith disposed of. We are not allowed immediately to see in this seacoast the antidote to Sicily that it thematically becomes, although soon enough the resources of Bohemia begin to appear.

The clown who finds the abandoned baby is a shepherd's son, and that shepherd is quick at thematics ("Now bless thyself: thou met'st with things dying, I with things new-born": III.iii.112-13).[50] The shepherds' ethos is, we discover, like that of "Jacke and Jone" in Campion's poem, entirely opposite to Leontes' life in more ways than just rank. Perdita is allowed to grow up a part of the natural cycle, in a natural and nature-bound family, where like the "silly Swaine" of Campion's final line, men live "securer lives" than "Courtly Dames and Knights." At least, this seems to be the case. Perdita lives happily with her shepherd-family, and when courtiers break in upon the shearing-feast, country lives are threatened. But the country idyll cannot be allowed to shine without some darkening. Like Jaques in the earlier play, but far more alienated than the unmanipulative Jaques, Autolycus destroys the pastoral sufficiency. A refugee-pirate from the city, Autolycus shows us the limitations in naivete and gullibility of the shepherd's restricted life. Though he pretends to earlier connections with Florizel, Autolycus the coney-catcher is no representative of the court itself; rather, of the city's underside, whose corruptions he spreads through the countryside as Vergil's *Eclogues* make clear that city-dwellers must.

Perdita, of course, is chosen by "Jacke and Jone" as their summer queen, the epitome of the pure country life. Time has ripened her into the mistress of the shearing-feast, where she presides over pastoral harvesting, surrounded by family and friends, admired by

50 Cf. Blissett, "'This Wide Gap.'"

her elegant suitor and other strangers from the town. Indeed, she seems very little less than the goddess they liken her to. In the matching of Perdita and Florizel, we find the mixing of social ranks appreciated by "modern" pastoralists experimenting with the mode's inherent democracy, and despised by stricter Aristotelian conceptions of socioliterary decorum.

Florizel, that romance-hero, reveals himself as irrevocably in love, recognizing the shepherdess' intrinsic value, ready ultimately to forgo his inheritance for her sake. And we are made to know that it is Perdita's essence which he values, even as France values Cordelia's. Florizel honors not only a pastorally benevolent human nature, but an almost perfect one, and is not afraid to celebrate it in those terms:

> What you do,
> Still betters what is done. When you speak, sweet,
> I'd have you do it ever: when you sing,
> I'd have you buy and sell so, so give alms,
> Pray so, and, for the ord'ring your affairs,
> To sing them too: when you dance, I wish you
> A wave o' th' sea, that you might ever do
> Nothing but that, move still, still so,
> And own no other function. Each your doing,
> So singular in each particular,
> Crowns what you are doing, in the present deeds,
> That all your acts are queens. (IV.iv.135-46)

For all his discriminating praise of her individually graceful acts, Florizel is aware that they all spring from Perdita's fundamental condition: he knows that all her delightful changes owe their beauty to her intrinsic being.

Florizel's disguised father acts as a bridge between tragedy and romance, his own behavior in the sheep-shearing scene partaking both of his son's admiration for Perdita and of Leontes' jealous tyranny. He too responds to the unutterably taking girl, and expresses his delight in her loveliness in narrowly social terms, professing himself unable to believe that anyone so beautiful could possibly spring from peasant stock. Polixenes is, then, ready to recast the girl before him, to rewrite her provenance, so to speak, to cast her in another play. In the magnificent exchange between the consciously disguised Polixenes and the unconsciously disguised Perdita, the resources of an immense tradition are exploited. Disguise itself, one property of the pastoral romance-plot, is requisite for such significant confrontations. Part of Perdita's disguise is that she is disguised to herself as well as to the others: her true origins are quite unknown to her. She believes herself a fictional queen, a queen for a day, and is quick to renounce her mock-royalty when she learns of Florizel's true estate—that is, she takes Sidney's or Denores' critical position about her place, refusing to approve "grafting" either of flowers or of social class.

For the audience, both in and out of the play, though, her disguise as harvest-queen represents her essence rather than covers or discovers her true self. She is, we hear, "no shepherdess, but Flora"—a shepherdess disguised as a queen, but apparently a goddess; as Flora, she distributes Flora's attributes, chosen with care to match her recipients' condition. For the playgoing audience, still more is involved: here is a boy playing a girl who, within this fiction, is a princess. The fiction requires disguise so that she also "is" a shepherdess, real enough as far as nurture is concerned; but in the fiction, there is an inner fiction, a play within the play, in which the boy-actor playing a princess (who thinks herself a shepherdess) must play the part also of a queen. We are reminded of Rosalind, a boy playing a girl disguised as a boy, etc.—who within her own playlet plays her real role in the drama. Perdita, unknowing where Rosalind had been aware, also plays herself: we are in on the illusionism, moreover, as she is not, since we know "what" she really is. As we shall see, this incident, so important for the pastoral theme of the play, also stands in contrast to the great scene of the statue of Hermione, where the audience is *not* in on the trick and does *not* know what strain upon its credulity will be levied.

Perdita establishes the terms of her debate with Polixenes by her gifts of rosemary and rue, matching middle age "With flowers of winter." She apologizes for having no flowers "o' th' spring" for Florizel's "time of day"—like Rosalind, this girl recognizes and reminds her hearers of time's passage and, even at the height of pastoral celebration, acknowledges the natural regulation of the seasons. She can accept, then, the melancholy fact that "twinn'd lambs" can become old rams; that men mature and age. Polixenes tests her, praising the cultivated garden flowers which Perdita, now in shepherd's ideology, rejects: the gillivors are for her "Nature's bastards," for which she will not "put/ The dibble in earth." That is, these flowers are mixed in kind, strive to be what

274

they naturally are not; Perdita behaves in accord with her flower-preferences when she lays by her queen's habiliments to return to shepherdhood, and thereby supports Polixenes' actual Aristotelianism about the mixture of modes in society (and thus in the play).

Still, she cannot help remarking that she has "heard it said/ There is an art which in their piedness shares/ With great creating nature": the *natura naturans*, which is for her the only legitimate creator, has been said to share with men its mysterious power.[51] Polixenes is a modern, Baconian ruler, in defending what he calls "improvement": gillivors are for him good flowers, although for Perdita they are adulterate. The topical terms of Polixenes' argument, with their wide implications beyond their literal meanings, run counter to the social theory he so violently imposes on his son, Perdita, and Perdita's family. When he speaks simply of flowers, though, Polixenes defends Guarini's view of mixing kinds:

> Yet nature is made better by no mean
> But nature makes that mean: so, over that art,
> Which you say adds to nature, is an art
> That nature makes. You see, sweet maid, we marry
> A gentler scion to the wildest stock,
> And make conceive a bark of baser kind
> By bud of nobler race. This is an art
> Which does mend nature—change it rather—but
> The art itself is nature.   (iv.iv.89-97)

On the face of it, Perdita argues the plain country position and Polixenes the sophisticated courtly one. She is a pastoral ideologue, pre- and anti-technological—she rejects, so to speak, Guarini's views. But in the reality of their situation, the two ideologues change places. Obviously, if we are to take this debate of kind in its specific application to the play, as well as to the broader social contexts sanctioned by literary traditions, we must face its contradictions and ambivalences.

In *The Winter's Tale*, so problematical a play, we must accept problems even in a pastoral interlude: Shakespeare faces the issues in his metaphors, made more complicated by their multitudinous

---

[51] G. Wilson Knight, " 'Great Creating Nature,' " in *The Crown of Life* (London, 1947). See also Foakes' remarks on nature and art in the play, in relation to disguises (pp. 134-37).

traditional use. He knows that we know who Perdita is, even if she does not. True to what she thinks she is—because her essence is truth—she argues against what she really is, because she can and will settle for simplicity. Therefore she must argue against what she most desires, that is, to be matched with Florizel. Polixenes' argument, of course, provides Florizel with the theory by which he chooses to match himself; and Polixenes' *behavior* certainly argues that his family needs some such mixture as the one he praises in plants. For instead of having learned Leontes' lesson or applied his own, by blessing his son's union with this perfect harvest queen, Polixenes rejects his own reasoning, his own metaphors, as if he had never enunciated them, to disown his son as Leontes had disowned his daughter so long before. As audience, we might have expected more of this king, especially since he had felt in Perdita's carriage "something greater than herself,/ Too noble for this place." But Polixenes cannot recognize the theoretical force of Guarini's dictum that the shepherd's life is ennobling, whether engaged in by shepherds or by nobles seeking some recreation from their busy life.[52]

Perdita (nobly) accepts the position she has enunciated in her part of the debate, with its implied corollary that shepherdesses may not marry with princes. But she nonetheless utters the equally ideological, but opposite, pastoral opinion:

> I was about to speak, and tell him plainly,
> The selfsame sun that shines upon his court
> Hides not his visage from our cottage, but
> Looks on all alike.   (IV.iv.444-47)

Florizel, a prince disguised as a lordling-shepherd, accepts the shepherd's ideals of democracy and love, which he recognizes as based on notions of natural rightness if not of natural right:

> It cannot fail, but by
> The violation of my faith; and then
> Let nature crush the sides o' th' earth together,
> And mar the seeds within! Lift up thy looks:
> From my succession wipe me, father; I
> Am heir to my affection.   (IV.iv.477-82)

[52] For this topic, see Guarini, pp. 51-52, and Michel-André Bossy, "The Prowess of Debate," pp. 37-38, and literature there cited on the *pastourelle*, where questions of social class are inevitably debated in sexual terms.

As so often in pastoral plays, the question of rank is not pursued to its final implications. Rosalind was a duke's daughter, Orlando a knight's son: like finally matches with like. Because Perdita is in fact royal, Polixenes' views about grafting are not in fact relevant to his son's union; and Perdita's hierarchical conception of rank, expressed in terms of gillivors, is confirmed, not challenged, by the ultimate arrangement of the plot. Such practical criticism of rank as we meet in this play actually runs *against* the notion of pastoral egalitarianism, as for instance in the exchange between clown and shepherd with Autolycus over Perdita's family's new-found gentility. The clown has been, as he says, a gentleman born these four hours, thus a gentleman (*vide* Lear's Fool) born before his father, now also an artificial gentleman. Perdita, for all her new-found royalty, nonetheless still calls the old shepherd "father," the clown still calls her "sister." The natural, generous response of her foster family is now officially assimilated to social gentility; the artificiality of social conventions of rank is underlined by the clown's comments. The clown plans to take advantage of his new privilege by *not* keeping his word— a satirical moment bespeaking nostalgia for a simpler ethics. Something as Audrey does in *As You Like It*, the clown reaches out of his pastoral world to snatch at aristocratic irresponsibility; his father, truly a shepherd and thus incorruptible, remains true to his word even though nominally converted into society's, as opposed to nature's, gentleman. The playwright once again has it both ways, as Perdita's rediscovered condition confirms the gentility she has always displayed, and the members of her family remind us of the loss incurred in giving up country manners for city behavior, their artless simplicity for the artifice and lying of sophisticated society.

Perdita's exchange with Polixenes touches on the nature-art debate in terms of nurture, training, and education; the social question of "making" a gentleman, either by his own means or the means society offers, the main subject of Castiglione's great book and fully explored in other plays of Shakespeare (notably in *King Lear*), is glancingly touched on here. As we have seen, Perdita is herself socially conservative, willing to relinquish Florizel for received reasons. And yet, because she is what she is, within the play itself the critical debate turns out to have been totally irrelevant. Shakespeare explores, and makes us explore, a major problem in pastoral thematics and pastoral literary theory, has made us consider the anomalies involved in the question—and then ripped the rug out from under the whole debate. To say this more grandly, he has chosen *not* to match his literary insight with an objective correlative within the play; the debate of kind is much ado about nothing.

All the same, Perdita somehow exemplifies some of the themes of her debate. Artless though she is as shepherdess, she is an artist in a different sense, sharing something with "great creating Nature": the flowers from which she would make appropriate garlands for her guests she has not to hand, but her poetry about those imaginary flowers is the richest of the play. She so excels nature—or, at least, nature's norm—that her imagination can dispense with the objects themselves. This scene, obviously in many ways crucial to the play, is highly ambiguous in its relation to the play as a whole: in it, the pastoral terms that inform the whole play are insisted upon so overtly, set in such relief, that we must expect to rely on them for interpreting the play. And yet we cannot: the debate is thrown away, its insights rejected as the plot turns out to have no use for them. What does it mean, then? Simply, I think, that the pastoral devices underscore what is fundamental to the whole play—underscore the frippery of the mode's metaphor and attribute—and at the same time make us see that, under all the conventional metaphorical prattle about nature-and-art, nature-and-nurture, what we must consider are questions of intrinsic human personality, of individual recognition of sharing in "kind" and in kindness.

The scene of Hermione's statue,[53] which raises the question of nature and art in terms entirely different from those of the Polixenes-Perdita debate, similarly cheats our expectation. The famous statue is a simulacrum of Hermione, an ecphrastic Hermione, Hermione transfixed into a memorial record of what she had

---

[53] See Tayler, *Nature and Art*, pp. 121-41; Grene, pp. 84-86; and Jean H. Hagstrum, *The Sister Arts* (Chicago, 1958), pp. 81-88. Though the statue is not in Greene's *Pandosto*, there may be some hints of the art-nature *paragone* in the source nonetheless: cf. Greene, *The Historie of Dorastus and Fawnia* (London, 1592, the Folear copy), f. E3ᵛ: Fawnia says: "Painted Eagles are pictures, not Eagles: Zeuxis Grapes were like Grapes, yet shaddowes; rich cloathing maketh not Princes; nor homely attire beggars: Shepheards are not called shepheards, because they weare hookes and bagges, but they are borne poore, and live to keepe sheepe: so this attire hath not made *Dorastus* a shepheard but to seeme like a shepheard." For discussions of this topic, I am indebted to Max Yeh.

been and symbolized in beauty, steadfastness, and integrity. Grateful for this much, Leontes accepts the figure as a statue; like another king mourning a wife lost through his own egoism, Leontes wishes to pretend that the statue is a real woman, promises to invest it with the same devotion Admetus would render Alcestis' statue.[54] We can recognize, beyond Leontes' confusion over the statue, another myth of the artificer as god, whose creations seem to live and breathe like living creatures.[55]

But this scene too removes from relevance the very question we are invited to rethink, for this work of art turns out to be nature after all. As in the Perdita-Polixenes exchange, our expectations of *paragone* are frustrated by the plot. The miracle Venus performed on Pygmalion's behalf is wrought for Leontes as well, as his statue moves, steps down from her pedestal, and embraces him. But this statue was never such—it was always the woman herself, "as like Hermione as is her picture," the real, restorative, forgiving Hermione, turned figuratively to stone, to linger like Persephone underground for a sixteen-year winter's tale, and warmed into reality only by her husband's repentance-quickened life: the statue's returning to life confers upon that frozen, suspended husband his full life again. The illusion here is not that art is an illusion, but that life is.

We may stop over the trick for a moment. Pygmalion offers one archetypal example in the *paragone* of nature and art, in which nature wins out; "favella, favella," Donatello is said to have said to his *Zuccone*, that almost-real figure of his invention. Why Giulio Romano, then, selected as the artist who can create "to the life"?[56] Who "would beguile Nature of her custom, so perfectly he is her

---

[54] Cf. Euripides, *Alcestis*, 348-54, 1143 (LCL ed.); see also Callistratus, "On the Statue of a Bacchante" and "On the Statue of Eros," LCL, pp. 380-87; Ovid, *Met.*, x, 243-97 (Pygmalion).

[55] Otto Kurz and Ernst Kris, *Die Legende vom Kunstler* (Vienna, 1934); and Gombrich, *Art and Illusion*, pp. 93-96.

[56] See E. H. Gombrich, "Zum Werke Giulio Romanos," *Jahrbuch des kunsthistorischen Sammlungen in Wien*, n.s., VIII (1935), p. 125, notes Aretino's praise of Giulio Romano in *Il secondo libro delle lettere* (Venice, 1542); see also Pietro Aretino, *Il Marescalco*, in *Quattro Comedie* (London, 1588), p. 40: the Pedant speaks: "Si pittoribus, vu Titiano emulus naturae. Immo magister, sara certo fra Sebastiano de Venitia divinissimo. Et forse Iulio Romano curie, e de lo Urbinate Raphaello allumno. Et ne la marmorarea facultate, che dovea dir prima (benche non è anchora decisa la preminentia sua). Un mezo Michel Angelo, un Iacopo Sansovino speculum Florentie." I am indebted to Professor Gombrich for this reference.

ape"? Giulio Romano's painted titans in the Sala dei Giganti in Mantua were said to have terrified viewers by their illusionism; from Vasari comes another comment on Giulio's miraculous illusionism: "a building, round like a theater, with statues of inexpressible beauty, finely disposed. Among them is a woman spinning, and looking at a hen with her chickens, wonderfully natural."[57] It is not quite clear from the text whether this miracle was a painting of a building, depicted as adorned with lifelike statues, or was a building with an actual row of such statues. Normally, statues were not painted, as Paulina says the statue of Hermione was: the *Zuccone* is marble, Pygmalion's lady was ivory, and though he decked it with fine garments and jewels, he did not appear to have painted it. In paintings, too, statues are generally distinguished from living people (as for instance in the painting of Lord Arundel and his gallery) by their grisaille, as opposed to the flesh-colored tints of those depicted as living. But in dramas, anyway, statues *do* tend to come alive. In *Friar Bacon and Friar Bungay*, in *The Old Wives' Tale*, in Campion's masque for Princess Elizabeth's wedding, statues speak and move. (In Campion's masque a row of women, fashioned by Prometheus, turned into statues by an angry Jove, step down from their niches into real life.)

Hermione was to be played by a real actor miming a statue, a not uncommon role in the repertory; this trick, then, is simply another *trompe l'œil* of legitimate stage-illusion. In other instances of this metamorphosis or pseudo-metamorphosis, however, there is no talk of naturalist human details, no pushing past the illusion's conventional cover. By mentioning Hermione's wrinkles, Shakespeare returns us to the undisguised artifice of this whole play, with its open, unmodulated combination of tragic with comic, its resolution of impossibility by metamorphosing tragedy into comedy. At this highest point of illusionism, illusion itself is abandoned, in the claim that reality is more startling, more miraculous, than any contrivance of art—that life itself, in its most significant moments, is hardly lifelike. Beauty's perfection, exemplified in Perdita's smooth cheek, gives way before the meaning and pathos of those wrinkles—even the ideal beauty of a mode emphasizing aesthetic ideals retires before the values attributed to suffering and feeling, validated by being experienced over time.

[57] Giorgio Vasari, *Lives* (Everyman ed.), II, 101; cf. comments pp. 103ff. on the decorations of the Palazzo del Té.

But turning his stress away from the artist's effort at mimetic matching, the playwright makes fun of the whole doctrine of *mimesis*—and thus strips illusionism from art. Giulio Romano had tried, thus, in Paulina's fiction, to play god and to supply a Hermione as she really would have been—hence he had to add the wrinkles that were so strange to Leontes. In terms of *mimesis*, Shakespeare forces the credible to the point where it is easier to believe the conventionally incredible than the "facts" of his fiction, of this play's plot. We are warned within the play that this is so, by an anonymous Gentleman: "This news, which is called true, is so like an old tale that the verity of it is in strong suspicion" (v.ii.27-29), a theme which runs through the last act (v.ii.62, 96-101; v.iii.115-17). By calling attention to the *vraisemblable* wrinkles, the playwright underscores his *invraisemblable*, and turns us back to rethink the convention of the "marvelous" in pastoral drama, the taming of a miracle to literary device. Where, outside of sanatoria, are pastoral interludes practical solutions to human destructiveness, of others and of self? The pastoral offers its artifact in substitution for life's consequential bitterness; in the statue-episode, as in the debate of kind, the artifice of the artifice forces us back upon the human resources such artifices symbolize. Hermione comes alive because she can forgive, comes alive when she does because Leontes is ready to receive at her hands what no man has a right to expect, the forgiveness that fulfills the utmost selfishness of his dreams.[58]

Hermione's statuedom is an outrageous device, fulfilling even more dramaturgical needs than the incredible transition from death to life. Not only is that statuedom the means by which this unashamedly artificial play is enabled to reach a proper reconciliation at the conclusion of the varied action, but the means as well by which both Leontes and Paulina can find some justification for themselves. Hermione-as-statue offers a moment of respite —the transition for Paulina from the vengeance-world, for Leontes from the wish-world, back to the world of personality and flesh and blood, where wives can be cherished and kissed without harming their fresh paint. Hermione is not painted but real (cf. gillivors), not stone but flesh. Some silence, some interlude, some symbol must stand between Leontes and the recovery of his human self, to preserve him from the total shock of joy which overcame

[58] See Robert K. Hunter, *Shakespeare and the Comedy of Forgiveness* (New York, 1965), pp. 185-203; Frye, "Recognition," p. 181; Tayler, p. 139.

Gloucester. He can say that he is "mock'd with art," but actually art mediates to let him speak what he feels, possible only as long as he thinks his wife a statue deaf and dumb. Of course he is in fact "mock'd," as the audience is too, by the dramaturgy: the point of the tricks in this play is that they are *not* in fact illusionistic, that stage-conventions are themselves unmasked and mocked. Of Hermione's wrinkles the playwright has made a symbol for all the failures of art to match reality. What can Paulina say, when Leontes remarks about how much older the statue looks than his wife did, sixteen years before? Only that the fabulous artificer was trying to outdo idealization to reproduce a specific natural creature. Paulina thus denies the value of the ideal in art, and undercuts *mimesis* too. The wrinkles show how simplistic are rigid distinctions between art and nature, between the ideal and the verisimilar.

The double insistence upon plausibility and actuality is symbolized by the almost-silent meeting of Perdita with her mother's statue: Perdita, that mother's child, recapitulates the mother's beauty, in her own living regenerates her mother's lost image. In that one scene then, we see before us both timelessness (statue: art) and time (living girl: nature)—and yet the statue's cheek is wrinkled and the girl's cheek is smooth. Wrinkles are the anti-romantic attributes of mature life: if Hermione is to be restored to Leontes with any significance to that restoration, she must return at time's full cost, her loss made calculable and conscious. The wrinkles are signs that suffering really *means*.

But one can also see in the wrinkles just the playwright's game with the thematics of his mode, his game with the possibilities of his theatrical and literary craft. If he sticks to verisimilitude, and it turns out that the wrinkles are on the cheek of a living woman, who can rate him for the implausibility of the statue-device? By pointing to life as it is, he points away from the illusionism of his craft to the illusions men make of their lives. By translating his pastoral into time, he can stress the imaginative value of the pastoral ideal in lives by their nature subject to the ravages of time. Only by a fiction—a statue, a play—can one immediately grasp the enriched, concentrated meaning attributed to life, drawn from life, by the imagination. The statue can become a woman, the woman can be a statue, in a fiction, in this play; the *mode* of this play is important to this particular issue of art. Within the thematics of pastoral such an examination of the relative values of nature and art is one of the mode's dictates: the relationship between the two is reversed and at the same time reaffirmed in *The Winter's Tale*, which owes its particular being to the permissiveness of the pastoral dramatic conventions, by which a woman can pretend to be a work of art, and can be one as well. With the contrivance of art's turning into life, the pastoral, so questioned and qualified throughout the play, resumes its proper habitat, as Leontes' Sicily is permitted once more to partake of all the symbolic gifts of art and nature.

Because she is so fine a piece of work as a human being, Hermione can come to life and redeem her husband, herself, the play: in her, "Dear life redeems" by means of the statue-device. Art is not what it seems in this play, where it turns out not to be art: but, as we can see in its ending at once emblematic and enigmatic, life is not what it seems either. In human crises, human beings need the resources both of their natures and their creative powers, the resources of nature and of civilization, with its arts. In this extraordinarily proud, self-confident play, which flaunts its artfulness and its sublime contempt for mere art, the interchange of art with nature is affirmed, as art offers human nature a chance to civilize its brutalities.

7

"Nature's Above Art in that Respect": Limits of the Pastoral Pattern

I

THE PASTORAL PATTERN in drama (of extrusion, sojourn in a natural environment, return in increased strength) is surely a mythic
one, involving deep human hopes and fears. At the same time, for
the writer it is a thematic *schema* easily manipulated, easily recognizable even when detached from anything to do with shepherds and sheep: it becomes a celebration, in varying degrees of
devotion, to what is "natural" and sustaining in human life and
human environment. This pattern, further, abstracts and formal-
izes into "plot"—sometimes a very exiguous plot, but a continuing story all the same—one aspect of the pastoral *paragone*, in
which nature (only occasionally sheepish) is the restorative agent
for the personal, and sometimes the collective, sufferings inflicted
by a highly artificial and self-conscious society.[1] Another way of
saying this is, I think, that pastoral always carries a suggestion of
the court-country dialectic, sometimes sharply stressed (*Cymbeline,
The Winter's Tale*), sometimes merely called up to offer a counterpoint to a non-pastoral theme, as in the history plays, where
Henry VI yearns for the shepherd's life in the midst of a deplor-
able battle, and Richard II for sheep and a little plot of ground.
Thematically, these pressures from *urbs* urging a return to at least
the *idea* of nature[2] are absorbed into the unspoken dialectic of
pastoral and inform much pastoral writing in the Renaissance. In
Shakespeare's plays, this pattern usually involves the removal of
good people, from a court somehow grown evil, to a rural or
woodland setting, whence the exiles return in triumph, often with
a train of natural or naturally-restored companions, to undertake
the human responsibilities appropriate to the renovation of the
court they had earlier left.[3] An essential attribute of this abstracted
pastoral is the unpastoral violence required to make persuasive

---

[1] Cf. Greg, op. cit.; Mack, *King Lear*, pp. 63-66.
[2] Poggioli, "The Oaten Flute"; and Rosenmeyer, *passim*.
[3] Cf. Lindheim, "*King Lear* as Pastoral Tragedy."

the regenerative pastoral interlude in any tale of restoration—so that one finds a high degree of cruelty and brutality (often very schematically and unemotionally wielded) around the edges of pastoral romance, in both narrative and dramatic forms.[4] Hence Sidney could find plausible his title, *Arcadia*, for a prose epic of chivalric doings in which so very much unpleasantness, and so very little sheep-herding, can be found. Actually, in the *country* of Arcadia things are peaceful, but within the *story*, violence is frighteningly common; even in Arcadia, its king and queen are hardly models of pastoral quietism. The pastoral or country interlude seems to have its chief meaning not so much as a lyric locus of *otium* (though that implication is never entirely lost) as an interlude thematically georgic[5]—an interlude which, whether literally or symbolically pastoral in setting, is as much educative and instructive as it is nutritive, recreational, and recreating, too. The pastoral interlude is the second chance offered men beleaguered by their complicated functions as men, a second chance to recognize, inform, and develop their creaturely human nature—their human kind and their human kindness.

Both Arden and Bohemian sheep-country serve that function in the plays we have just left; in very different ways, from these and also from each other, Prospero's magic island and the Welsh mountains of Cymbeline offer a second chance to the characters who harbor there, as well as to the larger society too ill to endure the virtues of the characters it exiled. Clearly, these plays offer commentary on the court-country paradigm, with an unashamed bias for the condition of "country," though with the obligatory return to the life of the court. At the outset of both *Cymbeline* and *The Tempest*, we witness or are told of courts dreadfully deteriorated. Cymbeline and Prospero have both relinquished their

[4] Indigenous violence in the pastoral world is allowed in animal shape (wolves, snakes); human violence swoops into it from outside to do its damage (e.g., the pirates in *Daphnis and Chloe*). The satyr-figure, half-animal, half-human, sometimes represents disorder and danger in the pastoral world and at other times exhibits heightened pathos. The ambiguity of this type is very important in aspects of Caliban's presentation. Sidney's *Arcadia* is an extremely interesting version of pastoral: in that book, most physical violence takes place or originates outside the country called Arcadia; but the internal uneasiness of Arcadia needs fuller attention, given the nature of its chief family. I am indebted to Sheldon Zitner and to Sears Jayne for discussions on this subject.

[5] Cf. the work of Alarik Skarstrom, mentioned earlier.

proper responsibilities and have thus relinquished their power: Cymbeline to his second queen, wicked stepmother *par excellence*, Prospero to his unnatural brother. Britain and Milan are no longer properly polite locales; the arts of true courtesy as delineated by Castiglione have given way to the artfulness of deceit and contrivance. The playwright chose, ultimately, to set this theme in the form of comedy, however potentially tragic such situations might seem. According to the plays' wonderful solutions, marriage and reconciliation promise that all shall be well, that Milan's daughter and Naples' son shall knit true hearts and true kingdoms; that Imogen's reunion with Posthumus shall frame the growth in both goodness and good sense necessary to restore the rule of Cymbeline and his variously purified children.

These are plays insisting on the comic mode, on pure fiction—pure fulfillment of human hopes of order—yet we must watch what the essential idea of pastoral form, nature itself, does and means for the maimed exiles from these tainted courts. *The Tempest* has, as Miss Lea has beautifully shown,[6] many of the cliché elements of low-style pastoral comedy, as practised in the *commedia dell' arte*: a shipwreck, an enchanted island, a magician, lovers wholly or partly disguised. Sheepless as it is, *The Tempest* may seem a very odd example of pastoral, with little to remind us of its place in the mode save the *pattern* of exile, natural sojourn, and return which it shares with more manifestly pastoral works. Precisely because of its removal from all that external nature usually implies in the pastoral mode, by its investigation of the power of nature (both external and human) and the relation of the one to the other, *The Tempest* deals with one extreme of the pastoral mode, while at the same time adhering to its fundamental dramatic scheme.[7] An arrangement in ingratitude and grace, in unkindness and kindness, the play also stresses, by means of its fundamental magic-metaphor, the problematics of art itself.[8] Prospero is a magician: he commands not just the natural

[6] K. M. Lea, II, 201-203, 334, 443; and see Angelo Ingegneri, *Della Poesia rappresentativa Discorso* (Ferrara, 1598), pp. 12-13, on pastoral "place" as an island.

[7] Kermode, Introduction to the Arden *Tempest* (London, 1954), xxiv, lix-lxii.

[8] *Theatrum mundi* now has considerable critical currency in several aspects, in particular as a metaphor for particular plays and the role-playing social world outside the play's limits; further, in the development of the self-refer-

world, but the supernatural one as well; he is an artist, in both the Renaissance and the modern senses of that tricky word. In this play, the notion of a pastoral environment, a natural countryside where men may find, recognize, and confirm their true nature, has been pushed to such an extreme as almost to contradict itself: "nature" has become supernatural. Here, as in so much else, Shakespeare manages to get it both ways. All that nature is and does is implied in the play, but all that it is or can do, in the play, far exceeds the possibilities of the nature we know in our everyday lives.

In *The Tempest*, humankind is emblematically presented, flanked by abstracted figures borrowed from the literary environments of masque and entertainment:[9] Ariel, spirit of air who can control both water and fire; Caliban, creature of earth, misshapen, brutal, and curiously in touch with the realities of his natural world, is a salvage man with a peculiar ambiguity of his own.[10] Ariel is sexless, Caliban sensual; Ariel superhumanly effective, Caliban simple and slow; Ariel unendowed with particular affections but with a strong sense of duty owed, Caliban unable to enter into equal intercourse with figures more fully human—not even, sadly, with such degenerate samples of mankind as Stephano and Trinculo, whose worthlessness shows up his own environmental fitness. Ariel is in charge not only of "real" nature but also of illusory nature; as his master's instrument, Ariel makes possible the illusions Prospero conceits—and Caliban, with old

---

ential topic of the uses, in a particular play, of announced dramatic techniques (dumb-show, play-within-a-play, language of "act," "scene," "exit," etc.). For this see Thomas F. Van Laan, "Acting as Action in *King Lear*," *Some Facets*; and *The Idiom of Drama* (Ithaca, 1970); John W. Erwin, "Narcissus Ludens: Person and Performance in Baroque Drama," doctoral dissertation, Yale University, 1970; Harry Berger, Jr., "Theater, Drama, and the Second World," *Comp. D.*, II (1968); and "Miraculous Harp: a Reading of *The Tempest*," *S. Stud.*, III (1967), 253-83.

9 See Kermode, Introduction, Arden ed., xxi-xxiv; Enid Welsford, *The Court Masque* (London, 1927), pp. 336-49; Stephen Orgel, *The Jonsonian Masque* (Cambridge, Mass., 1965), p. 14; Righter, *Idea of the Play*, pp. 201-203; Allardyce Nicoll, "Shakespeare and the Court Masque," *Sh. Jhrb.*, XCIV (1958), 51-62. R. A. Foakes, in *Shakespeare: The Dark Comedies to the Last Plays*, pp. 157-64, is particularly good on the functions of the masque in this play.

10 See above, fn. 4; Kermode, Introd., Arden ed., xxiv-xliii; Bernheimer, *Wild Men*.

or new master, cannot carry out even his own political programs.

Between these two extremes of figures like human beings but not quite human is displayed a row of human beings from Trinculo to Prospero, simple to complex, dishonest to honest, innocent to guilty, irresponsible to responsible, ungrateful to forgiving, unnatural to gentle—in the fullest sense of that last word. In various ways, all the characters, high and low, are held up to the standards of nature as well as to the even higher standards of human self-conquest by which Prospero's island measures human beings. Trinculo and Stephano are easily duped, not by Ariel's illusions only, but by wine, by Caliban, and by their own farcical ambitions as well; the revelation of their minimal characters is total, and easily accomplished. Antonio and Sebastian, by birth privileged and "gentle," educated by human sophistication, are shown to be characters even less scrupulous toward their relatives, friends, and associates—and, even though they are forgiven, they are thoroughly exposed as what they are. Antonio and Gonzalo offer contrasting comments, as they are contrasting specimens of it, on human nature, Antonio's attitude wholly expediential, Gonzalo's one of innate kindness and idealism, expressed in his curious hankering after a simpler commonwealth than the one in which he serves. Over against this set of experienced characters, Ferdinand and Miranda exist to prove that both court and country, however distorted, limited, and unnatural, can produce human beings of exceptional moral fineness. Prospero—disappointed ruler, benevolent magician—is ready to reform himself as well as to offer reformation to those under his spell. Gonzalo has done what good he could in the cruel situation in which he was cast, but imagines the natural utopia of which Prospero can offer us a glimpse, as everyone is brought to a judgment in which mercy is the judge's chief quality. Miranda admires what she sees in the world of men (with an irony remarkable in the circumstances) and is admired in turn as the "wonder" she is, preternaturally beautiful and good as she is beautiful. Ferdinand proves, in spite of heredity and environment, that he is truly and nobly gentle by his submission to Miranda's father for Miranda's sake. And Prospero, again, with whom the play begins and ends, is unlike the standard magician of pastoral drama, unlike that Sycorax brought into the play's discourse only to underline Prospero's responsibilities as magician, in that he practises only a pure white magic, a "natural magic,"[11] and is stern only as a means to moral betterment.

From the convincing illusion of the first episode, the tempest itself, in which the audience like the *dramatis personae* experiences violence and death, only to discover that the whole spectacle is "merely" art, we are made to understand that in this play an extraordinary man stands in an extraordinary relation to nature; that nature here not only offers creatural and human solace to exiles from harsh civilizations—that is, restores their human powers temporarily curtailed—but also is subject to human power of a very particular kind. Furthermore, although Prospero drowns his book and breaks his staff, reducing himself, as he says in his Epilogue, to the same status as everyone else in the play, we can see that for Prospero and for his creator (in this play, at least) nature "most plain and pure" is not enough to effect the kind of reformation of human beings here dealt with. More is needed than nature's art alone: an art controlling nature evokes from her all her possibilities of solace, support, and recreation. Art is called in, to smooth and to speed up natural processes to their necessary good ends—in this play, obedient to the unities, there is no time for the natural passage of Leontes' sixteen years to set all right. Art is invoked, then, to do what nature cannot do of herself, to illude the senses of men of sense, to alter natural laws so as to make implacable a restoration which nature by herself cannot guarantee.

And art is what we get, even though the supernatural in the play is nicely domesticated to the status of local nature. Ariel is always about, part of the family, and Caliban was to have been part of the family as well. Prospero's art is not anti-natural, but works from well within the natural processes—his art is, literally, natural magic. The storm he conjures is certainly "like" natural storms—the sailors and other victims have no difficulty in believing in its reality, and neither has its unwilling witness Miranda. The island-escapades are, in many cases, realistic enough:

---

[11] D. P. Walker, *Spiritual and Demonic Magic from Ficino to Campanella* (London, 1958), esp. Part II, Introduction (General theory of natural magic), pp. 75-84; D. G. James, *The Dream of Prospero* (Oxford, 1967). pp. 45-71; Stephen K. Orgel, "New Uses of Adversity: Tragic Experience in *The Tempest*," *In Defense of Reading*, ed. Reuben A. Brower and Richard Poirier (New York, 1963), 110-32.

men commonly get lost when drunk or in shock and, in pastoral landscapes, even a shepherd is not safe from the misleading will o' the wisp or can follow a moving light into the mire. Potential victims do, sometimes, awaken in time to avert the dangers threatening them; violent men are from time to time paralyzed in the pursuit of their villainy. Prospero's magic is an art, but an art like God's (in Sir Thomas Browne's view of the matter, anyway), according to which Nature is, quite simply, the art of God.

Prospero is of course notably a directorial, theatrical magician:[12] he chooses to effect his didactic or restorative ends by more dramatic means than nature usually provides. In many cases, the theatrical arts of illusion become, hypothetically and metaphorically for us as reconsidering critics, but naturally and actually within the play's fiction, the "art" compared and contrasted with nature. Indeed, this art is made to seem natural in more ways than one, since Prospero's benevolent magic in this play replaces the customary pastoral *numen*, capable in itself of supernatural restorations, but here heightened as the whole island is, more obviously and overtly than a conventional pastoral landscape, permeated with supernatural power. By stylizing Prospero's magic in theatrical terms and by referring it to theatrical metaphors, the playwright keeps us aware of his own use of dramatic illusion and of the literary imagination generally—though he nowhere forces such identification of his particular art with that of the magician or of nature. From this very strategy, we may take it that the poet had thoroughly understood another aspect of the pastoral fiction, by which the poet controls the pastoral nature he makes up, by which nature is entirely plastic to the poet's imagination. From the start, certainly, we are faced with Prospero's powers of imagination: we recover from the impact of the immediate tempest to discover that Miranda takes for granted that it was a real storm and that her father had a part in its creation; to hear in turn Prospero's reasons for calling up such an illusory storm and Ariel's report of how the illusion was put on. We watch, again and again, gestures arrested so that their normal consequences may not take place and their morality, or rather their immorality, may be understood; the significant tab-

[12] For material on this, I am indebted to Gavriel Moses; see also Righter, *Idea of the Play*, pp. 134-35; Berger, "Harp," p. 255; and Erwin, "Narcissus Ludens."

leaux of masque and anti-masque animate moral emblems and abstract in visual form the play's recurrent themes.

This, then, is Prospero's "art": to heighten nature's effects so that the miraculous achievement of human kindness, human solidarity, and human gentleness may be seen for the rarity it is: the patient, gifted work of self-civilizing men and women who, on the one hand, pull themselves out of a bestial life and, on the other, resist the moral temptations omnipresent in the complexity of any society and civilization.

The Tempest exposes the ideal pastoral pattern at its abstract and irreal extreme, choosing as the locale an unnamed island which is, like Tunis, ten leagues beyond man's life, an island whence, after exposure to it, men can return strengthened in their etymological kindness to places we know, Milan and Naples, there to undertake the business of government as comedies conceive it. In this play, we never see the courtiers, good or bad, at home; that "home" was imperfect we must infer from Prospero's narrative and Gonzalo's immediate image of a garden-state—as well, of course, as from the behavior of Antonio and Sebastian and their counterparts in travesty, Stephano and Trinculo. Whatever the court may be or have been, it is in another world from Prospero's island: we know it from narrative and remembrance only, recognize it only as it surfaces in mental experience or in the peculiarly warped "nature" of some of the courtiers. The island itself wipes clean of conditioning circumstances, though even on its enchanted shores, we see that what men have been relates to what they are and to what they may become. The island is their second chance, offered to Prospero and offered by Prospero, the once and future duke; on the island's oasis, it is given to each man (including the master of the revels himself) to find himself "When no man was his own." The play concerns forgiveness, or grace, granted to others and granted also to one's self:[13] atonement achieved, the island may be left behind. For such grace, ordinary nature is insufficient—as in *A Winter's Tale*, in *The Tempest* more is needed for real restoration, which provides a reason why the pastoral myth is raised to a supernatural level of discourse, ennobled even beyond its habitual purities.[14]

[13] Hunter, *Comedy of Forgiveness*, pp. 227-45.

[14] For this reason, many critics have seen Prospero as a figure for God, the play as a highly Christian allegory. Though there are certainly struc-

The schematization and abstraction of that pastoral myth are correspondingly powerful: the poet has stripped down his received, conventional plot to its bones, to reclothe it in another flesh far more spiritual than the usual legacy of natural birth.

II

In *Cymbeline*, which opens at a court and closes with the court's reconstitution, no such thing happens. We are at once made acutely aware, for good as for ill, of that court's sophistications, duplicities, fissures, and general unkindness. Posthumus is banished because he has overlept rank—in spite of the fact that he was raised as companion to princes and as cynosure of the King's household, he may not aspire to the King's daughter. Natural love between two persons considered to be naturally good, then, is denied at the play's beginning; "nurture" is also rejected, since the very King who raised Posthumus does not consider his own education of the young man a sufficient counterbalance to lack of "rank." Rank has replaced both nature and nurture; and rank itself is a matter of occasion. Cloten is distasteful to the courtiers among whom he moves, but as the new Queen's son, he is free to indulge his personality as he wishes. The Queen's machinations in the garden with the poisonous flowers, an inverted pastoral procedure, are matched and neutralized by the Doctor's mitigations: we see nature tampered with and restored in the successive incidents over the poison.[15] There are parallels to the Queen's artifices in other ranges of the court life—even Imogen's high Renaissance chamber has an overblown decorativeness that makes it seem an appropriate setting for Iachimo's schemes. Little here is natural, save the punished love of Imogen and Posthumus: that is, whatever is of the court is made to seem artificial if not positively invaded by artifice.

---

tural parallels between Prospero's place in his world and God's in His, though the rituals of Prospero's world may be seen as sacramental, and though there is an extensive literature, from Plotinus to Puttenham, likening the poet's creation to God's, the relationship here (as in the theory) seems to me more metaphorical than surrogate. Verbal references to Christianity are notably absent from *The Tempest*.

[15] See the interesting commentary on *Cymbeline* by Terry A. Comito, in his doctoral dissertation, "Renaissance Gardens and Elizabethan Romance" (Harvard University, 1968).

Caught between the Queen's calculated tricks on one side and the gratuitous stratagem of Iachimo on the other, Imogen can only flee the place—and flees to what is thematically, schematically, the opposite of the court, to a rocky cave in the wild hillsides beyond the boundaries of "civilization." Disguised as Fidele, Imogen takes refuge in the Welsh mountains, in a cave empty of inhabitants where, of course, the two young huntsmen whose home it is gladly take her in. That these two representatives of her kind turn out to be her kin as well is simply a stock arrangement in pastoral drama and in romances generally, where changeling situations abound. The reconstitution of a fundamentally noble family is a standard romance resolution, too, as it is a pastoral-comic resolution as well.

In *Cymbeline*, the moral thematics of pastoral receives considerable emphasis as, throughout the play, a concealed debate of court with country is carried on, in many thematic mutations. Imogen finds that courtiers have no monopoly on human deceptions, when she is misled by beggars; but she recognizes that their poverty and rusticity may offer an excuse for the beggars' unkindness which courtiers have not. In this as in much else, Imogen iterates her natural goodness, her recognition of other people's conditions: her wish to be a shepherdess (I.ii.79-81) is of a piece with her natural understanding. By far the most important doctrinal statement is that made by Belarius: insisting on the ideological purity of the life he has lived with his foster sons (in a rocky cave so stark that Imogen first takes it for a beast's lair), Belarius urges natural religion on his charges, as well as the spartan simplicity of

> this life
> . . . nobler than attending for a check:
> Richer than doing nothing for a robe,
> Prouder than rustling in unpaid for silk. . . .
>
> (III.iii.21-24)

The boys, however, will not join with him in his assertion that there is "No life to ours!" Like those primitives in the earliest stages of Lucretius' cyclical development of human polity, the boys have evidently tired of eating acorns and want something more in their lives.[16] Lucretius' lines describe a primitive race of

---

[16] See Lucretius, *De rerum natura* (LCL), v, 925-87.

men very like Belarius' ideal for these boys, a race far hardier than the present sort, men "maioribus et solidis magis ossibus," who ate acorns and drank the pure water of the stream, who lived in caves, hunted game, and slept on the ground: flint was their pillow, as it was for Belarius' boys. Otherwise primitive, these men had an immense integrity, a complete and finished humanness, qualified by their further "development" toward civilization. Guiderius' words echo another stage in the Lucretian account of social progress, that is, the rejection of cave life, and cave ecology. Acorns would no longer do ("sic odium coepit glandis"),[17] and a greater refinement in diet and life came to seem necessary. As Guiderius says to Belarius, not everything is perfect in the cave, either:

> Haply this life is best
> (If quiet life be best) sweeter to you
> That have a sharper known, well corresponding
> With your stiff age; but unto us it is
> A cell of ignorance, travelling a-bed,
> A prison, or a debtor that not dares
> To stride a limit.   (III.iii.29-35)

These boys, like Orlando, yearn for a nurture of which they are deprived: they are, like Orlando, inland bred and something in them craves for that inland cultivation:

> What should we speak of
> When we are old as you? When we shall hear
> The rain and wind beat dark December? How
> In this our pinching cave shall we discourse
> The freezing hours away? We have seen nothing:
> We are beastly: subtle as the fox for prey,
> Like warlike as the wolf for what we eat.
>
> (III.iii.35-41)

Like animals in their self-sufficiency and their physical hardness, the boys do not admire themselves as beasts; nor do they care for the winter weather, which they recognize as part of their discontent. Theirs is, truly, the classic life of hard pastoral—but which they, unlike proper ideological hard-pastoralists, criticize precisely for its want of nurture. Belarius makes haste to assure them of the comparative merits of their lot, recalling the injustices that

---

[17] Lucretius, v., 1416.

are—as the audience knows from the earlier parts of the play—
"the art o' the court":

> Then was I as a tree
> Whose boughs did bend with fruit. But in one night,
> A storm, or robbery (call it what you will)
> Shook down my mellow hangings, nay, my leaves,
> And left me bare to weather.   (III.iii.60-64)

In this organic metaphor, we feel the unnaturalness of the husbandry which so stripped Belarius. In the mountains he can claim
at least that in "this rock and these demesnes" he has "liv'd in honest freedom"—that primary requisite, as Rosenmeyer has pointed
out,[18] of the pastoral condition—without fearing the "poison,
which attends/ In place of greater state." And the audience must
agree with him, against the noble stretching of the boys, having
seen his metaphor unmetaphored earlier in the play, as the Queen
gathered simples in her garden with which to do away with
Imogen.

However their aspirations may reach, though, the boys must
bow each time they enter the cave, in a stoic *topos*: just as Hercules bent to enter mortal houses and Aeneas to enter Evander's
little palace, these boys acknowledged their humility every time
they take shelter. But they are proud, too: they hunt the hills,
Belarius the plain—and not just because they are nimble and he
is stiff, but also because elevations are their symbolic habitat,
properly sought according to the inevitable pastoral correspondence of real rank with character. However stern the doctrine he
tries to implant in them, Belarius does not quite believe in the
totality of his ideology, and cannot help delighting in the boys'
aspiring to a life beyond the one they lead. Noble as it is as a
refuge from the unjust, artificial, and deceitful court, this landscape is very far from the nourishing pastoral landscape to which
Theocritus turned, nor is it the ironically idealized background
of the Forest of Arden, delightful in some ways and harsh in
others. This is unmitigated hard pastoral, a rocky, difficult ter-
rain training its inhabitants to a spare and muscular strength
sufficient to wrest their nutriment from its minimal, ungenerous,
exiguous resources. No fruit here bends from the boughs to the
eaters' mouths; there is no leisure here to play on pipes and lie

---

[18] Rosenmeyer, pp. 98-129.

in the shade—and as for Neaera, she casts no shadow over the boys' lives. Here, the homely must prove savory, as they say, and flint offer the only pillow; hunger must be satisfied with cold meat till the catch be cooked. The boys are, in a word, cave-dwellers, troglodytes, quite innocent of the city's "usuries." As such children of nature, they instinctively scorn "pelf": when Imogen-Fidele offers them money for what she had taken from their larder, Arviragus answers like the natural aristocrat he is:

> All gold and silver rather turn to dirt,
> As 'tis no better reckon'd but, of those
> Who worship dirty gods.   (III.vii.26-28)

Again and again, the boys respond as nature's noblemen, and Belarius, for all the stoic moral instruction he gives the boys, takes pride in their mysterious elevations beyond their present condition:

> How hard it is to hide the sparks of Nature!
> These boys know little they are sons to th' king,
> Nor Cymbeline dreams that they are alive.
> They think they are mine, and though train'd up thus meanly,
> I' th' cave wherein they bow, their thoughts do hit
> The roofs of palaces, and nature prompts them
> In simple and low things to prince it, much
> Beyond the trick of others.   (III.iii.79-86)

Naturally courteous, then, the cave-family takes in the exile freely, shares what it has with her in hospitable kindness: bare gentility, but liberal. That the boys recognize some kinship with Fidele, and she with them, is of a piece with the kind of miraculous recognition in which this mixed drama is cast. Like calls to like; disguise is no bar to human recognition, the recognition of kind which is, in this kind of fiction, recognition of kin as well. Furthermore, Imogen-Fidele knows at once the natural gentility of these boys:

> These are kind creatures. Gods, what lies I have heard!
> Our courtiers say all's savage but at court;
> Experience, O, thou disprov'st report!   (IV.ii.32-34)

In contrast to her considerate nature, Cloten recognizes no such thing: unfortunately for him, he sees Guiderius simply as a villainous and rustic mountaineer, and comes to his death at the hands of this touchy aristocrat, who will not be condescended to, still less insulted. Once more, Guiderius' behavior, this time manifestly in line with the codes of courtly honor, elicits Belarius' praise of the goddess Nature, who has invested these boys with their birthright—

> royalty unlearn'd, honour untaught,
> Civility not seen from other, valour
> That wildly grows in them   (IV.ii.178-80)

corroborates their fundamental nobility. In another style, Arviragus proves as courtly as his brother, in his uttering the wonderful flower-catalogue of Fidele's beauty; in the dirge for her (learned from their foster mother?) the boys offer no simple country ditty, but a complex poem balancing off simplicity against sophisticated awareness of simplicity's power, a poem entirely in the pastoral mode if not in a pastoral vocabulary.

The plot itself permits the boys to prove their chivalric qualities: the murder of Cloten brings the British threat, so long staved off by Belarius, closer to the cave; the advent of the hostile legions menaces their outlandish privacy as well. Prudent in the boys' welfare, Belarius counsels retreat to the hills ("higher to the mountains") whither, he is sure, neither party shall pursue his "hot summer's tanlings," his "shrinking slaves of winter." But Guiderius has heard the call to arms, and the boys seize the chance to outrun the skimpy, barren life to which they had been bred— "Than be so," says Guiderius, "Better to cease to be." Off they go, and in the chaotic battle that follows, the boys and their foster father manage such deeds of valor that they are knighted in the field for their gentlemanliness at arms. Gradually, the concealments unwind until the boys are restored to their father, their foster father is forgiven his theft of them, and justice and mercy are distributed to everyone gathered for the play's proper ending. The self-consciously reformed court world takes them all in, as the court's recognized means of restoration; everyone turns his back on earlier error and harder landscapes elsewhere. The fine young men, schooled to endurance by their teacher and their habitat, take their places among the other courtiers naturally enough, their youthful discipline offering the promise that Cymbeline's kingdom will be reorganized on new and different moral lines. Nature has raised these boys so that they can return to a birthright compromised in their absence and purify it by the simple strengths of their natural characters.

In this paradigm, the country interludes, whether on a supernatural island or in the Welsh mountains, affirm nature's preservative and restorative powers, her capacity to reconstitute whatever may be wrong with the human constitution, personal or social. To this extent, the country interlude permits human beings to come into contact with Nature, and to assimilate from her such creatural strength as human nature requires in an unnatural social world.

The "oasis," as Poggioli has called it,[19] need not be perfect: it simply offers respite and recreation—that Prospero's island is not edenic, Caliban exists to demonstrate, for whatever else he is, Caliban remains a sample of mankind at the bestial end of the scale, still in that morally primitive naturalistic condition in which women were held in common and incest was the normal ground of sexual relations.[20] That is, Caliban reminds us, with details from hard pastoral, what some of the drawbacks were in the Age of Gold; Prospero's magic combines with a puritan's disgust at such unceremonial rites of conjunction, and his distrust of Ferdinand's sexual intentions has something in it of overcompensation against this aspect of the myth of earthly paradise. Cloten offers us a courtly Caliban, the incest-theme suggested by the relation of his mother to Imogen's father. From such attitudes, the good recoil—Prospero, Miranda, Imogen. Perhaps because there is so much of the marriage-masque in *The Tempest*, we are never allowed to forget the mysterious values of virginity surrendered only in a loving, lawful marriage bond.

Indeed, the bracketing of the human beings in *The Tempest*, between the passionate, brutal Caliban on the earthy side and the supersubtle Ariel on the elevated side, stresses the problematical within the human condition: as Pico della Mirandola put it, a man can become all air, to forget other human beings altogether (Prospero in Milan), or he can sink to bestial level, either from high place (Antonio, Alonso, Sebastian) or from high place parodied (Stephano, Trinculo). For a time Prospero seems to equate Ferdinand with Caliban, as if both equally designed to rob his daughter of herself by rape; Ferdinand must prove himself to be something other. To be Caliban is not enough, but to be Ariel

---

[19] Poggioli, "Pastoral of the Self."   [20] Lovejoy and Boas, p. 14.

will not do either—man must fulfill his *human* nature. To be human is, certainly, a natural thing: Miranda and Ferdinand are figures for an unspoilt humanity, capable for all its innocence and goodness of further development, education, and improvement. Nature and nurture marry them—but under the auspices of art.

We must wonder at much in *Cymbeline*, but the quality of our wonder is utterly different from the wonder experienced in *The Tempest*, where "wonder" is frankly written into the whole play, its *maraviglia* more than the wondrous and wondering Miranda. In the case of this uncharted island, its associations with the "still-vex'd Bermoothes"[21] and with Mediterranean islands like Corfu only serve to make its locale more mysterious, its magic qualities truly leagues beyond ordinary life. The island is far from simple: in the midst of its strange, transubstantiating perfections, Caliban is after all at home, part creatural and part bestial, like those miraculous primitives of the New World in Peter Martyr's account.[22] The island can nourish both the natural and the supernatural in man, but must be well-ruled, well-regulated, to become the gracious state that it symbolically is in *The Tempest*. Shielded as it is from cartography and from history, the island suggests ideals for human behavior rather than imposes them. Even Prospero cannot guarantee moral regeneration: had Ferdinand not loved Miranda, he would never have carried logs for her father; and we cannot be sure (as W. H. Auden has shown in his masque) of Antonio's and Sebastian's reformation.

All the same, Prospero is the only person conscious of history, his own history and history's effect on him; the only person, then, who is self-conscious. Prospero must call up her past for Miranda, to surround her with her original high born ambience; he can identify, having once known them, the people from the real world who make up the island's strange new population. He arranges for his daughter's future, testing Ferdinand by symbolic menial

---

[21] See Kermode, Introduction, Arden ed., xxx-xxxiv; and James, *Prospero*, pp. 72-123; J. P. Brockbank, "*The Tempest*: Conventions of Art and Empire," *The Later Shakespeare*, pp. 183-200.

[22] Richard Eden, *The History of Travayle in the West and East Indies* (London, 1577; [I was fortunate in using William Strachey's own copy: Beinecke Library, Yale University: Eca/555Eb]). Peter Martyr, *De Novo Ordo*, tr. Richard Eden and M. Lok (London, 1612), pp. 138-40, 298-301. For an analogue to Gonzalo's natural utopia, see Erasmus, *The Praise of Folie*, tr. Thomas Chaloner (London, 1549), Aiiij[v].

tasks of rural servitude, the bearing of logs and the drawing of water. These tasks stress both the natural and the supernatural in any environment: from the logs come fire, from water purification, and from both, as the biblical echo reminds us, comes survival.[23] Prospero can control the "now" of what happens on the island, and reach out as well to conjure other people's memories, impressions, hopes, and even their futures. In a metaphor made active and animate, this island *is* Prospero's, to dispose imaginatively as he will, just as the pastoral landscape is the poet's, to dispose as he will.

But this is drama, not lyric, and Prospero's animate landscape is, in the play's terms, actually *disponible*, not merely metaphorically so: this landscape transforms itself not only to suit its chief inhabitant's mental needs, but also to satisfy his moral aims. The metaphorical magic of pastoral landscape becomes the metamorphosing magic of its theatrical master, as before our eyes we behold nature turning into something more. An underlying assumption of lyric pastoral, then, has been adapted to drama, and by that adaptation enlarged and made more wonderful: we see Prospero, as master of the revels and as poet-playwright, in relation to his attendant—and necessarily attendant—landscape.

Prospero is presented as self-aware, self-critical, self-controlled: he abjures his magic when its purpose is fulfilled; he can go back confident into the life at which he had failed before the play began. By their sojourn on this island, the other characters gather and regroup their moral forces—are recomposed, recreated, before they return to the less manipulable world of their origins. Each person is given a chance at self-consciousness, a chance to reconsider and even to redraft his own personality to fit, to meet again the self he has lost or compromised in the *negotium* of his ordinary life. With guilts recognized and repented, innocence confirmed and re-embraced, the pastoral oasis sends its guests refreshed on their journey back into brazen society: Prospero's island is golden, the most golden of all Shakespeare's natural interludes, because a maker and a translator, a poet indeed, is in charge of it all—the shepherd has become magician.

The Welsh mountains of *Cymbeline* are no such magic place. Indeed, if we were to imagine a natural environment opposite to Prospero's island, we might come up with just such a stark, rocky,

---

[23] I owe this formulation to Sheldon Zitner.

isolated cave as Belarius has made his home. The strictness of that locale, as habitat and as symbol, simply guarantees the innate and confirmed rectitude of Cymbeline's sons, savage noblemen so totally in control of their inhospitable landscape that they can question the values of the life it offers even as they go about fulfilling its severe requirements. They are the hard pastoralists extolled by stoic and cynic, those plain men who, pared down to their essentials by the environment with which they must all their lives compete, make of themselves touchstones for moral and social truth. Their nobility may be rugged, even rude, but it is true because tried; so Guiderius knows that the proper way to deal with a boorish creature is to kill him; so both princes, unpractised in warfare, acquit themselves as knights when they sally forth from their restrictive cave. In all of this, Shakespeare manages to get it both ways, for "the court" is never condemned, though particular courts may be: he shows us how courtly men may and do degenerate, but at the same time he invariably associates natural nobility with actual social aristocracy—Orlando, Perdita, Miranda, Arviragus, Guiderius are noble, even royal, by birth. By the plays' ends, it turns out, there is no distinction and no competition between nature and nurture; these aristocrats need their pastoral interlude far less than the characters in the play who do not attain it, or who only unwillingly succumb to it. To their social condition, the mental landscape of pastoral matches the decorum of its moral condition.

Imogen-Fidele in fact shows how important the pastoral interlude is in such a play, for she was not in a landscape suited to her nature at court; how else could she have stayed alive but by the human kindness affirmed in the life of those gentle cave-dwellers? She dies to live again by their means, after her crucial and supportive experience of the unvarnished human values confronted in the cave, demonstrated by the cave-family. She is reborn by the limited, generous nurturing this family can afford and freely offers. In turn, the court is restored because these, its best members, return to it, their humanity corroborated after profound contact with an unremitting stark and inhospitable nature, a testing nature for their characters. They better and best themselves against this rock-hard life, to find their integrity as firm as the landscape.

In these two plays, the playwright brings us up against the extremes of pastoral myth: we are forced, in each play, to recognize the absolute qualities of the pastoral environment of received tradition, but the formula itself is altered, stretched, and modified to show how differently external nature may serve human nature—to show, really, that the fundamental question is man, as maker of his own environment. In *Cymbeline*, the "oasis," the natural environment, is as unpastoral as possible, offering no quarter to the human beings stationed in it—until we remember the long classical tradition, largely stoical, which A. O. Lovejoy and George Boas called "hard" pastoral, the tradition of a harsh but reliably supportive external nature which trained man in endurance and in self-knowledge. In *The Tempest*, the whole play *is* the oasis; the theme of pastoral recreation has been animated into setting and into plot as well. We see the poet-magician working his creative and recreative wonders by means of a nature wholly impossible, even more impossible than the usual pastoral dream-setting: we see the metaphor turned into dramatic actuality and dramatic action.

III

With such radical revisions of the pastoral pattern before us, it comes as less of a surprise to find, even more schematically, the same pattern in *King Lear*, another tale of exile and return, of flight from courtly corruption into the uncompromising simplicity of the country. Again and again in this play, "court" and "country" are played off against one another: in the nonsense between Oswald and the disguised Kent; in the contrast between Regan and her husband and the solicitous tenant, so opposed in their treatment of Gloucester. The courtiers Kent and Edgar turn "plain" in their exile: to do what they have to do, both simplify themselves radically. Kent speaks the flattest country speech to Oswald in the courtyard (as well as the golden courtier's speech, rejected by its parody, to Cornwall); Edgar snaps into the countryman's accent when the foppish Oswald later comes seeking Gloucester's life. As in *Cymbeline* and *The Winter's Tale*, the court is not safe for good men; courtiers forget all courtesy and choose to deal wholly in violence and savagery. Not for nothing does the subplot come from Sidney's *Arcadia*, that harsh shepherd's story where we learn so much about brutality. The inset tale of the Paphlagonian king, dispossessed and blinded by the natural son he unnaturally favored, tenderly led through the countryside by the true son he unnaturally persecuted, is one incident in a string of violent episodes reconciled at their end by brotherhood. But Arcadia was, in Sidney's book as elsewhere, a showcase and testing ground for questions of humanity and humankind: in this story, as in *King Lear* as a whole, generosity, generation, even genes themselves, are the issues, and are recognized as the issues of mankind. Nature and nurture are, in various ways, scrutinized and emblematized.[24]

As Maynard Mack has said in his provocative book on the play,[25] *King Lear* is an enormous anti-pastoral, a reversal of the usual pastoral correspondence between the shepherd and his peaceful environment. Yes and no: it is, certainly, in its unpastoral, even anti-pastoral, stress on violence and savagery, a reversal of the pastoral tone, an inversion of many traditions within the pastoral modes. But at the same time it maintains many elements of the pastoral pattern: there *is*, as a generation of students has learned from Theodore Spencer and E.M.W. Tillyard and their faithful *epigoni*, a correspondence between Lear's mental state and the meteorological conditions of his world—it is the ideology that is reversed, not the convention of pastoral; the decorum, not the device. Certainly, in Lear's wild nature, we are not led to expect reformation or recovery: precisely its *lack* of nurturing capacity distinguishes the nature of *King Lear* from the pastoral norm.

In true pastoral, however disordered nature might appear, nonetheless if a shepherd died or a shepherdess rejected his love, seasonal regeneration is consistently invoked to promise redress of present imbalance. Not so here: chaos is come, and nature gives no indication of future reconstitution, even promise of the seasonal round. All the same, there is a sense in which the storm gives comfort to the desperate King, even in its denial to him of a comforting antidote to his condition: in just its wildness and intractability, nature seems to Lear indifferent throughout to human fate, but sympathetic in providing him with a dramatic background tonally appropriate to his mood and his mental state. Like Lear, to whom he is often likened, Prospero was extruded from his sovereignty, though, we must note, that deed was done in secret; by means of his art, Prospero entered into intimacies with

[24] On "nature" in *King Lear*, see John Danby, *Shakespeare's Doctrine of Nature* (London, 1949); and, among much else, H. A. Mason, *Shakespeare's Tragedies* (London, 1970), pp. 136-37, 195-98.

[25] Mack, *King Lear*; and Lindheim, "*King Lear* as Pastoral Tragedy."

nature which enabled him to promote total restoration of the human and social disorders of his environment. Prospero's sojourn in nature involved an *otium* very active indeed: Lear's self-chosen abandonment of kingly duty and royal *negotium* left him (literally) without resources. In *King Lear*, too, there is no such inscrutable, backdoor solution to the exile's critical condition: his daughters are open in their persecution, he is open in his flight from the persecuting, peripatetic court. And nature is correspondingly open in this play. The storm proclaims extremity over the whole region: Regan sees it coming, and men publicly recognize its bitter significance for the old King. Though he runs out into the terrible night clad in his regalia, Lear has none of the protection offered by Prospero's cloak; he meets nature undefended and resourceless.

The nature which receives King Lear, which receives the reduced Edgar, is even more niggardly than the rocky wilderness to which Belarius fled with his charges. In *Cymbeline*, wild creatures may have threatened the boys, but they learned to hunt them for food. In *King Lear*, the wild creatures, as Albany says, are all human, and they do the hunting until it seems to Albany that "Mankind preys upon itself." In contrast to its mysterious, unlocated, pursuing court, *King Lear* offers a nature bare, hard, unpeopled, unresponsive, a nature as reduced as are the human beings it entertains, a nature pared down to its most abstract qualities, an ecology indifferent to its inhabitants. Nonetheless, it is a nature appropriately arranged to correspond to human beings concerned exclusively with extremity: it is an absolute, a stoic landscape.[26] We cannot even frame questions about life on this heath, so abstracted is it: did Edgar actually eat newt and toad, like Macbeth's witches? How was Lear nourished, if at all, Lear, who in the old world cried for his dinner the moment he came in from hunting? This heath is too stark for such workaday considerations; this heath is, simply, the minimal ground for existence, the plainest possible area on which men may work out such justifications as they can for their bare existence.

But even in this, Shakespeare has covertly offered us one comfort inherent in the thematics of pastoral: such nature as we have

[26] For Lear's stoicism, see William Elton, *"King Lear" and the Gods* (San Marino, 1966), pp. 97-107, 272-76, and the literature cited. Cf. Seneca, *Medea*, 426-28 ("Sola est quies,/ mecum ruina cuncta si video obruta;/ mecum omnia abeant"), for an analogue to Lear's relation to nature.

in this play is invoked in relation to Lear and the Lear party. The storm is an unmetaphored metaphor for *Lear's* state of mind—no natural parallel is offered, for the equally turbulent and far crueler minds of his daughters. However askew the "natures" in question, external and human, it is only to Lear and his friends that even an adumbrated suggestion is vouchsafed of the contact possible between man and nature. Thus, on the heath, where the playwright makes no effort to delineate a specific natural landscape (such as was provided in the harsh cave of *Cymbeline*), he does offer a fit landscape all the same for a debate so crucial and so abstract as that on the nature of man. All the pastoral words are critical in this play: "nature," "natural," "unnatural," "kind," "kindness," "unkind," "unkindness," "generous" and "ungenerous" recur, as each scene reveals more evidence for the question's consideration. But rarely are these words used in connection with landscape, and never in connection with a possible pastoral nurturing scene. It is with human nature that the play concerns itself, and the metaphoric, supportive thematic possibilities of "nature" are correspondingly reduced.

Nonetheless, as Maynard Mack has said, the pastoral pattern *is* in this play, which also investigates, at a level far deeper than the customary, more overt pastoral debate, the problems of nature and nurture, of court and country, of human kind, kindness, and unkindness, which are classically themes of the pastoral mode. First of all, in *King Lear* civilization itself is called into question, far more radically than in Leontes' Sicily or Cymbeline's Britain. In *King Lear*, neither nature nor nurture turns out to have much to do with kindness: family offers no guarantees, nor is there a recognizable generic gentility either. Edmund had been "out" nine years—that is, his father, like Oliver's brother, had not proffered him a nobleman's training. We might on these grounds incline to excuse his parody of courtly behavior, but no such excuse can be found for Goneril and Regan, to say nothing of Cornwall and even of the Duke of Burgundy, all bred to their station. If they "should" have performed better in a world of gentility, why then, so "should" Lear have done; in terms of protocol, even his good daughter is rude (though her silence makes her seem polite, in contrast to her father's response to that silence).[27]

[27] For Cordelia's speech, see Sheldon P. Zitner, "*King Lear* and its Language," *Some Facets*; and Emily W. Leider, "Plainness of Style in *King Lear*," *SQ*, XXI (1970), 45-53.

"Nature" means different things to the different people in this play, as fine commentators have taught us. Edmund invokes nature as his authority for the dog-eat-dog life upon which he sets out; Lear invokes an equally heartless nature when he curses Goneril with the sterility he, too late, wished he had had himself; later, he invokes the Lucretian version of Epicurean nature in his remarks upon universal generation. Kent and the nameless Gentleman note that the natural tempest is too great for human "nature" to bear; Gloucester takes nature to be simply fate, a cryptic determiner of man's destiny. No one in this play thinks of appealing to a generous, nourishing, supportive nature; only in the play's *structure* can we see a remnant of this philosophical view of nature's relation to mankind.[28] We hear and see much of what is both natural and unnatural, kind and unkind; again and again, characters consider birth and breeding. The bond of kind is variously recognized: by Gloucester in the play's opening exchange; by Cordelia in her stiff, limited, but absolute answer to her love-greedy father; in the exchange between Edmund and Gloucester in ii.i; in Lear's appeal to his second daughter's "kindness," the "bonds of childhood" due him now. "Breeding" is both the biological begetting of a child (as Gloucester speaks of Edmund, and Cordelia of her father's having bred her) and the bringing-up, the nurture and education, of that child. In Edmund's case, for instance, Gloucester was responsible for "breeding" in the first sense and utterly failed his responsibilities in the second. The same may have been true of Lear, although all we know from the play is that his elder daughters were not brought up to be what he had wished. The First Servant, loyal to an order of nature higher than Cornwall's, speaks of his service to the Duke "since I was a child," and was spoken of as having been "bred" or brought up by Cornwall—but all the same, in spite of that environment, the Servant has roots in kind and kindness which Cornwall clearly never put down. A narrower view of things (such as Regan's) responds with shock to the Servant's treatment of Cornwall, but we, with our attention drawn to the deeper implications of breeding, may well wonder how the Servant's sense of values was as true as it was. Kent marvels at Lear's get, that "one self mate and make" could "beget such different issues"; and

28 Paul J. Alpers, *"King Lear* and the Theory of the 'Sight Pattern,'" *In Defense of Reading*, pp. 133-52, deals with the primacy of feeling over understanding, as does Lindheim, op. cit.

Lear marvels, too, even to considering the possibility, only dimly fantasized, that he had been cuckolded by his wife. Rather a cuckold, then, than to have fathered from his own loins such unkindness.

Class and caste are in this play no warranties of courtesy, kindness, or gentleness, whatever the derivations of these words may suggest: the Fool asks if a madman be a gentleman or a yeoman, implying insanity's democracy; from Tom we hear, and in Edmund we perceive, that the Prince of Darkness is a gentleman. Certainly this would appear true enough, as we watch the blinding of an earl by a duke, his guest, hear Edmund claiming so brutally his "rank" against an unknown challenger, see Goneril and Regan harry their father into despair like the wolfish sheepdogs they are. In the world of rank and privilege, the world by tradition called "gentle," there is considerable reassurance in hearing Kent assert to a stranger-gentleman his own gentle birth and breeding, his actions so clearly corroborating the point. As a gentleman, through a gentleman, he sends his message offstage to that symbol for truth and gentleness, the lady Cordelia.

No wonder, then, that amidst all this whirligig of custom, behavior, and ideas, King Lear becomes obsessed with the idea of "breeding," lawful and unlawful. Tom keeps the notion alive for him in his own talk of Pillicock, and for us in Gloucester's incorporation of "the foul fiend Flibbertigibbet," "a walking fire," as he enters with a lantern as an emblem of his old self, burning in lust. Lear's great speeches later, in iv.vi, on lechery and adultery, reach a thematic crescendo of all this material: everything goes to 't, from the small gilded fly to great ladies. Epicurean nature, unnatural only in its obsessive singleness of purpose, justifies for the moment all that Lear must undergo. Though these are the clichés of Renaissance naturalism, for Lear as for Edgar, behavior so limited to the naturalistic comes to seem, simply, monstrous, below and thus beyond the capacities of human beings. "Down from the waist they are centaurs,/ Though women all above" draws one line of that mounting appeal to concepts and images of monstrousness, savagery, and predation so constant through the play. That monstrousness is harbored in the hearts of great ones is irony enough, but that (as in *The Winter's Tale*) such savagery should cluster in the place traditionally at the center of civilization, at court, whence law, courtesy, graciousness traditionally emanate, compounds the bitterness of Lear's situation.

Men are beasts; of these beasts, courtiers are particularly savage; of courtiers, the greatest are the most brutal. It is part of Edgar's disguise, not of his fundamental nature, to say of himself that he was (like those left at the court) "hog in sloth, fox in stealth, wolf in greediness, dog in madness, lion in prey." Like Guiderius', Edgar's self-disgust at these animal qualities in him speaks through the lines.

The pattern of predation—the pattern Jaques sentimentalized over and Cymbeline's sons follow as a matter of survival—is reversed in this play, to offer yet another version of the play's anti-pastoralism. At the same time, the nearly unbearable inhumanity at the center of power reinforces the very myth exemplified in pastoral drama, that civilization brings corruption and cruelties from which the only refuge is nature, a countryside beyond the reach of such uncreatural sophistications. In *King Lear*, good men are proclaimed outlaws, and the only "nature" for them to flee to is the last resort of the afflicted, exiled, and persecuted, a landscape so inhospitable that no one else will inhabit it, so hard and uncompromising that it can offer solace (if that is what mere "philosophers" are offered) only to the mind.

The self-acknowledged tempest in Lear's mind is such that he does not seem to have missed the roof he has abjured; but both Fool and Kent realize the insufficiency of the shelter they find, prefer it though they do to the "hard house" from which they have been barred. In the hovel the Fool (a natural) and the King (who has acknowledged and will again acknowledge his folly) find an emblem of their own and all human misfortune, a man evidently so reduced in wits, social status, and material condition that to them he appears literally a "naked soul," "the thing itself, unaccommodated man." As we know, Edgar-Tom has deliberately erased in himself all visible characteristics of his early life, has chosen the role and the condition of social outcast, bedlamite and beggar. In the topsy-turvydom in which he is trying simply to survive, to be safe at all Edgar must undertake a condition normally, in the real world, quite unsafe. But such is the situation of this play that only as outcast, only as outlaw, can he find protection against human beings turned beasts of prey. From this figure of Tom, the real Fool flees as from a savage creature or a fiend. The destitute King, however, moves toward him at once, as if recognizing in this new outcast a case of his own kind. The speed with which Lear turns to philosophizing on the nature of man is at once a naturalistic sign of his intelligence, even when under the siege of the madness he so feared. Edgar is the emblematic figure for such discussion, its subject and its illustration. In his scanty costume[29] he actualizes Lear's earlier generalizations about "naked wretches" with "homeless heads and unfed sides," with the "loop'd and window'd raggedness." With the guise and garb of madness, Edgar reduces himself by another level, to the "worst" of all social conditions.

Certainly, the heath scenes are of the utmost importance in the play's consideration of "man"—who is, as Lear says, "no more than this." No more than *what*? We know, as Lear does not, who and what Edgar actually is. Whatever he may seem, he is not the unaccommodated man Lear takes him for, but rather is disaccommodated, in much the way Lear himself is. Edgar was *someone*, and though he has had to exchange his identity for a role, he remains throughout someone far more complex and significant than his role characterizes. Emblematically, the question is valid enough: is man no more than this?—than a self-deposed, dispossessed king and rejected father, cut off from his family, his environment, his society, from all the holdfasts he had ever known? than a court Fool, never so foolish and never so great as when choosing to follow his master into the wilderness? a man, then, designated as a "natural" in a specific and limiting sense? or, than a disguised madman, destitute like the King and like the King ejected from a highly privileged position in the deference society into which he was born? All three of these are certainly at the extremity of their experience. And more: we are brought to feel that their extremity is the limit of human suffering as well—and yet not one of these figures is unambiguously what he seems, not one is the reduced human being hypothesized in Lear's speech about the poor naked wretches. The pastoral conventions of disguise work even here, in this extraordinarily hard-pastoral scene. These men are not what they seem, to the audience or to each other—what they *are* beyond their appearances is what is important, valuable, even great about "human nature."

Just this very ambiguity, unstressed and unforced, points to the deeply problematical in human nature—in a man's relation to himself, and in his relations to anyone else in his world. The reduction of any man to "the thing itself" forces us to consider those systems, institutions, and habits which keep any man from being

[29] See Maurice Charney, "Nakedness in *King Lear*," *Some Facets*.

simply human: as in the frankly pastoral plays with which these chapters are concerned, *As You Like It, The Winter's Tale, Cymbeline, The Tempest*, we must draw on our ideas of the relations between nature and nurture, between man and his environment, his culture, his civilization. In *King Lear*, the naturals before our eyes, those extreme figures of basic if stripped and warped humanity, cast and self-cast as moral emblems of necessity and destitution, are exposed as the absolute human minimum and displayed against a background of minimum nature as well. We are forced to think not only of the relation to humankind of external nature, but of the importance (at court, in the country, anywhere at all) of human kindness, the only quality distinguishing man from beast. We see it, startlingly, working even in the perverted court, as Gloucester's servants seek homely remedies for their master's eye-sockets; we see it in the country, as the tenant helps his landlord and the frightening "naked one" with him; we see it on the heath, in Lear's "In, boy, in." Much later, at the other end of the social scale from servant, peasant, and outcast, we see it in Cordelia's remarkable charity[30] and unquestioning forgiveness, for a moment sufficient counterbalance to the planned ferocity of her court-bound sisters.

Between these charities, themselves set within a frame of shocking savagery spontaneous and premeditated, is set the animate debate on the nature of man, on human nakedness and naked humanity. Is man no more than this? In his rags, self-mutilated,[31] Edgar-Tom stands for "this," nearly an animal and yet, as Lear sees, independent of the creatures as well ("Thou ow'st the sheep no wool, the cat no perfume"). At the bottom of the human scale, isolated, aloof, Edgar-Tom is nonetheless human—he stands out like a man from his stark environment. So reduced, Edgar bears a wry, comforting message underneath his horrifying report on human degradation. After all the earlier talk of gorgeousness and garments, the handy-dandy with garb and attribute already displayed on the stage with Edgar, Kent, Lear, and the Fool, the two-facedness of the powerful and the seekers after power, it comes as a relief to think, if only for a moment, of man irreducible, or man as "poor, bare, forked animal," "no more than this."

30 Cf. Sears R. Jayne, "Charity in *King Lear*," *Shakespeare 400*, pp. 80-88.
31 Cf. Zitner, "*King Lear* and its Language."

Extremity forces Lear to philosophy, and he then attributes philosophy to his speculative stimulus, Tom, his figure for extremity, "this philosopher," "good Athenian," "this same learned Theban." Not only has the association of madness with philosophy to do with the long tradition, exemplified in both the Fool and in Lear himself, of *docta ignorantia, idiotes,* and holy folly, but it derives as well from the stoical and cynical defenses of man as properly naked and poor, properly delivered from "accommodation."[32] Lear's recognition of Tom as a man is symbolic of his recognition of kind: men had argued for centuries that a minimal humanity be recognized as equally human as the greatest urbanite. In the pseudo-Lucianic dialogue *The Cynic,* an Edgar-figure debates the merits of an extremely hard pastoral morality against an *agora*-type, Lycinus, a representative of *urbs, civitas,* and *negotium.* Lycinus opens the dialogue by asking,[33]

> You there, why in heaven's name have you the beard and the long hair, but no shirt? Why do you expose your body to view, and go barefooted, adopting by choice this nomadic anti-social and bestial life? Why unlike all others do you abuse your body by ever inflicting on it what it likes least, wandering around and prepared to sleep anywhere at all on the hard ground, so that your old cloak carries about a plentiful supply of filth, though it was never fine or soft or gay?

The figure so garbed is the Cynic, who as Lycinus says, is "no better than the paupers who beg for their daily bread."[34] The Cynic invites his interlocutor to enter with him upon what is essentially a debate on reason and deed. "What need one?" Regan had asked, about Lear's servants. The Cynic would have been, for quite different reasons from hers, on Regan's side: his feet are more suited to their function, he says, than the average man's, likewise the rest of his body, made stronger by his diet (this is "the food that comes first to hand"—Edgar's "swimming frog, the toad, the todpole, the wall-newt, and the water"). Lycinus complains of the Cynic's habits: like a dog, or like Tom, he eats whatever he finds and sleeps on straw. The Cynic then demon-

32 For material on holy folly, see Kaiser, *Praisers of Folly,* chapter 1; and *Paradoxia,* Introduction, and chapter 15.
33 Lucian, "The Cynic" (*Works,* LCL), VIII, 381.
34 Lucian, VIII, 383.

strates that the clothes Lycinus wears scarce keep him warm, that his rich food and fine house merely publish his greed.[35] The Cynic goes on to say, as if providing an epigraph for this play,[36]

> Gold and silver may I not need, neither I nor any of my friends. For from the desire for these grow up all men's ills—civic strife, wars, conspiracies, and murders. All these have as their fountainhead the desire for more. But may this desire be far from us, and never may I reach out for more than my share, but be able to put up with less than my share.

The paradigm of sufficiency, material and moral, lies behind another element fully exploited in this play, the working-out in the play's action of those Renaissance restatements of the stoic paradoxes designed to question the material requirements of civilized society. *The Cynic* offers another point of reference for the connection of physical endurance with moral strength, a question debated, illustrated, and counter-illustrated throughout *King Lear*. Considering the background to all this talk of stripping, we must acknowledge anew that the pastoral skeleton of this play has indeed been stripped of its Arcadian lendings. As in the prose epic from which he took such a significant part of this play's fiction, Shakespeare has used the notion of Arcadia allusively, to force the memory and the meaning of pastoral nature as a norm against which, our awareness tripped of its presence here, we can measure the barbarity of the play's dominant predatory culture. The bare bones of the pastoral paradigm and of pastoral ideology support the many other intellectual and literary elements given voice in *King Lear*: without apology, and without customary generic cryptic coloration, the pattern and its themes are developed throughout. Perhaps the pastoral ideas are the stronger here for their very reticence. Another decorum, a nature either so uncompromising or so uncompromised as to be anti-pastoral, offers the ground—the scene, the costume, the language —for this ultimate confrontation of men with a nature so harsh that most men choose never to acknowledge its existence.

But "kindness" is not simply the recognition of humanity so schematically presented on the heath; it is also the acknowledgment of humanity's needs, such as the "naked fellow's" kindness to Gloucester in seeming at once to do the old man's will and at

---

[35] Lucian, VIII, 397-99; and Lucretius, V, 1423-29.
[36] Lucian, VIII, 405.

the same time preventing the self-destruction he sought. Edgar shifts, even here, from role to role,[37] the more easily for his father's blindness; but his symbolic affirmation of humanity's kindness is the greater because of his anonymity to his father onstage and his specific identity of disavowed son, known to the audience watching. In the scene at Dover cliffs, the dramaturgy expresses with wonderful economy the generosity exchanged which, in Sidney's prose version, had all to be described and explained in a long, rhetorical narrative by the Paphlagonian king. In keeping with his technique elsewhere, here too the playwright has condensed radically, called on his whole technical vocabulary of poetics and stagecraft to enrich his model. As with Cordelia's behavior to her father, Edgar's relation to Gloucester expresses both the enormous complexity and the basic simplicity of human connections. Through these specific characters, in this specific situation, we know general human needs and how they can be coped with; we see that in human beings, such recognition draws forth specific, appropriate responses of human support.

In Gloucester's suicide-attempt, we have the emblematic enactment of what we have earlier sensed in the heath-scene, with its debate of kind. The old man seeks his (unstoical) death, but learns—a surprise to him, a surprise to us—stoicism after all. As in the case of Antaeus, Gloucester's gesture of self-abandonment to natural forces, to nature itself, restores his strength. He rises from his grotesque contact with the earth capable of endurance, capable of life, and (how unlikely this is!) capable even of further moral growth and insight. His gesture, flinging himself down upon the earth,[38] makes graphic the symbolic content of the earlier, differently visual debate: however unyielding and unresponsive, nature in this play nonetheless offers to human beings a rigorous, severe, but reliable support.

His suicide thwarted, Gloucester is shortly brought to face, in the King running mad, another man's resolution to the same predicament that had brought him to the edge of suicide. Blind man and madman must somehow recognize in each other their

[37] Cf. Zitner, "Language"; and Van Laan, "Acting as Action."

[38] For a full interpretation of the poetics of the morality-function in this scene, see Bridget G. Lyons, "The Subplot as Simplification," *Some Facets*; as well as Harry Levin, "The Heights and the Depths," *More Talking of Shakespeare*; Alvin B. Kernan, "Formalism and Realism in Elizabethan Drama: the Miracles in *King Lear*," *RenD*, IX (1966).

own and each other's human extremity and, through their mu-
tilated perceptions, somehow communicate that recognition of
common humanity. Gloucester must, as Lear says, "look with
[his] ears"; and, though he cannot see the King's mad parody of
Whitsun pastoral festivity ("fantastically dressed with weeds"),
Gloucester knows soon enough who it is that speaks so. Lear too
has run back again into "nature"—to a natural scene, though,
very different from the barren heath on which he met unaccommodated man. Now, as we learn from Cordelia, the weeds
are tall, and "our sustaining corn" is highgrown for the harvest
—so high that it is easy to lose the King in the fields. Lear himself speaks in this scene in pastoral terms, and Gloucester refers
to his "nature." "No, they cannot touch me for coining," Lear
says cunningly; "I am the King himself"—that is, whatever artificial kings may have sprung up in Britain, only he is irrevocably
royal, by birth and breeding, whose right it is to sanction mintage.
Then, by a verbal leap which nonetheless demonstrates that
"reason in madness" his hearers recognize, he adds the classical
judgment of the pastoral *paragone*: "Nature's above art in that
respect." He is, then, intrinsically the King. No counterfeit, of
coinage or of kingship, will do. The arts and crafts of those who
usurp his position are no more than those artifices held up to
criticism and for rejection in the pastoral rivalry of nature with
art—mere imitation, mere fancy, mere illusion.

Gloucester's response to the King's words—"O ruin'd piece of
nature!"—presses us past the proud assumptions of Lear's assertion of nature's supremacy to art: nature decays, after all. Whatever else has happened in this play, the King powerful in kindness and in wrath has vanished, leaving only this ridiculous,
farcical figure, singing through the fields to recall in disjointed
phrases the force, for good and for ill, once characteristic of Lear.
Natural king he is still, but in a sense other than the one he
chooses to honor: he is now a natural fool of fortune. Gloucester
is equally a ruined piece of nature (as Lear cruelly perceives),
restored by his faith-keeping son only to perish in mixed joy and
sorrow when he learns that his guide has been, after all, that
dutiful child. The two old men are emblematic too: standing,
manifestly at the depth of their lives, in the open fields, and all
the same the better for their exposure to the elements, the storm,
the heath, and the Dover cliffs, the better for their confrontation
with each other in the wheatfield. It is true that Lear is now

finally mad, but relieved thereby of some of his worst anguish and about to be rewarded by the fantastic forgiveness of his kind daughter. Like Lear in the storm and on the heath, Gloucester too has touched the bottom of his nature at the imagined cliff-side; Edgar like his elders has emerged from the philosophical demonstration on the heath to resume, by degrees, his function and his identity. He works through his remaining family obligations, reordering his disordered kin as he rescues his father and punishes his brother, ready at last to undertake the social responsibilities laid on him at the play's end. Lear, Gloucester, Edgar: all three touch natural reality at its farthest remove from their normal lives, and build back from that contact to a renewed, if painfully qualified, understanding of their own humanity and the nature of humankind. The hard pastoral of this play, with its rigid version of irreducible nature, serves them as the pastoral interlude serves Rosalind and her father, as his pastoral interlude serves Prospero, his daughter, and the others, or as theirs serves Perdita, Florizel, and Sicily and Bohemia as well. From such contact with nature, men gain strength to re-enter the world of their inheritance. *King Lear's* nature is geologically and emotionally hard, like the rocky space that serves its pastoral function in *Cymbeline*, where the landscape supports death as readily as life, and is designed to train men for exceptional undertakings. Nature in *King Lear* is far harsher and more inhospitable than Belarius' cave-nature, however: in *King Lear*, the characters find nature no less hard than the "hard house" which Lear fled and where Gloucester lost his eyes, but its reliable neutrality and consistency offer support to exiles nonetheless. This nature, unlike the human beings in their lives, does not persecute men, even in their extremity; indeed, for all its forbidding severity, this nature, like the conventional pastoral vacation, offers men pressed to the utmost another chance to recover their sense of reality and their sense of themselves.

Lear is right, of course. The elements are not organized along familial lines:

> Nor rain, wind, thunder, fire, are my daughters:
> I tax you not, you elements, with unkindness;
> I never gave you kingdom, call'd you children,
> You owe me no subscription. (III.ii.15-18)

Mad as the speech sounds, it says something very important about the play's underlying schemes. Nature affords man a sufficiency, his life—no more than that, but that. Whatever else a man have, achieve, receive, or acquire, he must get from human beings, from himself and from others, must build from his social awareness. The late eclipses of the sun and moon have nothing whatever to do with generational conflicts or with a man's dealing with his friends; the harvest of this play is not of the sustaining corn through which the mad Lear runs, but of great figures dead of violence and heartbreak. Nature is not the "opportunity" with which Edmund's invocation equates her, as we watch the opportunists go down with the generous. Cornwall, Oswald, Regan, Goneril, Edmund, all die with their moral betters, and die in ways fitting their contempt of law, of custom, and of emotional claim. Nature simply *is*, as the stoics conceived of the matter, offering the support only of her stringent simplicity. And yet the play is paradoxical, in this as in so much else: from contacts with this inhospitable, inhuman, remote nature, maimed men are able to reassert their humanity and their kindness in the face of nearly insuperable emotional odds, and to draw (even in madness) on their own persistent human-kindness. To those who have the wit to risk themselves to nature's handling, this hard-pastoral nature offers the benefits of hardness—uncomfortable, barren, and unyielding support to those who can recognize it for what it is, and can take it.

8

Forms and Their Meanings:
"Monumental Mock'ry"

IN TROILUS AND CRESSIDA, the reader faces problems much like
those presented by *Love's Labour's Lost*: working with many
different devices and forms, the playwright brings them seriously
into question, showing up their emptiness and challenging their
meaning. The poet has made his double plot[1] in *Troilus and
Cressida* out of the metaphor so common in erotic poetry, that
love is "like" war; has given us a full war-plot (and how laden
with accrued meanings this particular warplot is!) played off
against a full love-plot, from which the play's name is taken; and,
in case we should miss this counterpoint, has provided us with a
critical commentator, Thersites,[2] who reminds us of the parallel
and counterpoint again and again: "war for a placket"; "All the
argument is a whore and a cuckold"; "Lechery, lechery; still wars
and lechery."

In addition, Shakespeare has attacked literature itself at its very
source, turning upside down the Homeric values, neither making
them problematical (as we might expect from his usual practice)
nor humanizing them, but degrading them to trivial hypocrisies
designed to cover appetite.[3] Nor has he chosen only to travesty
the epic that, according to much Renaissance theory, fathered all
literature;[4] he also undermines the greatest of English poets
among his own predecessors, stripping Troilus, Cressida, and

[1] For a discussion of the double plot, "complementary" in a special sense,
see Norman Rabkin, *Shakespeare and the Common Understanding* (New
York, 1969), pp. 30-57.

[2] For Thersites, see O. J. Campbell, *"Comicall Satyre" and Shakespeare's
"Troilus and Cressida"*; Alvin Kernan, *The Canker'd Muse*; Robert C. Elliott,
The Power of Satire (Princeton, 1960).

[3] The degradations of the Troy-legend in the Middle Ages is an important
part of the background of this play: see Robert Kimbrough, *Shakespeare's
"Troilus and Cressida" and its Setting* (Cambridge, Mass., 1964), chapter III
and relevant references.

[4] Cf. for instance J. C. Scaliger, *Poetices*, pp. 10-11 (comedy and tragedy),
p. 43 (*funebres*), p. 45 (rhapsodies), p. 46 (parody), p. 149 (satire), p. 215
(generation of other forms from the *Iliad* and the *Odyssey*).

Pandarus of the recognizable, rich, highly complex humanity with which Chaucer had endowed them[5]—one would have thought, forever.[6] Even allowing for the facts that there was medieval precedent for derogating Homer as an authority on Troy and morality, and that contemporary stage-references handle the Trojan story comically,[7] Shakespeare's management of the material remains obviously puzzling and daring, offering as he does a low version of the Homeric story in a period which openly idolized Homer, a low version of the Chaucerian narrative in a period when Chaucer's reputation was reaffirmed, and a satire on romance and epic just as romance and epic had found their great exemplars in Ariosto's, Tasso's, and Spenser's poems.

One critic has suggested that the reason for the great variety of artifices from different decorums, so many of them travestied, in *Troilus and Cressida* was that the play is Shakespeare's effort to encapsulate and anthologize the dramatic techniques of his period;[8] though this seems an inadequate answer to all the play's puzzles and problems,[9] we must at the very least recognize the comi-tragic mixture in the play, as well as the powerful satiric line that has led some critics to class the play as primarily satire.[10]

[5] See Muriel C. Bradbrook, "What Shakespeare did to Chaucer's *Troilus and Criseyde*," *SQ*, IX (1959), 311-19; J.S.P. Tatlock, "The Siege of Troy in Elizabethan Literature," *PMLA*, XXX (1915), 673-770; Hyder E. Rollins, "The Troilus-Cressida Story from Chaucer to Shakespeare," *PMLA*, XXXII (1917), 383-429; Robert K. Presson, *Shakespeare's "Troilus and Cressida" and the Legend of Troy* (Madison, 1953).

[6] But see Kimbrough, pp. 27-28, for a qualification of Miss Bradbrook's view.

[7] See Kimbrough, chapter II.

[8] William W. Main, "Dramaturgical Norms in the Elizabethan Repertory," *SP*, LIV (1957), 128-48; "Character Amalgams in Shakespeare's *Troilus and Cressida*," *SP*, LVIII (1961), 170-78. On the mixture of forms in the play, see Madeleine Doran, *Endeavors of Art*, pp. 366-67; and R. A. Foakes, "*Troilus and Cressida* Reconsidered," *UTQ*, XXXII (1963), p. 154; and his recent *Shakespeare: From Dark Comedies to the Last Plays*, pp. 43-62. J. N. Nosworthy's comments (in *Shakespeare's Occasional Plays*, New York, 1965, pp. 54-85) are useful; as is Jarold Ramsey's "The Provenance of *Troilus and Cressida*," *SQ*, XXI (1970), 223-40.

[9] The term "problem play" came into use with F. S. Boas' *Shakespere and his Predecessors* (New York, 1896); and has been variously used since: see W. W. Lawrence, *Shakespeare's Problem Comedies* (New York, 1931); E.M.W. Tillyard, *Shakespeare's Problem Plays* (Toronto, 1949); William B. Toole, *Shakespeare's Problem Plays* (The Hague, 1966).

[10] Cf. above, note 2, and O. J. Campbell, *Shakespeare's Satire* (London, 1943).

Indeed, the playing-off of the love story (comedy) against the war story (heroic tragedy) would sufficiently indicate satire, even without Thersites' at every point forcing on us his generic satiric interpretation of events. Besides these large generic references, the play makes use of many motifs, devices, and conventions from other decorums: the orations of the Greek rulers, Agamemnon, Nestor, Ulysses, have literary origins in the forms of actual political rhetoric and in the consults so represented in epic literature; the debate questions propounded by Priam call forth a dialectic of temperaments acted out for us as we watch reason go down before impetuous adherence to one and another interpretation of honour. The Prologue—"arm'd" and thus properly epic, as well as pointing to the conventions of the theater-war[11]— promises an epic construction to the forthcoming story:

> our play
> Leaps o'er the vaunt and firstlings of those broils,
> Beginning in the middle—   (Prologue, ll. 26-28)

although the play actually opens, not upon the *medias res* of the war, but on the beginning of the chamberers' affair. Even there, though, epic decorum is parodied and travestied, as Cressida draws out of her uncle a catalogue of heroes: "That's Aeneas." "Who's that?" "That's Antenor. . . . That's Hector," etc. Throughout the play, the war-theme and the love-theme, the events of the war-plot and the events of the love-plot, fold over each other, in an overlapping that manages to cut off our expectations of both: instead of supporting one another, they subtract from each other's dramatic force and interest.

Not that separately the different themes can stand in dignity, either: epic, for instance, is travestied in more than Cressida's childish questioning. The Prologue's conspicuously heightened, archaic language makes mock of the grandiloquent tradition: "princes orgillous," "strong immures," "war-like fraughtage," "crownets regal," "massy staples/ And corresponsive and fulfilling bolts" offer a pomposity to which Troilus' contrasting language of love puts a welcome end. But Troilus' language, though recognizable at once, is hardly original:

11 See Campbell, "*Comicall Satyre*"; Alfred Harbage, *Shakespeare and the Rival Traditions* (New York, 1952); John J. Enck, "The Peace of the Poetomachia" *PMLA*, LXXVII (1962), 386-96; and Harry Berger, Jr., "*Troilus and Cressida*: The Observer as Basilisk," *Comp. Drama* II (1968), 122-36.

> Why should I war without the walls of Troy
> That find such cruel battle here within?   (I.i.2-3)

Though the decorum shifts from epic to romance, language remains unrefreshed. In Troilus' words, the Homeric subject is "starv'd." Its deadness is confirmed by the orgulous language of the Greek chieftains, resuming in I.iii. the play's epic career:

> The ample proposition that hope makes
> In all designs begun on earth below
> Fails in the promis'd largeness; checks and disasters
> Grow in the veins of actions highest rear'd,
> As knots, by the conflux of meeting sap,
> Infects the sound pine, and diverts his grain
> Tortive and errant from his course of growth.
>
> (I.iii.2-9)

The convention of epic simile, irrelevant if formally correct, is observed by Nestor too:

> The sea being smooth,
> How many shallow bauble boats dare sail
> Upon her patient breast, making their way
> With those of nobler bulk!
> But let the ruffian Boreas once enrage
> The gentle Thetis, and anon behold
> The strong-ribb'd bark through liquid mountains cut,
> Like Perseus' horse. Where's then the saucy boat,
> Whose weak untimber'd sides but even now
> Co-rivall'd greatness? Either to harbour fled
> Or made a toast for Neptune.   (I.iii.34-45)

As Ulysses notes, both chiefs speak "high in brass," in the orthodox language of official heroism—here, parodied in the emptied, automatic magniloquence of men too long in authority.

Ulysses' great oration on order is no better than Agamemnon's and Nestor's pompous, bumbling efforts to speak as kings. Not only is it made up of *topoi*—hive, bees, honey; planets, sun, comets; communities, schools, cities; birth, age; crowns, scepters, laurels; tune and discord—but by its *copia* it empties these *topoi* of their potential charge, reducing them merely to the clichés of a redundant argument from authority. Compared to the same commonplaces in *King Lear*—Lear addressing the storm; Lear

320

facing the revolt of children against father; Albany realizing what his wife and her sister are doing—Ulysses' use is "rhetorical" in the worst sense. Where the analogous passages in *King Lear* (III.i.1-3; III.iv.1-3; IV.ii.48-49) express specific situations and psychological conditions, the *topoi* in *Troilus and Cressida* call attention to the fundamental commonplaceness of Ulysses' mind —*this* is the wily Ulysses, who spent ten years outwitting his enemies, human, divine, monstrous, and natural, here reduced to a version of Gloucester or Polonius, mouthing the unexamined platitudes of a doctrine of order which the play itself consistently subverts.[12]

This peculiar treatment of a staple from the Renaissance moral repertory may stand for what goes on in the whole play, where things are *un*done. The systematic barbarity of Hector's death brings down more than an exemplary champion and the reputation of the godlike Achilles: something fundamental to the heroic dream is murdered along with the unarmed hero; in spite of the rents in the heroic illusion which the play has already torn, from the Prologue's swollen rhetoric onward, we feel real pain at its loss. However vulnerable to modern political and psychological analyses it may be, the epic world offered a model for elevated behavior which, when reduced to these vulgar acts, leaves us no alternative glory.

As with the heroic in this play, so with its comedy: the love affair is denied its conventional resolution in union, since to a world in which values are so askew comedy offers no appropriate decorum, no therapeutic purgation for such widespread infection. And yet the play does not preach, either: we know from accrued literary tradition that Troilus must die and Cressida be cast out as a leper, but from the melodrama and morality inherent in such endings Shakespeare shields us, leaving us with a coda combining rampant vengefulness and inconclusive bawdy complaint, a coda far more ironically bitter than even Troilus' enigmatic, distanced reflections at the end of Chaucer's poem. In spite of the fact of war, the deaths, and the personal failures of hero and heroine, this play denies its tragic component; in spite of its city-setting and the pimping citizen Pandarus who trades in his niece's flesh, the play offers no comic opportunity for resolution and reunion, no society with which a firmly linked

---

[12] See Kimbrough, Chapter VII, and references.

hero and heroine may be identified. As satire, the play's inherent inconclusiveness (extending even to reticence about the *kind* to which it belongs)[13] finds some parallel in the poetic satires of Donne, Marston, Guilpin, Hall, and the rest, with their *personae's* atomized, neurasthenic presentation of experience, here dramatized into Thersites and Pandarus. Thersites' invective brings epigrammatic and Juvenalian railing to an extreme baseness, and Pandarus' unrelieved innuendo has something of the uncomplicated viciousness attributed by those *personae* to all other men in their society.

In the manner of much Renaissance satire, Continental and English, this play awakens our sense of the world's faults and offers no solace or retreat from them, no model for improvement. In *Troilus and Cressida*, there is none of the redeeming hope of Shakespeare's darkest plays, that from the brutal and calculating world some retreat is possible in a private construction of love and faith—the "little room" of personal love so long sought by Antony and Cleopatra, the prison of Lear and Cordelia. Both love and war are despoiled, not by Thersites' peculiarly dominant voice only, but by the actions at war and the behavior in love of the figures who, above all others in western literature, should command unqualified respect.

And they are despoiled by literary means—as if the playwright were showing us how automatically and uncritically we take Achilles and Hector, Helena and Ulysses, Ajax and Agamemnon as paragons in their kind. Instead of animating his literary clichés into actual characters, as he did with the *commedia dell' arte* troupe in *Love's Labour's Lost*, as he did with the lyric and epigrammatic genres in his *Sonnets*, Shakespeare chose here to *reverse* that process, to show how human situations can be stripped of their personal and general meanings to be no more— and to deserve to be no more—than the clichés with which literature presents us.

Let us begin, like the Prologue, in *medias res*, with Pandarus' speech[14] typing himself and the lovers: "If ever you prove false to one another . . . , let all pitiful goers-between be call'd to the

---

13 The problem of the play's kind (see note 8) was recognized as early as the Second Folio; it appears as a "tragedy" there.

14 This whole scene is well-characterized as "gaudy" by Bernard Evans, *Shakespeare's Comedies* (London, 1967), p. 175.

world's end after my name—call them all Pandars; let all constant men be Troiluses, all false women Cressids, and all brokers
between Pandars" (III.ii.194-200). As chorus-commentator on this
action, knowing his audience to be as thoroughly in the know as
he is himself, Pandarus states the morality principle behind the
characters' actions, their names already proverbial by the time
Shakespeare composed *Troilus and Cressida*. By this means, the
audience's expectation itself is titillated but thwarted: in fact, as
the play unfolds, the audience is granted only the same tautological substitute for awareness that is given the characters in the
play. *This* is what was expected: so much, and no more, is provided. Indeed, the minimum turns out to be *less* than what is
expected: we see the figures in the drama, by their own conniv-
ance, reduce themselves from life to figures of speech[15]—and
that reduction is sworn to religiously:

> *Pandarus*: Say "Amen."
> *Troilus*: Amen.
> *Cressida*: Amen.
> *Pandarus*: Amen. . . . (III.iii.200-204)

Within the play's context, fictionally and without our hind-
sight, Pandarus is of course within his rights to ask for religious
corroboration to a love-vow traditionally taken in religious terms.
That this triple "Amen" is so particularly empty, its emptiness
suggesting the emptiness of all such vows in an outworn conventional mode, is a function of our knowledge of what these
lovers, this broker-between, "mean" as mere norms, mere cate-
gorizing terms. Like Thersites who, as Mr. Kimbrough has so
well said,[16] had become no more than a figure in the rhetoric-
books, these three lose their significance as people to become mere
nouns. The "Amen" further links Pandarus to Thersites, who in
II.iii kept associating disease and prayer and ended his major
speeches in "Amen," too.

Of course Pandarus' prose-speech merely picks up and encap-
sulates the serial assertions of devotion Troilus and Cressida
have already made to one another:

---

15 I am much indebted to Sheldon P. Zitner for help in shaping my conceptions of the play in respect to this problem.

16 See Rollins, *passim*; and Kimbrough, pp. 38-39, 75.

> Yet, after all comparisons of truth,
> As truth's authentic author to be cited,
> "As true as Troilus" shall crown up the verse
> And sanctify the numbers,   (III.ii.176-79)

he has already said, and she:

> If I be false, or swerve a hair from truth, . . . yet let memory
> From false to false, among false maids in love,
> Upbraid my falsehood. . . .
> Yea, let them say, to stick the heart of falsehood,
> "As false as Cressid."   (III.ii.180-85, 186, 191-92)

The characters (mere rhetorical terms though they are) speak in proper decorum. It is no accident that Troilus speaks in terms of literature and Cressida in terms of action; in the play Troilus' experience derives from his romantic, literary understanding of what love should be. Hers, though it takes its cue temporarily from his diction and the emotional context his interests give the episode, has its haphazard basis in her previous lived experience. Troilus declaims in terms of poetic values, speaking of and to those "true swains in love" who

> shall in the world to come
> Approve their truth by Troilus, when their rhymes,
> Full of protest, of oath, and big compare

—that is, the "swains" turn out to be poets writing in the style Troilus deems proper for love, a style he has himself so enthusiastically appropriated. When these swain-poets, then,

> Want similes, truth tir'd with iteration—
> As true as steel, as plantage to the moon,
> As sun to day, as turtle to her mate,
> As iron to adamant, as earth to th' centre,
>
> (III.ii.169-75)

then the phrase "As true as Troilus" shall relieve them of further search for proper bombast—that is, he kills literary creation, too, as he pronounces his simile the height of literary creation.

Cressida's "false maids in love" can, like herself, speak the same language of conventional simile:

"As false
As air, as water, wind, or sandy earth,
As fox to lamb, or wolf to heifer's calf,
Pard to the hind, or stepdame to her son"

(III.ii.186-90)

but her images are somewhat less literary than her lover's—and "stepdame" unfigures and deromantizes the whole proceedings. These lovers (like Berowne and his friends, like Lorenzo and Jessica, like Romeo) speak by the book; their fluency in its lovely clichés threatens love-language at its center, as they empty their utterance of the very meanings they strive to express. But unlike Berowne, Romeo, Jessica and Lorenzo, these two have no sense of their failure with language, no sense that language might fail them, might be inadequate to the crisis of their lives. If they can say things right, that is all that is required.

By the time Cressida must leave Troilus, she speaks of her fidelity only in terms of the "falsehood" *we* know she must come to exemplify:

O you gods divine,
Make Cressid's name the very crown of falsehood,
If ever she leave Troilus!   (IV.ii.98-100)

Unwitting as they are of themselves and their decorum, the lovers demonstrate the reduction of expressive intentional language to social and linguistic counters. As they milk language of meaning, so their names lose private, individual meaning too, to signify impersonal morality-functions. Their verbal oaths require, furthermore, a knowing audience to have any meaning whatever, even if that meaning is the opposite of what the lovers imply: what tension these clichés exhibit results from our knowing the sadly-declined truth of these once-noble traditional fictions.

Of course, to write a play about Troilus, Cressida, and Pandarus is to stack the cards against these characters and their languages. After these lovers' history, perhaps Shakespeare was wise to strip them of all qualities requiring an audience's identification, understanding, and empathy. By choosing such stock figures as his characters and in deliberately laying stress on their figurative functions, the playwright seems to examine the situation under which their particular behavior became typical and turned into stereotype—but even *that* he throws away, together with the opportunity for persuasive and permissive understanding so brilliantly exploited in Chaucer's romance, to accept the stereotypes *before* their defining action occurs, and to examine the implications of such stereotyping for the whole epic legend with which his own literary system began.

Unlike *Love's Labour's Lost, Troilus and Cressida* presents us with characters refusing to live up to personality, refusing altogether to conform to the conventions of psychological illusionism we have come to expect from drama, particularly from Shakespeare's plays: these characters are and remain flat, two-dimensional, cardboard figures. Indeed, for this treatment Thersites offers a model: from Erasmus' famous self-help textbook to humanism, the *Adagia, Thersitae facies* was known to schoolboys all over Europe,[17] and *faedior Thersite* was a common proverb put to literary uses.[18] Thersites had become a rhetorical and proverbial figure, as Pandar had become a grammatical term: both were, in every sense of the word, commonplace references. This word-game works with other characters too: Helen, for instance, provides us with one measure of the play's inadequate language and thus its inadequate value-system. As cause of a war now seven years old, Helen comes up for reconsideration and reassessment. Obviously Priam hopes that Hector's initial (and at first unequivocal) "Let Helen go" will prevail upon his warriors; though we must notice that, in his own city, the old King has no voice among his argumentative sons. Others have taken over the war: kings follow others' advice. When Troilus cries out against Hector and Helenus, both willing to return Helen to the

<hr/>

[17] Desiderius Erasmus, *Adagiorum Chiliades* (Basel, 1551), IV.iii.lxxv: "Thersitae facies. . . . De prodigiose deformi dici solitum, quod Homerus scripserit hunc omnium qui ad Troiam venissent, foedissimum fuisse. Ac totum hominem, a capite, quod aiunt, usque ad pedes ita graphice depingit, & corporis vitia & animi morbos, ut dicas pessimum ingenium in domicilio se digno habitasse." The *Adagia* reliably record Erasmus' dislike of wars, even of Homer's classical warfare: see III.ix.lxxvii (Helen); I.vii.xli, and I.vii.vii (Achilles); III.iii.cii; IV.iv.lx; III.v.liii (Patroclus); II.vi.lx (Agamemnon); I.iii.i (Agamemnon and Achilles); I.ii.i. (Diomedes); I.iii.xxvi (Paris and Helen); I.iii.xxxv (Helen and Ajax). In the combination of things discussed (i.e., *Patrocli occasio, sive praetextus*; Helen and dung[-cosmetics]), one can see the elements of the paradox, as well as a pattern of disgust similar to that, enlarged and enlivened, in Shakespeare's play. See also Erasmus, *The Praise of Folie*, tr. Sir Thomas Chaloner, ed. C. H. Miller (EETS, 1965), p. 30.

[18] Cf. Kimbrough, p. 39.

Greeks, Hector can still rejoin, "Brother, she is not worth what she doth cost/ The keeping," and mean it, since "every tithe soul 'mongst many thousand dismes" had fallen for her sake. At this point, we may remember Troilus' apparently irrelevant statement in i.i. (the italics are mine):

> Helen *must needs* be fair,
> When with your blood you daily paint her thus.
>
> (89-90)

But at that point, Troilus did *not* mean it: he was denying then the concept of chivalry he here prepares to force into decisive collective action: Hector's realistic view is argued down by the fiery young lover as yet totally inexperienced in the love he extols as a source of honor. Troilus offers a display of passionate nonsequiturs to illustrate his fundamental point, "What's aught but as 'tis valued?" "Value" has been much commented on in this play.[19] Troilus speaks out not for intrinsic or objective value so much as for the psychological value of valuing. And yet we know he does not mean it, any more than Hector means his humanitarian realism in wanting to send Helen back. Troilus requires, and forces upon others too slack to contest his romantic illogic, a literary justification for warlike action, an incredible prettification for the slaughter that tithes Trojan and Greek forces alike. The echo of Marlowe carries its ironies in Troilus' context:

> Why, she is a pearl
> Whose price hath launch'd above a thousand ships,
> And turn'd crown'd kings to merchants.   (II.ii.81-83)

This computation of Helen's value, however vague, manages in spite of its flabbiness to overgo Faustus' simple "thousand" even as the chapman's metaphor[20] degrades both lady and the claimants to her person. But this fustian outburst is enough: great Hector rejects "the moral law" he seems to defend, to agree with his beardless brother's view of chivalric theory: that inex-

---

[19] See, e.g., Winifred M. T. Nowottny, " 'Opinion' and 'Value' in *Troilus and Cressida*," *Essays and Studies*, v (1954), 282-98; Philip Edwards, *Confines*, pp. 102-104.

[20] Cf. Robert Ornstein, *The Moral Vision of Jacobean Tragedy*, esp. pp. 243-45; Terence Eagleton, *Shakespeare and Society*, p. 19; and Raymond Southall's identification of this play with the market-economy: "*Troilus and Cressida* and the Spirit of Capitalism," *Shakespeare in a Changing World*, ed. Kettle, pp. 217-32.

perienced warrior restates "his" Helen in terms designed to persuade anyone who has for a moment taken seriously the need to reappraise this ostensible cause for war:

> She is a theme of honour and renown,
> A spur to valiant and magnanimous deeds,
> Whose present courage may beat down our foes,
> And fame in time to come canonize us. . . .
>
> (II.ii.199-202)

She is a *theme* for fame in time to come: that is, Troilus knows what Helen symbolizes, this woman whose beauty was so extraordinary as to cause a ten-year carnage that brought down a great civilization and brutalized another; a woman the possession of whom made seem worthwhile such uprooting, by the civilized, of civilization itself; all that—but to Troilus, simply a topic for *epideixis*. Troilus knows the conventional values, then, of the long literary culture between Homer's war and Shakespeare's play, and is determined, whatever actuality may be, to make beautiful those dangerous fictional values that lie at the basis of romance. We might believe this, if he had not in exasperation spoken of the inadequacy of Helen as a theme in his very first appearance: though he works to make his own life and the lives of his friends conform to what he recognizes as the value-laden sources of literary creation, we know that he *chooses* to believe these fictions, belying himself to do so.

In the Greek camp, the warriors doggedly pursuing victory have no respect for Helen, the ostensible cause of this activity. For Diomed, she is "a flat tamed piece" with "whorish loins" (IV.i.64-68); like Thersites, he sees her as whore, and in his brutish way makes no concessions to the effeminate minion Paris, now so proudly holding her in Troy. As for Menelaus, cuckold to the whore, on whose behalf the expeditionary force has come to Troy, he can answer Hector's sly reference to his "quondam wife" only with, "Name her not now, sir; she's a deadly theme" (IV.v.179-81). For both sides, she is a "theme"—but this mere theme, it turns out, is quite enough to justify brutalities on both sides.

As if to make sure that we understand the irony implicit in Troilus' evaluation of Helen and the selfish crudity in Menelaus', we see the lady herself with Paris, who is reduced to a pet she keeps by her from the dirty business of the war. "I would fain have armed today, but my Nell would not have it so," he tells us. From a "theme" to "my Nell": this is that unique mortal woman of fable, reduced in both literary and domestic terms. She deserves little else, this particular Helen: her bawdiness, like Cressida's, underscores her trivial worldliness, her trivial sensuality. Like Cressida's, hers is a pastime love, not the fatality of Cleopatra's obsession with Antony.

As with the characters, so with larger literary themes and traditions, for instance, that rich sonnet-tradition in which Shakespeare had worked so constructively. Here his originality shows once more, but the playwright is his own Thersites, his own Pandarus, showing that tradition to be no more than the argument of a whore and a cuckold, its wars merely metaphors for lechery. Young Troilus has read enough literature to know that, having gone to war, he must take a mistress. Further, that mistress must be in the high style, a sonnet-mistress. He stages himself as the high-minded lover whose petrarchan language rings out in his first speech, spoken as he unarms himself and, taking off his arms, internalizes the "war without the walls of Troy" in "the cruel battle here within." After running through the *blason*-topics, he produces a copious comparison of her hand—

> O, that her hand,
> In whose comparison all whites are ink
> Writing their own reproach; to whose soft seizure
> The cygnet's down is harsh, and spirit of sense
> Hard as the palm of ploughman!   (I.i.54-58)

Troilus, like his lady, asks questions which are not real, hence he already knows the answer:

> Tell me, Apollo, for thy Daphne's love,
> What Cressid is, what Pandar, and what we?
> Her bed is India; there she lies, a pearl. . . .
>
>   (I.i.97-99)

He makes up his own metaphors:

> Between our Ilium and where she resides
> Let it be call'd the wild and wand'ring flood;
> Ourselves the merchant, and this sailing Pandar
> Our doubtful hope, our convoy, and our bark. . . .
>
>   (I.i.100-103)

He is his own poet. Then, Troilus considers his language with care—but the language he finds (riches, merchant, sea, bark) is merely the highly conventional, overfamiliar vocabulary of the petrarchistic sonneteer. In Troilus' hands, too, language just misses the mark, degrading both lady (merchandise) and "this sailing Pander" who trades between the lovers. The imagery of chaffering returns in iv.iv., when Troilus and Cressida part, who "with so many thousand sighs/ Did buy each other" and now "must poorly sell ourselves/ With the rude brevity and discharge of one" (iv.iv.38-40). Again and again, sonnet-language sounds, just discordant, just out of tune: matching, of course, a plot in which high sonnet-love cannot be accommodated.

In this play, there is further irony in Troilus' sonnet-speech, for he uses not just the flat common figures from the tradition, but the very themes, language, figures from Shakespeare's own sonnets. What we learn from Troilus' use of words is that context counts—for on his tongue, the words that used almost to tell Shakespeare's name (and undeniably told Will's) seem to tell Troilus' name now, trivial Troilus who is himself no more than a name. In "I am giddy, expectation whirls me round," the solo of iii.ii before Troilus gets into Cressida's house, he expresses his virgin sense of inexpressible glories in still-untasted sexuality. His phrase for the experience is "love's thrice-repured nectar": it will be like

> Death, I fear me;
> Swooning destruction; or some joy too fine,
> Too subtle-potent, tun'd too sharp in sweetness,
> For the capacity of my ruder powers.　　　(iii.ii.21-24)

He presents the requisite mixture of *mel* with *sal* ("thrice-repured nectar"; "joy . . . too sharp in sweetness"), and the oddly-innocent analogy to war—

> I do fear besides
> That I shall lose distinction in my joys;
> As doth a battle, when they charge on heaps
> The enemy flying.　　　(iii.ii.25-28)

which shows where Troilus *has* had some real experience. In the *Sonnets*, the poet had likened distillation to life, not death; the beauty and sweetness of his love were distilled for continuance and memory, not for Troilus' dispersion and dissolution. The *Sonnets'* distillation was to essence: Troilus expects to lose the essence altogether. In Sonnet 114, the poet-lover can turn even monsters into cherubs by means of true love's epideictic: for Troilus, the same figure works the other way on, and "Fears make devils of cherubins." Troilus is not really in control of his language, although (of course) the foreboding he unwittingly conveys sorts well with what we know of his, and the love-affair's, ending. In his poet-role, as in his lover-role, Troilus is just undertaking his apprenticeship; he seizes upon his art too headlong and impetuously, just as he seizes upon his beloved. He cannot stop to realize what language, or what a woman, can mean to a man.

And yet he *almost* realizes: he has a real sense of the "monstruosity" in love and in love's language. Lovers' "undertakings when we vow to weep seas, live in fire, eat rocks, tame tigers" are the verbal derring-do of men who know themselves to be less than omnipotent. Execution *is* confin'd, as Troilus recognizes, the act a slave to limit: for a mature Troilus, "Th' expense of spirit in a waste of shame" might have expressed real insight; but Troilus can never reach such maturity. He almost hesitates at his entry into love, acknowledging a young man's fear of overpromising: but he plunges in, insisting that Cressida expect from him more than mortal man can give.

Cressida's rejoinder to all this bespeaks her experience; in her coarseness with her young lover lie the intimations of the experiential world of love from which she has entered the play.[21] But she shares a lot with her lover: coarse though she is, she too rises to hyperbole; and however highflown Troilus' speech, it is not always so innocent as his reiterations of his own "truth" would have us believe. His "what truth can speak truest not truer than Troilus" overstates in just the fashion he otherwise recognized as monstrous. Later, when Cressida asks, "My Lord, will you be true?" he answers in a couplet[22]—

[21] But see Tucker Brooke, "Shakespeare's Study in Culture and Anarchy," *Essays on Shakespeare and Other Elizabethans* (New Haven, 1948), pp. 71-77; and Ornstein's sensible comments on Cressida's plight, p. 245.

[22] Troilus speaks in "couplets" more sonnet-like than the usual sonnet-ending to a scene, and persists in maintaining sonnet-themes, even to the chapman-imagery noted above, fn. 20.

> Fear not my truth: the moral of my wit
> Is "plain and true"; there's all the reach of it.
>
> (IV.iv.106-107)

designed to clinch the earlier

> Whiles others fish with craft for great opinion,
> I with great truth catch mere simplicity;
> Whilst some with cunning gild their copper crowns,
> With truth and plainness I do wear mine bare.
>
> (IV.iv.102-105)

From the conclusion, we read Troilus' sense of conviction of his own truth, but qualified by the fish-craft-catch-cunning-gild imagery of his major image.

Troilus' oath is sworn before he is tested. Sonnet 105, the "fair, kind, and true" tautological poem, speaks to a love affirmed after severe testing. In the poet's bending of his greatest pride, that is, his skill, there is a glad humility, as the voluntary iteration limits ideas, images, and vocabulary. In that sonnet, the poet was willing to pay a professional price for reconciliation understood and thus earned. After his usual high-sounding asseverations, Troilus promises the plainness the sonneteer had worked and suffered for: faced with separation and Cressida's infidelity, his own constancy is at once forgotten, as he undeclares plainness in the fancifications of his outcry against Cressida and Diomed.

Context matters. So the scene between the sensualists and the voyeur, Helen with Paris and Pandarus (III.i), rings the changes on the words "fair" and "sweet," those simple English terms of praise and endearment which, against the more ornate background of sonnet-imagery, sound so true in Shakespeare's or Spenser's sonnets; here, it is no more than a verbal tic:

> *Pand.*: Fair be to you, my lord, and to all this fair company!
> Fair desires, in all fair measure, fairly guide them—
> especially to you, fair queen! Fair thoughts be your fair
> pillow.
> *Hel.*: Dear lord, you are full of fair words.
> *Pand.*: You speak your fair pleasure, sweet queen. Fair prince,
> here is good broken music. (III.i.41-47)

Mel drips: Helen calls Pandarus "honeysweet lord" and Paris "sweet lord"; she is called "sweet queen" eleven times. Merely by repetition, the words sink back into mere sounds, conventional gibberish, and meaninglessness. "As true as Troilus" is no more than a refrain; Cassandra, similarly, is reduced to a slogan— "Cry, Trojans, cry!" Meaning drains out of words reduced to mere sounds.

So also with larger traditions: Pandarus undoes love and love-language in his cynical song, grossly mimetic of the act, with its deerslaying bawdy quibbles; here too iteration of mere syllables makes nonsense of the emotion.

> These lovers cry, O ho, they die!
> Yet that which seems the wound to kill
> Doth turn O ho! to ha! ha! he!
> So dying love lives still.
> O ho! a while, but ha! ha! ha!
> O ho! groans out for ha! ha! ha!—hey ho!
>
> (III.i.114-19)

And outside, a war is going on! But within, Paris' choplogic continues to reduce the deed on which these three count so much: "He eats nothing but doves, love; and that breeds hot blood, and hot blood begets hot thoughts, and hot thoughts beget hot deeds, and hot deeds is love" (III.i.122-24). The logic looks all right, but it turns out to be tautological—the circularity leaves us where we always were, at a center of non-definition and meaninglessness.[23]

The reduction of a thing to itself, as Paris does here, is to re-move outside reference and thus to cancel context. Though in some cases this argues for the poetic expression of ontological reality, just as repetition as a form of *copia* can enrich a sentence, a line, a whole text,[24] in this play Shakespeare makes no such grand attempt. In *Troilus and Cressida*, the reiterated reductions to nonsense isolate more and more from what is normally—in a play, in life—the fabric of common understanding. The play's frequent, apparently irrelevant, questioning of identity has some-thing to do with this same isolation of person from person, from society, from his own name, that is a major tendency of the play. Cressida asks a question which, considering the length of time she has lived in the city, is unbelievable:

23 Cf. Eagleton, pp. 22-23, 27-28; and Edwards, *Confines*, p. 102.

24 For *logos*, see *Paradoxia*, Chapter Five; for repetition, see the sensitiv ranging essay by Kathleen Lea, "The Poetic Power of Repetition," *Proc. Br Acad.*, LV (1969).

> *Cress.*: Who were those went by?
> *Alex.*:   Queen Hecuba and Helen.

She keeps on questioning, apparently at random:

> *Cress.*: And whither go they?
>   What was his cause of anger? . . .
>   Who comes here? . . .

The answer to this question is indeed startling:

> *Alex.*: Madam, your uncle Pandarus.

The questioning goes on, with a new answer:

> *Cress.*: Who's that?
> *Pand.*: That's Antenor. . . .
> *Cress.*: Who's that?
> *Pand.*: That's Helenus. I marvel where Troilus is. That's
>   Helenus. I think he went not forth to-day. That's
>   Helenus.   (I.ii.182-213)

The point of all this is not any of these separate heroes, Antenor or Helenus, but Pandarus' preoccupation with Troilus, the absent one. Pandarus only *seems* to designate, only *seems* to compare these people with the hero he has chosen for his niece: he repeats Helenus' name so often because he is *not* thinking of that young man, but only of his trade with Troilus. Helenus becomes more insignificant than Antenor (so significant in Cressida's chancy life) although more often mentioned, precisely *because* he is so often mentioned. He becomes a mere name, and naming here does not identify—without reference to distinguishing qualities, names are nothing. Cressida's interrogation, a joke and a tic, is part of the general questioning that runs through the play— "Who's that?" "Who comes here?" "What's Agamemnon? . . . What's Achilles?" "What's Thersites?" "Patroclus, what art thou?" Aeneas, who has for seven years been fighting the Greeks, must ask "Which is the high and mighty Agamemnon?"—a question Agamemnon feels to be a bit odd, too, in the circumstances. He in turn questions this messenger from Troy: "Sir, you of Troy, call you yourself Aeneas?" After more exchange, Agamemnon admits to being himself and listens to Aeneas' proclamation of Hector's challenge. There is no particular point to the delayed identification within a context of serious warlike business: this is comedy, and confusion.

And, when it is given, nothing could be sillier than Hector's challenge, cast in chivalric terms of devotion to feminine beauty: we know that he "chid Andromache" when she begged him to stay away from the field; we soon know what he thinks of Helen. That is to say, Hector at each point contradicts himself; the thrust of the play is turned as soon as it is declared, our expectations thwarted as soon as they are raised. The foolishness of the challenge is met with an endearing folly from Nestor, who creakily proclaims his mistress—that is, his ancient wife—the fairest of all women and worthy reason for answering Hector's invitation to single combat.

Later, when Achilles addresses Aeneas without identifying himself, Aeneas says to him, "If not Achilles, sir,/ What is your name?" Achilles' answer is significant in terms of the play's building theme: "If not Achilles, nothing" (IV.v.75-76). Achilles, hero of the ancient world, the model for Alexander, who was in his turn the model for Augustus Caesar: this Achilles we have seen already as "nothing," sulking, playing with Patroclus, bantering and railing like Thersites, blustering to Ajax. We will see him far worse: ordering his thugs to murder the unarmed Hector. So far short of heroic measure, this Achilles, whatever his name, in this play, proves not to be "Achilles" but the "nothing" of his own alternative.

Later, when Hector visits the Greek camp, Menelaus and Nestor must be identified for him, but he can guess the name of the proud warrior who has, during the earlier exchanges, "with exact view perus'd" him: "Is this Achilles?" "I am Achilles"—but Hector will learn how little the great name means. Questioning is constant: identities are insecure, together with the rules of the whole heroic convention, based after all on a man's "name," his reputation for living up to himself. "Name" guaranteed value in the heroic world; the opposite is true here. Wherever names are fixed, there value is denied (Pandarus, Thersites, Cressida, Troilus); and except for the major figures, names are unfixed. Unreasonable doubt prevails: people keep asking the names of people they know very well. When no other strange woman is expected in the Greek camp, Agamemnon must still say, "Is this the lady Cressid?" Others are less easily confused. After watching her for a bit, both

Ulysses and Thersites know who and what Cressida is, even down to those potentialities she has not yet realized.

Her own question, early on, about Ajax, provokes a tautological answer that denies all qualities to the man: "They say he is a very man per se./ And stands alone" (I.ii.16-17). We come to know how little Ajax is a man, how little he knows himself, how brutalized he is and can be—but in the play it is not worth trying to put this nonentity into words. As the characters are reduced to mere token-names, the tautologies rob them of context and reduce intelligible, distinguishable qualities to nonsensical sameness. Comparison, normally the figure of *copia* which shows the manysidedness of something, enriching, varying, filling in and out mere words, here fails altogether: it is thwarted to become mere tautology itself, as the copious comparisons all turn out to be meaningless or false. One by one, rhetorical devices are reduced in function to emptiness and sameness. In the exchange of I.ii, as Cressida forces her uncle out of his tendentious comparisons, she shows that they are in fact tautologous—in this case significant indicators of her uncle's own emptiness:

> *Pand.*: Who, Troilus? Troilus is the better man of the two.
> *Cress.*: O Jupiter! There's no comparison. . . .
> *Pand.*: Well, I say Troilus is Troilus.

Cressida does not let her uncle off:

> *Cress.*: Then you say as I say, for I am sure he is not Hector.
> *Pand.*: No, nor Hector is not Troilus in some degrees.
> *Cress.*: 'Tis just to each of them: he is himself.
> *Pand.*: Himself! Alas, poor Troilus! I would he were!
> *Cress.*: So he is.
> *Pand.*: Condition I had gone barefoot to India.
> *Cress.*: He is not Hector.
> *Pand.*: Himself! no, he's not himself. Would 'a were himself!
> (I.ii.59-73)

In making him agree that Troilus is not Hector, Cressida forces Pandarus to admit that Troilus is and is not Troilus, forces him into simultaneous assertion and denial even about Troilus' coloring: "Faith, to say truth, brown and not brown." She offers the final paradigm for this sort of statement, "To say the truth, true and not true." Both Cressida and Pandarus speak the language of is-and-is-not, the terms of the familiar Liar-paradox;[25] both of them are, like the Cretan liar, equivocators, not quite liars but as certainly not truth-tellers either. In the same fashion, Troilus finally makes the same statement about his Cressida, refusing to choose, once for all, between a Cressida who is in fact true and one who is false. Their equivocal syntactical formulations make sense in a world where tautology unnecessarily affirms and questions unnecessarily interrogate the world of unstable, problematic epistemology called up by the Liar-paradox, the world of is-and-is-not. It is just the play's suggestion of epistemological confusions which has given rise to a long (and in my view wrong-headed) critical quarrel over the degree and nature of the "philosophy" contained or expressed in the play.[26] Cressida's "true and not true," spoken in jest as she whets her wits on her uncle's purpose, is the clear statement of the is/is-not theme which culminates in Trolius' desperate and determined "It is, and is not Cressid," as he sees her giving herself, in game and willy-nilly, in earnest and acquiescent, to another lover.

In crucial matters, men do not and cannot name things as they are. Yet we have seen how, in the catalogue of heroes, naming mocks the epic decorum in which the name was the man and the man the name. For this play, such naming is meaningless; that heroic world has gone in which a man's name signified his stock, his homeland, his deeds. In this Troy, Trojan and Greek alike deliver up the dear mythifications with which tradition has endowed their names. Through Thersites at first, later through confirming action, we are brought to learn, not just that Troilus is not Troilus (—for who was that Troilus, anyway, outside of romance?), but that Hector is not Hector, who pursues and kills a man *for his armor*! And Achilles, who in the *Iliad* becomes almost a god as he dons his god-made armor, is here reduced to the chief of a gang of thugs.

The audience begins, then, by thinking the context familiar, but must soon abandon its conventional associations with Greeks

[25] See *Paradoxia*, Introduction, and literature cited.
[26] Cf. Una Ellis-Fermor, *The Frontiers of Drama* (London, 1945), pp. 56-76; G. Wilson Knight, "The Philosophy of *Troilus and Cressida*," in *The Wheel of Fire* (New York, 1957), pp. 47-72; L. C. Knights, *Some Shakespearean Themes* (London, 1956); S. L. Bethell, *Shakespeare and the Popular Dramatic Tradition* (London, 1944); W. W. Lawrence, *Problem Comedies*, p. 119.

and Trojans—small wonder that the people within the play have difficulty in recognizing each other and themselves. Even Ajax, that simplest of characters, does not recognize himself: he huffs and rants, struts and curses, as only Ajax can and does. In a huffing, railing, cursing play, he has the simpleton's dulled invective, distinct from all the other huffings, railings, and cursings in the play because less articulate than they. Thersites recognizes that "He is Ajax" and thus has no self-knowledge; and Ulysses must tell him how to "be as Ajax," to recover himself and to behave as "Ajax," the hero of a known name, ought to behave. Ulysses tries to heroize Ajax, not in his own terms but for other purposes, to metamorphose this Ajax into Achilles. In his duping of the dolt, Ulysses plays on the concept of heroic naming, so that Ajax must come to believe himself that "to be as Ajax" means to be like the Homeric Achilles. (Thersites, of course, knows better.) In the play, too, Ulysses recognizes that the heroizing of Achilles, the abstraction of his name from the man, is what has destroyed him: by creating a false Achilles in Ajax, Ulysses hopes to reheroize the real Achilles. "Naming" here becomes only another way to manipulate men fundamentally unpossessed of personality or awareness of personal choice. Ajax is, as Thersites calls him, following a well known joke, a jakes.[27] When Troilus, Cressida, and Pandarus offer up their names as stereotypes, they abdicate their claims on both individual personality and human stature, permit themselves to become the dross that Thersites thinks all men and women to be.

Men unname themselves, and unname their names; women too give up their social qualities for a single function: Cressida and Helen are both, simply, whores. The recurrence of invective epithets (cur, elephant, dogfox, cuckold, cuckold's whore, daughter of the game, etc.) insists on the voluntary reduction of human beings to single qualities. Perhaps such a view of the world, perhaps such metamorphoses of humans to something less than human, is what happens in the random, nearly motiveless behavior of wartime, as official standards of behavior, both the real protections of social respect and order and the propaganda mouthings of honor and courage, decay and dissolve. In this play, people flatten out to attributes, even to just *one* attribute—Pandar be-

[27] Cf. John Harington, *A New Discourse of a Stale Subject Called The Metamorphosis of Ajax* (1596), ed. Elizabeth Story Donno (New York, 1962), a remarkable example of the literature of paradoxy.

comes *only* a bawd, Cressida *only* a whore, Ajax *only* a braggart soldier, Nestor only an "old chronicle"; or they are redefined, Hector as greedy brute, Achilles as gangster. And thus they become meaningless: it is not this Hector for whom one mourns but the idea of the other, the "real" Hector; we cannot sympathize with Troilus' loss of Cressida any more than we can pity, for more than a moment, a Cressida soon to be cast off by Diomed.

"As true as Troilus" has its own meaninglessness. A dozen lines before his proclamation of this, his essential attribute, Troilus explains "himself":

> I am as true as truth's simplicity,
> And simpler than the infancy of truth.
>
> (III.i.165-66)

He is, indeed, infantile,[28] as he had promised us at the very beginning:

> But I am weaker than a woman's tear,
> Tamer than sleep, fonder than ignorance,
> Less valiant than the virgin in the night,
> And skilless as unpractis'd infancy.   (I.i.9-12)

He predestines himself to be what he is; and so does Cressida predestine herself, false before the play begins by the power of a predestinating tradition, but false also because of the extreme triviality of her character. They speak as they are, Troilus in redundancy and cliché, Cressida with a greater sense of irony that leads her to declare herself in the form of the Liar-paradox. Like Cressida, the Liar-paradox is both betrayer and self-betrayer.

The railing Thersites transforms himself into a single tautological term, too: willing to be beaten by his fellow Greeks, he dares not fight with enemies who kill for keeps. When Hector challenges him in terms of rank, he says with exactitude, "No, no —I am a rascal, a scurvy railing knave, a very filthy rogue," and is amazed at the chivalric pride which, taking him at his word, turns away to seek a "better" foe. From this exchange he learns how to question potential combatants: "What art thou?" he asks Margarelon in the familiar interrogation, who unexpectedly proclaims his own bastardy. Thersites gleefully outbastards this bas-

---

[28] But see Willard Farnham, "Troilus in Shapes of Infinite Desire," in *Shakespeare, Modern Essays in Criticism*, ed. Leonard Dean (New York, 1967), pp. 283-94, for another view of Troilus.

tard son of Priam: "I am a bastard too, I love bastards. I am a bastard begot, a bastard instructed, bastard in mind, bastard in valour, in everything illegitimate" (v.vii). But all this is rhetoric too: long since accepted as privileged railer, bitter truth-teller, satiric fool, Thersites moves in vain into the area of actual living, cannot really persuade us that he is a man generated, like other men, by fathers and born of the wombs of mothers. Rather, the unconnected and disconnected is what is stressed—a man without a family, outside social context.

What the play offers us is a set of names in substitution for things, for personalities, for values. The o'erleaping rhetoric of the play falls on 'tother, into mockery and farce, and calls everything into question. The languages of love and of war are stretched far beyond their strengths, leaving great holes where meaning falls through; the famous "corresponsive and fulfilling bolts" of Troy's great gates merely open and close as Aeneas, Cressida, Troilus pass in and out: a mock-epic dramatic exercise, this play displays lordliness taken leave of its senses, words unmatched to real referents, words as justification for irresponsible action.

The war is, when we enter the scene, paralyzed. Seven years have passed and nothing at Troy is changed, save that men die every day in the ritual slaughter. The Greeks—or Ulysses anyway—search for a way to win; the Trojans seek no more than justification for continuing the war at all. The is/is-not language reflects that paralysis of will; in the play, such language *is* that paralysis, by which men submit to accident and contingency as if it were fate. So Cressida submits to Troilus and to Diomedes, the one courtly and idealizing, the other brutalizing and blunt. Diomed, needing a woman and seeing this one, reduces Cressida to what fighting men need; and this, finally, is all she is. His poetic speech on her "value," in iv.iv, is not made to praise her, but to annoy Troilus. When, after their rhetorical flyting in Cressida's praise, Diomed says "to her own worth/ She shall be priz'd," we are sent back to that ominous comment of Pandarus in the first scene, "Let her be as she is."

"As she is" is precisely what Troilus cannot bear, both before he has entered upon his love affair and after he has lost her. Indeed, "as anything is" was always insufficient for Troilus, who had to make Cressida more than Helen, the act of love more than that act, Helen into the sum of romantic significance; and in this

heightening of fancy, he speaks for Troy, as all come to agree
with him. More than most, Cressida seems to know what she is, as
she speaks neutrally of her own nature in I.ii and bitterly of it in
v.ii. Diomed recognizes her and pitilessly takes advantage of her
weaknesses; Ulysses recognizes her too, at the kissing as Cressida
arrives in the Greek camp—but Troilus never does. In keeping
with the whole play's tone, he consistently converts persons into
topics for the deployment of style and figure, as well as for larger
deployments of action and mode of behavior. So Cressida becomes
a theme for him, as Helen was a theme for Troy: and finally a
theme for hatred and violence, a justification for self-brutaliza-
tion—which, in effect, though expressed in idealizing language,
was what Helen was, too.

When his *topoi* fail Troilus, so do his actions. Paralyzed for a
time by his realization of Cressida's infidelity, he sees in it a total
fragmentation of ideals. He, who has tarried the requisite time for
a lady "stubborn, chaste, against all suit," must watch her bullied
and degraded to campfollower status by a man who reserves his
chivalric pose (guerdon, horse) to taunt Troilus, not to honor his
lady. Troilus' astonishment expresses itself in an overblown
rhetoric of abstractions:

> To make a recordation to my soul
> Of every syllable that here was spoke.
> But if I tell how these two did coact,
> Shall I not lie in publishing a truth?

(The language of is/is-not emerges in the familiar paradox.)

> Sith yet there is a credence in my heart,
> An esperance so obstinately strong,
> That doth invert th'attest of eyes and ears;
> As if those organs had deceptious functions
> Created only to calumniate.   (v.ii.114-22)

In a series of staccato questions, to which, when Ulysses' answers
displease him, he supplies his own responses, he tries to assess
the truth:

Troil.: Was Cressid here?
Ulyss.:   I cannot conjure, Troyan.
Troil.: She was not, sure.
Ulyss.:   Most sure she was.
Troil.: Why, my negation hath no taste of madness.

341

Ulyss.: Nor mine, my lord. Cressid was here but now.
Troil.: . . . Rather think this not Cressid. . . .
　　　　Nothing at all, unless that this were she.

(v.ii.122-26; 131; 133)

Finally he reaches the climax of his argument:

This she? No; this is Diomed's Cressida.
If beauty have a soul, this is not she;
If souls guide vows, if vows be sanctimonies,
If sanctimony be the gods' delight,
If there be rule in unity itself,
This was not she. O madness of discourse,
That cause sets up with and against itself!
Bifold authority! where reason can revolt
Without perdition, and loss assume all reason
Without revolt: this is, and is not, Cressid.　　(v.ii.135-44)

"This is, and is not, Cressid": like the tautologies, the paradoxes, psychologically true to the young man's acceptance and refusal of his own sense-evidence, reduce to meaninglessness and nonsense, deny what *is*. Cressida becomes—was she ever more?—merely a reason for reacting, a term to justify, as Helen justified for the Trojans, commitment to hatred and carnage.

The imagery of fragmentation, too, reaches its peak in this speech of Troilus', as he copes with a shattered vision:

Instance, O instance! strong as Pluto's gates:
Cressid is mine, tied with the bonds of heaven.
Instance, O instance! strong as heaven itself:
The bonds of heaven are slipp'd, dissolv'd, and loos'd;
And with another knot, five-finger-tied,
The fractions of her faith, orts of her love,
The fragments, scraps, the bits, and greasy relics
Of her o'er-eaten faith, are bound to Diomed.

(v.ii.151-58)

In the literature of paradoxy, such atomization of things is a regular *topos*. It is by "Instance, O instance!" that Montaigne brought down the beautiful cosmic structure of Raimond de Sebonde, that Robert Burton undermined the cosmic psychology of the humors.[29] Detachment from context is as effective in destroy-

---

[29] See *Paradoxia*; and Ellis-Fermor, p. 73. W. W. Lawrence, in "Troilus,

ing orderly truths as is annihilation of context: for Troilus, Cressida has done both. By these means, we come back to the play's major theme, its imbalances of balanced badness, its undermining of secure holdfasts, personal, social, and moral. Both means and ends are called into question; no "instance" is seen whole, no action properly finished. "Received opinion" is undone by this play's workings.

When we consider what has happened to received opinion in *Troilus and Cressida*, which undermines by instance and counter-commonplace the common security afforded by "received opinion," we may not be surprised that so many of the Homeric characters played parts in another ancient form, the paradoxical encomium, designed to challenge, test, and to subvert received opinion and received values, exactly as these values are debated and questioned in the play. According to its prescription, the paradoxical encomium praised things unworthy of praise, according to the conventional value-system: Helen, civilization's destroyer, was one famous subject for the paradoxist;[30] Ajax,[31] Thersites,[32]

Cressida, and Thersites," *MLN*, xxxvii (1942), 422-37, noted an essential paradoxical function of the play (which he did not name), in saying that here Shakespeare leaves it to the audience to draw its own conclusions about the play.

[30] For Helen, see Theodore C. Burgess, *Epideictic Literature* (Chicago, 1902), pp. 118, 159, 166; Aulus Gellius, *Noctes Atticae* (Paris, 1532), f. xxv (scholion): Gorgias "cuius et hodie extat in hoc genere encomium Helenae meretricis festivissimis argumentis oppletum." See also *Amphitheatrum Sapientiae . . . Joco-seriae*, ed. C. Dornavius (Hamburg, 1619), ii, pp. 5-8. Not surprisingly, it is difficult to determine in some cases whether an encomium of Helen is paradoxical or not.

[31] Besides Harington's specialized paradox which pays tribute, *inter alia*, to the classical tradition of mock-praise, Alcidamus' *Aias* is not a mock-encomium, although it was often referred to as if it were: cf. scholion to Aulus Gellius (Paris, 1532, p. 126[v]) likening Ajax to a fly. (I owe these references to R. A. Hornsby.)

[32] Thersites is the most complex of all: a paradoxical encomium on him is referred to by Polybius (xii.26b); another is attributed to Favorinus by Aulus Gellius (xviii.12). In the scholia to the *Noctes* by Jodocus Badius, Thersites is likened to a monkey (9) and to Achilles (126[v]). In Leonard Cox's *The Arte or Crafte of Rhethoryke*, ed. F. I. Carpenter (Chicago, 1899), p. 53, the following comment on Thersites occurs: "Nowe if one wolde take upon hym to make an oracion to the prayse of [t]his losel [Thersites]/ whiche mater is of litle honesty in it selfe/ he must use in stede of a preface an insinuacion. That what thyng poetes of commune fame doth eyther prayse or disprayse ought not to be gyven credence to/ but rather to be suspect"; his

Agamemnon, Paris[33] were others. Heroes were praised for their bad qualities, or bad people were praised for their characteristics —often interpreted expedientially and parodically as leading to some unexpectedly good end. In the prefatory epistle to his *Lenten Stuffe*, after a long list of paradoxical authorities, Nashe speaks of Helen paradoxically:[34]

> The Poets were triviall, that set up *Helens* face for such a top-gallant summer May-pole for men to gaze at, and strouted it out so in their buskind braves of her beautie, wherof the onely *Circes Heypasse*, and *Repasse* was that it drewe a thousand ships to *Troy*, to fetch her backe with a pestilence. Wise men in *Greece* in the meane while to swagger so aboute a whore.

Thersites had a place in the paradoxical encomium even before he became a rhetorical term, and we can recognize him in the play as the standard rhyparographer, the crier-up of filth, the crier-down of virtue, whose *persona* speaks in paradoxical encomia:

> A slave whose gall coins slanders like a mint,
> To match us in comparisons with dirt   (1.iii.193-94)

that is, with anything vile, such as sickness, excrement, and rubbish. The boils, botchy cores, murrains, the camel, etc., of Thersites' vocabulary exactly fits this rule: indeed, we discover also that Thersites' topics are also those of the standard paradoxist—diseases, listed in the catalogue of v.i.16-22, in which epic catalogue a whole human being is reduced to his disgustingly-infected parts; small things, trivia, miniatures—"thou skein of sleid silk, thou green sarcanet flap for a sore eye, thou tassel of a prodigal's purse . . . such water-flies—diminutives of nature! . . . Finch egg!" (v.i.29-34). A louse, another such topic, is not low enough for Thersites; he must prefer being "the louse of a lazar" to being Menelaus. So the hero Ajax can be called "Mars his idiot," a camel, a draft ox, a mongrel dog, a cur: in his first appearance, Thersites' description of Ajax is an interrupted inversion of encomium, and, farther back in the play, Alexander, Cressida's

---

example is Erasmus' "prayse of folysshenes." (Cox's example of Thersites derives from Melanchthon's *Institutiones Rhetoricae*.)

[33] For Agamemnon, see Burgess, p. 166; for Paris, Aphthonius, *Progymnasmata*, tr. Rudolph Agricola (Frankfurt, 1598), pp. 231-33.

[34] Thomas Nashe, *Nashes Lenten Stuffe* (London, 1599), p. 31.

man, has mentioned Ajax first in a standard paradoxical dispraise.

The same Achilles who can proclaim to Hector, "I am Achilles" is to Thersites a "full dish of fool"; Patroclus, who late in the play recovers more honor than could be expected of such a man, is "Achilles' male varlet" and his "masculine whore." Menelaus, Agamemnon, Nestor, "the dog fox Ulysses" come off no better: Thersites provides for these heroes the language of baseness customarily applied to what—we discover finally—these heroes are, the "things without honour" celebrated in the paradoxical encomium. Shakespeare has once more unmetaphored a literary term, and unmetaphored it on a very large scale.

Nor is Thersites the only speaker of paradoxes. Speaking of the "orts," "The fragments, scraps, the bits, and greasy relics" of Cressida's love and faith, Troilus is well on his way to becoming a rhyparographer himself. And so, of course, are they all: Patroclus' parodies of the Greek lords were, as Ulysses had said, "paradoxes." In that speech, Ulysses gives us the clue to the dramatized equivocation of the whole play. The Graeco-Trojan crisis is travestied by its supposed heroes themselves (the italics are mine):

> All our abilities, gifts, natures, shapes,
> Severals and generals of grace exact,
> Achievements, plots, orders, preventions,
> Excitements to the field or speech for truce,
> Success or loss, *what is or is not*, serves
> As stuff for these two to make paradoxes.
>
> (I.iii.179-84)

Against the background of paradoxy, we can make considerable sense of the chaotic and countereffective elements of *Troilus and Cressida*. From first to last, received opinion is called into question: about Homer, about literary grandeur, about Chaucer, about war and love, and, finally and fundamentally, about literary expression. The incessant questioning starts up a sense that either comparison or identification will orientate us, but the answers, given according to paradoxical techniques, turn out to be irrelevant, self-referential, or untrue. Of a piece with the paradoxical mode is the fragmentation and atomizing of things, topics, persons, destroying customary shape and customary context, upsetting altogether common measurements of value. This too is reflected in the playing-off of various decorums against each other, so that the war's irrationality, for instance, is "explained" by unreason in love. Finally, the relentless reduction to tautology (cf. Folly's praise of folly) cancels context even more radically than the fragmentation does, so that normative patterns are merely affirmed, in such idiotic grammatical and logical forms that they are immediately perceived as ridiculous. With the loss of normative patterns, expectations are frustrated until expectation itself collapses, and nothing can be judged at all. This is paradoxy's declared function, to dislodge things from their context, to challenge common notions of order, connection, logic, cause and effect—of intellectual arrangement. So the play thwarts our ordinary sense of sequence: Troilus knows (we know) Helen's merely opinion-worth, but acts to confirm opinion-as-worth by his own and others' blood; Hector knows that Helen should be returned but reneges on his conviction. Cressida will not, she cries, leave Troy—and does so, immediately on being sent for; Troilus' mighty devotion to her turns into a desire to enjoy her at night only. We are brought to expect some climax as Hector and Ajax begin their much-vaunted fight, only to find that fight called off even as it begins, with much prattle of blood-relationship, cousinship, and aunts. We await Hector's heroism and get the killing for armor; we await Achilles'—and get what we get.

Like the paradox, the play insists on thwarting expectation, on shaking us out of our ordinary ways of perceiving; like the paradox, it serves equally "what is or is not." No wonder the play everlastingly calls into question what "is" or ought to be, when for the characters involved "is" and "is not" make so little difference. This is one of the play's problems; but the problem has, if its manifestations have not, a proper context in the epistemological mode of paradoxy, where questions of utmost importance are discussed in terms of trivial matters: a nut, baldness, the ague; and trivial matters are raised to the dignity of philosophical language. No wonder so many critics have felt the voices of "philosophy" and "metaphysics" in this play: the voices are there, as in paradoxy: as in paradoxy, it is precisely philosophy and metaphysics which are discovered to be wanting.

Under such conditions, things conventionally honored are easily brought low—Homer, Hector, *arete*; Chaucer, Troilus, codes of love; civilization itself can easily be reduced to an amalgam of barbarism, stupidity, brutality, hypocrisy, self-satisfaction, and sadism. In this play, the paradoxical method has been pushed as far as it will go, has been expanded into dramatic structure, varied into many kinds of theatrical language and gesture. Further, as in paradoxy, the very terms are challenged by which opinion is received—that is, language itself, that web by which cultures interpret and project themselves, by which cultures live, and literature survives at all. When language is broken apart from its referents, anything goes—as it does in this play, at this Troy. "This is, and is not, Cressid": is and is not Helen, Hector, Achilles, Odysseus, Ajax—and either way it doesn't matter. Even the occasional truth—Thersites' self-description to Hector, Margarelon's to Thersites—is too "occasional" to count: it too becomes contextless, as we realize that self-reference is by definition unreliable. So Troilus, cardboard lover, pasteboard soldier, stuck in his stereotyped code, cannot learn; there is no question in his case of knuckling under, as the speaker in the *Sonnets* learned to do, to his nature's overwhelming need for a fictional beloved who was really a betrayer. After the abstracted speech expressing his intense confusion (which matches, after all, the confusion in his happier "expectation" speech), Troilus still finds relief in vast overstatements, now in terms of his role in war:

> That sleeve is mine that he'll bear on his helm;
> Were it a casque compos'd by Vulcan's skill
> My sword should bite it. Not the dreadful spout
> Which shipmen do the hurricano call,
> Constring'd in mass by the almighty sun,
> Shall dizzy with more clamour Neptune's ear
> In his descent than shall my prompted sword
> Falling on Diomed.   (v.ii.167-74)

In the "expectation" speech, he himself was dizzy with anticipation; now he shall dizzy Diomed forever by his violence. To achieve such "dizziness" is one aim of the paradoxist. The love that seemed like war in Troilus' first speech becomes war in earnest—and, since his love was corrupted at its origins, he enters the war corrupted, love's motivations giving him scope for ignoble action. His defense of Helen as an excuse for fighting is proper prelude for his translating Cressida from love object to object of hate and excuse for killing.

So other actions turn out to be ignoble too. Hector's chivalrous challenge is belied by his killing the unknown Greek for his armor; Diomed's presentation of Troilus' horse to Cressida is merely a point scored off Troilus, now self-propelled out of chivalry: he and Diomed exchange roles. Throughout the play, its elements, from the most commanding themes governing love and war to the smallest, least significant figures of speech, pull apart from one another. The love-theme does not exploit the real poignancy implicit in its metaphysical and metaphorical association with the war, as we have seen the same association enriched in *Romeo and Juliet, Othello,* and *Antony and Cleopatra.* The conduct of the war is not only not enriched by a love like Othello's for Desdemona or Antony's for Cleopatra, it is made sordid by its inception in sexuality. The expediential, brought to a horrible climax in Hector's murder, seems only a little viler than the lack of conviction of the chief heroes, or the trumped-up justifications of warriors and lovers in both camps. Paris offers one spectacle of effeminacy; Patroclus another; Ajax one kind of brutal folly, Achilles another; Achilles' manhood is qualified from the beginning by Thersites' apt assessment of him, and Hector's honor allows him to murder for possession. For Helen the war seems to exist only because occasionally her Paris must leave her for a time; Cressida cares as little for politics and public affairs, although she knows that her own arrangements are at the mercy of the war's turns of fate. The many-childed Priam is an impotent ruler; Agamemnon cannot control his captains. Nestor bumbles through to his superannuated wisdom, and Ulysses is only a little less prolix. Ulysses' wiliness is parodied in Pandarus' bedroom manipulations; and the implicit acceptance of the world's scurviness which governs Pandarus' actions needs little deepening to become the railing of Thersites. We are not let off, in any confrontation, from realizing the superficiality, triviality, and egocentricity of the situation, the actions, and the personalities of this play.

All the same, we are conspicuously prevented from assuming a "moral vision,"[35] either, though we are constantly reminded that such a thing is needed: we are aware of significance, and we know what is sick, but denied by the disordered, unstructured, brainsick sequence of actions the opportunity to grasp any co-

[35] The phrase comes from the title of Mr. Ornstein's valuable book.

348

herent remedial plan. Even the emptied, emptying language of
the play denies us holdfast: again, the policy of the paradoxist
rules in this play. "I speak no more than the truth," says Pandarus, and Cressida, "Thou dost not speak so much." We are
deprived of a measuring-rod—if for a time we are tricked into
taking Thersites as the rule for the play's moral dimensions, we
are soon disillusioned of that, as he acts out the final self-cancel-
lation of the rhetorical paradox by undercutting his own authority to speak. Like the others, he takes the path of least resistance to reduce himself to his lowest common denominator.

Important though it is that Shakespeare reverses his usual practice in this play, reducing human beings to verbal counters, the
point of the play is that these characters *live* that way: live by
the book, by the rule, by forms only. In this play, Shakespeare
shows us—unflinchingly, since words were his livelihood and his
life—the dangers in words, in their "mereness," their automatic
substitution for real response and engagement, and in their
tricky grandiloquence as well. As paradoxy instructs us, words
can be made to do anything—the source, this, of Plato's quarrel
with the Sophists, masters of paradoxy. Words can annihilate as
well as create: characteristically, we have watched how Shakespeare recreates language by enriching its outworn ground, by
replanting it with newer, finer referents. Here, he shows us how
words detached from their received referents can unmake even the
values celebrated in the greatest literary tradition the world has
known; can show us Troilus, Cressida, Pandarus, Thersites, Ajax,
Hector, Achilles, and the rest conniving at that dismantling,
trading their enriched inherited identities for counters in a game
without rules, impoverishing themselves and their tradition. Self-
deniers (like the formal paradox) they become mere commonplaces: words, words, words. The proud *epideixis* on which ancient civilization's memory is based is turned back on itself by
self-referential, self-questioning, self-denying paradox, identical
in technique with the rhetoric of praise it here destroys.

Epilogue

Troilus and Cressida is a limiting case in Shakespeare's work, darker than the other "dark comedies," more problematical than most of the official "problem plays," presenting a morality so negative and in such negative literary terms as to pry us loose from our usual comforts in conventional commonplace, to say nothing of richer forms of value. Such an exercise in "undoing" allows us to see, even more clearly than without its contrasts, Shakespeare's customary habits of "doing," of examining and enriching traditions. His renewing and reanimating of literary forms by realigning them with a more imaginatively conceived mimetic reality become even more remarkable when we realize, by studying the emptying-out of *Troilus and Cressida*, how fully he understood what he was doing, understood how precarious the relation is between morality and literary technique, between "life" and "literature." By forcing the technical achievements of his craft to their bottom limit of expressiveness, he offered a paradigm of life (like Ajax) "languageless, a very monster," an exercise in non-mimetics.

But one cannot end a book like this one with *Troilus and Cressida*, brilliant and absorbing though that play is—one cannot end a study of fruitful literary traditions with a play dismantling them, and doing so by the very means by which traditions are customarily preserved and transmitted, any more than Shakespeare could end his career on such a play. In *Troilus and Cressida*, we can see a genuine exercise in matching: the linguistic tricks, the puzzles, the mixtures of genre and decorum can be seen to have their rationale in a play which expresses systems undone and orders overthrown, which shows how easily, under the conditions of wartime, any system can be undone, any order overthrown. Having worked down to the minimum of meaning in *Troilus and Cressida*, the playwright turned back to the problem, more normal for him, of finding forms for meanings customarily beyond expression, rather than beneath it.

In *King Lear*, another play in which normal order is overturned and men consistently draw attention to its overturning, there is just as much mixture of genre and decorum as in *Troilus and Cressida*; but mere juxtaposition and mixture of these elements do not mean the same thing in both plays (need not ever mean the same thing, from work to work). In *King Lear*, such mixtures do not express, though they certainly represent, annihilated connections between human beings—quite the contrary, finally. *Lear* deals with both the consequences of detachment and the meanings of attachment affirmed, and does so unequivocally, in spite of all it shares in technique with *Troilus and Cressida*. The paradoxy which in *Troilus and Cressida* detached every-thing from everything else to leave a fragmented and meaningless existence plays as important a part in the themes, motifs, and even plot-structure of *King Lear*.[1] The *Lear*-paradoxy, though, is in many ways more orthodox than that of *Troilus and Cressida*, where paradoxy was so remarkably translated into most of the ranges, dramatic and poetic, of the play. But where paradoxy demonstrates the potential emptiness of words, of grammatical, rhetorical, and logical systems in *Troilus*, in *Lear* it performs a very different function, working not to detach one meaning, one idea, one person from another such, as much as to connect them all in a web of significances in which the paradoxes of poverty, blindness, folly, bastardy, barrenness, and the rest are interrelated and interrelate meanings, ideas, and persons in one firm structure.

As in *Troilus and Cressida*, paradoxy in *King Lear* serves to keep us off balance, to thwart expectation, and to hold in tension the contradictory and counteracting meanings of the play. In *Troilus and Cressida*, audience and readers are thwarted in their efforts to identify and to draw conclusions, prevented from taking a fair share in any transactional understanding, but *not* in *King Lear*. There, the intervolved paradoxes move audience and readers smoothly along from one level of meaning and understanding to the next—as, for instance, Folly does in Erasmus' exemplary paradox—so that, as in *The Praise of Folly*, we are allowed, even forced, to penetrate ever more deeply into the dark implications of the play. In this way, paradoxy inverts its usual aim of detachment and inconclusiveness to plunge the reader, almost before he is aware of it, deep into feeling. In *Troilus and Cressida*, the playwright explored the implications of paradoxy's inversion of *epideixis*; in *King Lear* he transcends

[1] *Paradoxia*, chapter 15.

the limits of paradox by paradoxy's own means, to make the form do what, by its own definitions, it ought not to be able to do—to make it, then, express the heights and depths traditionally expressed in the magniloquent conventions of praise.

In this respect, then, the play is quite other than *Troilus*, and much more like those plays of the major Shakespearean line, in which various literary devices and conventions are "sprung" beyond their own limits to do something unexpected. As far as the extraordinary mixture of *King Lear* is concerned, Maynard Mack's book[2] suggests how rich the play is. That book shows us how folkish and chronicle materials inform it; how it fulfils Polonius' repertory of comical-tragical-historical-pastoral; how it reaches from paradigmatic and commonplace figures to the most startling naturalism. From Mack's book more work of this sort has consciously come. Martha Andresen's study of the functions of *sententiae* in *Lear* opens up our awareness to how specifically enriching such tags can be;[3] related to this same topic, we can find Scriptural imagery in both the language and the action of the play.[4] Bridget G. Lyons has examined two puzzling scenes, Gloucester's would-be suicide at Dover and the duel between Edmund and Edgar, to show the function of these archaic insets, a morality playlet and a romance *judicium*.[5] Long ago, Miss Welsford pointed to a formal analogue, in the *sottie*, to the judgment scene in which Lear arraigns his daughters,[6] and there is much in the Renaissance folly-tradition to be worked out in this play.[7] Mr. Mack's comments on the play's pastoral have been further enriched by Nancy Lindheim's study of the meanings of pastoral thematics in *King Lear*,[8] and I have tried to show in an earlier chapter how an orthodox but recessive pastoral pattern is one structural element of this comical-historical tragedy.

[2] *King Lear in Our Time.*

[3] " 'Ripeness is All,' " in *Some Facets of "King Lear."*

[4] See John Rosenberg, "King Lear and his Comforters," *Essays in Criticism*, XVI (1966).

[5] Bridget G. Lyons "The Subplot as Simplification," *Some Facets.*

[6] Enid Welsford, *The Fool* (London, 1935).

[7] See principally Kaiser, *Praisers of Folly*, and literature there cited.

[8] Mack, op. cit.; Lindheim, "*King Lear* as Pastoral Tragedy," *Some Facets*; and above, Chapter Eight. Katherine Stockholder's article, "The Multiple Genres of *King Lear*: Breaking the Archetypes," *Bucknell Review*, XVI (1968), 40-63, is an extremely valuable and sensitive discussion of some of the interpenetrating genres of the play.

Another way of seeing on what extraordinarily diverse resources Shakespeare has drawn for this play is to look at the *dramatis personae* and to hear them all speak: Edmund is a machiavel as well as the presenter of interludes and the vice of morality-plays;[9] Childe Edgar moves from requisite innocence by ritual steps to adulthood and responsibility, accomplishing the anonymous impossible in the romance-test of the duel. As he proceeds to his ultimate and unexpected kingship, he turns himself into various Theophrastan characters, an emblematic bedlam and a trueborn cudgel-wielding countryman. Cordelia, that fair catastrophe of the old play, has her morality character,[10] as have her sisters as well, those machiavellian, smartly retouched forms of Appetite and Will. Goneril and Edmund play out a romance love affair in little, in the style of Jacobean court-tragedies of intrigue: in this self-casting they show, once more, their particular modernity. Kent is Good Counsel, Oswald the Theophrastan foppish new man; the Fool emerges from an environment of comedy, farce, and festival; France speaks the sane sonnet-language of romance.[11] Cornwall and Albany both seem the standard conspirators of history plays and court-tragedies, engaged in getting power, until their characters diverge, and the one loses his life for the power he has brutally schemed to get and the other at the last minute relinquishes the power for which he has been as eager. Gloucester is an easygoing *senex*, conventional, sententious, easily duped, but (like Albany) able to see his allegiance purely at last. And Lear —what is he? A king maddened and mad, upsetting decorum altogether; a king prattling the lunatic language which the theater assigned the mad—and, at the same time, never failing to express the fundamental human reason of madness which Edgar recognized at once in his disordered speech.

Like *Troilus and Cressida*, *King Lear* works in travesty: characters are again and again *en travesti*, dressed up as something else either literally or spiritually—Kent as Caius, Edgar as Tom, Edmund as true son and brother, Goneril and Regan as loving daughters. Gloucester is thrown out of his own house—not quite on the dungheap of Regan's charming suggestion, but quite low enough—blinded and outlawed, reduced in a moment from

[9] Cf. Spivack, *Allegory of Evil*.

[10] Cf. Sears Jayne, "Charity in *King Lear*," *Shakespeare 400*, ed. McManaway, pp. 80-88. I owe much on this point to Sheldon Zitner.

[11] So far as I know, France is little discussed: but see Zitner, "*King Lear* and its Language," *Some Facets*.

secure status to none at all, like the son he himself proscribed. That son is hidden from the father whom he leads, as his real nature was hidden by his supposed treachery; later, for a time, Lear does not recognize, or affects not to recognize, Gloucester in the squinying "blind Cupid" he engages in his harangue on justice. Cordelia loves and is silent, seeming to withhold affection we know to be real: once more, the King seemed (like Gloucester and Edgar) never to have taken in the quality of this daughter, in spite of his favoritism for her. And Lear, like Gloucester reduced by a child and succored by a child, is *en travesti* too—and literally so, tearing off his clothes in the storm, weed-crowned at Dover, redressed by Cordelia. He chooses to divest himself of kingship and must therefore take on other clothes, other roles, other decorums. His symbolic social and political gesture is, then, unmetaphored: only in a very special sense does Lear remain "the King himself." But "vestment," however important a theme in the play, is not a key to type: the Fool counters his own practical philosophy in denying himself to be "knave"; Kent is never more himself than when he is Caius. And Oswald dresses in the character-garb of the new man climbing to higher place, but is (as Caius sees) no man at all, a tailor's dummy. Cornwall's servant turns into outraged avenger from nothing, from no proper assigned role in the play, to strike down his lord in a gesture of immediate superhuman justice. The travesty is there, but it is not a consistent system by any means.

Another way of saying this is that characters take on, try out, experiment in various roles, voluntarily and involuntarily.[12] They act beyond received and assigned decorums to "be" other than themselves, or other than what others take them to be. Part of our engagement with the play lies in just this unexpectedness and multiplicity, in the disguise and the representativeness of these roles. Kent is the true servant for which Caius is a character-type; in spite of his explicit denial of himself ("Edgar I nothing am"), Edgar is Edgar through all the disguises, speaks through all transvested roles, however brilliant and antic their conception is, however distant from the earl's son's frank courtesy which had invested him in his original, simple role.

As Muriel Bradbrook has rightly said of *Hamlet*, so we can say of *Lear*: the play offers a recapitulation of the range of drama from interlude and morality to the most sophisticated forms of

---

12 See Thomas F. Van Laan, "Acting as Action in *King Lear*," *Some Facets.*

modern coterie-plays.[13] It is a powerful, integrated dramatic anthology, as Mack's book teaches; it is also, according to a modern prescription, an "anatomy," a world viewed from a particular intellectual point of inspection, presented in terms of its anomalies and problems, with a clear understanding of the predicaments of outsiders, the disinherited, the outlawed, the madmen, and the fools denied proper place in that world.[14]

What the outsiders' parts can be in such a world is stressed by the play's conspicuous breaches of decorum, none more considerable than the reduction of the King to destitute madman and fool, chief player in an impromptu *sottie*, chief speaker in an impromptu dialogue between madman and blindman. The quality of the imaginative act of making the King run mad can be read from the sources, for the madness of Lear is Shakespeare's shocking revision of his texts. In the earlier versions, though Lear was considerably persecuted by his elder daughters and had irrationally deprived his youngest daughter of her place in his love and in the country, the King had retained his reason, ratifying his good sense by seeking reconciliation with his daughter across the Channel. Here, he rants from the beginning in King Cambyses' vein; his invocation of "the barbarous Scythian, who makes/ His generation messes" out-herods Herod, that other wanton destroyer of innocence. In Shakespeare's play, Lear is variously primitivized[15]—archaized, made to behave in a primitive way, and reduced to childhood (*puer senex*)—but he is also as remarkably humanized, civilized, made sensitive to his own and others' plights.

His abrupt break in style from the sarcastic, bombastic rage of

> The King would speak with Cornwall; the dear father
> Would with his daughter speak, commands, tends service:
> Are they inform'd of this? My breath and blood!
> Fiery! the fiery Duke! Tell the hot Duke that—

to

[13] For this, see the forthcoming study by John Reibetanz, as well as his "Theatrical Emblems in *King Lear*," *Some Facets*.

[14] For the concept of anatomy, see (of course) Northrop Frye, *Anatomy of Criticism* (Princeton, 1959).

[15] For primitivism, see Mack, op. cit.; and F. D. Hoeniger, "The Artist Exploring the Primitive," *Some Facets*; for the problem of sensibility in the play, see Lindheim, op. cit.; and Paul J. Alpers, "*King Lear* and the theory of the 'Sight Pattern,'" in *In Defense of Reading*, ed. Brower and Poirier.

No, but not yet; may be he is not well:
Infirmity doth still neglect all office
Whereto our health is bound; we are not ourselves
When Nature, being oppress'd, commands the mind
To suffer with the body. I'll forbear. . . .   (II.iv.100-109)

marks a break in personality too, an instant of insight in which he can generalize from his own to others' conditions, indeed reversing the habits of a lifetime. In the figure of Lear, Shakespeare offers us, by the symbolic indicators of literary device which his contemporaries were trained to understand, an analogue to his analytical techniques with literary forms. A character, this time, is scrutinized from many different points of view (i.e., compared and contrasted with other characters, put into different situations), broken down into its parts (the onset of madness), reconstituted and revivified from the implications latent in its original composition, this reformation manifestly the result of the playwright's analytical decomposition. For once, breakdown is breakthrough, as our mid-century vulgar commonplace has it. The "character" of Lear, the King's personality, is what the playwright says it is, a mixture of human qualities rendered by literary forms which alter to match the alterations of a conceptual personality,[16] and by altering, "create" a new personality and mediate it to the audience.

The technical means by which we are offered the complex case of Lear can be seen even more clearly in the comparison (which Shakespeare leaves us no option to ignore) of the King with his Fool. Like the figures of Falstaff and Hamlet, the Fool is made up of a range of stereotypical follies: he speaks in archaic rhymes and doggerel, in the riddles and patched proverbs of social and stage-fools; he is the wise simpleton attached to courts, privileged to speak true; like Erasmus' Folly, this Fool points to "things"—that is, to the problematic, perspectivist world of men acting in different ways, where madness is constant only in its name, is various and unique in all its many instances. The Fool acts as child and teacher, as satirist and comforter, detached from and attached to his master's person and plight. He works to share with Lear both the intolerable burdens of that plight—thus,

16 For discussions of this problem, I am indebted to June Fellows and William A. Watterson. The contrast here with *Troilus and Cressida* is clear: in *Lear*, characters are "filled in," in Troilus gradually emptied of personality.

tries to make it bearable for the stricken King—and the insights of wisdom his social detachment guarantees him. Each utterance of this Fool, at the same time, fits its specific interlocutor and occasion; bitter-sweet, the Fool measures out the truth of things.

How much more problematical "the King himself," invested in a fool's weaknesses and strengths, a fool's folly and wisdom! He takes on, too, something of the fool's simultaneous detachment from actual life:

> *Kent*: Your eldest daughters have fordone themselves,
> And desperately are dead.
> *Lear*:   Ay, so I think.
>
> (v.iii.291-92)

and total attachment to it:

> No, no, no life!
> Why should a dog, a horse, a rat, have life,
> And thou no breath at all? Thou'lt come no more,
> Never, never, never, never, never!   (v.iii.305-308)

A ranting, an antic King, whose exercises of power have crowded justice and love out of his immediate world, a berserker tearing his clothes off on the heath, a parodied philosopher consulting the natural fool about first causes, a weed-crowned lunatic offering prescriptions for social justice, a "child-chang'd father," this Lear comes to his end having fully experienced what it means to be detached—deracinated, rationally and irrationally distanced —from life, and (far more painful) what it means to admit overwhelming connections and attachment to a living human being. From "Howl, howl, howl" to the pitifully courteous "Pray you, undo this button," Lear recapitulates his violence and his conversion, as well as his capacity for immense feeling and gentleness: in the undoing of the button—his? Cordelia's?—he relives the unreason, in a different mode altogether, of "Off, off, you lendings!" to express himself, simply, as unaccommodated man seeking help from another: "Thank you, Sir."

Lear dies, like Gloucester, on an instance—"Do you see this?" —which neither he nor we can fully interpret. "Look on her, look, her lips,/ Look there, look there!" Cordelia's breath is all that is real to him now, and we cannot know surely whether he thinks she lives or is dead, can know only that he wants her to live more than he has ever wanted anything else in his life. The love he craved from her he has finally learned to give. And, in the play's awful unmetaphoring, "for nothing": that is, he gives it freely at last, but her silence now only acts out the uttered "nothing" of the first scene. He had banished her, and now, she'll "come no more,/ Never, never, never, never, never!"[17]

In *Troilus and Cressida*, negation denied life; here, negation affirms the meaning of living and of having lived. The "mortal no" refuses to accept what at the same time must be accepted, in this case, another, dearest person's death for one's own fault. As fits the profound paradoxy of this play, Lear dies on an ambivalence that expresses human resistance to and welcome of death, bringing them into question. As Sheldon Zitner has said,[18] the final scene of *Lear*, like so much else in the play, violates decorum entirely, moving out of generic possibilities to something indefinably but recognizably different and new. Albany makes an effort of will to impose the generic decorum upon events dreadfully out of hand: after Lear has entered with his dead child in his arms, after the news of Edmund's death has come in, Albany can say in pompous desperation for orderliness:

> You lords and noble friends, know our intent;
> What comfort to this great decay may come
> Shall be appli'd. . . .

He attempts to reduce to common expectations, then, the conditions around him. He refuses, then, to "see" Lear and Cordelia:

> for us, we will resign,
> During the life of this old Majesty,
> To him our absolute power. . . .

Not only Albany's insensitivity and selfishness must strike us, as he attempts to rewrite events to his own limited understanding of what should be, but also his grandiose, unearned verbal habits —"*we* will resign," "*our* absolute power." In this reversion to the language Lear used at the play's start, Albany demonstrates his total unfitness to rule, unfitness even for the play. He goes on, this time addressing Edgar and Kent,

17 Once more, the contrast with *Troilus* makes plain the importance of controlling contexts: there, repetition was deployed to rob words of their simplest meanings; here, the word becomes even more charged with repetition. See K. M. Lea, "Power of Repetition."

18 "*King Lear* and its Language," *Some Facets.*

> you, to your rights,
> With boot and such addition—

"addition!" fatal word—

> as your honours
> Have more than merited. All friends shall taste
> The wages of their virtue, and all foes
> The cup of their deservings.

This may be an orthodox moral ending for a tragedy, but such platitudes simply will not do here. Even Albany must give in to the meaning of the horrible emblematic tableau before him which belies forever his efforts to restore convention:

> O! see, see!   (v.iii.296-304)

What he "sees," finally, overturns and blots out his words: no one has listened, no one remembers what he has been saying. But (again, unlike *Troilus and Cressida*) in *King Lear*, however words, devices, and conventions are shown to fall short of extreme situations, words are not debased by being substituted for what actually happens. Albany cannot put over his trivial vision: he must bow to "the general woe" and speak in plainer words. Kent, whose consistent moral values were always clear to him and to us, declines the role Albany offers him, to return us to the tragic ambience with his image of life as "a journey to go";[19] and Edgar, in a remarkably muted, anti-dramatic *sententia*, quietly closes off the play.[20]

How can such sentence, such quietness befit a play like this one, changing, whirling, interrupting, violent, and unexpected as its action is? Robert Heilman has shown one way that Shakespeare's "mind and hand went together" in this play,[21] as its images, motifs, and themes reliably knit to make a substantial net for all that happens. In quite a different way, the paradoxes conjoin disparate notions, ideas, themes, and values to weld together the disparate parts of this play. Counterpoint works steadily, as symbolic ritual is set against naturalistic representativeness,

[19] See Martha Andresen, unpublished dissertation (Yale University, 1973), Chapter Three.

[20] Zitner, "*King Lear* and its Language."

[21] Robert B. Heilman, "The Unity of *King Lear*," *Sewanee Review* (1948), reprinted in Casebook *King Lear*, ed. Frank Kermode (London, 1969), pp. 169-78.

as ornate style is played off against plain style, and complex plot against simplified subplot.[22] From "real life," in general and in specific cases,[23] analogues to the play can be found, as well as in many ranges of the manifold formalities of literary art. "His mind and hand went together"; or, as Maynard Mack has said, "Shakespeare is like the wind over a field; everything goes the same way." Having seen the counterexample in *Troilus and Cressida*, we can appreciate the more precisely and poignantly how *King Lear* knits up its parts. Here, the most disparate techniques of craft are called upon to make sense—literally, to make *sense*—of the consequential casuistry of living. Here, to paraphrase another kind of critic, from the strengths of his self-conscious tradition, the poet could achieve a form for his tragic vision which is also and fundamentally "classic" because it comes to terms with, and finds terms for, life and the daily, critical business of living.[24]

For Shakespeare, clearly, craft was livelihood and life. By submitting to its regulations he became ingrained with its strengths ("the dyer's hand"); by weaving (like Bottom) farce and comedy, nightmare, dream, and vision into magnificent patterns he came, like Edgar after experience, to "speak what we feel," to make out of his perceptions of his craft and his experience a "living art."

[22] Lyons, "Subplot"; and Burckhardt, "The Quality of Nothing," *Shakespearean Meanings*.

[23] Colie, "Reason and Need," *Some Facets*; C. J. Sisson, "Justice in *King Lear*," reprinted in Casebook *King Lear*, pp. 228-44; and G. M. Young, "Shakespeare and the Termers," *Proc. Brit. Acad.*, XXXIII.

[24] Murray Krieger, *The Classic Vision* (Baltimore, 1971).

Index

Index

Index

Index

Index

Updike, John, 54
Ure, Peter, 214n

Valency, Maurice, 135n
Van Laan, Thomas F., 287n, 313n, 355n
Varchi, Benedetto, 85
Vasari, Giorgio, 280
Vauquelin de la Fresnaye, Jean, 89
Vellutello, Alessandro, 55
Venus and Adonis, 96, 152
Vergil, 98, 246; *Aeneid*, 179n, 258n; *Eclogues*, 246, 248, 249, 253, 272
Vickers, Brian, 172n
Vitruvius Pollio, 264
Vittorino da Feltre, 34
Voltaire, François Marie Arouet, 7
Vyvyan, John, 136n

Waddington, Raymond B., 179n, 195n
Waith, Eugene M., Jr., 196n, 225n, 231n, 252n, 254n, 257n
Walker, D. P., 289n
Walker, J. B., 214n
Waller, G. F., 268n
Watson, Thomas, 70, 76, 80
Watterson, William A., 357n
Watts, Robert A., 147n
Webbe, William, 89
Weever, John, 93, 96

Weinberg, Bernard, 17, 262
Wells, Stanley, 269n
Welsford, Enid, 19n, 287n, 353
Wenkel, Karl-Heinz, 135n
Whipple, T. K., 77n, 8on, 85n
Whitehead, Alfred North, 22
Wilamowitz-Möllendorf, M. von, 171n
Willcock, G. D., 32n
Williamson, George, 172n
Wilson, J. Dover, 19n, 208n
Winny, James, 51n, 76n
Winters, Yvor, 68, 70, 96
The Winter's Tale, 6, 8, 9, 10, 16, 17, 18, 23; as pastoral, 247, 253n, 261, 265-83, 284, 291, 302, 307, 310
Wittkower, Margot, 209n, 214n
Wittkower, Rudolf, 209n, 214n
Woogewerff, G. J., 209n
Wordsworth, William, 54
Wyatt, Sir Thomas, 57, 70, 76, 85n, 155

Yates, Frances A., 32n, 34
Yeh, Max, 278n
Young, G. M., 361n
Young, Richard B., 56n

Zitner, Sheldon, 3, 4, 24, 170n, 213n-214n, 215n, 224n, 238n, 285n, 300n, 305n, 310n, 313n, 323n, 354n, 359, 360n